Mobile Learning

Norbert Pachler · Ben Bachmair · John Cook

Mobile Learning

Structures, Agency, Practices

with contributions from
Gunther Kress, Judith Seipold, Elisabetta Adami
and Klaus Rummler

Norbert Pachler
University of London
Institute of Education
20 Bedford Way
London
United Kingdom WC1H 0AL
n.pachler@ioe.ac.uk

Ben Bachmair
Universität Kassel
FB Erziehungswissenschaft/
Humanwissenschaften
Nora-Platiel-Str. 1–5
34127 Kassel
Germany
bachmair@uni-kassel.de

John Cook
London Metropolitan University
166-220 Holloway Road
London
Tower Bldg. North Campus
United Kingdom N7 8DB
john.cook@londonmet.ac.uk

ISBN 978-1-4419-0584-0 e-ISBN 978-1-4419-0585-7
DOI 10.1007/978-1-4419-0585-7
Springer New York Dordrecht Heidelberg London

Library of Congress Control Number: 2009938820

Printed on acid-free paper

Springer is part of Springer Science+Business Media (www.springer.com)

To three special 'native experts': Benjamin, James and Daniel

Acknowledgments

Gunther Kress, Elisabetta Adami, Judith Seipold, and Klaus Rummler took part in regular meetings of the London Mobile Learning Group; they contributed to the development of the book overall. Specifically, Elisabetta Adami and Gunther Kress authored Chapter 7 against the background of the conceptual work of the LMLG. Judith Seipold led on the writing of Chapter 4. Klaus Rummler contributed to the discussion about at-risk learners in Chapters 1 and 10; he led on preparing the artwork contained in the book and on permissions.

Contents

List of Figures

List of Tables

Part I
Big picture and Examples

Chapter 1
Charting the Conceptual Space

The 'Mobile Complex'

'Mobile learning' is an emerging, and rapidly expanding field of educational research and practice across schools, colleges and universities as well as in the work place. It is also gaining increasing importance in what is frequently referred to as 'informal' (as opposed to 'formal') learning (see e.g. Cook et al. 2008a) and it is starting to attract the interest and imagination of practitioners in all phases of education as well as that of researchers. In response, a number of national and international conferences have been established, some as annual fixtures, to share growing insights into attendant pedagogical practices. However, there exist as yet no comprehensive theoretical and conceptual frameworks to explain the complex interrelationship between the characteristics of rapid and sometimes groundbreaking technological developments, their potential for learning as well as their embeddedness in the everyday lives of users.

In view of the increasing portability and functional convergence of technologies, as well as the reduction in their cost, and the cost of services available for them, mobile devices have become more and more central to, and at the same time invisible in the life-worlds of users. It is the growing significance of mobile devices in learners' everyday lives, i.e. their ubiquity and personal ownership of them, as well as their increasing use for engaging with, and making sense of the world that motivates our interest in them.

This book was written by members of the London Mobile Learning Group (LMLG) (www.londonmobilelearning.net), convened by Norbert Pachler and housed at the Centre for Excellence in Work-based Learning for Educational Professionals (www.wlecentre.ac.uk). The LMLG comprises an international, interdisciplinary group of researchers from the fields of educational, media and cultural studies, social semiotics and educational technology.

As authors, we are concerned about the difficulties of the education system to keep pace with social developments and with the life-worlds of young people, both of which include, importantly, the shape of the media landscape. We argue the need for a purposeful engagement with mobile learning in all sectors of education, among other things in order to avoid a potential disconnection between the ways young people operate in their daily lives and the ways educational institutions interact with

N. Pachler et al., *Mobile Learning*, DOI 10.1007/978-1-4419-0585-7_1,

them. Educators in all phases are having to face up to the challenges posed by the normalisation of mobile technologies and devices and their integration into everyday as well as professional practices and through our work we aim to make a meaningful contribution to understanding the complex processes involved as well as to propose possible ways forward.

Focus on Socio-cultural Conditions, Avoidance of Technological Fetishisation

In recognition of this convergence the book aims to initiate a new phase of thinking, research and practices around mobile learning, which problematises the notion of learning and its socio-cultural conditions. Its focus is on socio-cultural conditions and *not* on technological innovation, not on the adoption in schools of ever new waves of technologies, in this instance of mobile devices, in the context of a paradigm of 'efficiencies' and 'productivity', as was, arguably, the case with personal computers. There, cost-benefits were assumed, in terms of notions of transmission and 'delivery' as well as in terms of effectiveness and efficiency of students in relation to their (future) contributions to the world of work. Rather, our aim is to provide means for a discussion of fundamental changes relating to the contexts of learning and (the role of) associated, so-called 'mobile' technological tools (in it). We propose a focus on the processes and artefacts, that is, on cultural resources, on the knowledge, skills and understandings that underpin an analytical engagement with media of all descriptions, but in particular with mobile devices, by individuals. This focus is premised on an examination of cultural resources and practices, an attempt to describe how cultural resources are distributed and an assessment of whether that distribution is 'fair'. Our aim is to support individuals in the use of such resources in their everyday life-worlds, which includes a critical stance on resources and practices where that seems called for.

Questions arise around who can be helped and how, who needs to be protected, how and from what. There is a need for a theoretical – and from that, a practical – response in a society of individualised risks, which no longer has the school as the dominant institution guiding appropriation. We see learning as one mode of appropriation among others with regard to mobile devices. We assume also that there exists a need to connect present conditions with, and to build on the long tradition of 'appropriation' in mass communication.

'Mobile' Learning

Definitional Bases and Key Characteristics

Mobile learning is slowly establishing itself as a field in its own right. However, there still exists a lack of clarity about what best be understood by the term and if there is, in fact, a need for a separate field of enquiry on mobile learning. The question arises whether attendant phenomena can be adequately discussed under the umbrella of 'technology-enhanced learning' or 'information and communication technologies' (or similar generic labels)? Is there really a need to add to the seemingly endless list of prefixes to be found in the literature already for the word learning: e-, online-, ubiquitous-, virtual- etc.? Do these prefixes point to a different kind of learning or to different conditions and environments for learning, particularly bearing in mind affordances and characteristics of mobile technologies? For a detailed discussion of these questions see Kress and Pachler (2007). We intend to show here that mobile learning has to be, and can only be fully understood in the context of the fundamental societal and cultural transformations currently taking place, to which we see it inextricably linked. One defining feature of mobile learning for us is the need for individuals to go beyond the acquisition of knowledge relevant to issues encountered in the world but also to shape their knowledge out of their own sense of their world (Kress and Pachler 2007, p. 22). Consequently, we see learning as the result of the transformative engagement with an aspect of the world that is the focus of attention by an individual, on the basis of principles brought by them to that engagement leading to a transformation of the individual's semiotic/conceptual resources. We see meaning-making as an integral part of learning and we are content with using a (new) prefix even if we agree that, at best, it merely qualifies aspects of 'learning' rather than represent a new 'kind' of learning. However, the use of a prefix requires a detailed discussion of definitional bases to which we turn next.

Much of the work that is currently being done on mobile learning all over the world tends to remain ephemeral and comparatively scattered as it is still often only reported in the form of unpublished presentations or papers at conferences or it is documented in reports published fairly unsystematically on blogs or websites. Only few books on mobile learning have been published to date (e.g. Kukulska-Hulme and Traxler 2005; Metcalf 2006; Pachler 2007; Ryu and Parsons 2008; Ally 2009; Vavoula et al. 2009), and those that do exist tend to be collections of chapters from a range of contributors rather than authored titles if they don't focus more on the technical, rather than educational and pedagogical dimensions of the field in the first place. This, among other things, makes it very difficult for interested parties to gain an overview of dominant discourses.

Kukulska-Hulme and Traxler (2005) provide an introduction to the field through essays and case studies. Metcalf's text (2006) focuses on the corporate and general reader and on technology-related issues, rather than the educational professional and pedagogical matters. Pachler's (2007) collection brings together chapters on conceptual and theoretical issues around definitional bases as well as socio-cultural and pedagogical practices and reports on some mobile learning projects. Ryu and Parsons (2008) present cases of emerging use together with some reflections on attendant pedagogies and design. Ally (2009) offers a collection of practical examples with reference to some theoretical considerations. Vavoula et al. (2009) by comparison provide a collection of chapters focussing on frameworks, methods and designs of researching mobile learning.

The basic principles informing work on mobile learning are by no means new: 'learning' in general, as well as its mediation by and through technology, is a hugely contested and much written about field and it can hardly be claimed that the concept of 'mobility' has not been a concern of researchers, scholars and education practitioners for a long time. What is new, however, is the capability and the functionality of the technology usually associated with 'mobile learning', in particular the convergence of services and functions into a single device, its ubiquity and abundance, portability and multi-functionality; abundance in particular in the sense of a shift away from educational institutions having to provide technological devices towards the learner doing so. What is also new, and very significant in our view, is the boundary- and context-crossing mobile technologies and devices enable in relation to learning.

Mobile learning – as we understand it – is not about delivering content to mobile devices but, instead, about the processes of coming to know and being able to operate successfully in, and across, new and ever changing contexts and learning spaces. And, it is about understanding and knowing how to utilise our everyday life-worlds as learning spaces. Therefore, in case it needs to be stated explicitly, for us mobile learning is not primarily about technology.

Definitions of mobile learning in the literature are manifold but they tend to revolve around the mobility of the technology or the mobility of the learner with a clear change in emphasis of late from the former to the latter. Some commentators also point to the importance of the increasing mobility of information. This is viewed by some as liberating and as enabling greater scope to examine the complexity of the field.

Winters (2007, p. 7), in his definitional piece on mobile learning, comes to the conclusion that as a concept, mobile learning – at least at that time – was ill-conceptualised and he delineates the following conceptual perspectives:

- technocentric,
- relational to e-learning,
- augmenting formal education and
- learner-centred.

He sees the enabling of knowledge building by learners in – and we would add across – different contexts as defining and advocates a move away from viewing mobile learning as a process of information transmission predicated on a model of 'anytime, anywhere' access towards a notion of a guiding intervention in the learner's knowledge construction process with mobile devices being viewed as mediating tools (pp. 7–8). Traxler (2007a, p. 5) asserts that 'learning that used to be delivered "just-in-case", can now be delivered "just-in-time", "just enough" and "just-for-me"'. The attributes Traxler identifies are relevant even if they are framed, probably more inadvertently than deliberately, in transmission-based terms, which is not a pedagogical frame we would advocate in the context of mobile learning.

This view is closely aligned to that of Sharples et al. (2008, p. 5), who conceive of mobile learning as a 'process of coming to know through conversations across multiple contexts amongst people and personal interactive technologies'. Whilst we find this definition attractive, we consider it to be too narrowly focussing on 'conversation', which, we feel, foregrounds the link to people but underplays the linkages to systems better expressed by the broader term 'communication'.

Laurillard (2007, pp. 156–157) defines mobile learning as 'digitally-facilitated site-specific' learning, and she considers it to possess a degree of inherent motivation because of the degree of ownership and control afforded.

In his talk at mLearn 2007 in Melbourne, Traxler referred to the dual paradigm of 'the world in the box' versus 'the box in the world' noting that no longer do educational practices have to focus on reducing the real world to sanitised versions of reality that fit neatly into text books and other representational tools, but that with mobile devices it is possible to locate the learning experience in the real world. In the written version of his paper, Traxler (2007b, p. 257) describes a mobile society in flux, not just in quantitative terms, i.e. doing things faster, better etc., but also in qualitative terms, i.e. being characterised by profound and fundamental changes in many aspects of people's activities, e.g. in terms of social norms, commerce, the economy, the world of work, entertainment, the arts etc. We strongly agree with this analysis of socio-cultural structures governing mobile learning.

Another question in need of clarification here is what counts as 'mobile device' and what doesn't. Given our emphasis on convergence, the normalisation of technology and its seamless integration into the fabric of everyday life and into users' life-worlds, we consider laptops to lie outside the range of devices we focus on in the context of mobile learning as they mostly still lack true portability and ubiquity as well as penetration of a wide range of social contexts. The main focus in this book is on mobile/cell phones and personal digital assistants (PDAs) as well as to some extent also music players, game consoles and similar pocket size computing devices.

Some Important Characteristics of Mobile Devices

In the following we briefly examine some important characteristics of mobile devices, which make them attractive to us from an educational perspective given the affordances they provide for meaning-making, for engagement with and for mediating the world around us as well as for communicating with it. They include among other things increasing portability, functional, multimedia convergence, ubiquity, personal ownership, social interactivity, context sensitivity, location awareness, connectivity and personalisation.

In relation to portability, we consider the socially acceptable 'penetration' of every-day life-situations by mobile devices to be significant. These tools make a wide range of cultural resources, content and functionalities available as well as disposable to users in everyday situations: mobile devices readily allow us to document situations as well as stand back and reflect critically on them. At the same time, connectivity affords the user ubiquitous access to people and services, what De Waele (see http://www.m-trends.org/2009/05/mobile-social-contextual-applications-services. html) calls 'contextual communication', which he sees characterised by

- presence (psychological environment),
- location (physical environment) and
- communities (social environment).

Also, more and more services are becoming available on a single device as well as integrated into online services available over the internet.

Important for us is, of course, also the device as a physical object. In Chapter 7 we offer a social semiotic analysis of a device to problematise some key issues in relation to 'unlocking' the potential for meaning-making inherent in the device, its functionality and design, how meaning-making and different representational forms are supported, or indeed hindered by the device, its appearance and physical form, the software tools and applications available on it etc. The multimedia and multimodal affordances and characteristics of mobile devices can be seen as important, particularly how images and sound-related functionality impact on the input, process and output dimensions of interactions as well as on the representation of information and knowledge.

Through mobile devices, and their convergence, services and tools/functions/media come together and through them the world comes to the user and s/he can impact on the world. The mobile device makes the world move at the user's behest and the user moves through the world with and through using it. The user no longer depends on a stable context: contexts are becoming mobile and there is an increasing diversity of use not only in terms of content but also in and across contexts. As such, devices also support individualisation and tendentiously work against canonicity.

In his reflections on personal information technologies, Traxler (2008) makes the point that harnessing personally owned devices, particularly high specification ones, such as smartphones and games consoles, might help overcome problems educational institutions tend to experience with the large-scale and long-term deployment of mobile device due to resource implications, even if the diversity and transience of mobile devices (currently) pose real challenges for the technical infrastructure for educational institutions.

> (Users) invest considerable time, effort and resource choosing them, buying them, customizing them and exploiting them. These devices express part or much of their owners' values, affiliations, identity and individuality. They are both pervasive and ubiquitous, both conspicuous and unobstrusive, both noteworthy and taken-for-granted in the lives of most people... (p. 1)

In terms of context-sensitivity, an important affordance of mobile technology is that of digital augmentation (see e.g. Price 2007), whereby contextual data is added to objects to enable a deeper understanding of them and richer meaning-making. Context-sensitive mobile learning holds great potential for enabling learners to engage in meaning-making through interactive practice. We can distinguish between location-aware services, which use systems that are able to detect the exact physical location of mobile device. Context-sensitive systems are aware of the activities of learners and can offer to give assistance. Thus, an interaction-based approach to context should, ideally, continually derive what intervention is appropriate and provides relevant services to aid learning.

Opportunities and Challenges for Mobile Learning

Just like the Sesame Workshop Joan Ganz Cooney Centre, we are interested in the question of how emerging media can help children learn. And with the Centre's Carly Shuler (2009) we consider mobile technologies to possess educational potential for today's generation akin to that of television some 40 years ago or so. Shuler identifies the following key opportunities and challenges in mobile learning, which summarise arguments in the debate about mobile learning aptly:

> O1. *Encourage 'anywhere, anytime' learning* Mobile devices allow students to gather, access, and process information outside the classroom. They can encourage learning in a real-world context, and help bridge school, afterschool, and home environments.
> O2. *Reach underserved children* Because of their relatively low cost and accessibility in low-income communities, handheld devices can help advance digital equity, reaching and inspiring populations 'at the edges' – children from economically disadvantaged communities and those from developing countries.
> O3. *Improve twenty-first century social interactions* Mobile technologies have the power to promote and foster collaboration and communication, which are deemed essential for twenty-first century success.
> O4. *Fit with learning environments* Mobile devices can help overcome many of the challenges associated with larger technologies, as they fit more naturally within various learning environments.
> O5. *Enable a personalized learning experience* Not all children are alike; instruction should be adaptable to individual and diverse learners. There are significant opportunities for genuinely supporting differentiated, autonomous, and individualized learning through mobile devices. (p. 5)
> C1. *Negative aspects of mobile learning* Cognitive, social, and physical challenges must be surmounted when mobile devices are incorporated into children's learning. Disadvantages include: the potential for distraction or unethical behavior; physical health concerns; and data privacy issues.
> C2. *Cultural norms and attitudes* Though many experts believe that mobile devices have significant potential to transform children's learning, parents and teachers apparently are not yet convinced. A 2008 study done by the Joan Ganz Cooney Center in collaboration with Common Sense Media found that most teachers see cell phones as distractions and feel that they have no place in school.
> C3. *No mobile theory of learning* Currently, no widely accepted learning theory for mobile technologies has been established, hampering the effective assessment, pedagogy, and design of new applications for learning.
> C4. *Differentiated access and technology* Wide diversity among mobile technologies represents a challenge for teachers and learners who wish to accelerate academic outcomes as well as the producers who seek to facilitate such learning.
> C5. *Limiting physical attributes* Poorly designed mobile technologies adversely affect usability and can distract children from learning goals. Physical aspects of mobile technologies that may prevent an optimal learning experience include: restricted text entry, small screen size, and limited battery life. (p. 6)

The report affirms the need to conceptualise mobile learning not simply within a traditional 'technology-in-education paradigm' (p. 34), but to recognise the distinctiveness of the affordances of mobile devices compared with other (digital) technologies. In Chapter 3 we discuss and analyse the key issues emanating from debates about mobile learning in various domains and in Chapter 7 we explore their pedagogical implications without, hopefully, falling into the trap of being constantly pulled by the lure of the latest technology but instead, in pursuit of scalability, being guided by the notion of ubiquity, i.e. by features that are common also on less expensive phones.

The Need for a Coherent Theoretical/Conceptual Frame for the Field

The single most important motivation underpinning the writing of this book was the perceived need – also evident in the report from Joan Ganz Cooney Centre discussed above – to develop a coherent conceptual/theoretical frame in the emerging field of mobile learning. There is at the moment a proliferation of perspectives and approaches used by various researchers and commentators in trying to understand, analyse, explain and theorise examples of mobile learning practices. In our view, that shows the liveliness of the field on the one hand and on the other represents a danger to the development of a coherent framework, the possibility of constructive debate and eventual agreement in broad outline on major features.

Building a Larger Frame for Understanding

In its recent Task Force Report on 'Cyberlearning', the National Science Foundation of America (Borgman et al. 2008; see Fig. 1.1 below by Roy Pea and Jillian Wallis), traces the historical advances in ICT for human interaction. They discern five waves of resources, which increase in complexity of the media from basic, physical interaction around transient oral communication towards social networking and Web 2.0 characterised by cybernetic mediation, cloud computing, sensor networks etc. The report argues (p. 11) that the set of actions and interactions possible has changed with each new wave of mediating technologies. Mobile technologies and devices very much have to be seen as part of this developmental trajectory.

Dillenbourg (2008, p. 132), in a piece on integrating technologies into educational ecosystems, shows how the field of technology-enhanced learning has been structured around clusters of applications, including

(a) courseware with a frame-based structure inspired by programmed instruction or a modular structure inspired by mastery learning approaches,
(b) microworlds with their constructivist inspiration,
(c) hypertexts based on an awkward combination of *instructionalism* and exploration,
(d) simulations founded in guided discovery approaches,
(e) modeling tools that strangely grew independently from microworlds and simulations, and
(f) collaborative learning environments based on social-cultural theories.

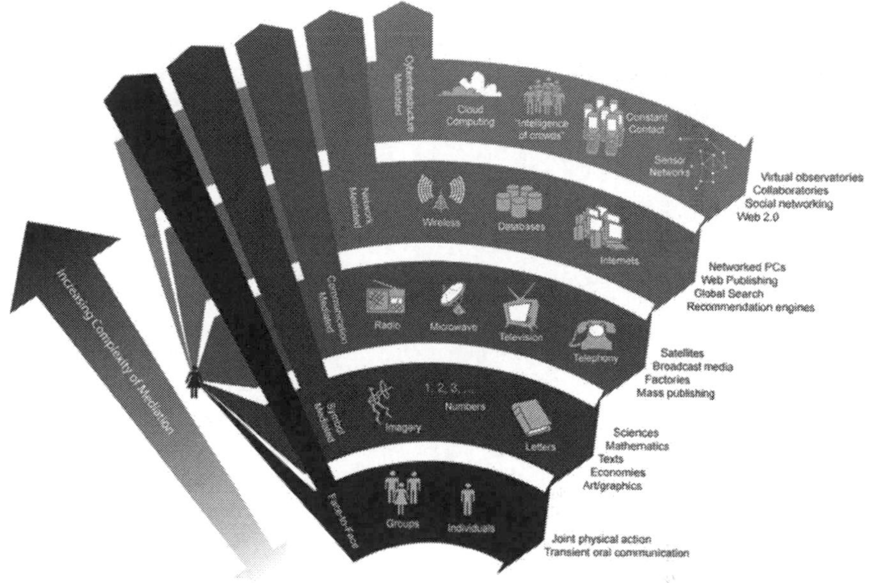

Fig. 1.1 Advances in communication and information resources for human interaction (Source: Borgman et al. 2008, p. 11)

And, he puts forward the view (p. 133) that, progressively, these clusters are converging into a common set of educational practices. This is a perspective we share: we, too, consider convergence to be a noticeable, and highly significant trend, which fundamentally informs the context within which educators work and against which we write this book. The 'mobile complex', therefore, is characterised by an exciting infrastructure in flux, which is at best only partially understood in terms of its educational potential.

Education in the Context of Societal and Cultural Transformations

A World Marked by Provisionality

Our approach attempts to provide a conceptual framework for an educational response to current social and cultural trends in a world marked by fluidity, provisionality and instability, where responsibilities for meaning-making as well as risk-taking are firmly located with the individual. It also attempts to take into account current changes in the authority over education from state to the market, changes to consumption and production as well as current characteristics of the media landscape like participation, distribution, local and global content, ubiquity and multimodality.

One of the fundamental tenets underpinning our rationale for the socio-cultural ecological approach to mobile learning delineated in this book is that of the need of an educational response to the current social, cultural, media-related, technological and semiotic change. This is particularly the case if the aims of education include the preparation of young people for active, and meaningful participation in their social, cultural, political and economic life-worlds for their own benefits as well as those of the community. The world in which we live is characterised by fluidity, provisionality and instability and the attendant risks increasingly fall to the individual.

From an educational perspective, this fragmentation poses serious questions in relation to the equitable provision of, and access to learning resources, be they conceptual, curricular, cultural and/or technological. It also brings to the fore changes in the means for the making and communication of meaning, for example in terms of multimedia and multimodality. Furthermore, it poses the challenge of pre-empting social isolation. And, it requires a deliberate stance of the education system and its agents, stakeholders and organisations in relation to the increasing importance of market principles and control, which in turn are characterised by principles of consumption and fragmentation into niche markets, rather than cohesion, integration and homogeneity. Traditional explanatory frames, such as 'social class', no longer provide sufficient analytical power. Instead, we use the notion of 'life-worlds' in this book, which recognises the clustering of different factors such as socio-economic background, gender, age/generation, ethnicity, regional background, profession etc. Traditional boundaries of various kinds are being blurred, abolished and they dissolve and disappear. Also, these trends have a lasting effect on meaning-making and learning.

Fragmentation and provisionality also find expression in the changing structures of power towards more open and participatory relations and adoption of agency on the part of young people, in particular in relation to participation in, and meaning-making through the production of cultural resources as well as their media habits. Consumption and audience are replaced by participation and production. The relationship between producers and users of artefacts is becoming increasingly blurred and the relationship of the user with the cultural artefacts they engage with in the process of knowledge production is frequently one of re-use underpinned by a fundamentally different attitude towards text as open, instead of fixed, and subject to constant modifications as well as text as comprising different modalities to be (re)contextualised according to specific situational requirements. In other words, 'text'-making is being governed by new practices, aesthetics, ethics and epistemologies. Text-making in this context needs to be understood as semiotic (form as content), cognitive (content as concepts) and affective (reflecting on interest and personal investment). And, there are boundaries, which include what counts as knowledge, what genres are permissible and what is considered to be culturally relevant. The characteristics and potential of new technologies also bring to the fore the question where the boundaries between information and knowledge lie (see Kress 2009).

'Participatory Culture': the Significance of Mobile Devices in the Life-Worlds of Users

The MacArthur Foundation in the US has published two interesting reports in recent years, Jenkins et al. (2006), Mizuko et al. (2008) and Ito et al. (2008), which, on the basis of empirical studies, illuminate the cultural practices of teenagers and young adults, which in turn relate to, and are conditioned by, changes to the media landscape, which we discuss below. Jenkins et al. use the notion of 'participatory' culture in order to shift the focus in debates about the digital divide away from questions about technological access to opportunities to participate and to develop the necessary 'cultural competencies and social skills' (p. 4). In terms of literacy practices, they see the notion of participatory culture shift the focus from individual expression to community involvement around: play, performance, simulation, appropriation, multitasking, distributed cognition, collective intelligence, judgment, transmedia navigation, networking and negotiation. And, they posit the need for policy and pedagogical interventions in relation to the following three concerns:

> *The Participation Gap* – the unequal access to the opportunities, experiences, skills, and knowledge that will prepare youth for full participation in the world of tomorrow.
> *The Transparency Problem* – The challenges young people face in learning to see clearly the ways that media shape perceptions of the world.
> *The Ethics Challenge* – The breakdown of traditional forms of professional training and socialization that might prepare young people for their increasingly public roles as media makers and community participants. (p. 3)

Ito et al.'s report (2008) argues that young people are struggling for autonomy and identity in a digital world in and through online spaces, which creates new opportunities for them to grapple with social norms, to explore their interests, develop skills and experiment with new forms of self-expression. The authors distinguish between 'friendship-driven practices' and 'interest-driven networks', which characterise young people's use of online media and around which new genres such as 'hanging out', 'messing around' and 'geeking out' are emerging. For us these findings have important implications for education.

Outside in and Inside Out

New converged media and associated cultural practices are having transformative effects on learning outside formal learning institutions. New technologies, such as the mobile/cell phone, and their widespread availability and use, affect cultural practices and enable new contexts for learning. For example, new media, such as YouTube, are changing traditional media practices, learners outside formal environments/institutions are able, actively, to select, appropriate and implement solutions to meet their own needs thus generating their own contexts for learning. These everyday learning practices, which make use of digital cultural artefacts, can be viewed as cultural resources for learning to be brought from outside into formal education. This is viewed as an 'outside in–inside out' relationship, where cultural practices involving new digital media can be brought into the school, these practices can be enhanced inside school and in turn feed back into the digital world at large. Thus new digital media can be regarded as cultural resources that can enable the bringing together of learning contexts in the world outside the school, and other formal educational institutions, with those processes and contexts that are valued inside the schools and formal education more generally. According to Davies (2008), young people, who by-and-large fail to be impressed by their general experience of technologies in schools, are happy to build technologies into their lives. Davies posits that the preferred mode of technology for young people is 'as resources that they exercise in ways that enable them to choose, to some extent, how they manage those aspects of their lives over which they have some degree of control' (p. 10).

From Distinct Media to Ensembles of Cultural Resources

In the context of the ongoing, and accelerating, process of fragmentation of mass communication and its increasing integration within everyday life interactions and communication, a wide range of media and mobile devices is (becoming) available and being utilised. Even a cursory look exposes a blend of media, services, events and mobile devices. This development represents an evolution from discrete media such as books or films. Beside this blend, the dramatic increase in the number and the variety of mobile devices is striking. Media are just one element within mass communication, albeit an important one. These developments we see aptly captured by the notion of media convergence.

The blending of media, commodities, events, sites, contexts etc., together with the increase in the availability of mobile devices, we argue, requires a broadening of our view of media and similar products towards a focus on their functions within contexts. Our long-standing cultural experiences with the media of mass communication has made those contexts more or less invisible; in particular the fixture of the TV set in home settings and the invisible transfer of content from centralized and remote production and broadcast units to stationary local TV screens tended to lead to a definition of media by its content, as 'programmes'. Today, the proliferation of devices and media applications opens a new view on context and activities within environments including the production, storage, presentation and interactive communication of content. Furthermore, the new portable and often, but not necessarily, multifunctional devices are becoming integral elements of flexible contexts which can be, and increasingly are being, generated by users. Indeed, the fragmentation of our society is inextricably bound up with (socially) flexible contexts: 'mobility' allows for, and demands flexibility within and beyond spaces for and contexts of activities. Not as visible as spatial mobility, but similarly important, are contexts which derive from the interrelation of internet offerings with user activities. Mobile devices work as interfaces for user-generated content and contexts.

In the context of this complexity, which has become normalised in everyday life, we find it helpful to search for adequate terminology, which goes beyond the restricted term of one medium. We think that a suitable term is 'cultural resource' as for us it integrates media, mobile devices, internet tools and services under the functional description of *resources*. In media and cultural studies the equivalent term is 'cultural products' (see e.g. Du Gay 1997).

Until now, by-and-large, the school has not really considered mobile devices and attendant content and context generation as relevant resources for teaching and learning. The term 'school' is used here as the label for institutionalised teaching and learning practices, which transmit a society's relevant knowledge, competences and habits from one generation to the next. In the context of lifelong learning (policies), learning is becoming a ubiquitous social feature, which goes beyond traditional school contexts. We see our line of argument located in this trajectory.

Why then do schools, as the agents of institutionalized teaching and learning practice, not take up these new resources? We think that there are two main reasons:

The first derives from the traditional perspectives of schools towards the media of everyday life in which media are viewed as objects of enquiry and the educational aim is for students to obtain critical (media) literacy. This approach to media is orientated towards offering students a critical understanding of how media work and endeavours to teach them how to use media creatively, and in a self-determined and expressive way.

The second reason results from the contrast between a disappearing world of discrete, bounded and clearly framed media compared with the complex of modes inherent in the emerging resources. When the photograph, the film or the video became available for use in schools, it was comparatively easy to integrate these media in curricular terms as functionally clearly defined media. The distinct media could work in the school context because of their precise functions: film, for example, allowed the presentation of the outside world in the school, as did video, photography or audio recodings. Discrete media were viewed either as tools for learning or as tools for teaching. Their specific representational features – the still photo, the moving image etc. – defined their curricular 'media' function for learning and teaching. Curricular application followed representational affordances.

Media convergence facilitated by, and characteristic of the web and its flexible platforms and services are far more difficult to control and hence to integrate or to subsume into the purposes of a traditional curriculum.

Apart from representational affordances, a second type of use tended to be in evidence, namely media as means of replacing specific teaching tasks, either to support or to replace the teacher, e.g. showing slow motion pictures of a complex physical experiment. Media in this paradigm were pedagogic tools or tools for learning and followed the model of the workbook with associated tasks for homework.

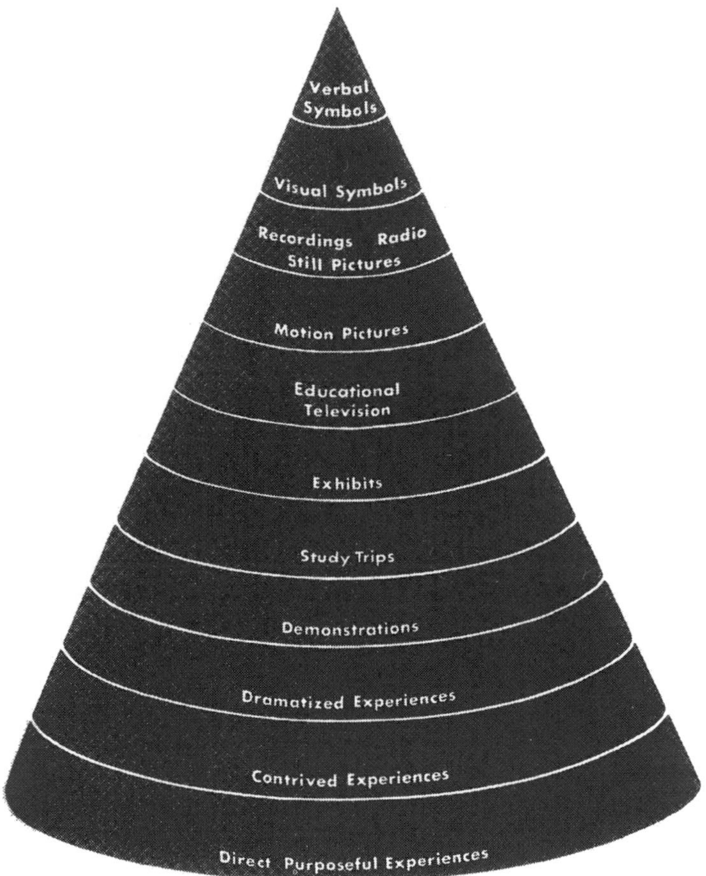

Fig. 1.2 Cone of experience (Dale 1969, p. 107)

A theory to deal with the way in which experiences can be, and are being linked to the outside world with these representational features was developed in the 1960s. Dale (1969) defined curricular applications in relation to the available range of media, in terms of their proximity to the real world, which students can experience. Dale's 'cone of experiences' (Fig. 1.2) placed media in a progressive sequence of realistic modes of representation, which comprised 'direct purposeful experiences, contrived experiences, dramatized experiences, demonstrations, study trips, exhibits, educational television, motion pictures, still pictures, recordings, radio, visual symbols, verbal symbols' (Dale 1969, p. 107). This approach was based on the representational functions of media and their relevance for students to gain and process experiences.

The 'cone of experiences' follows a one-dimensional rationale, which leads from the concrete ('direct purposeful experiences') to the abstract ('verbal symbols').

Along this spectrum between concrete and abstract, the media and the programmes they offered had the function of supporting experiences, which were seen as equivalent to contexts. Today, difficulties around a differentiation of media according to representational modes make such an evaluative rationale from the concrete to the abstract rather difficult if not meaningless. Also, current communication works not only through media but also, in an ensemble, by way of combinations of media, products, events, activities, settings etc. In (mass) communication, the available representational modes reach from 'spin-offs' such as the coffee cup, the t-shirt, the book and the casting event coupled with TV shows to web-events, communities, blogs etc. The personal computer with the representational tools film, image, sound and text has increased the diversity of representational functions.

In such a complex media landscape, the curricular functions of a 'mobile' video on YouTube for teaching and learning are difficult to discern. As noted above, for us the concept of cultural resources opens up an integrative view on mobile media or, put differently, on mobile devices within the context of media convergence and its integration within everyday life and attendant commodities.

Such a broad view of media and media-related phenomena requires detailed examination. The concept of cultural resources includes object/commodities as well as (moving) images, hardware, software, and, of course, the contexts provided by websites, such as media platforms or social networking sites. Here, a student's engagement with school learning through web offerings, for example in the form of a mobile video as homework in a Maths community on YouTube, works first of all as user-generated context.

In this discussion the concept of *situated learning* comes into play. Lave and Wenger (1991), the main proponents of situated learning, emphasise the situated character of meaning-making. They view learning as a mode of meaning-making in contexts, which can transgress the school in the same way an apprenticeship does in work-based learning contexts. Meaning-making is viewed as more than just the production, the decoding and the memorising of signs. Signs and learners depend constitutively on situations as otherwise meaning does not come about. But the situated character of meaning-making in the school is rather delimited by the range of situations the school can offer. 'Old' cultural resources, such as distinct media and 'new' ones, such as Web 2.0, are differently related to the situational aspect of meaning-making.

In contrast to the very stable learning practices of the school, communication is currently in a dramatic transition away from its former stable structures of programme production, broadcasting and reception/consumption, via TV channels and in front of TV sets. In contrast to the former transmission function of the TV or radio within a notion of broadcasting, mobile devices function within contexts. Examples for contexts are user-generated web contexts or differently combined geographical and communicative 'mobile' contexts. For example the mobile capacity of an iPod enables individually chosen geographical context. In combination with iTunes an iPod also offers a 'virtual' shopping context. Therefore, complex, individualised contexts are becoming available as distinct from, or overlapping with each other.

The question arises how to utilise this capacity in the school. In Chapter 12 on pedagogical approaches to ubiquitous mobility we make detailed proposals how to 'dock' school learning onto mobile contexts by taking up 'conversational threads' from students' everyday life. These proposals are premised on an understanding of the interrelation of media and context as cultural resources with the social constitution of child development and the formation of identity und subjectivity.

In the following we offer a brief, and invariably condensed discussion of the theoretical and philosophical underpinnings of our line of argument by way of background information for those readers wishing to engage in more detail with the perspectives we draw on in our argumentation, in particular in Chapters 9, 10 and 11.

The Social Construction of Culture, Child Development and Learning as Appropriation in 'Responsive' Contexts

Our wide conceptual and terminological approach to media, which is linked with commodities and contexts as cultural resources, refers deliberately to an interpretation of culture, which goes back two centuries to Georg W. F. Hegel and the conception of subjectivity by Wilhelm von Humboldt. Their leading ideas concerned culture and subjectivity as *social constructs*. The Hegelian concept of cultural manifestations sees culture as the externalisation of the collective human mind. The secular interpretation of the social construction of culture is based on human activities, which are mediated by objectified human activities. In terms of contemporary cultural studies, these objectified human activities are the cultural products of society. In terms of Georg W. F. Hegel (1807), the 'manifestations of the human mind' form the basis of a culture. In more contemporary terms, the human mind contains the symbolic activities of people, which lead to an objectively existing society and culture. The objectivity, what we perceive and interpret as real, consists of cultural products as manifestation of collective symbolic activities. Whilst this concept focuses on the objective world as a social construct, the educational approach to modernity and the emerging industrial age explained the development of children analogously as socially mediated formation. Appropriation can be seen to work as the central dynamic of the socially mediated formation of outside reality. A child appropriates outside reality, which is constructed by the parental generation in and through its symbolic activities. Appropriation begins with the internalisation of objectified symbolic activities of the parental generation. From an educational perspective, the appropriation of cultural products defines the social character of the development of the human being. Parallel to the social construction of the world within symbolic activities of externalisation and objectification, the educational theory of Wilhelm von Humboldt (1793/94, 2002a) describes the process of child development within a pre-given culture. Here the process of development depends constitutively on appropriation, which is a reflexive and personal internalization of the pre-given cultural manifestation. The development of a child, in modern terms, the development of identity or subjectivity, is possible only by appropriating external cultural products. The original German terminology for this process of a reflexive personal development by appropriation is 'formation', *Bildung*.

Against the backdrop of such a model of appropriation, Vygotsky investigated child development. Working in the 1930s, he stressed that child development is not an unfolding of innate, inherited capacities within certain time periods but, instead, an appropriative process, which is socially negotiated. This idea of social negotiation includes the internalization of the pre-given world of cultural products. In other words, learning is a mode of appropriation through the socially negotiated internalization of cultural products.

Essential for the social negotiation of learning of children with cultural products is the availability of what we call here 'responsive situations' in their development (see below for our rationale for preferring an alternative term to that established in the literature, i.e. 'Zone of Proximal Development', ZPD). This is one of Vygotsky's central ideas, who criticised the dominant learning practices of schools. His main argument was that school-based teaching did not respect the rationale behind child development. Child development happens in phases of the life-course. Vygotsky (1930/1978, p. 84 ff.) speaks of 'zones of development'. He argues (p. 81 f.) that the school and 'educational movements' emphasised formal discipline and urged the teaching of 'classical languages' etc. without considering their relevance for the daily life of pupils and their mental development. This critique makes the point that the cultural products, which have to be learned and dominate the process of teaching and learning, are insufficiently grounded in children's development. Moreover, school children merely had to internalize in a standardized way by memorizing. This kind of school learning did not aim at a negotiation of the child's 'responsive phases' of development (the original English translation speaks of *zones of proximal development*, Vygotsky 1930/1978, p. 84) with the pre-given cultural products of the curriculum. Despite the school's institutional power to command a specific internalization of cultural products, the specifics of child development also have to be taken into curricular account.

Following Wilhelm von Humboldt's idea of appropriation and Vygotsky's idea of developmental phases of a child and their specific rationale, we argue that children's subjectivity has to be respected in fostering learning. In the dominant educational discourse the negotiation of curricular subject and child development is seen as *scaffolding*. This concept was proposed by Bruner (Woods, Bruner and Ross, 1976); it views learning as internalization of cultural pre-givens and is deemed to succeed only if it is negotiated with respect to the respective developmental stage of the child. From this perspective, curricular scaffolding takes the form of negotiating activities in relation to the child, his/her actual stage and his/her susceptible phases of development.

As noted above, Vygotsky described children's developmental stages as 'zones of proximal development', in which the internalization of cultural products is possible in a scaffolded mode. But in the light of recent cultural developments, and the shift to symbolic spaces and flexible contexts, such as socio-cultural milieus or media convergence, the concept of developmental zones no longer has only the meaning of temporal zones. Stages of cognitive development were a special focus of Jean Piaget (1955). In the context of a cultural and social approach to appropriation, and of a view of the processes of learning as internalization of cultural products within zones of child development, the notion of zones has to be revisited. Also, the concept of cultural products, we argue, has to be reconsidered and extended from objects to situative contexts. Ongoing cultural and social transformation promotes contexts as highly relevant cultural products. Contexts comprise user-generated contexts in the field of media as well as of socio-cultural milieus to which traditional and new media are connected. With the emergence of mobile devices, contexts receive a visible and tangible interface as well as, of course, tools for navigation, communication and action.

Life-Worlds, Social Fragmentation and the Habitus of At-Risk Learners

Vygotsky's view on child development and learning in categories of time and phases in the life-course in our view requires a cultural re-interpretation. This re-interpretation has to fit into structures of individualised and mobile mass communication as well as into the society of individualised risks (Giddens 1991; Beck 1986). Of course, the social negotiation of child development and the internalization of cultural products have to be reconsidered with the aim of matching learning with meaning-making in disparate, fragmented situations. Such new situations for meaning-making and development are socio-cultural milieus. These milieus result from the process of individualisation and fragmentation, which lead to a fragmentation of meaning-making. This fragmentation of meaning-making in turn is a result of the range of available contexts in the sense that meaning-making belongs to a variety of social contexts, among them socio-cultural milieus. In Chapters 4 and 10 we depict such a milieu in the form of an ethnographic case study of an 18 year-old young man from a migrant family, who comes into conflict with society because of the nature of his media use. The socio-cultural context of a migrant boy is as relevant for learning as his bodily and cognitive development over the life course and its phases. But as far as milieus are concerned, our consideration focuses first and foremost on life-worlds and their developmental function and not on temporal phases.

Already in the first third of the last century, individualisation and fragmentation were an emerging dynamic, which led to a discourse around life-worlds (see Schütz 1932; Schütz and Luckmann 1984). Life-worlds have to be constructed by the people themselves and are their own responsibility. A life-world comprises more than just the environment in which people live. Life-world stands for lifestyle and habitus, which depend on people's individual way of living, which frames their life-course. Life-worlds result from individualization, which has led to fragmented worlds; they have to be configured personally. The responsibility for one's own life-world is to be carried by people individually. People in European countries organise their life-worlds within and by way of stable socio-cultural milieus. Milieus do have the function of individualised life-worlds, which are structured by the hierarchical variable of differentials in income and formal education. This is the traditional social stratification. But there is also a second important variable, which combines people's value orientation with the process of modernization of society.

For Central Europe the milieu fragmentation depicted in Fig. 1.3 is empirically valid:

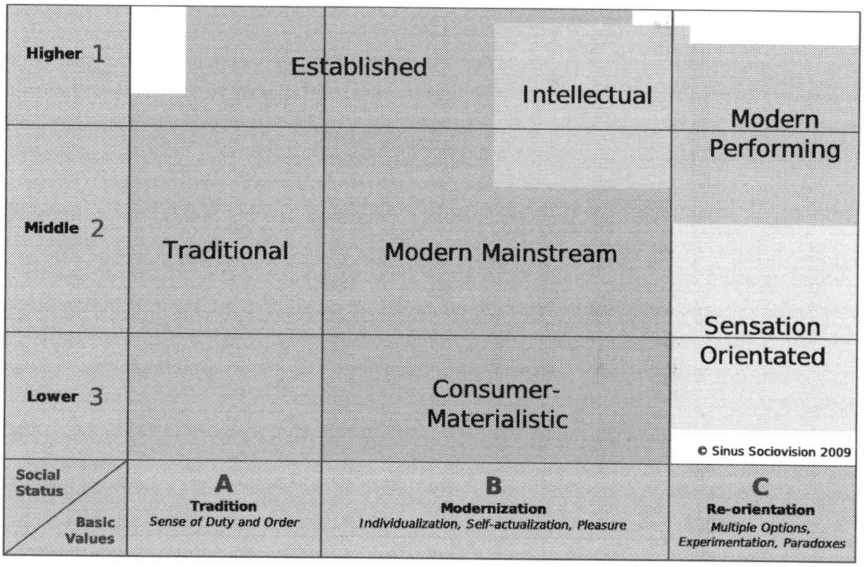

Higher 1
Middle 2
Lower 3
Established
Intellectual
Modern Performing
Traditional
Modern Mainstream
Sensation Orientated
Consumer-Materialistic
© Sinus Sociovision 2009
Social Status
Basic Values
A Tradition Sense of Duty and Order
B Modernization Individualization, Self-actualization, Pleasure
C Re-orientation Multiple Options, Experimentation, Paradoxes

Fig. 1.3 Sinus-Meta-Milieus® in Europe (Sinus Sociovision 2009, p. 22)

Figure 1.3 depicts along the vertical axis/variable *social status* (formal education, profession, income) and along the horizontal axis/variable *basic values (traditional, modern, re-orientation)*. Seven milieus exist: *established, intellectual, modern performing, traditional, modern mainstream, consumer materialistic, sensation orientated.* Children and young people from a low-income milieu differ dramatically in their way of living, which is a result of the value orientation of their social environment. For example, a child in a context with multiple and not very coherent options for decision-making is familiar with paradoxes in relation to their life accomplishment and the attitude towards experimenting (*Basic Values: C Re-orientation*). Such a child will deal differently with mobile and convergent context compared to a child from a traditional value system (see the value differentiation A, B, C for the low-income groups in Fig. 1.3). Of course, they also deal differently with learning inside or outside the school. And, they will configure different activity patterns for the use of traditional and new media and their related contexts.

In the process of this socio-cultural differentiation and fragmentation, the school has lost its defining power for all socio-cultural milieus on what counts as learning. This is clearly visible for boys of migrant families with low income and low formal education. Their learning experiences match primarily with the habitus of their milieu, that is, a life-orientation towards consumption and multiple risk-taking on the economic basis of limited material means. In the low income milieus the new mobile cultural resources obtain a compensatory function to the usual market for commodities. Commodities with a money value and resource with non-monetary values, e.g. social risks, are compensatory. They are also interchangeable. A key question for education is whether school, with its teaching and learning contexts, comes into contact with these resources. By that we mean that they contribute to the development of children in categories of learning.

We wish to re-emphasise at this point our view that mobile devices facilitate mobile contexts including user-generated contexts. In view of this we propose the assimilation of 'mobile contexts' as *responsive zones of child development*. The concept of assimilation derives from Piaget, who, with reference to Vygotsky, brought adult concepts of thinking into the relevant developmental zones of children. In terms of our terminology, the new cultural products of mobile contexts provide options for the development of a child if the child appropriates these contexts as cultural products.

What are these options? How can schools connect assimilative mobile contexts with school learning? Our answers to these questions are discussed in Part II of the book on the educational frame for mobile learning. Schools, we argue, should focus on *conversational threads*, which lead from learners' life-worlds into school. Furthermore, schools can relate curricular learning to user-generated contexts as 'zones of proximal development'. Conversational threads, which are determined and initiated by children or young people, are the thematic options enabling the connection of the fragmented life-worlds outside of school with curricular-based learning inside the school. Also the connection of contexts inside and outside of formal education can succeed if there is thematic accordance.

The references in our educational frame for mobile learning to thematic options and affordance link us to Paulo Freire (1970) and his generative themes. Freire succeeded with the alphabetization of adult workers and farmers in South America because the adults applied the intended reading and writing to their life-themes. Our educational intention is to 'knot' and 'dock' thematically with and at the new user-generated, mobile contexts, activities and devices as cultural products to and with the school and its learning intention. Mobile contexts offer the option of reaching students' responsive zones of development in their life-course as well in their everyday life.

Key Implications of Societal and Cultural Transformations for Learning with Mobile Devices

Following this historical and theoretical discussion, which we believe to be foundational for our line of argumentation, we briefly wish to re-iterate two key aspects we consider to be central to an understanding of the significance of mobile learning and its successful adoption.

Learner-Generated Contexts: Paradigm Change from Learning-as-Content to Learning-as-Contexts

We are currently witnessing a significant shift away from traditional forms of mass communication and editorial push towards user-generated content and individualised communication contexts. These structural changes to mass communication also affect the agency of the user and their relationship with traditional and new media. Indeed, we propose that users are now actively engaged in shaping their own forms of individualised generation of contexts for learning. For example, broadcasters have traditionally been 'in editorial control': commissioning programmes and broadcasting them through a predefined schedule that is transmitted on television. Now we are seeing a trend where the 'user' can generate their own content with a mobile/cell phone or other digital device in the form of text, pictures or video clips; they can then go on to publish their content almost immediately on the internet via media platforms such as Wordpress (for blogs), Flickr (for annotated photographs), Twitter (for micro blogs or 'diary like' social messages around the question 'what are you doing' in textual form no longer than 140 characters), FaceBook (a social networking site) or YouTube (for video clips and commenting). YouTube, for example, is not a traditional form of mass communication, it is essentially a lot of individuals publishing user-generated content (in the form of videos that users have produced themselves or copied from some other source, the latter may be subject to copyright restrictions). Consequently, what is emerging can be described as an 'individualised communication context' and it is interesting to note the response of traditional media organisations. Many have been slow to respond whilst others have begun to adapt. For example, the introduction of the BBC's 'iPlayer' and similar services by other broadcasters (e.g. ITV, Channel 4, ZDF) allow an individual to create their own schedule that can be watched outside normal schedule time.

New relationships between context and production are emerging in that mobile devices not only enable the production of content but also of contexts. They position the user in new relationships with space, the physical world, and place, social space. Mobile devices enable and foster the broadening and breaking up of genres, e.g. homework produced with the help of mobile/cell phones interlaced with humour. Citizens become content producers, who are part of an explosion of activity in the area of user-generated content.

But, one might ask, is there a direct relationship between user-generated content and learning? Undoubtedly the link is currently still more obvious in certain areas, such as music, media studies etc., than others. Yet, if not planned for, failing to explore how educational institutions can cope with the more informal communicative approaches to digital interactions that new generations of learners possess, we argue, could lead to a schism between learning inside and outside of formal educational settings. We see the notion of 'learner-generated' as a paradigm shift where learning is viewed in categories of context and not content and as a potential. Learning as a process of meaning-making occurs through acts of communication, which take place within rapidly changing socio-cultural, mass communication and technological structures that we have briefly outlined above.

Appropriation

The second key issue is how students appropriate mobile devices to set up specific learning contexts for themselves. How do they generate contexts for learning? Forming contexts with and through mobile devices outside of, as well as within existing educational sites of learning, we consider to be a key feature of appropriation. We see it related to the significant ongoing changes in terms of socio-cultural practices and approaches to learning. The concept of situated learning (see Lave and Wenger 1991) emphasises that learning as meaning-making occurs in situations (Hanks 1991), which are now 'in the hand', i.e. at the disposal of learners (cf. agency) through their use of mobile/cell phones within social structures.

We define appropriation as the processes attendant to the development of personal practices with mobile devices and we consider these processes in the main to be interaction, assimilation and accommodation as well as change (Cook and Pachler 2009). Whilst clearly terminologically linked, these are not the same as the development stages that are described in Piaget's (1955) theory of development, which are sensorimotor, pre-operations, concrete operations, and formal operations. However, our work is aligned with Piaget's (1955) description of learning and perception as a constant effort to adapt to the environment in terms of assimilation and accommodation. Thus, assimilation in the context of learning means that a learner takes something unknown into her existing cognitive structures, whereas accommodation refers to the changing of cognitive structures to make sense of the environment. Furthermore, for us, the context of appropriation is emergent and not predetermined by events; centrality is placed on practice, which can be viewed as a learner's engagement with particular settings, in which context becomes 'embodied interaction' (Dourish 2004).

We see appropriation as governed by the triangular relationship between agency, practice and structures. This inter-relationship manifests itself as emerging cultural transformations and appropriation provides a lens through which to view and analyse these changes. Indeed, we suggest that media convergence, together with the fluid socio-cultural structures of milieus and their respective habitus, lead to modes of appropriation as the individualised generation of contexts for learning. The spaces thus created differentiate everyday life into individually defined contexts as well as overarch different and divergent cultural practices such as entertainment and school-based learning. We envisage that at a foreseeable future point the socio-cultural developments described above will lead to a situation where there is no longer a need for a differentiation between media for learning inside and outside formal educational settings.

Our notion of appropriation also provides a conceptual frame to understand the growing gap between the literacy practices outside and inside formal educational environments. By 'literacy practices' we refer here to the cultural techniques involved in reading and producing artefacts to make sense of, and shape the socio-cultural world around us. The key point is that learners are evolving practices and meanings in their embedded interactions, i.e. interactions embedded in cultural artefacts that are found outside formal learning systems. A key challenge is to support learning between and across contexts outside and inside of educational institutions. To do this as educators, we need to make use of emerging cultural transformations that mobile devices afford and bring about as well as of the resultant cultural products that enable the individualised generation of content and contexts for learning. See also Pachler et al. 2010 for a detailed discussion of appropriation.

An Overview of the Socio-cultural Ecology: Agency – Cultural Practices – Structures

The analytical engagement with mobile learning we propose in this book takes the shape of a conceptual model in which educational uses of mobile technologies are viewed in ecological terms as part of socio-cultural and pedagogical contexts in transformation.

In the main, the following aspects characterize our proposals for an ecological approach (see Fig. 1.4):

Agency: young people can be seen increasingly to display a new habitus of learning in which they constantly see their life-worlds framed both as a challenge and as an environment and a potential resource for learning, in which their expertise is individually appropriated in relation to personal definitions of relevance and in which the world has become the curriculum populated by mobile device users in a constant state of expectancy and contingency (Kress and Pachler 2007);

Cultural practices: mobile devices are increasingly used for social interaction, communication and sharing; learning is viewed as culturally situated meaning-making inside and outside of educational institutions and media use in everyday life have achieved cultural significance;

Structures: young people increasingly live in a society of individualized risks, new social stratifications, individualized mobile mass communication and highly complex and proliferated technological infrastructure; their learning is significantly governed by the curricular frames of educational institutions with specific approaches towards the use of new cultural resources for learning.

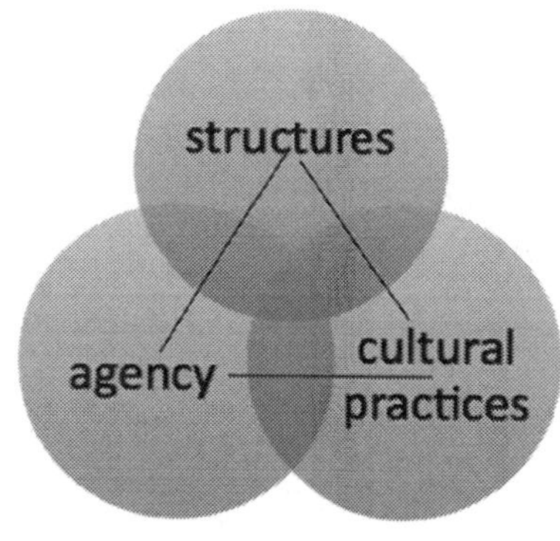

Fig. 1.4 Key components of a socio-cultural ecological approach to mobile learning – a typology

We, therefore, see learning using mobile devices governed by a triangular relationship between socio-cultural structures, cultural practices and the agency of media users/learners, represented in the three domains in Fig. 1.4. The interrelationship of these three components: agency, the user's capacity to act on the world, cultural practices, the routines users engage in their everyday lives, and the socio-cultural and technological structures that govern their being in the world, we see as an ecology, which in turn manifests itself in the form of an emerging cultural transformation.

The diagram in Fig. 1.4 is deliberately non-hierarchical, i.e. it can be read clockwise or anticlockwise and each one of the three branches of the concept map can be read first. It seems important to us that none of the domains is dominant over the other, and that their relative importance is determined by the specific context in which the model is used.

Overview of the Structure of the Book

Overall, the book attempts to take stock of developments in the field to date as well as to provide a developmental trajectory.

As could be seen, Part I starts off in Chapter 1 with an overview of the key issues discussed throughout the book, in particular an exploration of the 'mobile complex' and the definitional basis of mobile learning, the educational implications of social and cultural transformation as well as an overview of the socio-cultural approach to mobile learning, which provides the conceptual and theoretical underpinning for our discussion. Chapter 2 offers a diachronic overview of the development of the field of mobile learning, introduces some examples of mobile learning in practice, provides an overview of specialist conferences, events, journals and organisations and offers a discussion of key issues emerging from an in-depth analysis of the literature in the field. Chapter 3 explores the characteristics and potential of mobile devices for learning, adoption trends as well as constraints and challenges. Chapter 4 offers a number of cases of mobile learning as well as an analytical frame to describe and discuss them. Finally, Chapter 5 provides a detailed, and critical examination of the theoretical and conceptual approaches to mobile learning to be found in the literature to date, in particular Activity Theory and the Conversational Framework.

Part II offers an educational and social semiotic frame for dealing practically with the mobile complex. Chapter 6 presents the key concepts for a critical educational discussion of how school-based, and school-related learning could respond to the mobile complex. In Chapter 7 a semiotic analysis of one of the main mobile devices, the mobile/cell phone, leads to a consideration of mobile habitus. Since we conceive of the mobile/cell phone as a resource for meaning-making, we analyse the tool and its applications in terms of their semiotic functionality. In so doing, we pay particular attention to the issue of convergence. In Chapter 8 we offer a general discussion of the 'mobile complex' from an educational perspective. In Chapter 9 we examine the implications of the mobile complex for learning as personal appropriation and in terms of child development. In Chapter 10, we focus in particular on the learning options for at-risk learners. This discussion reveals a specific habitus for learning and media use in different socio-cultural milieus. Chapter 11 raises the question how schools could assimilate learners' user-generated contexts. We argue that mobile devices play the role of resources from the life-world as well as of interfaces between the life-worlds of young people and school. Our proposal to assimilate mobile learning from everyday life focuses on the recommendation for schools to develop reflexive context awareness in students. In Chapter 12 we discuss two mobile learning projects on the basis of four didactic parameters, which we have developed as a tool for analyzing and planning teaching and learning with mobile devices within the mobile complex.

Part III of the book comprises three chapters. Chapter 13 briefly sets the scene for the discussion in Part III. Chapter 14 attempts to provide a medium-term perspective for mobile learning, particularly in terms of emerging technologies and explores their implementation horizons as well as their implications for pedagogy. In the final chapter, Chapter 15, we programmatically explore possible futures for mobile learning inside and outside of formal educational contexts.

At the end of the we provide some suggested further readings with a brief annotation signalling the significance of the resources in question, in our view, in relation to the ideas covered in the book.

All URLs were live as of July 2009 unless otherwise stated.

Chapter 2
Mobile Learning: A Topography

So here is the paradox: the lived always seeks to be represented in some way and thus sacrifices the sense of life for the sense of words and meanings in order to relive. The journey is thus a double structure: one is the life of bodily engagement with the world; the other track is the life of reflection in order to represent textually, through images, through signs of all kinds, the experience of the journey. The double-tracked journey demands commitment, is often uncomfortable, takes too long and yet opens up new vistas, gives glimpses into different lives and can offer new possibilities for changes in direction, self-growth. (Schostak 2002, p. 2)

Introduction

In many ways writing this chapter, which attempts to provide a brief overview of the 'history' as well as the most pertinent current issues in mobile learning (research and practice) – as opposed to summarising the issues covered and foregrounded in this book, which we do in Chapter 1 – is like the double-tracked journey John Schostak describes in the quote above. Inevitably, no description, least of all the largely textual one possible within the confines of this book, can do justice to the breadth and depth of the rich tapestry that is the field of mobile learning with its many conference papers, presentations, case studies, project reports and pilots as well as its research papers and longer scholarly texts. The research underpinning this chapter necessarily involved attendance at, and the organisation of specialist conferences and engagement with relevant blogs and other social networking tools. And it is because of this 'bodily engagement' as well as the multimodal nature of the artefacts encountered – with video-enhanced PowerPoint or wiki presentations being the norm rather than the exception and with real-time blogging and podcasting of conference presentations being common – that it is difficult to do justice to the experiences and insights gained in a more traditional representational form. The reader, particularly if she is immersed in the practices of the field, rather than seeking initiation through the reception of this text, might well ask about the appropriacy of the chosen form of presentation. Yet, traditional academic discourse, even in the

N. Pachler et al., *Mobile Learning*, DOI 10.1007/978-1-4419-0585-7_2,

field of technology-enhanced learning, is not dead, we feel. In fact, it might be argued that in order to achieve maturation, the field – in view of the external drivers and gatekeepers of reified knowledge or canonical status – requires the adoption of a more traditional scholarly form of communication as a necessary precursor to ensuring transcendence into an established academic discipline.

We feel that sufficient work has taken place now in the field of 'mobile learning' to warrant, and require of us in writing this book, to take stock of the key debates taking place in the field before setting out our own perspectives and deliberations. This chapter, therefore, is an attempt to provide an overview of the field, in terms of practical examples as well as key conceptual issues, in an attempt to sketch a broad context for the remainder of our discussion. That is, it attempts to summarise, present and comment on the main developments in mobile learning in order to provide a baseline for our own theoretical stance, which we have outlined broadly in Chapter 1, and which we will delineate more fully in Part II of the book. In this chapter, then, we offer a state-of-the-art overview of and commentary on the most pertinent discussions in the field. We neither analyse the issues raised in any detail nor do we necessarily discuss them in relation to our own conceptual and theoretical perspective, although such links are, of course, made from time to time.

A Brief 'History' of Mobile Learning

We want to start our topography with a diachronic overview using a structure proposed by Mike Sharples at the Becta seminar 'Future Gazing for Policy Makers' held in 2006 at the BT Government Innovation Centre, UK. Sharples outlined three phases of mobile learning at this event characterised respectively by:

- a focus on devices;
- a focus on learning outside the classroom; and
- a focus on the mobility of the learner.

We attempt here to delineate the affordances that mobile devices and attendant technologies can provide across these three phases by providing highly selective, yet illustrative, examples from both inside and outside of school. It seems important to stress that the respective foci are not exclusive to any one phase, but that each phase is arguably characterised by an emphasis on one focal point. For example, of late we detect a resurgence of interest in devices with the introduction of new devices such as Apple's G3 (S) iPhone and phones that run Google's Andriod Open Source Operating System.

The First Phase of Mobile Learning: A Focus on Devices

The beginnings of widespread experimentation with mobile devices for learning happened from the mid 1990s. The first phase is characterised by a focus on what devices, in particular PDAs, tablets, laptops and mobile/cell phones, can be used for in an educational context for instruction and training. This first phase makes productive use of the affordances of mobile devices and technologies such as e-books, classroom response systems, handheld computers in classrooms, data logging devices and reusable learning objects.

Perry (2003) describes a UK project that took place in 2002–2003 in which some 150 teachers in 30 schools in England were given a selection of devices, mainly PDAs, to evaluate. The first phase of the project focused on senior management teams and how the devices support their work. The last phase involved a small number of schools being equipped with devices for the majority of staff and providing teachers with access to class sets in order to support their teaching. The project reported that the advantages were seen as being: portability, size, instant on (no start-up time), cost (relative to laptop computers), battery life (relative to laptop computers), and outdoor use. However, the disadvantages were seen as being: small screen, possibly not robust enough for schools, lack of technical support, data loss due to battery problems, problems with linking to networks. It would seem that even at this early stage, the concept of mobile/cell phone usage as a mediating tool for learning in the school context seemed to find positive advantages. Some of the disadvantages, like robustness and linking to networks, have diminished in the intervening years. However, as we shall see below, new challenges for learning with mobile devices have also emerged.

Also in the UK, McFarlane and colleagues conducted research on two ambitious initiatives, 'Learning2Go' in Wolverhampton and 'Hand-e-learning' in Bristol. These projects have enabled every pupil in a year group and their teachers to have a mobile device. These projects use considerable parental support to provide funding for these initiatives. The first report from the study (McFarlane et al. 2007) identified three issues as key contributors to the problems encountered and a less positive take-up than had been hoped for: lack of infrastructure in the schools – wireless capacity in particular; rushed initial training for teachers; the choice of science as the subject through which to promote device use (in science the majority of teachers were too preoccupied with a new curriculum to take on another challenge). However, following a project re-launch, McFarlane et al. (2008, p. 9) have subsequently reported that whilst 'the introduction of 1:1 mobile devices has been more problematic and complex in secondary schools than in primary',

> since the re-launch there are encouraging signs of success. The size of the devices makes it possible for them to be taken from a pocket or bag and accessed very easily in class, in a car or bus on the way to and from school, even to be taken comfortably to bed. Large amounts of material (provided or learner-created) can be stored in one place on a device. Combined with these points, the instant-on facility means that access to stored material or the internet is immediate. The intimacy of the device in the hand seems to be attractive, especially to learners in the primary phase, and the size of the screen appears less daunting to some writers. Observations of primary phase learners record children writing curled up in chair or on cushions, walking around the class, standing in line waiting: all situations which would not support traditional writing tools or larger/heavier technological tools. (p. 9)

It is interesting to note in the above quote that affective issues such as 'the intimacy of the device' play a part in the appropriation of the device in the children's life-worlds and for meaning-making.

The above McFarlane et al. quote mentions the fact that 'large amounts of material (provided or learner-created) can be stored in one place on a device'. A project that explored the increasingly sophisticated converged multimedia capabilities of smartphones as platform for storing learning resources is based in the UK's Centre for Excellence in Teaching and Learning (CETL) in Reusable Leaning Objects (http://www.rlo-cetl.ac.uk/). This work uses smartphones as a desk-top, placing rich multi-media mobile learning objects in the phone's memory to scaffold (Wood et al. 1976) different types of learning. This work originates in Higher Education but the learning support/tasks are also appropriate for 14–19 year olds; a perspective confirmed by various presentations of this approach to school leaders in the South East of England (e.g. see Cook and Smith 2004) who are involved in the multi-billion pound Building Schools for the Future programme (see e.g. http://www.teachernet.gov.uk/management/resourcesfinanceandbuilding/bsf/). Briefly, a selection of the 200+ internet based Reusable Leaning Objects (RLOs) that the CETL repurposed for mobile/cell phones have been evaluated with consistently positive results (see Bradley et al. 2007; Smith et al. 2007). For example, in a pilot evaluation of the 'self-tests' and 'basic guides' shown in Fig. 2.1, Bradley et al. (2007) found that there were indications from students that they would use mobile learning objects. One thought it was 'a good idea' as you could look at something you needed to on the way home from class (this theme was echoed by other students, see below). In this sense, there is a link through to the Bitesize learning material from the BBC also described below; this moves the RLO approach into a context where the learning can take place outside the school or educational establishment in a way that is convenient to the learner.

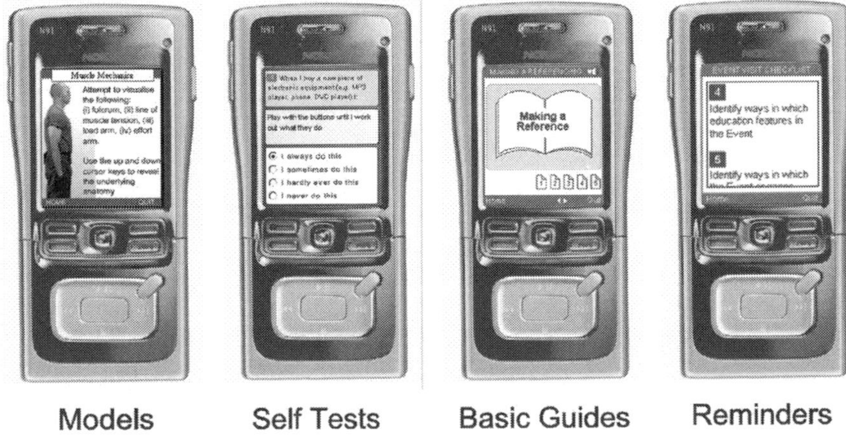

Fig. 2.1 Different types of learning support

Figure 2.2 shows students evaluating sports science learning objects. Smith et al. (2007) obtained some interesting results in the focus group when the students had a chance to use and evaluate a mobile RLO for muscle mechanics (which is also

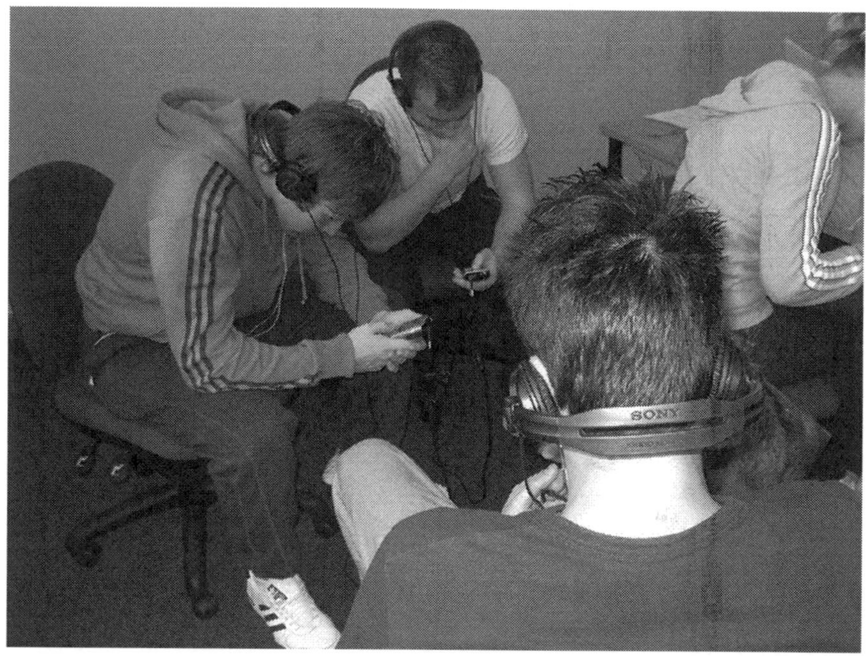

Fig. 2.2 Students evaluating sports science RLOs

available as an internet version). Of particular interest was the observation that the mobile version complimented the web version of the RLO in a number of respects. Firstly, it was observed that having already seen and completed the web-based version, the mobile version could be used to reinforce and memorise what was learnt before an exam 'because, if you were on the train or whatever, to Uni... it would be perfect'. Secondly, it was agreed that the addition of audio in the mobile version added to a sense of immersion in the content and an increase in the level of involvement in comparison with the web version. 'It's more like you're in class.... you are able to concentrate more'. Indeed, Fig. 2.2 illustrates that with headphones on, this form of learning enables immersion in the learning task. The subjects are completely engrossed in their learning activity. A number of students mentioned some other advantages of the mobile version, citing the element of distraction with computer versions: 'Because when I'm on the internet to be honest, I've got loads of different pages open and just flicking through – on the mobile you're just looking at the work' and 'I just think it's much better when you're travelling or whatever, when you're on a train going somewhere... If I had it on my phone, I'd look at it definitely'. Students also agreed that they would use the mobile RLO in context, e.g. in the gym to observe muscle mechanics.

Possible criticisms of the RLO approach include that it simply replicates the desktop experience, it is simply extending traditional pedagogic practice, it is not taking advantage of the ability of mobile devices to enhance context-to-context learning or, indeed, conversations across contexts. However, one advantage of the

RLO approach is that it provides rich, bite-sized learning that can be used outside and inside the classroom to reinforce learning; as such, this approach can be seen to be reaching into the second phase of mobile learning. The design of these mobile learning objects is not simple (see Bradley et al. 2009) and, as we saw above in the students' comments, sound is used more than in the internet versions in order to avoid having lots of text on a small, match-box sized screen. Indeed, this approach allows learners to take a 'proxy' of the teacher off-site with them as they engage in a field-study learning task (e.g. 'Reminders' were used in the Cook et al. (2007) study). This ability of pre-installed guides to scaffold off-site learning is something that is difficult to 'fit' into Laurillard's (2007) recent re-mapping of her own Conversational Framework, described and critiqued in detail in Part II of this book, to accommodate on-site and off-site learning. Furthermore, it is noteworthy that the ability to watch films, videos, etc on small screens was not generally seen as having much potential for success around 2005–07; however, such a view has proved incorrect as we have seen with Apple's iPod Touch and iPhone, and other equivalent mobile devices. Such devices are used in vast numbers to watch content on the move which can be downloaded through fast wireless networks like 3G, or indeed be sat waiting to view having previously been downloaded to a computer via the internet and then 'synched' to the mobile device. Mobile/cell phones that have the ability to combine rich multimedia, scaffolding guides and context awareness would seem to have a rich future, as we will see below. There is, however, one other important drawback to RLOs, which needs to be acknowledged here: compared with digital video recordings their production normally lies outside the scope of teachers and learners.

The Second Phase of Mobile Learning: A Focus on Learning Outside the Classroom

A focus on learning outside the classroom is a characteristic of the second phase of mobile learning. In order to reify our model of socio-cultural ecology, with its focus on socio-cultural practices and bringing those found outside educational establishments inside, in our discussion we attempt to highlight the meaning-making that is possible for a person in situations outside institutionally framed educational contexts. The affordances in the second phase can include field trips, museum visits, professional updating, bite-sized learning and personal learning organisers.

An early second phase project in the UK was 'HandLeR' (Handheld Learning Resource) (Sharples 2000; Sharples et al. 2001; Sharples et al. 2002). 'HandLeR' addressed issues of user interface design for mobile learning and developed software for a field trip (see Fig. 2.3). The system was designed to have multiple functions. According to Sharples et al. (2001), the generic HandLeR system had four main components:

- a set of tools to capture and annotate events,
- a web browser,

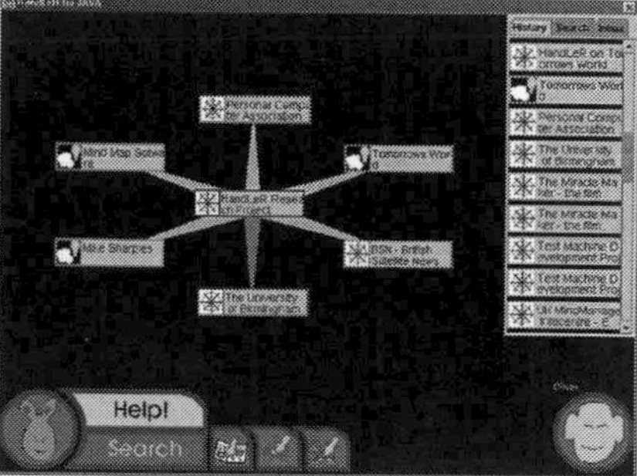

Fig. 2.3 Main screen and concept mapping tool from the HandLeR children's field trip interface (Source: Sharples, Corlett and Westmancott, 2001)

- a database manager to organise and relate the events as a knowledge structure, and
- a communications manager to support synchronous voice and data communication and asynchronous sharing of knowledge

and the capture tools included:

- a notepad with handwriting or voice recognition,
- an integral still and video camera, and
- a drawing package.

'HandLeR' used a 'mentor' that was intended to act both as a learning guide and to initiate activity, but which appears in reality as a screen metaphor. For example, clicking on body parts launches tools, such as the eyes for a camera, hands for a writing pad, and brain for a concept mapping tool. Figure 2.3 shows the main 'HandLeR' screen and the concept mapping interface.

An important conclusion from trials of the 'HandLeR' system was that the technology at that time (2000–2001) had severe limitations, which made it almost impossible to use. However, its main success was to establish the concept of mobile and contextual learning outside the classroom, for field trips and professional development.

A significant project in this phase was 'MOBIlearn'. This research and development project ran for 33 months from January 2002 to March 2005 and involved 24 partners from academia and industry in ten countries (http://www.mobilearn.org). This project provided access to knowledge through appropriate learning objects, mobile services and interfaces. One aspect of the non-formal learning that the project tested extensively was with users at the Uffizi Gallery in Florence (http://www.mobilearn.org/results/trial.htm; Lonsdale et al. 2004) (Fig. 2.4).

Thus, the 'MOBIlearn' project realised the shift in focus from learning with handheld devices towards support for the mobility of learning as it started to make use of location aware systems, i.e. the system deployed was able to provide information and guidance depending on the users' location. Furthermore, the lead partner, Giunti Labs, has subsequently developed a mobile extension to its 'Learn eXact'

Fig. 2.4 A student with a mobile/cell phone in front of one of Signorelli's paintings in the Leonardo room (Source: http://www.mobilearn.org/images/museum_trial/PIC_0024.jpg)

system based on results from 'MOBIlearn' that enables context aware learning; this approach is being utilised in the 'CONTSENS' project (see discussion below in Phase 3).

The converged functionality that is now commonplace with mobile/cell phones (e.g. see the smartphones described in Phase 1) has led to their extensive use for learning outside the classroom. The technology simply could not support the pedagogy when 'HandLeR' was formulating its support for student learning. A recent example of a project that has taken advantage of the converged media affordances of mobile/cell phones is the 'Learning Lab Initiative' discussed in detail in the examples chapter later in Part I of this book. This project was conducted in Bangalore, India, at a government school with 13–15 year old pupils and consisted of several activity-based stages, where 'students were encouraged to move out of the classroom and bring into play new ways of exploring and understanding their environment, and visualizing this new knowledge' (CKS 2005b). Pupils were equipped with mobile/cell phones, ranging from GPS devices to multi-media capable mobile/cell phones (see Fig. 2.5). At the beginning of the project, students were supported with workshops and training sessions. The learning that took place with these mobile devices was evaluated impressionistically only by the Learning Lab team and, in general, the results appear to be optimistic with regards to learners and parents: learners were able to use the mobile devices in a competent way to organise their self-directed learning. Parents appear to support the use of mobile devices in curricular contexts and were, thus prepared to 'invest in any promising educational technology' (CKS 2005b). However, and is in the work by McFarlane et al. (2007) reported above, the teachers' role, as well as administrative aspects, were considered to contain challenges: teachers prefer hierarchical over peer-to-peer communications because there is a perceived loss of authority and communicative control. Also, from the teacher's perspective, there was a perceived inability to keep up with technology. Furthermore, from the administrator's viewpoint, there was a

Fig. 2.5 Students using image capture for a science assignment (Source: CKS 2005a)

perceived lack of control over the use of technology in the school. This project highlights a common theme in the literature, that teachers are struggling to keep up with the new modes of technology and digital media appropriation and that this may lead them to take measures to retain control in teaching and learning situations.

SMS alerts are starting to find a use in schools for communicating with students and parents, although the approach tends to take a one-way push mode as it is seen to provide benefits for co-ordination and management, for example students (and even parents) receiving notifications about aspects of school life, such as parent evenings. However, there is considerable scope for development in the use of this technology. For example, in Kenya there is a widespread availability of mobile/cell phones as well as no reliable fixed telecommunications network and no prevalent computer availability; Kenya also, like much of Africa, has unreliable surface mail. This has led to explorative work (e.g. Traxler and Dearden 2005a) that has examined the potential for using SMS to support learning and organisation in sub-Saharan Africa. The potential of this 'low-tech' approach seems enormous. SMS thus has the potential to reach parts of the world that traditional media, including the computer-based internet, is not able to reach.

The University of Wolverhampton, for example, has used SMS to improve retention and progression by extending and enriching the contact and support of higher education students on- and off-campus (see e.g. http://www.jisc.ac.uk/whatwedo/programmes/elearninginnovation/melas.aspx). The University of Dublin carried out a project which enabled students to send SMS to lecturers' laptops to anonymously ask questions without interrupting the class. It is up to the lecturer to respond immediately, wait until a number of questions arise or respond after class (see http://www.cs.tcd.ie/crite/projects/mobile/Txt%20IT.php). Griffiths University in Australia carried out a project learning Italian with SMS where 2–3 messages a day were sent about grammar, vocabulary news, literature and administration, homework etc (see http://www98.griffith.edu.au/dspace/handle/10072/186).

Traxler and Dearden (2005b) propose that it is possible to provide support for the curriculum through SMS: study guides giving week-by-week support; content in the form of hints, tips, outlines, lists, summaries, revision; reminders about assessment, contact, broadcast, discussion, video, meetings; discussion including feedback, seminar, query; pastoral support, and encouragement; urgent messages about cancellation and change.

The BBC Bitesize's (http://www.bbc.co.uk/schools/gcsebitesize/) is a secondary school revision resource for students studying their GCSEs (General Certificate of Secondary Education) in the UK that is made freely available to the world. Figure 2.6 below illustrates some of the features offered by this resource, which includes written content, interactive content, audio, video and games. Sometimes Bitesize allows revision questions to be sent to mobile/cell phones.

Fig. 2.6 BBC Bitesize (Screenshot taken September 14, 2008)

This form of push-learning has proved very popular, with 2.6 million unique internet users in May 2006, as a BBC press release dated August 15, 2006 suggests (http://www.bbc.co.uk/pressoffice/pressreleases/stories/2006/08_august/15/bitesize.shtml):

> ... last year 70% of all GCSE students used the service. It is the most innovative multi-platform revision tool there is. Bitesize fits teenagers' lives because it's available in so many different formats – online, on your mobile/cell phone or by pressing your red button [on the TV]. New technologies offered this year included downloadable MP3 s for English and Science, a multi-player revision game, RSS feeds, and a mind-mapping tool called Revision Map. Bitesize provides different ways of revising and helps to break up the monotony of what is an onerous and stressful period, but also provides an alternative angle to subject areas which may have been unclear before.

The Bitesize facility to download to mobile/cell phones appears to have been withdrawn, possibly because of the large number of hits that the service was getting. The way in which learners incorporate these resources into their learning habitus is not clear and more research is needed. However, a qualitative appreciation of the worth of such a resource for the meaning-making of school children can be gained form the quote below, taken from McFarlane et al. (2008, p. 10); for us this quote illustrates from a student's perspective why Bitesize and similar resources are helpful for mobile learning:

> The one thing that has got me through my exams is Bitesize. So if there's anything in lessons that you don't understand or the teacher is busy with other things, instead of just sitting there, you can check – its got all the possible subjects for GCSE e.g. in RE its got all the subjects in religious studies... so Buddhism, Christianity, if you go to revise, its fairly quick the internet on this [the mobile device]. [Jake (Year 11)]

Although students at the moment do not tend to have phones with web browsing capability like Jake, there is a trend for them to have this affordance on the mobile devices they use outside of school (see Part III). Indeed, learning outside the classroom is now making use of the multimedia affordances of mobile/cell phones in increasing sophisticated ways. An approach that goes well beyond the RLO approach described in phase one above is the 'Skattjäkt project' (Treasure Hunt; http://www.celekt.info/projects/show/15) (Figs. 2.7 and 2.8), developed at Vaxjo University, Sweden. Treasure Hunt is a mobile game that is designed to encourage young people to solve a mystery surrounding a castle:

> The game is inspired by treasure hunts and the sport of orienteering. Up to 6 teams can compete currently. The game starts with a video detailing the mystery of why the ghost of Anna Koskull has come back and now the players need to help her solve the mystery of her late husband Frederick Bonde in order to free her spirit from limbo. After the players get briefed they are split into teams. The game starts and each team gets a different location on the campus to find. The locations are shown on the phone via the Flash Lite Application

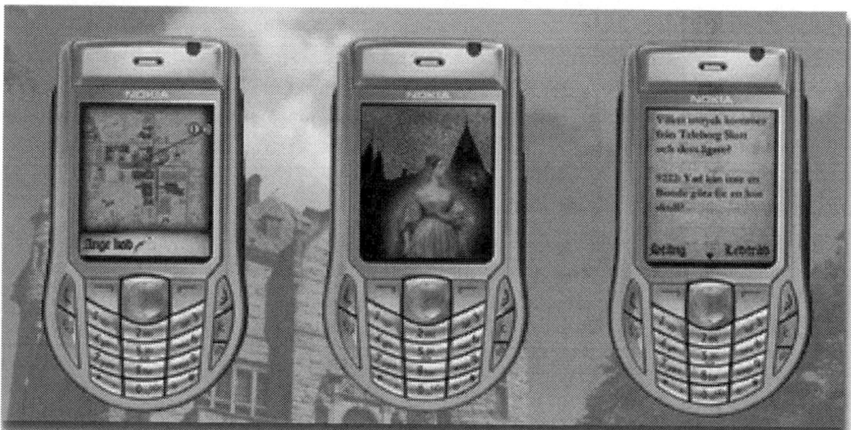

Fig. 2.7 Screen shots from the 'Skattjäkt project': the map, the ghost audio clue, and a question screen (Source: http://www.celekt.info/max/content/game_collage.jpg)

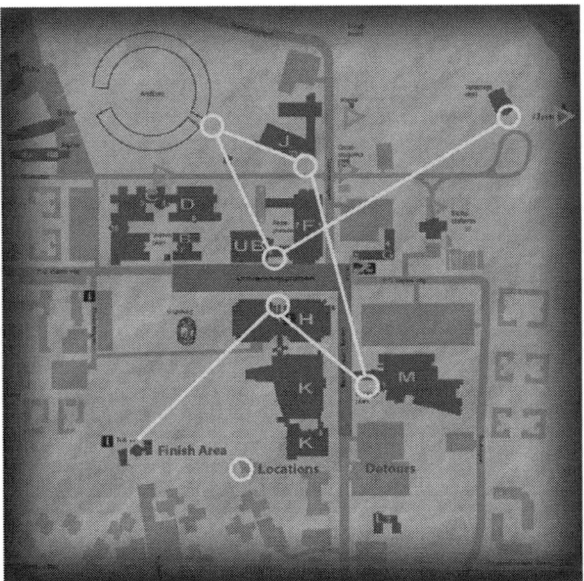

Fig. 2.8 Game map (Source: http://www.celekt.info/max/content/full-map.doc)

> [Adobe multimedia software]. They receive a clue to find a 4-digit code, for example look for lion's feet at the castle. When they arrive to the castle the can see 2 large lions at the feet of the right lion is sticker with a code, they enter the code into the phone and then they get the question what is on the family shield of the castle. They go up the steps of the castle to look at the shield, if they answer correctly they get a clue to the next location, if not they get a detour location. Of course they don't know it is a detour until they get to the location.

Spikol (2008) describes an evaluation of Treasure Hunt using co-design principles. Co-design is described as a 'highly facilitated, team based process in which students, teachers, researchers, and developers work together in defined roles to design an educational innovation, realise the design in one or more prototypes, and evaluate each prototype's effectiveness in addressing an educational need'. This approach was used to guide two completed trials over the 2007–2008 with a third trial in progress at the time the paper was presented. Preliminary indications from the study suggest that, from a methodological perspective, the co-design approach can assist researchers in 'understanding how informal mobile games can be used as learning tools in traditional educational settings through the active involvement of students in the design of their own learning activities. This can provide ways to understand the learning practices of the students by utilizing the different assessment techniques' (Spikol 2008). In a similar vein to Treasure Hunt, various commercial systems are now available on the market that enable field trips. For example, WildKey (http://www.wildkey.co.uk/) provides a good example of software for fieldtrips. WildKey is essentially set of software tools that enables the learner to identify, record and capture data on a range of handheld devices. In this way the learner is drawn into a practice of meaning-making and knowledge construction.

The focus on learning outside the classroom has become an active area of mobile learning practice and research. The diversity of learning in this phase is striking: from the Italian art gallery experience in 'MOBIlearn', the use of Bitesize for revision in the UK, SMS-based learning across the world, through to game-based learning in the context of a mystery surrounding a castle in the Swedish Treasure Hunt project. Furthermore, the focus on the learner through co-design is coming to the fore, as is the emergence of an interest in context sensitive learning. And it is the latter to which we turn now.

Third Phase: A Focus on the Mobility of the Learner

The third phase is characterised by a focus on the mobility of the learner, the design or the appropriation of learning spaces and on informal learning and lifelong learning. Three important affordances can be distinguished: mixed reality learning, context-sensitive learning and ambient learning.

Mixed Reality Learning

Mixed reality learning, or mixed modes of representation, attempts to augment a learner's meaning-making by enabling them to participate in a media-rich environment rather than view the learner as consumer of content. Augmentation is intended here as a positive notion not as making up deficiencies. The provision of visualisations enables the learner to see aspects of the world in a new light and to discover facets of this augmented environment that are not easily perceived in the 'non-augmented' world. New environments and visualisations are created where the physical and digital interact and inform one another in real time.

Learners are enabled to construct content and 'place' it in context using mobile devices where other learners can access, and add to it. Meaning can, for example, be built around the specifics of a place and learning trails can be developed to foster meaning-making across and between multiple contexts. For example, a user with a camera phone and free reader software can scan Quick Response (QR) Codes (http://en.wikipedia.org/wiki/QR_Code) and automatically convert them into URLs, small books, images or videos etc. This act of linking from physical world objects is known as 'physical world hyperlinking'. Users can generate and print their own QR Codes and create their own physical learning environments very quickly (Fig. 2.9).

The 'MyArtSpace' project provides an example of a sophisticated mixed reality project (e.g. see Sharples et al. 2007; http://www.cultureonline.gov.uk/projects/in_production/my_art_space/). The aim of the project was to make school museum visits more engaging and educational. In one part of this project, school students explored a D-Day museum using mobile/cell phones to help them discover information about exhibits, take photos, and record audio and text notes. Photos and notes were sent automatically from the phones to their personal museum visit webspace, thus allowing students to construct personal narratives to share with family, friends and the general public. MyArtSpace, therefore, combines a learner's personal space (mobile/cell phones), physical space (museum, classroom) and virtual space (online

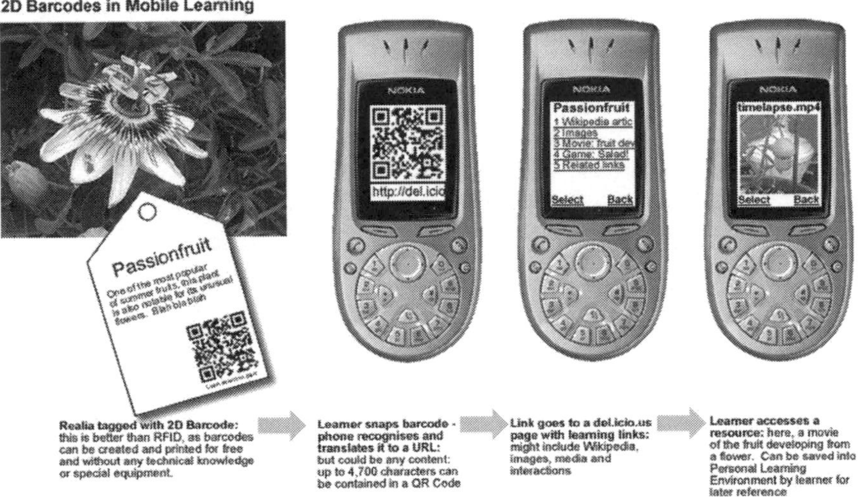

Fig. 2.9 QR codes (Source: http://farm1.static.flickr.com/96/214538909_0b5f7a233d_o.png)

repository and gallery). Sharples et al. (2007), who acted as external evaluators to the project, reported that

> continuous evaluation and fine-tuning of the new technology in concert with the learning practice (including lesson planning, IT support, and activity planning) resulted in a system that met the initial design aims and provided a generally reliable service to museums. The study also identified issues that will need to be addressed in future services for museum or field trips, including the need to orient teachers and students to the experience, how to re-create the context of the visit back in the classroom, and finding a suitable business model for museums and schools to support a continued service.

Given the above comments it would appear that a co-design approach may be a productive way forward as a way of building learning systems that fit into the practices of both learners and teachers. Within a co-design perspective use and purpose are in the foreground, hardware and software design are brought together and it is acknowledged that client and beneficiary may not be using the artefact being designed. (See http://en.wikipedia.org/wiki/Co-Design) Furthermore, the key issue of orientating teachers points to the emerging need for staff development for those involved in such projects.

Other interesting work in the context of 'MyArtSpace' is that by Kevin Walker around 'personalised learning trails' (see e.g. http://www.archimuse.com/mw2007/papers/walker/walker.html) where visitors to museums, botanic gardens and cultural heritage sites aged 9 years and up created learning trails through the capture, editing and sharing of audio, photos and text during visits. The notion of personalisation in this example refers to conceptual frameworks into which information and experiences captured during a visit are placed in order for learning to be fostered.

Another approach to mixed-reality is provided by the 'CONTSENS' project (http://www.ericsson.com/ericsson/corpinfo/programs/using_wireless_technologies_for_context_sensitive_education_and_training/), funded by the European Commission's Mobile Learning: A Topography Leonardo Lifelong Learning Programme. The two year project, which started in April 2008, involves a European-wide consortium headed by Ericsson Education Ireland, with Giunti Labs, London Metropolitan University, ECLO (Belgium), Plovdiv University (Bulgaria) and Corvinno (Hungary). The project focuses on the development of appropriate training/learning materials for mobile learning enhanced by context sensitive and location-based delivery. In one work package, based at London Metropolitan University, consortium members are working on new environments and visualisations that are created where the physical and digital interact and inform one another in real time. This Cultural Heritage Learning work package extends work done on an earlier Cistercian Chapels project for archaeology students hosted by Sheffield University, UK, (http://www.shef.ac.uk/hri/projects/projectpages). Virtual reality representations of heritage sites can offer innovative solutions to the challenges which exist when learning about our cultural heritage. In order to allow for the greatest degree of flexibility in learning, the outputs of the Cistercian Chapels project are visualised in multiple ways (via multiple media);

Fig. 2.10 Visualisation in the Cistercian Chapels project

these include the web and site visits equipped with handheld devices including mobile/cell phones which use GPS to locate the user and present the appropriate reconstructions. Figure 2.10 gives an indication of visualizations that are used for this project.

Mixed reality learning is a powerful approach as it enables the learner to visualise something that may not have been seen in reality for centuries. The field-trip is a great tradition of school learning and mobile devices add new digital affordances to it.

Context-Sensitive Learning

Context-sensitive learning is a fascinating area that holds great potential for enabling learners to engage in meaning-making through interactive practice (Dourish 2004). 'Interactions' is taken here to be a term that encompasses conversation and non-verbal communicative acts like gestures and mouse clicks etc. Location-aware services, already used by emergency services, which use systems and tools that are able to detect the exact physical location of mobile device. For example, if a learner is stood in front of a painting by Picasso in an art gallery, the location-aware system can offer to transfer background information on the painting and the artist. In addition to services such as finding places and giving directions, location-aware systems can also help identify potential interactors in physical proximity of the learner. Applets on mobile devices such as the iPhone or iPod Touch utilise location awareness inter alia to tell the user which of their 'buddies' and friends are in physical proximity. Context-sensitive systems are aware of the activities of learners and can thus offer to give assistance. For example, if a student's course work is due in soon, the context-sensitive system can send a tip giving the location of resources that may help with an assignment. Thus, interaction-based approach to context should, ideally, continually derive what intervention is appropriate and can provide relevant services to aid learning. Context-sensitive systems, therefore, enable the delivery of appropriate learning content. Sharples (2006) pointed out that examples of context-aware learning could include: location-based guides and customised help systems; systems that enable activities in context, e.g. data logging; game learning offering services and options such as communication and awareness of other game players; customise content; adaptive interface and interaction, where the level of detail and order of presentation can vary and be made appropriate for context and for display on different devices.

'CAGE' is a system with an interaction model of context (Lonsdale et al. 2004), where context is seen as a dynamic and historical process that enables appropriate action (learning). 'CAGE', which stands for Context Aware Gallery Explorer, was developed as part of the 'MOBIlearn' project. This model of context is constructed through interaction between people, technology, objects and activities as proposed conceptually by Dourish (2004) (see below).

The 'CONTSENS' project, also already mentioned above, is one of several follow-ups to 'MOBIlearn'. It examines the use of wireless technologies for context sensitive education and training in museums and galleries, for language learning and for workplace learning. One 'CONTSENS' partner, again at the UK's London

Metropolitan University, has developed a series of mobile learning applications that are being used to support student teachers in exploring their knowledge and understanding of urban education in a meaningful context (Smith et al. 2008). An urban area close to London Metropolitan University is being used to explore how schools are signifiers of urban change and continuity of educational policy and practice from 1850 to the present day. The learning content developed for the mobile devices is directly relevant to the context of the learning needs and the location of the learners. It provides evidence of how the organisation and (re)structuring of urban space worked alongside educational discourses and policies to support participation in civic urban life and educate generations of working class children. The intention is to examine the community from the past, in order to engage, understand and inform the present, as urban space and society are made and remade. The project uses a complex interplay between mobile learning technologies, iconic physical infrastructures and educational discourses to visualise urban education through various collective images and representations. Many of the historical media are sourced through the British Film Institute, thus avoiding copyright issues. The project has created a digital 'technoscape' (Appadurai 1996; Sheller and Urry 2006; Urry 2007), essentially a visualisation that represents urban land, archaeological space, and subjects using a combination of social and cultural scripts. This resource is also appropriate for older school children. The idea in the project described here, however, is to scaffold the teachers' understanding of what is possible with mobile learning. The 'Urban Education for Trainee Teachers' project uses high end mobile/cell phones: HTC diamond (running Mediascape [http://www.createascape.org.uk/] on the Windows Mobile operating system) plus Nokia N95 (with QR codes running the Symbian operating system). These are used by small groups of two or three students at a time. They allow real research to be done on the move. The voice recorder on the phone is used to allow report writing and note taking for final presentations to be captured quickly and efficiently. Students can also produce video podcasts of themselves and even edit the videos they make on site using the phones. Finally QTVR (QuickTime Virtual Reality) movies of the structures under investigation can be viewed and manipulated in real time (see below).

Key questions that learners are asked to consider when on the tour are (Figs. 2.11–2.14):

- As you take the tour, identify continuities and change as evidenced by the educational settings.
- What do you learn about the socio-economic conditions over time? Which social class has been educated in this area? What indicators are there that the area has changed?
- What do you think has been the influence of religion in the area? How can you tell?
- What can the education of the past tell us about the present?
- What do you think have been the educational challenges faced by those living and working in the area?

Script segment 1 from the actual mobile tour:

- The school is different in design from the London 3-decker style of the time, with the hall at the centre and classrooms coming of this central point. What do you know of class sizes at the time?
- What does the close proximity of church and school buildings suggest? Can you see any indications of the relationship between education and religion in the architecture of the building itself?

Script segment 2 from the actual mobile tour:

- In the 1920s this area was known as the Ring Cross Estate and was in the second highest criterion for overcrowding and squalor, with people living in some of the worst slums. Why do you think the area was so heavily populated?
- What does the past and present housing stock suggest to you about the socio-economic status of the local community?

Script segment 3 from the actual mobile tour:

- The school is built in an open style, giving each classroom some access to the playground. When do you think it was built? What does the architecture suggest about the educational approaches at that time?
- Task: Looking at the exterior of the school, what changes do you think have been made to the school recently? What effect do you think this has had on the environment and the education of the children?
- Task: Using the local maps and old photographs sketch the road layout of the area in the nineteenth century.
- As you continue to walk down Georges Road you will come to St. James' School flats on the right hand side. This was an early attempt at change of use of a building as part of gentrification of the area.
- Task: Compare the structure of this building with those you have seen earlier. Can you see where the different entrances for boys, girls and infants would have been. How has the architecture changed? Why do you think this is?

The 'CONTSENS' project uses the IP Multimedia Subsystem (IMS). We will explore IMS in more detail in Chapter 14. Here we simply want to note that Erickson have developed a facility in some of its phones to use IMS positioning data to track group members. Zone-based notifications can be set to be sent when a specified person either enters or leaves the selected area. Clearly, in addition to certain affordances for learning, these forms of tracking and surveillance have major ethical implications; we will return to this point in Part III.

Ambient Learning

Ambient learning makes use of digital artefacts to augment the environment and enable learning (see e.g. Price 2007). In essence, digital artefacts are placed within the real world, the ambience, in order to enhance that world. Thus, technological tools are used to augment user activity in context. This view of context invests effort in designing a rich environment that in turn mediates innovative forms of learning

Fig. 2.11 The location of the Urban Education for Trainee Teachers project

Fig. 2.12 Images from the Urban Education for Trainee Teachers project

and teaching. For example, Rogers et al. (2004) describe approaches to bridging the gap between outdoor fieldtrips and computer-based indoor learning activities with such devices as the PDA pinger

> which was programmed to show sporadically an image of a plant or animal together with a voice-over about an aspect of its habitat. This happened whenever the children walked passed a pinger that was hidden in a pre-determined place in the woodland. The information displayed was intended to draw the children's attention to a part of the woodland at pertinent times for them to think and reflect upon it. (Rogers et al. 2005)

Fig. 2.13 Images from the Urban Education for Trainee Teachers project

Fig. 2.14 Images from the Urban Education for Trainee Teachers project

Essentially, a learner walks up and uses learning support (e.g. large screens to share information from mobile devices). Such an approach could potentially lead to technology-enabled learning spaces, a theme we will return to in Chapter 14.

The latest trends in mixed reality at the time of writing involve a blurring of distinction between virtual and real worlds and ambient learning. For example, the 'Mobile Augmented Reality Applications' (MARA) project from Nokia (http://research.nokia.com/research/projects/mara/index.html), is designed to identify objects viewed on the screen of a camera phone (Fig. 2.15). Augmented reality in this context indicates that supplementary information is overlaid onto the camera picture of the real world. Thus, MARA explores how to make use of camera equipped mobile devices as platforms for 'sensor-based, video see-through mobile augmented reality'. Developments like these could one day make it easier to navigate the real world by superimposing virtual information on an images of your surroundings. If a phone has the appropriate software and hardware set up it would be able to identify restaurants, hotels, and landmarks and provide Web links and basic information about these objects on the phone's screen. In addition, the system

Fig. 2.15 A prototype Nokia camera phone, equipped with sensors and MARA (Source: Nokia Research Center at http://research.nokia.com/files/maraobj.bmp)

could also be used to find nearby friends who have phones with GPS and the appropriate software. David Murphy, an engineer at Nokia Research Center, Helsinki Finland, has described 'MARA' as being

> able to pull together the information from the three sensors to pinpoint the location and orientation of the phone. The software then scours a database of objects–which can be loaded onto a phone or can be accessed through a network connection–to determine which object would be visible to the camera. Once visibility is determined, MARA highlights the objects and provides extra information and hyperlinks if available. So, if a nearby restaurant is in the database and within view, the software could display the menu and wait time, and by clicking on the hyperlink, you could visit the restaurant's website... This capability becomes particularly compelling when people, as well as buildings, are incorporated into the database. If you have a GPS sensor in your mobile device and elect to share your location... people could click on you to link to your blog... You could go to a football match and be able to see information on the players, or ball movement, or tactics by looking at the field with your device... MARA has an additional feature to access a satellite view of your location and nearby landmarks, simply point the phone's camera at the ground. The software infers the orientation and displays the map. (http://www.technologyreview.com/Biztech/17807/)

Thus, we can see a shift towards mobile devices capable of enabling mixed reality and ambient learning. In this sense we are seeing the interpenetration of the real world and the digital world. Such affordances will enhance our ability to teach a vast range of subjects, from biology to chemistry through to history and geography. However, as we pointed out above, there are ethical considerations when enabling tracking and when broadcasting personal information; clearly care must be taken when children are exposed to these technologies, issues we return to in some detail in Chapter 14.

Interim Summary

We conclude from our discussion so far that there is much to commend mobile/cell phone usage as a mediating tool for learning inside and outside of educational institutions. Emerging trends over the three phases of mobile learning are, as we have seen, the enhancement of the desktop, support for learning outside the classroom and the notion of learner mobility with location and context sensitive systems that enable life-long learning transitions across multiple contexts. Ambient and mixed-reality systems and environments may soon be teaching us about themselves. Wide area educational gaming may draw in learners who may be at distance to the school. Also, we saw in the 'CONTSENS' project that zone-based notification provides a form of tracking and surveillance that has major ethical implications.

There is still much work to do if mobile devices are to be widely adopted for learning in educational institutions. As Sharples (2006) pointed out, there are many issues that for schools to resolve, these include:

- How will schools respond to children bringing in their own mobile multimedia communications devices?
- How can schools manage the tension between informal networked learning and formal institutional learning?
- What types of mobile learning are appropriate and cost-effective for schools, colleges and universities?

Our approach throughout this book is to try to provide compelling arguments, both theoretically and through practical examples, for the inclusion of mobile/cell phones in the curriculum. Of course it is for educational institutions and the professionals working in them to decide. Looking into the future, Sharples (2006) points out that lifelong learning support is needed; specifically we need to design a mobile lifelong learning environment; simply providing a mobile office environment, which is how for example a laptop is typically set up, is not the most effective way forward as far as education is concerned.

Let us now turn to the next part of our topography, namely an examination of conferences, events, organizations and journals in the field.

Specialist Conferences and Events

mLearn

mLearn, arguably the main international event on the annual mobile learning calendar, which is attended by delegates from across the world, first took place as the 'European Workshop on Mobile and Contextual Learning' at Birmingham University in 2002 and has since become the most important academic conference in the field of mobile learning internationally.

Long papers are reviewed by an international panel. In addition, conference organisers tend to welcome short papers and poster presentations. It has taken place in London (2003; http://www.lsda.org.uk/events/mlearn2003/), Rome (2004; http://www.mobilearn.org/mlearn2004/), Cape Town (2005; http://www.mlearn.org.za/), Banff (2006; http://www.mlearn2006.org/), Melbourne (2007; http://www.mlearn2007.org/), Telford (2008; http://www.mlearn2008.org/) and Orlando (2009; http://www.mlearn2009.org) and authors of this book have attended, and presented at various mLearn conferences in recent years. In 2010 the conference will take place in Malta and focus on the future of mobile and contextual learning (http://www.mlearn2010.org).

mLearn 2007 in Melbourne focused on 'making the connections' and stimulated debate about theories, approaches, principles and applications of mobile devices supporting learning. Papers explored conceptual questions around mobile learning, pedagogical considerations, educational affordances of mobile devices, standards for mobile learning, findings from and evaluations of small- and large-scale mobile learning projects across phases and sectors including informal learning or guides for practitioners.

In 2008 mLearn was under the metaphorical banner of 'the bridge from text to context', in part motivated by the location of the conference, Ironbridge in Shropshire, the birthplace of the Industrial Revolution, as well as the increasing importance of location awareness. The choice of conference theme, unsurprisingly, reflected changing priorities in the field. In part, the 2008 papers show that the growing functionalities of mobile devices are leading to an extension of traditional notions of context, normally bound up with spatial proximity, through social networking tools across existing geographical and socio-economic boundaries. Among other things, the 2008 conference problematised issues around the relationship between discourse, identity and knowledge in ever more global contexts in learning with increasingly ubiquitous mobile technologies in and across formal, informal and work-based contexts. Whilst the number of practical examples of use of mobile devices for pedagogical purposes in and across a number of spheres and sectors of education is undoubtedly growing – most noticeable in 2008 we saw the growth in the number of large(r) scale projects (city-, Local Authority-, sector-wide) reported on –, the extent to which that work is underpinned by explicit theoretical considerations remains limited as does the number of papers that address conceptual and theoretical considerations. Nevertheless, the number of conceptually and theoretically underpinned papers is growing with a number of presenters, for example, trying to use Activity Theory as analytical frame for explaining their data. This might well have been linked to Yrjö Engeström bring one on the keynote speakers in Telford. Judging by the 2008 proceedings, whilst mobile learning has clearly matured and consolidated, it still has some way to go before it can be said to be theoretically grounded.

The 2009 conference was divided into the following four strands: global development, contextual learning, emerging technology integration and emerging vertical application. Noticeably, the field of language learning attracted a number of papers.

IADIS Mobile Learning

IADIS is the International Association for Development of the Information Society (http://www.iadis.org/). It is a non-profit association focusing on technological developments and human computer interaction. IADIS publishes journals and sponsors several annual conferences, one of which is International Mobile Learning Conference. The themes of this conference series have become more concrete over the years and reflect the move outlined in the diachronic overview away from general issues surrounding the device towards an understanding of the mobility of the learner. The first IADIS Mobile Learning Conference took places in Qawra, Malta in 2005 (http://www.iadis.org/ml2005/). The second event was held in Dublin, Ireland in 2006 and encouraged in 'particular empirical research informed by theories of learning such as collaborative, contextual, constructivist and constructionist approaches, which are well suited for mobile learning experiences and scenarios' (http://www.iadis.org/ml2006/). Mobile Learning 2007 took place in Lisbon, Portugal. The 2007 event in particular, but not exclusively, aimed 'to enrich the Big Issues in Mobile Learning debate with an international perspective and with empirical research that will further contribute to forge understanding of the Big Issues in Mobile Learning' (http://www.mlearning-conf.org/2007/). Mobile Learning 2008 took place in the Algarve, Portugal and in particular aimed 'to further our understanding of mobile learning from the standpoint of learner mobility' and it sought to explore how the multiple perspectives of mobility and the interactions among these influence and enhance current definitions, design, and evaluation of mobile learning (http://www.mlearning-conf.org/2008/). The 2009 event, in Barcelona, Spain, explored the 'transition from content consumer to content creator in experiences that take advantage of the learning opportunities this provides'.

Handheld Learning

Another important event on the annual mobile learning calendar is Handheld Learning (http://www.handheldlearning.co.uk/), an annual conference for mobile learning practitioners from schools, further and higher education as well as adult learning and policy makers taking place in London. The conference offers themed workshops, seminars and plenaries hosted and supported by relevant organisations and companies as well as keynote addresses by experts in the field. The focus is very much on practice and the event is also a showcase for companies and service providers to present their wares and services. The event is also a forum for (government-funded) organisations involved in education technologies to present their work. The Handheld learning website features an online discussion forum in which some pertinent issues around mobile learning are discussed between conferences and also makes some of the talks available for online viewing.

Budapest Mobile Learning Conference Series

There is also some very interesting and important work on mobile learning taking place in Continental Europe, some of which is documented in English some is not. In particular Kristóf Nyíri, in association with the Hungarian Academy of Sciences, has been running a series of annual conferences on mobile learning with a particular focus on philosophical issues for a number of years (http://www.socialscience.t-mobile.hu/). A recent conference in September 2008 in Budapest focused on mobile communication and the ethics of social networking and brought together an inter-disciplinary range of speakers from Hungary, Germany and beyond, in particular the US and the UK. The proceedings were published as Nyíri 2009.

WMTE

The Workshop on Wireless and Mobile Technologies in Education or WMTE series began in Vaxjo, Sweden in 2002 (http://lttf.ieee.org/wmte2002/). This event led to the series of international conferences held in Asia and in Europe in the field of mobile learning. Being associated with the IEEE has meant that WMTE has taken a technical design and development perspective, but this has not precluded other perspectives. The second workshop was held nearly two years later in Jhongli, Taiwan in 2004 (http://lttf.ieee.org/wmte2003/). The conference theme for this second meeting was 'Mobile Support for Learning Communities'. The third workshop, held in 2005 at the University of Tokushima in Tokushima City, Japan (http://lttf.ieee.org/wmte2005/netscape/) focused on 'Learning Everywhere: Design and Challenges for Ubiquitous Learning Society'. The fourth WMTE 2006 workshop in 2006, Athens, Greece (http://www.ask.iti.gr/wmute/2006/others/) had a diverse set of themes. The fifth WMUTE was held two years later in 2008 in Beijing, China (http://www.wmute2008.org/). The proceedings from some of these conferences are available at: http://csdl2.computer.org/persagen/DLPublication.jsp?pubtype=p&acronym=WMTE

Professional Association

International Association for Mobile Learning (IAMLearn)

Out of the work of the mLearn community and Kaleidoscope (see below) a professional body, the International Association for Mobile Learning (http://www.iamlearn.org) has emerged. IAMLearn, which organises mLearn, is a membership organization which aims to promote excellence in research, development and application of mobile and contextual learning. Through its website, the association collates and disseminate information about new projects, emerging technologies, and teaching resources.

Organisations with a Particular Interest in Mobile Learning

WLE Centre: Mobile Learning Symposia and the London Mobile Learning Group (LMLG)

Since 2007 the Centre for Excellence in Work-based Learning for Education Professionals (http://www.wlecentre.ac.uk) at the Institute of Education, London, which sponsors the work of the London Mobile Learning Group (http://www.londonmobilelearning.net/) of which the current authors are members, has organised a number of mobile learning symposia leading to important publications in the field. The February 2007 event (http://www.wlecentre.ac.uk/cms/index.php?option=com_content&task=view&id=105&Itemid=39) aimed to contribute towards the emerging research agenda for mobile learning and featured papers concerned with definitional aspects of mobile learning, emerging functionalities such as digital augmentation as well as pedagogical issues and led to the publication of Pachler (2007), which can be downloaded free of charge from (http://www.wlecentre.ac.uk/cms/files/occasionalpapers/mobilelearning_pachler_2007.pdf) as part of the WLE Centre Occasional Papers series (http://www.wlecentre.ac.uk/cms/index.php?option=com_content&task=category§ionid=7&id=34&Itemid=50). In December 2007 the second symposium took place (http://www.milrm.wle.org.uk/), which was entitled 'Research methods in mobile and informal learning' and explored the challenges inherent in mobile devices for researching emerging practices and uses. The best papers of the symposium were published as Vavoula et al. (2009) by Peter Lang. The third symposium in the series in March 2009 (http://symposium.londonmobilelearning.net) looked at mobile learning cultures across education, work and leisure, in particular it considers experiences related to the learners' life worlds, agencies and cultural practices, in out-of-school, informal contexts and how they relate to learning and practices at work and formal education.

Not only did a number of publications emerge from this series of events but also did the idea of working group of researchers emerge which has since formalised itself and grown into the London Mobile Learning Group (LMLG; http://www.londonmobilelearning.net). The group brings together an international, interdisciplinary group of researchers from the fields of cultural studies, sociology, semiotics, pedagogy and educational technology. Since its inception, the group has worked on a theoretical and conceptual framework for mobile learning around the notion of a socio-cultural ecology documented in this book. The analytical engagement with mobile learning of the group takes the shape of a conceptual model in which educational uses of mobile technologies are viewed in ecological terms as part of a socio-cultural and pedagogical context in transformation. The members collaborate on various projects and publications with each other, and organise joint events. Over the years they have organised workshops and symposia at national and international conferences such as the annual conference of the American Research Association (AERA) (2009), the Kongress der Deutschen

Gesellschaft für Erziehungswissenschaft (DGfE) (2008 and 2010), the CAL biennial conference (2009) and the Alpine Rendez-Vous (2009). For details see the LMLG website.

Futurelab

Futurelab is a not-for-profit organisation that explores the potential offered by digital and other technologies through developing resources and practices that support new approaches to learning for the twenty-first century (http://www.futurelab.org.uk/). According to its website, Futurelab works in partnership with others to: incubate new ideas; share evidence and practical advice to support the design and use of innovative learning tools; communicate the latest thinking and practice in educational ICT; provide the space for experimentation and the exchange of ideas between the creative, technology and education sectors. As the screenshot from their home page shows (captured September 14, 2008), Futurelab's work towards achieving these aims through projects, resources, events and networks. It has produced several notable reports on mobile and informal learning, which we have drawn on in the research for this book (Fig. 2.16).

Fig. 2.16 Futurelab homepage

Interestingly, the above screenshot has as a speech-bubble/caption for their October 2008 conference which reads 'why can't I use my mobile/cell phone?', a student-centred theme that is central to this book.

Becta

Becta (http://www.becta.org.uk/) describes itself on its website as the UK's 'government agency leading the national drive to ensure the effective and innovative use of technology throughout learning'. Becta, focuses on schools and Further Education, has four main roles:

- strategic adviser to government;
- co-ordinating the government's e-strategy for education, developing and implementing an overarching delivery strategy and establishing effective programme management;
- providing insight through analysis and research;
- working to deliver specific elements of the e-strategy.

Becta funds various research reports on mobile learning that have been drawn upon in this book. Of particular interest to the themes of this book is the recent home access initiative:

> Over one million children do not have technology and access to the internet in their home and this perpetuates the social and digital divide and disadvantages children. To begin to address the imbalance the Government is now considering establishing a programme of activities to ensure that every family with 5- to 19-year-old learners in England, irrespective of their circumstances, has access to ICT resources and support at home. (http://live.industry.becta.org.uk/display.cfm?cfid=1476190&cftoken=29154&resID=37031&page=1714&catID=1620)

UK members of the LMLG have been working closely with Becta in support of the effective use of educational technologies in learning and teaching.

Kaleidoscope

Kaleidoscope was a European research network of excellence involved in shaping the scientific evolution of technology-enhanced learning (http://www.noe-kaleidoscope.org/pub/). The project was funded from January 2004 to December 2007. The network ran a Mobile Learning Special Interest Group (SIG), which turned into the International Association for Mobile Learning (IAMLearn). The SIG was supported by a website and generated two important reports: Big Issues in Mobile Learning Report (Sharples et al. 2008), and the report of the Alpine Rendez-Vous workshop (Arnedillo-Sánchez et al. 2007). The themes of the IADIS Mobile Learning Conference in Lisbon in 2007 were also based around these reports.

G1:1

G1:1 (http://www.g1on1.org/), pronounced as 'G one one', is a global network of research teams to which the authors of this book belong. G1:1 believe that every learner will soon have a personal mobile computing device that is wirelessly connected, and which will enable multimedia input and output. G1:1 propose that the 'fundamental infrastructures of education are being dramatically transformed with 1:1 technology together with other interactive media'. As we have seen elsewhere in this book, with the convergence of affordances onto a single mobile device our private, informal and formal spaces are becoming intermingled. Learning, community and social communications, working, entertainment, commerce, shopping and other actives are becoming intertwined. Currently, G1:1 aims at promoting the rapid advancement of research-based understandings of 1:1 technology-enhanced learning that will provide the foundation and disseminate information for progressively extending its impact throughout the world.

Specialist Journals

IJMBL

The International Journal of Mobile and Blended Learning (http://www.igi-global.com/ijmbl) is a new journal and, as a partner of IAmLearn, publishes papers from the MLearn conference. The journal aims to provide a forum for researchers in the field of mobile learning to share their knowledge and experience.

IJMLO

The International Journal of Mobile Learning and Organisation (IJMLO) 'intends to establish an effective communication channel among decision makers and policy makers in business, government agencies, and academic and research institutions which recognise the important role mobile learning may play in organisations'. (http://www.inderscience.com/browse/index.php?journalCODE=ijmlo). Since its inception in 2007 it has published four issues a year and covers a diverse range of topics, ranging from globalisation to ethical and copyright issues in the context of organisations.

IJIM

International Journal of Interactive Mobile Technologies 'aims to focus on the exchange of relevant trends and research results as well as the presentation of practical experiences gained while developing and testing elements of interactive mobile technologies. The objective of the journal is to publish and discuss fundamentals, applications and experiences in the field of interactive mobile technologies in learning and teaching as well as in industrial and other applications' (http://www.i-jim.org/). IJIM produced one issue in 2007 and is now generating 3/4 issues a year. In 2008, IJIM published a special issue of the mLearn 2008 conference papers.

Special Issues on Mobile Learning

A number of journals in the field of computer-assisted, technology-enhanced and distance learning have featured special issues on mobile learning to provide an in-depth perspectives. They include the *Journal of Computer Assisted Learning* (JCAL; http://www3.interscience.wiley.com/journal/118532977/issue) in 2007 (Vol. 23, No. 4), the *International Review of Research in Open and Distance Learning* (IRRODL) of Athabasca University (Vol. 8, No, 2) also in 2007, available free of charge at http://www.irrodl.org/index.php/irrodl/issue/view/29, and in 2008 the *Journal of the Research Centre for Educational Technology* (RCETJ) of Kent State University (Vol. 4, No. 1) also available free of charge at http://www.rcetj.org/?type=ci&id=5769. RCETJ will publish a special issue with selected papers from the research strand of Handheld Learning 2009.

Key Issues in Mobile Learning

In the third part of our topography, we turn to the key issues emerging from the literature in the field.

Challenges in the implementation of technology in education are plentiful. There is not the space here to discuss the generic issues, such as for example those around assessment, that are well documented in the burgeoning literature on educational technology. Instead, in the following we focus on those issues, which we consider particularly relevant to mobile learning, as well as ones which we deem to be central to the successful adoption of mobile devices in education. And it is the latter we will start with here.

Development for Educational Professionals and Mobile Learning

According to a recent teacher voice omnibus survey conducted by the National Foundation for Educational Research (NFER 2008) amongst 1,000 teachers in November 2007, a sizeable minority (33%) feel unprepared to exploit the technology available to them and say they lack the necessary skills. The report also suggests that there continues to be a demand for basic skills training in relation to what might be called established technologies such as personal computers and visual technologies such as interactive whiteboards. Kitchen et al. (2007, p. 11) report in a recent study that most teachers perceived a need for professional development in using technology, with primary school teachers identifying development needs in the area of the creation of digital video material whereas secondary teachers perceived a need for CPD in supporting learners' use of digital video.

The UK government has adopted the term 'educational e-maturity' of late, by which they mean the 'integration of technology-based applications and processes into all key aspects of... practice and operation' (BECTA 2007, p. 19), to capture the degree of preparedness by all stakeholders at all levels. Concerns about difficulties in realising the potential of mobile devices is shared by Shin, Norris and Soloway (2007, p. 33) who, writing about K-12 contexts, argue that substantive technical and instructional support for teachers is required to build the necessary skills and confidence.

These figures and findings pose some important questions for us around the 'm-maturity' of the education sector, in particular as regards compulsory education. The challenges in relation to the use of 'newer' technologies, such as mobile devices, can be assumed to be considerably greater and to represent an urgent issue to be addressed by the education system to ensure the successful implementation of these technologies; an issue, which we see closely linked to strategic leadership at meso (institutional) and macro (systemic) level. However, a recent small-scale study by Kukulska-Hulme and Pettit (2007) suggests that the situation is not much better in higher education settings. They argue (p. 114) that a lack of personal experience of mobile learning represents a major barrier to its uptake and integration in teaching and learning. The authors also make the valid point that compared with other technologies, such as personal computers, there tends to be a much greater degree of specificity in the technical skills required depending on the particular device being used.

In their report on teacher learning with digital technologies, Fisher et al. (2006, p. 2) note that there is very little research on how teachers might learn with digital technologies and they identify the activities in Fig. 2.17 as purposeful for teacher learning.

Knowledge building	• adapting and developing ideas • modelling • representing understanding in multimodal and dynamic ways
Distributed cognition	• accessing resources • finding things out • writing, composing and presenting with mediating artefacts and tools
Community and communication	• exchanging and sharing communication • extending the context of activity • extending the participating community at local and global levels
Engagement	• exploring and playing • acknowledging risk and uncertainty • working with different dimensions of interactivity • responding to immediacy

Fig. 2.17 Clusters of purposeful activity with digital technologies (Source: Fisher, Higgins and Loveless 2006, p. 2)

McFarlane et al. (2007, p. 6) note that across their sample of three schools different approaches to teachers' continuing professional development (CPD) are in evidence and that none of them has proved to be superior to date. The report identifies the following elements as beneficial: opportunity to explore how devices work hands-on prior to considering their application in teaching and learning; the ability to confer with mentors and colleagues; as well as starting small and building up slowly.

> Teachers' confidence, their relationship with their classes and their attitude to taking risks appear to be the factors having the greatest effect on the pace of implementation of mobile learning into teaching and learning. The pace of implementation increased when teachers found material and/or examples that they felt comfortable with. (p. 7)

Public, Personal and Intimate Spaces and Ethical Considerations

An ever more important issue in view of the growing ubiquity of wireless technologies and wireless communication (networks) by virtue of wireless functionality becoming cheaper and getting more readily attached to machinery, embedded in the environment and, as in the case of wireless medical devices for example, under people's skin, is the ethical dimension and the implications for the privacy of the individual user. Examples are machine-to-machine communication without the knowledge and specific consent of the owner/operator of mobile devices, such as the mining and exploitation of datalogs, or the transmission of location data through RFID (Radio Frequency Identification) tags in credit cards, passports or items of clothing. RFID tags are often applied to or incorporated into objects such as a product (e.g. on a parcel for tracking shipment progress), animals, or even a person for the purpose of identification and tracking using radio waves. An example of wireless technologies being used to develop new business models around so-called 'smart services' are pay-as-you-drive car insurance schemes. These developments have led to assertions by specialist commentators, such as the technology correspondent of *The Economist*, that the implications of wireless technologies are huge and that the world we will live in will be fundamentally different to the one we know now with machines, metaphorically speaking, getting eyes, ears and a voice, through interconnectivity by way of ad-hoc mesh networking (an approach to routing data, voice and instructions between communication nodes). This, it is argued, poses a considerable challenge for current models of privacy protection which are based, by-and-large on a bi-directional relationship between the consumer and service provider. (For details see *The Economist* Special Report on wireless technology April 26, 2007) There are also concerns about the commodification of users and the content they generate using digital technologies (see e.g. Hodgkinson 2008; Jarrett 2008; Petersen 2008)

In relation to learning, the use of mobile devices tends to be characterised by digital recording as well as sharing of experiences. These acts invariably leave multimodal trails of our lives, and that of others whose consent it might, or might not be possible to obtain. And, there are attendant issues of secure storage and use/exploitation by whom and for what purpose. Whilst the use of mobile devices and their ubiquity in learners' life worlds allows for new, and potentially very fruitful synergies between activities inside and outside formal education situations, there exist increasing anxieties about the potential negative impact of the use of records generated in the context of users' private lives for other purposes. Employers, for example, reportedly increasingly explore the digital trails available about potential employees on the internet. As mobile devices become more and more like desktop PCs, for example, enabling affordable internet access, the same challenges come to the fore in relation to user data and their storage that already exist in cyberspace in relation to things like users search profiles, the online storage of pictures and other data files (incl. e-mails, calendars, chat records, documents, maps, shopping habits and product preferences). (see e.g. WOZ Spezial 1+2, 2008 available at http://www.woz.ch/files/WOZ_1.08_google-spezial.pdf; Albrechtslund 2008; Zimmer 2008)

There is, of course, also the question about the extent to which the act of recording and documenting experiences digitally actually interferes with the nature of these experiences for participants, for example in terms of their uninterrupted enjoyment due to the creation of psychological barriers and inhibitions caused by the presence of mobile devices or psychological pressures in relation to information overload caused by the instantaneous nature of available information.

The use of mobile technologies has to be viewed as located within the contingencies of specific socio-cultural and economic environments which in themselves are bound up in geopolitical changes. With reference to work by Baumann (2000), Stone (2008, p. 177) discusses the notion of 'liquid modernity' which to him suggests a certain fluidity of individuals, 'increases everyone's self-consciousness and individualizes responsibility for well-being and self-attainment, encouraging less static modes of being'. Clearly, mobile technologies have a significant potential to contribute to this increasing freedom 'to choose our way in the world'. Another important role for mobile technologies is in relation to what constitutes individual identity. With Stone (2008, p. 179) we assume that individual identity is 'a work in progress, which reflects the dialectic relationship between self-reflexive understandings and externally enforced subjectivities', that they are 'multiple, fluid and contingent', but not underpinned by a 'true self' that finds multifaceted articulation according to different contexts.

> A project which is worked upon within the ordinariness of everyday life through a combination of moments of self-contemplation, familiar interactions with family, friends and colleagues, subconscious reactions to strangers and the discursive nature of structural influences.... For in 'liquid modernity' our lives are fragmented into a 'succession of ill-connected episodes', the narrative for which is no longer some notion of Cartesian transcendence nor the negotiation of conformity within the structured identities of modernity, but a desire and a need to communicate with some sense of who we are at each juncture. (Stone 2008, p. 179)

Traxler (2007b, p. 260) rightly notes the fluidity of social norms caused by the increasing co-presence of actual (face-to-face) and remote (technologically-mediated) social interaction. In his terms, mobile/cell phones have created 'simultaneity of place', which has led to a constant 'permeability' between public, private and intimate social spaces. Many readers will have found themselves astounded, for example, by the intimate nature of mobile/cell phone conversations conducted by others in their presence and have wondered about their intrusion into the private lives of others or/and perceived the inability of escaping the exposure to such conversations, for example due to them being held in a loud voice in a train carriage, as an intrusion into their private spheres. Or, what of the seeming inability of many users to ignore incoming phone calls even if they are in the midst of a face-to-face interaction with a co-present other? Mobile/cell phones have led to a redrawing of the boundaries between public and private talk and how we interact with our social world.

> Most young users... are able to establish intimate spaces for shared presence when they talk on the phone or have a text-message conversation.... The experience of presence is important in most interpersonal communication situations in order to establish a feeling of trust and social bonding. (Stald 2008, p. 154)

Another interesting point Traxler makes about the issue of privacy with reference to work by Bull (2005) from the field of leisure studies relates to the use of media players. He notes that the use of media players can be understood as an attempt by users to 'inhabit' and structure the spaces within which they move and to fill the spaces in between acts of communication. Stald (2008, p. 154) points out the potential of such devices to 'shut off the surroundings and establish a private space where one's psychological presence is transferred to another symbolic place of experience'. With reference to Biocca et al. (2003), she makes the distinction between physical and social presence with the latter defined as 'a state that varies with medium, knowledge of the other, content of the communication, environment, and social context'. Stald (p. 156) also refers to Gergen's (2002) notion of 'absent presence', which describes the phenomenon of someone being physically present in one space but mentally present in another.

Cooper (2002) asserts that the private 'is no longer conceivable as what goes on, discreetly, in the life of the individual away from the public domain, or as subsequently represented in individual consciousness' (quoted by Traxler 2007b, p. 260): in short, mobile technologies require a re-definition of what is private, what is public and what is intimate.

The educational establishment, we would posit, has yet to start to consider the implications – good or bad – of these fundamental changes.

Learner-Generated Contexts

One defining characteristic of mobile technologies is their potential, or affordance – a term widely used in the specialist literature, if contested by some commentators (see e.g. Oliver 2005; Chapter 3), who note, for example, that the concept tends to negate the wider context of the objects in question as well as their culture of use, i.e. for users to create contexts for learning. We use the terms 'affordance' deliberately in this book, as we do not subscribe to the view that the concept negates the wider context nor inhibits cultures of use. Instead, as we show in Chapter 7, we take the view that the potential and constraints of mobile devices, e.g. in terms of their functionality, whilst not determining them, nevertheless have a bearing on the actions that are possible with and around them, e.g. by constraining or fostering what meaning-making is possible in the context of their use. With reference to

Weilenmann (2003), Stald (2008, p. 145) stresses that mobile technologies do not make users independent of place, which she argues remains important because users are constantly negotiating their mutual understanding of the situations in which they find themselves. However, we would argue that mobile devices for example increase the students' ability to bring into fruitful synergy the knowledge distributed across communities of use. As such, using Vahey, Roschelle and Tatar's terms (2007), they make it possible for private cognition and public interaction to be and become linked. Most relevant for our line of argument in this book is the realisation that learning, understood broadly as meaning-making, is always situated (see e.g. Lave and Wenger 1991) and that even if movement in geographical space is foregrounded, meaning-making is still situated in contexts and situations, albeit in all probability ones that transcend specific geographical places and physical spaces.

In the literature about social networking and mobile learning, the notion of space is frequently discussed, within which, it is argued, the use of (mobile) devices and attendant learning processes have to be understood. (see e.g. Crook and Harrison 2008)

Sharples et al. (2008), for example, distinguish the following spheres of and for mobility: mobility in physical space, mobility of technology, mobility in conceptual space and mobility in social space. They also note the fact that learning is dispersed in time.

Kevin Walker, in his attempt to map the landscape of mobile learning (2007, p. 5), rightly notes that one of the defining characteristics is learning across contexts.

Matt Locke (http://www.test.org.uk/2007/08/10/six-spaces-of-social-media), in a blog posting in October 2007, distinguishes the following six 'spaces' of social media with examples:

- secret spaces (SMS, MMS, IM),
- group spaces (Facebook, Myspace, Bebo),
- publishing spaces (Blogger, Flickr, YouTube),
- performing spaces (Second Life, World of Warcraft),
- participation spaces (Meetup, Twitter) and
- watching spaces (mobile tv).

Locke does note some of the limitations of this conceptualisation, in particular the overlap between some of the categories as well as their existence offline as well as online. The particular appeal of this model, for our purposes, lies in its user- rather than platform- or application-centredness. In view of our earlier discussion, one might question the appropriacy of a term like 'secret'. One important weakness of Locke's conceptualisation for us, however, lies in the lack of clarity of the use of the term 'space', in particular with reference to our socio-cultural ecological approach as in our terminology what Locke lists are structures through which users generate contexts for meaning-making.

Luckin et al. (2005, pp. 1, 3–5) consider one of the advantages of mobile technologies to lie in their ability to overcome the constraints of specific educational cultures within which technology is used by enabling the linking of learners' experiences across multiple locations. Indeed, Rose Luckin and her group, the Learner Generated Context Group (http://en.wikipedia.org/wiki/Learner_generated_context) was one of the first to use the notion of user-generated context. They posit that context has both a static and a dynamic dimension. The static elements of content ('the stuff to be learnt'), process ('ways that stuff can be learnt') and place ('where stuff can be learnt'), they argue, interact with each other dynamically. In their paper, they identify the following 'linkages' (pp. 12–13) afforded by mobile technologies: linking learner to people, learner to knowledge, learner to knowledge and location, learner to location and its organization and people to people. In their final analysis (p. 19), they see the role of technology as 'helping to identify ways in which resources can be adapted to meet the needs of a learner rather than as a tool that can adapt itself to the context and to the learner'. And, 'it must be used as a means to provide continuity across locations'. If nothing else, Luckin et al.'s discussion reminds us of the importance of context in learning.

Hung and Chen (2007, p. 148) stress the importance of authenticity of and across context(s) and argue for the authenticity of practices, i.e. for the likening of learner actions with practitioner actions. They also foreground the issue of what they call 'identity enculturation' arguing that (learning) communities and domains are bounded by certain beliefs, attitudes, norms and roles, including epistemological orientations towards knowledge, which all have a bearing on identity construction and re-constructions as learners move between diverse communities.

Dourish (2004), in a conceptual piece which acknowledges the centrality of context, attempts to move beyond a view of context as being located in positivist, phenomenological and critical theory considerations. Instead of viewing context as a representational problem, he puts forward a view of context as an interactional problem. Dourish bases this view on four assumptions (p. 5): contextuality is a relational property that holds between objects and activities; the scope of contextual features is defined dynamically; context is particular to each occasion of activity or action; and context arises from the activity, it is actively produced, maintained and enacted in the course of the activity in hand. He raises a fundamental question which, we feel, is of central importance to an understanding of the potential of mobile technologies in learning: 'how and why, in the course of their interactions, do people achieve and maintain a mutual understanding of the context for their actions?' (p. 6) In his thinking, 'context isn't something that describes a setting; it's something that people do. It is an achievement, rather than an observation; an outcome, rather than a premise'. 'Context cannot be a stable, external description of the setting in which activity arises. Instead, it arises from and is sustained by the activity itself'. In other words, how, why and with whom mobile technologies are used become more constituent of context than is where and when they are used.

On a practical level, Dourish's interactional view of context is borne out by work carried out in Finland on the active construction of experiences through mobile media. In their study, Jacucci et al. (2007) focus on the role of technology-mediated memories in constructing experiences. They observed that users expended cognitive, social and physical resources supported by mobile technologies, particular the camera function of mobile/cell phones, to foster continuity and group identity, to reflect on the self and/in relation to the group. The study identifies a number of multimedia-mediated forms of expression, in particular: staging, competition, storytelling, joking, communicating presence and portraying others. The study is not only of interest in relation to our discussion of learner-generated contexts, but also because of its detailed discussion of the role of memory in the creation of experiences and, therefore, the process of learning. It posits that memory is an active and proactive participant in the process of producing acts of volition, and that it is not just a storage device for experiences and events in the past (p. 3). And, it raises the question of how mobile technologies, in particular multimedia devices, can be used prosthetically to support the recording of experiences as well as the active construction of experiences and actions. In the same way Dourish sees contexts as embodied, Jacucci et al. see meaning as emergent and not predetermined in events (p. 5). Ubiquitous multimedia, they argue 'could have an explicitly participative role enhancing, and thus shaping experiences by taking part in the emergence of meaning supporting shared interpretation, or assisting doing and undergoing'. Their work, we would posit, supports our view on 'affordances' in so far as it exemplifies the fostering role of mobile devices, in this instance multi-media functionality, in contexts of interpersonal communication in the process of meaning-making. And, the example demonstrates the capability of mobile devices to produce cultural resources that are significant in identity formation.

We believe in the importance of the situatedness of activities carried out with the help of mobile technologies – in our case for purposes of learning. We consider the spatial framing for learning, be it real or virtual, as less important. Instead, we consider the importance of situatedness to lie in the framing it provides for meaning-making. Very important in this context is for us the notion of agency, namely the creation by the user/learner together with other relevant parties, such as teachers and peers, of situations conducive to the use of mobile technologies as frames for meaning making. Like Dourish, we believe in the importance of practice, i.e. people's engagement with particular settings, in which context becomes 'embodied interaction' (p. 14).

Augmented Reality

Another important affordance of mobile technology for us is digital augmentation whereby contextual data is added to objects to enable a deeper understanding of them and richer meaning-making. Digital augmentation is particularly relevant for user-generated contexts, for example the provision of multimedia data about real objects or places through GPS. The data can be drawn from third parties but can also come from users themselves. In the literature the term 'ambient learning' is sometimes used to express the potential of digital augmentation, which is bound to grow significantly in the coming years with physical spaces and objects becoming increasingly 'learning-enabled' with the growth of wireless networks and the continuing fall in prices for associated technologies. Some useful examples of the use of digital augmentation to foster learning can be found in Price (2007) and Rogers and Price (2007). An interesting perspective on things to come is offered by theoretical physicist Michio Kaku in a 2008 programme in the BBC Four series entitled *Visions of the Future* in which he predicts an intelligence revolution in which artificial intelligence will become ubiquitous (see http://www.bbc.co.uk/bbcfour/documentaries/features/visions-future.shtml).

Affective and Motivational Factors

The high levels of intrinsic motivation normally associated with technologies make ICT an attractive proposition to educators. The levels of intrinsic motivation do decrease as technologies lose their novelty and are replaced by newer devices and greater functionality. This problem of hardware and software becoming constantly out of date poses a real challenge and has been referred to as 'dynamic obsolescence' (Davies 1997). However, the fact that ownership of mobile devices by the learner is statistically more likely than of desk-based ones, as well as because of the possibility, for the first time ever, of a 1:1 student-device ratio, motivation engendered by mobile devices can be higher and more sustained. Intrinsic motivation can also be pedagogically enhanced by the provision of challenge and complexity as well as curiosity in the design and choice of activities and tasks that allow for agency by the user. One effect that tends to remain strong, though, given the predominantly technophile orientation of modern society, is a high level of face validity of technological devices, which can be counter-productive in educational contexts, as it can create tensions in relation to the pedagogical leadership role of educators in the use of new technologies for learning.

Jones et al. (2007) posit that affective factors play a strong role in harnessing technology for learning and list six reasons why users find mobile devices particularly engaging: control over goals, ownership, fun, communication, learning-in-context and continuity between contexts (p. 18). Naismith and Corlett (2006), in their reflections on the successes of mobile learning assert motivational benefit inside and outside the classroom as well as high levels of engagement in learning activities and learners' environments. Peters (2007, pp. 3–4) identifies a number of 'unique educational affordances' of mobile devices, such as portability, social interactivity, context sensitivity, connectivity and individuality, which can all be seen as linked to intrinsic motivation for learners and their teachers. Studies about mobile technologies in use, for example that by Stald (2008), often stress the importance of mobile technologies, in particular mobile/cell phones, in establishing social belonging and norms and, in particular for young people, in relation to questions of identity and their place in their peer group:

> The mobile has become the ideal tool to deal with the pace of information exchange, the management of countless loose, close or intimate relations, the co-ordination of ever-changing daily activities, and the insecurity of everyday life. Hence the mobile becomes a learning tool for dealing with living conditions in modern society for young people, while at the same time it adds to the conditions they are trying to deal with. (Stald 2008, p. 144)

Evidence suggests (Stald 2008, pp. 149–150, 155) that adoption and appropriation of mobile technologies, loosely defined here with reference to Waycott (2004) as their routine usage for and integration into users' activities but not always necessarily for the purposes and in the ways envisaged by designers and service providers, are not only determined by practical issues such as availability, usability, functionality or infrastructure but also by socio-cultural factors, such as perceived need and trends. The socio-cultural dimension is particularly important as with the growth in social networking tools and applications, communication mediated by (mobile) technology is particularly prevalent with people from one's everyday life-world. And the mobile/cell phone can play an important role either in fostering a sense of co-presence, nearness and intimacy or it may be perceived as an alienating medium. Berson and Berson (2007, p. 291) note the importance of mobile/cell phones in shifting power dynamics between adults and young people: 'home and school have traditionally been adult-dominated spaces in which communication with peers was regulated by parents or teachers'.

Importantly also with respect to affective factors, mobile telephones can be viewed as a 'mobile extension of the body and mind' (Stald 2008, p. 158) with the devices always being in close proximity to the body. Interestingly, Stald asserts that the physical device holds no or little affective value but, instead, that it is primarily the content and the representations it contains that matters. This is not a view espoused by Berson and Berson (2007, p. 291) who argue that the physical object of the mobile/cell phone has social value and that characteristics of the device have become important status symbols. They believe that 'the device functions as a symbol of young people's connections with, and membership in, their peer group'. Stald also argues that the phones themselves are more like conduits for affective and social bonds between people than substitutes for them. This does not entirely tally with our own work (Cook et al. 2008) where ownership and the 'coolness' of a device appear to matter affectively to users. Stald does concede, though, that there tends to exist a certain degree of identification, which extends to the actual mobile/cell phone number as codes for intimate and social relations and access to networks.

Interface Between Learning in Informal and Formal Settings

One question we consider to be of great importance in relation to mobile devices is their potential to overcome the, in our view, unhelpful conceptual division between 'formal' and 'informal' learning. As we have shown in Chapter 1, the terms suggest differences in the processes attendant to learning, where, in our view, the differences pertain mostly to the sites of learning. We consider the socio-cultural practices developing around the use of mobile devices as a real opportunity for legitimising learning outside formalised educational frames, normally referred to as 'informal learning', and to validate them.

This issue of interface does emerge from our review of the literature. One important dimension of the attempt to overcome current conceptual and actual barriers is an effective technological infrastructure, which allows for the seamless transfer of artefacts from one context to the other. Another is the increasing embeddedness of information, and people online, which Breck (2007, pp. 52, 53) describes as ‘viral’ and ‘intertwingled’, by which she means a relationship characterised by a certain lack of hierarchy, categorization and sequentiality. From a conceptual and theoretical perspective this not only raises epistemological questions about what constitutes knowledge, but also ontological questions around conceptions of reality. Brodie, in his foreword to Fensel’s book on ontologies as the solution for knowledge management and electronic commerce (2004, p. vi), defines an ontology as ‘a community-mediated and accepted description of the kinds of entities that are in a domain of discourse and how they are related. They provide meaning, organization, taxonomy, agreement, common understanding, vocabulary, and a connection to the “real world”’. It is clearly much more difficult to achieve agreement of this kind in the context of an ever more spatially distributed group of users and learners.

One key component of such an infrastructure, in addition to ownership of appropriate interoperable mobile devices with affordable connectivity, is a learning object repository which allows for the easy storing, retrieving and re-using of dynamically created digital artefacts. According to Verdejo et al. (2007, 44–45), searchability enhanced by appropriate metadata is one key characteristic of an effective repository. Others, it is argued, are heterogeneity – the possibility of storing objects from a variety of resources –, automatic and contextual metadata generation, a community portal as well as the ability to synchronise distributed repositories in a network.

We argue here that the interface between sites for learning can also be greatly facilitated by some degree of meta-level awareness of the learner about the learning processes they engage in across spaces, time and sites of learning. The same can be said of purposefully designed learning networks and paths (see Koper et al. 2005). One possible model is that developed by Schenker et al. (2007, p. 172), who describe three interacting domains: external representations of knowledge, individuals’ internal conceptualizations of knowledge, and the social uses made of knowledge and through which it is constructed. Arguably the navigation across sites of learning is much easier if they are not viewed as opposing poles but rather as a continuum which invariably, and irrespective of where along the continuum one is positioned, is about a purposeful engagement with Schenker et al.’s three interacting domains rather than temporal or spatial positioning. The fundamental role for the educator is to consider how best to use technology, in our case mobile devices, to affect the engagement with these domains.

And, we posit that a learner-focussed locus of control and learner agency are key in ensuring the gap between learning in formal and informal settings can be successfully bridged.

Mobile Learning and Design Issues

Simply given the physical characteristics of mobile tools, such as their small size and portability and, therefore, the size of the screen and keyboard/input device, i.e. due to usability and accessibility issues, as well as the contexts within which they are being used, characterised at times for example by bad lighting, background noise or other types of interference, the issues attendant to design are not insignificant. In order to pack a high number of functions into a small device, great attention is required to the physical design of the handset as well as the graphical interface of the software applications running on the devices themselves. And, the size of the display requires careful packaging and chunking of content. Of late an increase in the number of mobile devices is discernible that have been specifically designed with educational use is mind, such as Ultra-Mobile PCs (UMPCs) and NetBooks.

The design of tools, including the software, is fundamentally predicated on the envisaged types of use. For example, in a conversation-based framework (see e.g. Laurillard 2007; Sharples et al. 2007), where mobile devices are viewed as tools for harnessing conversations between learners and learners and between learners and educators, connectivity for synchronous and asynchronous communication become very important with an emphasis on facilitation, rather than impeding or interference through distracting attention from the content to the process, for example by adhering to the 20 second interaction principle whereby it needs to be possible to complete all logical steps from start to finish of a task within 20 second (Jacucci et al. 2007, p. 29). Jaccuci et al. posit that even 20 second is often too long, which renders a service useless. Therefore, devices need to be easy to use and the process of learning how to use them needs to be intuitive and straightforward. Norris et al. (2007, p. 6), with reference to Moore (1991), use the metaphor of the need for mobile technologies to ‘cross the chasm’ from being niche products to becoming an integral part of the consumer mass market. And they consider design considerations to be crucial in the transition to ensure that the needs of mainstream users, as opposed to early adopters, are catered for. Norris et al. (2007, p. 7) argue that unlike early adopters, who tend to find new technology intrinsically interesting and who are willing to devise workarounds for any shortcomings, mainstream education practitioners are mainly concerned with the curriculum and its ‘delivery’ and they tend to see technology as a means to an end. One hopes that they are also concerned with processes of learning. Norris et al. also suggest that mainstream teachers are looking for simplicity and reliability rather than viewing technology as new opportunities.

The attentional aspect is also foregrounded by Beale (2007a, p. 14) who notes that, particularly when working in new, and often uncontrolled environments, in which greater situational awareness and alertness is needed than normally, ‘having to change a focus of attention from the ‘real world’ to a specific device can be problematic’.

Design issues are, of course, also very pertinent in relation to the integration of mobile devices into, and interoperability with teaching and learning processes and curricula, as well as the infrastructure for learning provided by educational institutions. Hoppe (2007, p. 33) distinguishes the following types of integration: media, process and knowledge.

O’Connell and Smith produced a very helpful manual for and guide to working with mobile learning standards published by the Australian Flexible Learning Framework in 2007. They draw on the work of the e-learning consortium at the Masie Centre NY which had outlined six ‘abilities’ that define standards in e-learning:

- interoperability (*ability of two or more systems to share information*)
- reusability (*ability to reuse or modify existing systems, data or code*)
- manageability (*ability to monitor and maintain systems, data or code*)
- durability (*ability of a system to endure over time*)
- scalability (*ability of a system to handle growing amounts of information and work*) and
- affordability (*ability of systems and data to remain in financial reach of users*). (O'Connell and Smith 2007, pp. 3–4)

These 'abilities' are considered to be of relevance for mobile learning design as well. The authors also advise their readers to ensure resources are cross-compatible with baseline delivery contexts, to exploit the capabilities of specific devices to maximise quality and usability as well as to exploit the creation capacity (p. 8). The latter point, i.e. the harnessing of the potential for knowledge creation by users, is also made strongly by Bruns (2007) who has coined the term 'produser' describing the ad hoc, on-the-fly user-and-producer position of learners. Bruns sees the difference between a user and a producer model as one of quantity as well as quality of participation.

And, of course, design issues also come into play in relation to the production processes teachers and learners themselves engage in when creating content for and with their mobile devices. For effective use in everyday situations or the hurly-burly of a classroom, features such as instant-on/instant-off are very important as without them the ephemerality of the here and now cannot easily be captured, even using mobile devices. With reference to the design of innovative educational activities, Milrad (2007, p. 30) suggest 'scenario-based design' which is thought to offer a rich description of the interactions of the settings, actors, goals/objectives, actions and events constituting a scenario. Of real significance here for us are the multimodal affordances and characteristics of mobile devices, in particular how images and sound-related functionality impact on both the input and output dimensions of interactions as well as the representation of information and knowledge.

Naismith and Corlett (2006, pp. 19–20), reviewing papers presented at *mLearn* conferences between 2002 and 2005, identify the following design principles:

- create quick, simple interactions;
- prepare materials that are flexible and can play to the heterogeneity of learners and situations;
- design access and interactions that account for the heterogeneity of devices and standards;
- consider the affordances and limitations of the devices;
- focus not only on delivery of content but also on facilitation of learning;
- apply a learner-centred design in view of the lack of fit of teacher-centred models with a diverse range of learning environments.

All of the above, clearly points towards the need for a theory of instructional design for mobile learning which, as Sharples et al. (2008) rightly note, has not yet been fully articulated. Our experience also suggests the need for an iterative approach to the design of artefacts, such as re-usable learning objects (RLOs), which is linked synergistically to theorising (Bradley, Haynes, Cook, Boyle and Smith, 2009). And Divitini and Morken (2007, p. 12), quoting Thackara (2005) suggest the need to design for 'new geographies of learning' by which they mean 'configurations of space, place, and network that respect the social and collaborative nature of learning – while still exploiting the dynamic potential of networked collaboration'. They point out that collaborative learning is increasingly taking place within and across looser communities (p. 13), which necessitates a focus on the seamless integration of different learning experiences (p. 14). Sprake (2007, p. 31) notes that mobile technologies can create conditions for 'spatial contiguity' and 'spatial dispersal' out of which 'new' learning webs, namely those that take in the world outside the classroom and which are characterised by lateral connections between people, objects and places, could emerge. The design of mobile learning tools, software, content and learning material needs to take account of that as well as of the needs of individual users. In order to support learning effectively, the design process needs to focus on the strength of mobile devices, such as immediacy of communication and access to information, context-sensitivity and location-awareness.

Researching Mobile Learning

Given the complexities of mobile learning delineated in this chapter, there emerges a clear need not only for sustained research into phenomena attendant to mobile learning but also for work on explanatory theoretical and conceptual frames, which enable a systematic analysis of all aspects of mobile learning. Indeed, as already noted in Chapter 1, we attempt to make a significant contribution to such an analytical frame in this book. We will discuss our deliberations in some detail in Part II of the book.

Based on the issues discussed above, it is also not difficult to imagine the challenges faced by mobile learning research. Given the (semi)private nature of much of the engagement with mobile technologies, studies are often based on the learners' own accounts and metacognitive analyses of their learning, by means of semi-structured interviews, surveys, and diary studies with all the limitations such methods entail. Also, given the social nature of much mobile technology use around acts of communication, the challenge for researchers is not just to make tangible cognitive processes taking place within an individual, which at best manifest themselves indirectly in the creation of certain artefacts, but also how these processes are embedded in social interaction and affect, and are affected by, cognitive process of co-learners. In any event, the research methods used will invariably reflect the research questions in focus as well as the broad theoretical orientation of the researchers.

Taylor (2007, p. 28) argues that the evaluation of mobile learning best be conducted from an activity analysis point of view, from whatever theoretical perspective, which is, of course, in line with the theoretical model she espouses in her writing (Taylor et al. 2006; Sharples et al. 2007). We discuss the merits, and limitations, of Activity Theory in some detail in Chapter 5 as a basis for our own conceptual/theoretical perspective.

Of particular importance in relation to mobile learning is also the capturing of learning over time, rather than of isolated instances, as well as of learning as context-bound; in view of the myriad of contexts within which mobile learning can take place, as well as their unpredictability, the latter issue poses a particular challenge. On the plus side, learning with and through mobile technologies leaves data trails which can be accessed and analysed by researchers. In view of the above, we see considerable merit in the use of qualitative, e.g. narrative and case-based approaches to data collection as well as data analysis. For a detailed discussion of research methods in mobile learning (see Vavoula et al. 2009).

Our attempt at a topography of mobile learning leads us to the conclusion that mobile learning can be seen as central to educational landscape of the twenty-first century. Needless to say, there is a need for more systematic research, which helps educators make informed pedagogical decisions in support of mobile learning, as well as for a sustained effort in synthesizing existing research in order to make reliable findings accessible to practitioners, researchers and policy makers (see also van't Hooft and Swan 2007, p. 350).

Chapter 3
Mobile Devices as Resources for Learning: Adoption Trends, Characteristics, Constraints and Challenges

Introduction

Most educators, and indeed parents, have been sceptical about the value of mobile devices as a resource for learning. However, over the last two, three decades large changes have taken place for children in society. The pressure of the market in societies dominated by neo-liberal economies is one of many factors (see Buckingham 2000). Children continue to gain ever increasing access to functionally convergent digital media and mobile devices; their bedrooms are increasingly becoming multi-media centres (a trend commented on already in the early to mid-1990s) (see for example Bachmair 1997, 1999) where they can engage in meaning-making that is personally motivating for them. For example, in the UK children aged 12–15 have an average of six media devices in their bedrooms and children aged 8–11 have an average of four such devices (Ofcom 2008a, p. 6).[1] Furthermore, 84% of people in the UK aged 8 or over use, or have access to mobile services (Ofcom 2008b, p. 5). In many places, however, children are asked not to bring phones into school or the use of these devices within school is limited because of e-safety or harassment concerns (http://news.bbc.co.uk/1/hi/scotland/glasgow_and_west/6334523.stm). Schools are cautious – anxious, maybe – about new digital technologies and media.

However, there are success stories for mobile learning in schools. For example, there has been positive press coverage in September 2008 about mobile/cell phones in schools from the Daily Telegraph Newspaper that ran the headline: 'Mobile/cell phones "boost school standards"' (http://www.telegraph.co.uk/connected/main.jhtml?xml=/connected/2008/09/04/dlmobile104. xml). The newspaper report is based on work carried out by Hartnell-Young (2008), presented at the British

[1] Ofcom, or Office of Communication, is the independent regulator and competition authority for the UK communications industries. Ofcom's statutory duties, as set down in the Communications Act 2003, are: '3(1) It shall be the principal duty of Ofcom, in carrying out their functions; (a) to further the interests of citizens in relation to communications matters; and (b) to further the interests of consumers in relevant markets, where appropriate by promoting competition'. Ofcom has responsibilities across television, radio, telecommunications and wireless communications services. http://www.ofcom.org.uk/

N. Pachler et al., *Mobile Learning*, DOI 10.1007/978-1-4419-0585-7_3,

Educational Research Association (BERA) conference. The study took place in schools where mobile/cell phones are banned in class. However, champions of change among teachers and students were still able to explore mobile/cell phones use in various ways. The study reports that in spite of policies and media pressure, teachers become confident enough to share their experiences and attitudes with groups of teachers realising that the taboo against devices in school is merely addressing surface issues. Furthermore, the recent comprehensive report from The Joan Ganz Cooney Center, already referred to in Chapter 1, has examined over 25 mobile device orientated projects in the U.S. and throughout the world, reporting that there already exist 'early evidence and examples of how mobile devices may help re-define teaching and learning in the decade ahead' (Shuler 2009, p. 4). Indeed, teachers are seen as innovators, where the co-construction of learning between teachers and students is regarded as a powerful vehicle for innovation (Visions 2007, p. 19). Our view is that it is very important for teachers to assume an obligation to see it as part of their role to sensitise young people to the need for a reflective use of new technologies. Consequently, given these emerging discourses it seems relevant and timely to look at the adoption trends, characteristics, constraints and challenges of mobile devices and digital media.

Adoption Trends of Mobile Devices and Services

The recent spate of Horizons reports (e.g. Johnson et al. 2008, 2009) provide us with a hint of what is to come in education, from a US and Australasian perspective over the next 5 years in terms of new digital technology and media we will use 'Ofcom' reports to provide a UK perspective. Specifically, over the next year or two we will see the deployment, in educational institutions, of innovations such as mobile broadband, cloud computing, collaborative webs, 'geo-everything' and context aware learning. Some of these trends are discussed below.

The Global and National Figures and Potential for Learning

According to the International Telecommunication Union, 3.3 billion people, more than half the world's population, now have a contract to a mobile/cell phone service, 'so the internet at last looks set to change the whole world' (The Economist 2008, p. 3). The present global economic downturn (dating from the second half of 2008) appears to have slowed down this rate of adoption. Furthermore, currently not all mobile/cell phones are internet enabled. Once a phone can easily connect to the internet the ability to browse web services makes such devices more useful for learning. Research for Intel suggests that the number of mobile internet devices, i.e.

devices that can browse the web, will increase to 1.2 billion by 2012.[2] Furthermore, the mobile sector in the UK is now larger by revenue than the fixed phone line and broadband sectors combined (Ofcom 2008b, p. 5). And, the number of people who report themselves involuntarily excluded from mobile/cell phone ownership in the UK is small, around 1% of the total population[3] (Ofcom 2008b, p. 75), i.e. about 609,750 people in the UK were not able to own mobile/cell phones for reasons other than personal choice. But, Ofcom (2008b) also identify gaps in network coverage, problems with callings plans and inequality of access for particular groups as significant among consumers.

Whilst we readily acknowledge that the figures for mobile/cell phone will be different in different countries and contexts, we feel the cases reported above are broadly generalisable across the industrialised world. That said, we draw on statistics from different countries where we consider them relevant to ensure breadth of coverage but we do not seek comprehensive coverage. A critical point here is that should society decide to use mobile/cell phones for learning, access to the network and internet services needs to become ubiquitous. Fast mobile wireless services, or broadband wireless, are becoming more widespread in the developed countries. This trend will encourage the use of mobile/cell phones for learning in and out of school. In this book we pay particular attention to the transformative effects of new media on learning, which is viewed as an 'outside in–inside out' relationship, where cultural practices involving new digital media can be brought into the school, these practices can be enhanced inside school and in turn feed back into the digital world at large. Thus new digital media can be regarded as cultural resources that can enable the bringing together of the informal learning contexts in the world outside the school with those processes and contexts that are valued inside the school.

Mobile Access Trends and Patterns of Usage

John Horrigan, Associate Director of the Pew Internet and American Life Project, in the report *Seeding the Cloud: What Mobile Access Means for Usage Patterns and Online Content*, gives details of the US trends. Horrigan (2008) points out that mobile/cell phone users in the US are more likely to be found in groups that have generally lagged in internet adoption, such as senior citizens, blacks, and Latinos. Some 84% of English-speaking Hispanics reported having mobile/cell phones and 71% of blacks had mobile/cell phones, compared with 78 and 63%, respectively, for online access (PC internet access). In the executive summary for the report, (http://pewresearch.org/pubs/754/cloud-computing) Horrigan points out that

[2] Maggie Shiels, July 25, 2008, Technology reporter, BBC News, *Boom times ahead for mobile web* http://news.bbc.co.uk/1/hi/technology/7522305.stm

[3] In mid-2007 the resident population of the UK was 60,975,000 (http://www.statistics.gov.uk/)

> More striking than access patterns is usage. For use of non-voice data applications on handhelds, Hispanics and African Americans lead the way relative to white Americans. Half of African Americans and 56% of English-speaking Latinos with cell phones, on a typical day, do at least one of 10 non-voice data applications such as taking pictures, accessing the internet for news, playing music, or texting. By contrast, 38% of whites do these kinds of activities on a wireless handheld device on the average day.

The UK Office of Communications (Ofcom) is the independent regulator and competition authority for the UK communications industries[1]. As we pointed out already, the recent Ofcom (2008a) report, *Media Literacy Audit – Report on UK children's media literacy*, highlights that 'children's bedrooms are increasingly becoming multi-media centres, with children aged 12–15 having an average of six media devices in their bedrooms and children aged 8–11 having an average of four' (p. 5) and that 'The correlation between age and mobile/cell phone use is particularly strong, with the proportion of children using a mobile almost doubling between the age of 9 (52%) and 15 (95%). While in 2005 we saw a sharp increase in mobile/cell phone use between the ages of 10 and 11 years, in 2007 the rise is more gradual and starts at an earlier age, with significantly higher usage levels among 9 and 10 year olds; children are acquiring mobiles at a younger age and using them more' (p. 5). Thus, in the UK at least, by the age of 15 we find that 95% of children use mobile/cell phones. Thus we can say that there is a strong trend outside schools for young people to use mobile/cell phones as part of their life-worlds.

The Ofcom report (2008a) suggests that

> Behaviour patterns and media preferences vary considerably by gender; boys of all ages are more likely than girls to use games consoles and to cite these as the medium they would miss the most. While the media preference of younger girls is dominated by television, older girls demonstrate particularly high levels of mobile/cell phone use and are more likely to miss their mobile/cell phone than any other medium (p. 5).

This can be relevant for teachers who, as in Hartnell-Young's (2008) study, have taken decisions against what appears to be the accepted norm of banning phones from schools; they are devising policies for best use based on emerging collaboration within the school community. New technologies, like the mobile/cell phone, and their widespread availability and use affects cultural practices and enables new contexts of learning. New media like YouTube are changing traditional media practice, informal learners are able to actively select, appropriate and implement learning solutions to meet their own needs.

The Ofcom (2008a) report also provides a useful insight into usage patterns of mobile device according to geographical location:

> Mobile/cell phone use is significantly higher among children living in urban areas compared to those living in rural areas (87% compared to 83%), while use of social networking sites is higher among rural children (61% compared to 54%) (p. 8).

The reasons for these urban-rural differences are not clear, but high usage of social networking sites in rural setting could be capitalised on by teacher working in such distributed communities. We will return to social networking at the end of this chapter.

This data provides a useful insight for teachers wishing to use mobile devices to assist learning for ethnic minorities, in that such groups may be amenable to some of the phases of mobile learning described in Chapter 2. Similarly, ethnic minority groups in the UK appear to lead the way on digital device take-up and use. Research from Ofcom (2008c) reveals that:

> Ethnic minority groups are at the forefront of digital communications in the UK, with high levels of mobile/cell phone, internet and multichannel television take-up. But, despite this, many people from ethnic minority groups lack confidence finding content online and are concerned about content delivered on digital communications.

This media literacy audit by Ofcom of UK adults from ethnic minority groups draws on quantitative research from the four largest ethnic minority groups in the UK: Indians, Pakistanis, Black Caribbeans and Black Africans.

The pattern of ownership in the US appears to be different to that in the UK. In the UK older people and disabled people, have disproportionately low levels of mobile/cell phone ownership. Those without access to credit or a bank account may not be able to obtain the most favourable prices or packages. As mobile devices become a more important way to communicate, these issues become more significant (Ofcom 2008b, p. 6). If mobile/cell phones are to be used for wider social uses, including for instance '(social) learning' these patterns should be built into policy and contingencies built in to support in targeted areas.

Trends in Any Where, Any Time, Any Device Learning

In the diachronic overview provided in Chapter 2 we saw that poor network access was an issue for some teachers. Currently, a learner needs access to fast broadband wireless if they are to take advantage of some of the more high-end affordances of mobile devices. Logistical and infrastructural issues thus have an impact on the adoption of mobile devices for learning. Choice and provision of devices, storage and retrieval capabilities, file categorisation and classification and sharing, plus the need for back-up contingencies all prey on the mind of the innovative teacher. However, this seems about to change with cloud computing and other innovations, which we consider towards the end of the book in Chapter 14.

Characteristics and Functions of Mobile Devices

If we foreground the functions of mobile/cell phones then the list expands as time goes by: a mobile/cell phone usually has SMS, MMS, MP3-player, photo and video, games; a mobile/cell phone may also include an organizer, radio and TV-set, Web-browser, navigation tool, personal identification and tools for paying, and so on. The point will come where the device will begin to be differently named; just as the horseless carriage eventually became a car. Below we discuss social networking in detail; here we mention that there is an increasing trend to use mobile/cell phones to access such sites. Furthermore, the increasing availability of different network services and applications is making use of location awareness, discussed in Chapter 2, an increasing possibility for learners and teachers. Indeed, the workspace for the Horizon Project (Horizon 2008, p. 17) points out that:

> Today, mobiles are increasingly about networking on the go. Better displays and new interfaces make it easier to interact with an ever-expanding variety of content—not just content formatted specially for mobiles, but nearly any content available on the Internet. Mobiles now keep us in touch in almost all the ways that laptops used to: with email, web browsing, photos and videos, documents, searching and shopping—all available anywhere without the need to find a hotspot or a power outlet... Newer, longer-lasting batteries keep our mobiles alive for longer trips between charges. Today's mobiles are smaller, slimmer, and more powerful than ever before. Storage capacity has significantly increased, and some mobiles can even store and play back multiple feature-length films—perfect for long airplane rides... Even the days of having to buy a new phone to take advantage of the latest features are coming to an end. As more features are embedded in the software, the physical device will become more flexible simply by receiving the latest software updates. Open APIs (application programming interfaces) are already encouraging the creation of special add-on software that will offer even more services; those "widgets," combined with the growing array of webware applications will make mobiles as capable as computers for doing many everyday tasks. Smaller and less expensive than a laptop, yet increasingly useful, the mobile is fast becoming the ultimate portable computer.

The distinction is blurring between emerging infrastructures and devices, and the social uses to which these technologies are put, it is still helpful to enumerate them. Furthermore, van't Hooft (2008, p. 33) points out that although the possible combinations of functionalities into a single device is 'mind-boggling', most people tend to use their devices for a limited number of tasks. The most important tasks include (source: van't Hooft 2008, p. 33)

- accessing and aggregating information online (such as news, sports, entertainment, hobbies)
- navigating the physical environment (mostly by using GPS devices, Google Maps, and Google Earth for maps and directions, or sites like Flickr for geo-tagged images)
- accessing or interacting with digital information embedded in the physical environment (as available through (combining) technologies such as GPS, RFID or QR tags, and NFC (near field communication))
- interacting with the physical environment (for example, using embedded chips to make payments or accessing public transportation; a good example of this is the use of mobile/cell phones for such activities in Singapore)
- communication (using a variety of channels such as SMS, IM, VOIP, email and yes, even voice calls)
- entertainment (games, music, and videos/movies)
- media creation (recording video and audio, and to some extent, editing and publishing from a mobile device, for example by moblogging – uploading pictures from a mobile/cell phone to a weblog)
- media tagging (labelling audio, video, and images with key words, or geo-tagging media for integration with tools such as Google Maps or Google Earth).

From a pedagogical perspective, Arnedillo-Sánchez et al. (2007, p. 6) have pointed out that mobile learning experiences and tools have been classified according to their educational objectives (Gay et al. 2002), potential activities (Roschelle

2003) and by the educational theory they support (Naismith et al. 2004). More recently, Patten et al. (2006) have proposed a more extensive framework encompassing functionality and pedagogy. Patten et al. (2006) propose a functional-pedagogical framework, which 'consists of seven distinct categories of application, which they term: administrative, referential, interactive, microworld, data collection, location-aware and collaborative. We argue that three categories, namely data collection, location-aware and collaborative, are particularly suited to learning with handheld devices when they are informed by collaborative, contextual and constructionist learning theories'. Thus, administrative, referential, interactive and microworld replicate learning experiences are enabled by 'static technology', whereas data collection, location-aware and collaborative 'are not attempting to replicate, or even augment, existing learning scenarios but rather they try to create new learning opportunities which would not be possible without (mobile) technology'.

Constraints and Challenges

Children and Mobile/Cell Phones

A report published by the Joseph Rowntree Foundation (a social policy research and development charity in the UK) (Joseph Rowntree Foundation 2008) proposed that owning at least a pre-pay mobile/cell phone is a prerequisite to adequate participation in society. As we mentioned earlier in this chapter, Ofcom has highlighted the fact that in the UK, 84% of people aged 8 or over use, or have access to, mobile services (Ofcom 2008b, p. 5). But should children in this age group be given access to phones? Is this a question for parents and schools? Do governments have a role to play here? Following the Stewart Report in 2000,[4] the UK's Department of Health recommended that, in line with a precautionary approach, the widespread use of mobile/cell phones by children (under the age of 16) should be discouraged for non-essential calls (Ofcom 2008b, p. 5). Yet the trend has been for increased access. Attendant public concern has not, however, receded; research undertaken as part of Ofcom's Media Literacy Audit (reported Ofcom 2008b, p. 79) identified a number of concerns among mobile users, many of which illustrate concerns about children and this technology. The unprompted responses were grouped into the following themes:

- risk to society/values – relating to responses such as misuse of camera phones, 'happy slapping', children having phones at a young age and paedophiles contacting children;
- affordability – relating to responses such as cost of calls generally and cost of calls when abroad;
- risk to health – relating to responses such as health concerns from using handsets and from masts;

[4] Independent Expert Group on Mobile/cell Phones. http://www.iegmp.org.uk/

- risk to personal safety – relating to responses such as being a target for stealing mobile/cell phones;
- risk to privacy – relating to responses such as intrusion into other people's space, a public space and the proliferation of junk and spam text messages; and
- offensive content – including access to inappropriate content by minors.

The comments from the Ofcom (2008b, p. 80) report below appear to reflect a growing awareness and anxiety about take-up of mobile services by children:

> Community concerns surrounding health risks, affordability and risk to personal safety have been reported by people in poll data for a number of years. Risks to personal safety are often reported in the context of street crime. Concerns surrounding society/values and the risk to privacy are more recent developments. This may reflect growing awareness and anxiety about take-up of mobile services by children... Issues regarding privacy and mobile/cell phones raise some questions for governments and, for example, the UK's Information Commissioner's Office... The data shows that the level of concern is roughly similar with the exception being in the 'offensive content' category which is currently not as significant a worry as the other areas – reflecting, possibly, the still-emerging nature of access to content on mobile devices and self-regulatory efforts to address these issues.

E-safety, as it is termed in the UK, is a complex issue and Becta, the UK Government agency leading on the use of technology throughout learning, has issued useful guidelines in this respect (http://schools.becta.org.uk/index.php?section=is): 'The virtual world opens up new opportunities for learning and creativity, but it also means thinking ahead of new risks'. The statutory context for e-safety in the UK follows on from the 2003 Green Paper 'Every child matters' and the provisions of the Children Act 2004, the publication entitled Working Together to Safeguard Children sets out how organisations and individuals should work together to safeguard and promote the welfare of children. 'Every local authority has now established a local safeguarding children board (LSCB) as the key statutory mechanism for agreeing how the relevant organisations in each local area will co-operate to safeguard and promote the welfare of children, and for ensuring the effectiveness of what they do... While the work of LSCBs contributes to the wider goals of improving the wellbeing of all children, it has a particular focus on aspects of the "staying safe" outcome'.

The 'staying safe' states includes that children and young people be:

- safe from maltreatment, neglect, violence and sexual exploitation
- safe from accidental injury and death
- safe from bullying and discrimination
- safe from crime and anti-social behaviour in and out of school
- secure, stable and cared for (http://localauthorities.becta.org.uk/index.php?section=esf&catcode=la_es_01&rid=14585).

Becta also provides generic advice to schools on developing an e-safety policy, the importance of an acceptable use policy, and the key considerations in creating one; on understanding good practice in keeping personal data secure; on finding out how to buy internet services and filtering products from suppliers accredited by Becta; on getting advice on how to educating staff and learners about internet safety, and online bullying and other issues (http://www.becta.org.uk/safeguarding.php).

On a more practical level, ThinkuKnow (http://www.thinkuknow.co.uk/ teachers/default.aspx) provide resources that have been produced to help teachers and trainers teach young people how to stay safe online. The resources have been developed largely with the direct help and advice from the UK's Child Exploitation and Online Protection Centres (CEOP) Youth Advisory Panel. For example, in January 2009 ThinkuKnow added 'Where's Klaus', (http://www.youtube.com/watch?v=-IOOn2wR8bU&feature=channel_page) an award winning film given to them by their German counterparts Klicksafe, (www.klicksafe.de) to CEOP's Youtube channel (www.youtube.com/ceop). This film raises awareness amongst parents about the risks that young people may be taking in an online environment. Other 'cybersafety' advice can be found, for example, in the Digizens blog (http://suz01.edublogs.org/2008/08/08/cybersafety-forum-developing-responsible-ethical-and-resilient-digizens/) and on the Worksmart Not Safe For Work site (http://www.worksmart.org.uk/nsfw/hub.php).

Teachers who are innovators will need to be aware that in projects like Learn2Go, described in Chapter 2 (McFarlane et al. 2008), parental 'buy-in' of phones was a prerequisite and may in part have contributed to the success that project has achieved. Such a model of parental contribution, or indeed general fund raising through school fairs common in the UK, is not necessarily part of cultural practice in other countries.

In terms of gender difference for digital devices, Becta (2008c, p. 5, bold in original) report that

> **Girls are more likely to own and use a webcam and to record video than boys. Boys are significantly more likely to own a Wii or PSP/DS and play more games.** There is no significant difference between boys and girls with respect to access to MP3-players, mobile/cell phones or PDAs. **Social networking and communication activity is more common amongst girls** and girls in Year 10 reported significantly greater rates than boys of receiving messages from people they did not know through instant messaging and via email.

From that analysis we can infer that girls in Year 10 (in UK schools approximately age 14) in particular may require e-safety guidance. In order to unpick the constraints and challenges facing teachers who wish to innovate with mobile/cell phones, we follow the headings used in the Ofcom (2008b) to structure and inform our review of the issues.

Opportunities to use Public Services

We are seeing the creation of a '*digital handbag*' or '*digital wallet*', with electronic or transactional services integrated into a single digital device. This technology, already developed, is getting closer to being a commercial reality for the mass market. There may be a number of long-term citizen concerns about the hidden impact on those who do not have a mobile device.

> The 'digital handbag'... brings a number of potential consumer benefits. However, alongside these benefits of device convergence come some understandable risks. The integration of transactional services, alongside other electronic services (key access to cars and the home) brings risks not previously associated with mobiles, for example, 'how do I get into my house if I've lost my phone?' The full scale of device convergence is uncertain – this is therefore one of those areas where rapid developments can spring surprises (Ofcom 2008b, p. 77).

The implications for learning will be various. Care will need to be taken to make back-ups of student work. For example a student may use their mobile devices as an integrated '*digital portfolio*', that is being updated and reflected upon over time and over different contexts. We can envisage a scenario where students will be using this digital portfolio inside the school, when working from home, when working in public spaces such as libraries and other public areas such as cafes that provide access to wireless networks. Learning in and across formal and informal contexts would be enabled by access to public spaces such as the BBC's online resources plus libraries, archives, galleries and museums that provide digital access to information for homework; these could be selectively accessed with an appropriate digital portfolio as and when the students need to do so. Such a near-future scenario could, as the above quote indicates, bring surprises. Ownership of the appropriate device that can host the digital portfolio and valid access codes may become a necessity for access to public services. For the moment it is the case that in the health service and elsewhere in business there is a trend not to store any date on portable devices precisely because of these problems.

Democratic Opportunities

If school children are to participate in the democratic process, assuming this is desirable, and in particular e-democracy, does it make sense to sensitise them to democratic possibilities as soon as possible in order to engage them in the political process?

> '**E-democracy**' can take many forms... It is possible that there may be a role for mobile devices in democratic processes – for example, as a tool in voter registration, or to alert voters about nearby polling stations using location information. Mobile services will also, inevitably, be used as an element of the communications between political candidates and parties, and the electorate. (Ofcom 2008b, p. 77)

E-democracy opportunities through schools and mobile/cell phones could, perhaps, assist communication and understanding between diverse social and ethnic groups. As Stephen Downes points out in an entry to one of his blogs:

> The problem [w]ith representative democracy is that your representative is often looking out for someone else's interests. Often his own. Internet technology creates the possibility for direct democracy, but this in turn requires a way of rethinking how we manage society. We want to connect people to government – but only those parts that affect them directly. We want to create mechanisms that allow people to govern themselves – but not to govern others. Collaborative and community-oriented systems for resource management and

> decision-making will be a fertile field in the future. (What Not To Build, January 4, 2009) (http://halfanhour.blogspot.com/2009/01/what-not-to-build.html)

A school based on collaborative and community-orientated systems using mobile/cell phones to enable pupils to participate in school decision making could provide an exciting opportunity to foster the life-long learners and citizens of the future.

Ambient Wireless Devices and Health and Learning Needs, Opportunities and Issues

In 2000 the UK's Department of Health issued an advice leaflet on mobile/cell phones and health (http://www.dh.gov.uk/en/Publicationsandstatistics/Publications/PublicationsPolicyAndGuidance/DH_4123979) in which it reports:

> Radio waves emitted above a certain level can cause heating effects in the body. International guidelines seek to ensure that exposure is kept below that level. All mobile/cell phones sold in the UK meet these guidelines.
>
> The balance of current research evidence suggests that exposures to radio waves below levels set out in international guidelines do not cause health problems for the general population. However, there is some evidence that changes in brain activity can occur below these guidelines, but it isn't clear why. There are significant gaps in our scientific knowledge. This has led a group of independent experts – commissioned by Government and headed by Sir William Stewart – to recommend "a precautionary approach" to the use of mobile/cell phones until more research findings become available. If you use a mobile/cell phone, you can choose to minimise your exposure to radio waves. These are ways to do so:
>
> - keep your calls short
> - consider relative SAR values... when buying a new phone.

It is possible to measure how much radio wave energy your body receives from each model of mobile/cell phone; this is called the specific absorption rate or SAR. SAR values are provided with each mobile/cell phone. The Guardian newspaper reported in September 2007 (http://www.guardian.co.uk/uk/2007/sep/12/mobilephones.health) that

> Mobile/cell phones do not pose health problems to adults in the short term, according to the results of a major six-year research programme published today. However the research also points to a "slight hint" of a cancer risk for long-term users.
>
> Experts warned they were unable, at this stage, to rule out the risks of brain or ear cancers for people who have used mobiles for more than 10 years. They said that further investigation of this result would be a priority for the next phase of their work, which would also study the effects of mobile/cell phones on children's health.

The World Health Organization, based upon the consensus view of the scientific and medical communities, states that health effects (e.g. headaches) are very unlikely to be caused by cellular phones or their base stations, (http://www.who.int/features/qa/30/en/) and expected to make recommendations about mobile/cell phones in October 2009. (http://www.gsmworld.com/health/programs/sciencemilestones.shtml)

As well as the health and safety concerns and considerations mentioned above, there are wider health opportunities and issues for mobile device usage

> Future developments in the healthcare sector, as indicated in Ofcom report “Tomorrow’s wireless world”, may include the use of in-body networks, on-body monitors and smart drug dispensing to help health professionals to diagnose and monitor at-risk patients in their own home. However, those who are poorer, older or disabled are less likely to own a mobile/cell phone – and these groups, for different reasons, often have relatively greater need to access health services than the general population. As more health services are promoted and delivered via mobile communications, not owning a mobile/cell phone or having access to a mobile network could affect the ability of, for example, public health initiatives to be fully effective – in the extreme, with the risk of those most in need of medical support missing out. (Ofcom 2008b, p. 78)

UK Patients with breathing problems such as asthma already receive SMS air quality reports to help them plan journeys. Students with specific health problems who want to decide if a trip outside school is appropriate could contact a service that then replies with advice personalised to their needs. If a student has a particular learning need that can be supported via mobile/cell phone, then not having a phone could be a barrier to learning. For example, if a learner is new to a country, mobile devices can be used to provide language learning support. In the Stephen Downes Blog cited above, he also talks about being connected to applications (walls, desks, fridges, toasters):

> OK, maybe not toasters, unless you really value weather maps on your morning toast. But with ambient wireless in an increasing number of homes it has become feasible to connect appliances to the internet. This creates a whole range of possible products – paper-thin displays that hang on walls, desks with smart, interactive surfaces, fridges that keep track of your food, automatic light switches that switch off when the room is empty, health monitors, and more. And it’s not just that these applications are connected to the internet, it’s that these applications can access *your* data, remember choices you’ve made, and interpreted and project your needs. What needs? That is where the room is for innovation. (What Not To Build, January 4, 2009)

In terms of schools we suggest veering towards imposing the personal on the technical; successful use of ambient wireless devices will be about making these tools about the person instead of about what the designers of the technology intended, which leads into agency and notions of consumption vs. production, discussed in the Chapter 1.

Social Opportunities

Web-based social networking has enjoyed a striking rise in popularity. School aged-children enjoy social interactions enhanced by social networking, which can also be used to provide opportunities for collective intelligence, thereby adding value to data and concepts. Developments in the area of user-generated content have meant that mobile devices can be used for capturing digital video and photographs; they have also made the downloading of music easier. Thus, the whole emphasis has moved away from the traditional editorial process, where media organisations push out a programme or a newspaper, towards a process of content creation and distribution by owners of these devices. Copyright of protected material is becoming a crucial issue. The UK's Joint Information Systems Committee (JISC), which is funded by the UK Higher Education (HE) and Further Education (FE) funding bodies to provide leadership in the innovative use of ICT to support education and research, provides a copyright service (http://www.jisc.ac.uk/whatwedo/themes/informationenvironment/scholarlycomms/copyright.aspx) and it points out that:

> Traditionally publishers have required authors to sign agreements transferring copyright of their publications to the publisher and managed copyright on their behalf. In the age of print-only publications, most authors went along with this practice. With the advent of electronic publishing and the Internet, the academic community started to question whether transferring all rights to the publisher was in the interests of scholarly communication. For example, this could limit an author's right to post his/her article on their web site or deposit it in an open access repository.

JISC have also produced an animation (http://www.jisc.ac.uk/news/stories/2008/12/web2rights.aspx) considering Intellectual Property Rights in their use and re-use of interactive Web 2.0 technologies. Becta also provide copyright advice for schools, pointing out that 'Students should be aware that plagiarism is not only cheating but where sufficient is copied, an illegal infringement of copyright also constitutes a criminal offence'. (http://schools.becta.org.uk/index.php?catcode=ss_to_es_pp_le_03&rid=9983& section=is)

The whole cycle of user-generated content is made much easier when we introduce social software, which is widely used for both business and leisure activities alike.

> These networks allow communications that would previously have been conducted face-to face, or over the phone, to take place in other ways. As online social networking sites grow and diversify their services, they are increasingly looking towards mobile as a way to offer access to their users. Many mobile operators are integrating mobile access within their packages, for example offering convenient access to social networking sites such as Facebook, Bebo and Myspace, (and related services like Twitter) as part of their tariff bundles. The ability to integrate such services with location information provides a new sort of immediacy: the prospect of services that integrate 'social proximity' ("who are my friends?") with physical proximity ("are any of my friends nearby?"). The social impact of these services could be significant. (Ofcom 2008b, p. 78)

Thus the addition of social software to mobile/cell phones adds a layer of complexity, with children who are in possession of such devices able search for friends based on their location.

From a school perspective, Becta (http://schools.becta.org.uk/index.php?catcode=ss_to_es_pp_com_03&rid=12065§ion=is) points out that social software 'provides new opportunities for personal expression, the creation of communities, collaboration and sharing'. Examples of social software is a catch-all term used to describe systems like moblogs, (http://news.bbc.co.uk/1/hi/technology/3658977.stm) which are single authored web-based journals, i.e. blogs, that are sent from a mobile/cell phone, modifiable collaborative web pages in the form of wikis, podcasting via subscription-based broadcast over the web, and social networking sites like Twitter (http://twitter.com/); with the latter providing a social networking and microblogging service utilising instant messaging, SMS or a web interface. Another Ofcom report (2008e) reported by Becta (http://www.dh.gov.uk/en/Publicationsandstatistics/Publications/PublicationsPolicyAndGuidance/DH_4123979) shows that

> just over one fifth (22 per cent) of adult internet users aged 16+ and almost half (49 per cent) of children aged 8–17 who use the internet have set up their own profile on a social networking site. For adults, the likelihood of setting up a profile is highest among 16–24 year olds (54 per cent) and decreases with age. The research shows that social networking is very popular with younger users, but also reveals that some are by-passing age restrictions to set up profiles. For example, although the minimum age for most major social networking sites is typically 13 (14 on MySpace), 27 per cent of 8–11 year olds who are aware of social networking say that they have a profile on a site.

As we pointed out above, one of the key benefits of social networking sites for school children is that they encourage young people to be creative users of the internet, publishing content rather than being passive consumers. Indeed, Becta (http://www.dh.gov.uk/en/Publicationsandstatistics/Publications/PublicationsPolicyAndGuidance/DH_4123979) points out that by adopting an online personality school children can express themselves and chat and socialize with peers. It is also possible for them to share self-generated, swapped or downloaded multimedia content. However, social networking sites can present some risks if not used in a safe and responsible way. As with most new technologies, key issues centre around content and contact risks. However, and as we pointed out above, Becta also points out that there are general concerns that young people may upload content that is inappropriate, offensive or even illegal to their online spaces, and that they may post inappropriate comments to the profiles of others, which can result in the bullying, slander or humiliation of others. Furthermore, many young people maintain very detailed online profiles, including a large amount of personal information, photos and accounts of daily routines, which could lead to them being identified or contacted in person. In extreme cases this can lead to young people being contacted by those that seek to harm or exploit them. There is mounting evidence that social networking sites are used as a way to contact and groom potential victims. There is also concern about the amount of time that children and young people may spend on social networking sites to the detriment of relationships with family, friends and peers in the real world.

Good principles for minimising risks have been provided by Becta (http://www.dh.gov.uk/en/Publicationsandstatistics/Publications/PublicationsPolicyAndGuidance/DH_4123979); they include:

- establishing with young people the sites they can sign up to
- establishing the minimum ages that sites will accept – generally over 14; 16 or 18+ – and abiding by these restrictions

• discussing the importance of privacy online, and encouraging young people to make use of privacy settings. A good principle is to only allowing access to friends known in the 'real world'
• regularly reviewing young people's online profiles along with them
• maintaining an ongoing dialogue about the issues, encouraging young people to seek help if they experience any problems online.

Digital Divide Among Citizens

The 'digital divide' (a phrase that stems from the early 1990s) refers to the gap between people or groups with effective access (and competent use) to digital and information technology and those without such access. Ofcom highlight the following.

> Given that not everyone has a mobile, there is the risk of a digital divide among citizens. One part of society, the mobile-savvy, could prefer to conduct the majority of their interaction via mobile and social networking, placing limits on their opportunities to interact with non-mobile users. The other part of society, non-mobile users, may continue interacting in a more traditional way, but with less interaction with mobile users than previously. As among groups of consumers, the fact that some people use mobile/cell phones or social networking and some people don't, may not be particularly significant. However, for us as citizens, the fact that some people don't interact with other people, as a result of their access to technology, may be significant. (Ofcom 2008b, p. 79)

Given the potential for this 'digital divide' to open further because of the ownership or not of mobile devices, it is interesting to note a study that has examined the use of mobiles to bridge this divide. The UK's Learning and Skills Development Agency (LSDA)[5] has published work on the way in which mobile learning inspires young adults who are 'not in employment, education or training' (the so-called NEETs). Attewell (2005) describes a project that has looked at how to motivate the large number of NEETs. Such learners are described elsewhere in the book as 'at risk learners' or 'at a distance from school'. The LSDA study used trials of games, learning materials and learning tools, designed to be used on a range of portable devices such as mobile/cell phones. The findings, the results of a three-year pan-European research and development project called 'm-learning', appear to be encouraging with respect to the use smartphones and PDAs as learning aids. The project, which trialled the use of mobile learning materials and systems involving nearly 250 young people (aged 16–24) in the UK, Italy and Sweden. Most were unemployed, many had dropped out of education (or were considered to be at risk of doing so) and some were homeless or travellers. One key finding was that mobile learning helped learners to improve their literacy and numeracy skills and to recognise their existing abilities

[5] In 2006 this agency was broken up: see http://www.lsc.gov.uk/Jargonbuster/Learning+and+Skills+Development+Agency+(LSDA).htm

> Although the learners were involved in mobile learning for fairly short periods of time, some mentors reported perceived improvements in their learners' reading, writing and maths skills. Most improvements were noted amongst those learners initially described as being 'less able' or having 'very limited ability'. Some of these improvements seem to have been due to mentors, and learners themselves, not recognising existing abilities. One mentor reported that a learner 'perceived reading to be a book based activity but he was able to read texts and information regarding the device very well... perhaps his biggest barrier to reading is his self-evaluation of his reading ability, and negative educational experience!' (Attewell 2005, p. 13)

Other findings from the project suggest that mobile learning:

- can be used to encourage both independent and collaborative learning experiences
- helps learners to identify areas where they need assistance and support
- helps to combat resistance to the use of ICT and can help bridge the gap between mobile/cell phone literacy and ICT literacy
- helps to remove some of the formality from the learning experience and engages reluctant learners
- helps learners to remain more focused for longer periods
- helps to raise self-esteem
- helps to raise self-confidence.

Security and Privacy Concerns are Growing

In our discussion above we have outlined the various concerns that new digital media bring with regard to security of our data and the privacy of our personal details. For example, in the UK in November 2007, HM Revenue and Customs lost computer discs containing the entire child benefit records, including the personal details of 25 million people – covering 7.25 million families overall (http://news.bbc.co.uk/1/hi/uk_politics/7103828.stm). If the digital portfolio becomes a wide-spread reality in schools, and not just the preserve of well-supported projects, then these issues deserve a more detailed consideration. Ofcom have pointed out that

> The risk to privacy that mobile/cell phones may bring is an area of growing concern for some citizens. A device that is carried by the individual, and that contains much information that is highly personalised, carries an inherent ability to compromise our privacy if it falls into the hands of others, or if the data on it is used without our permission. Recent issues concerning the loss of information by public organisations have brought the issue of data security to the fore. As mobiles become more sophisticated, incorporating payment functions and containing personal data, the types of information they store is becoming more sensitive, and the necessity of keeping that information secure is increasing. (Ofcom 2008b, p. 87)

The introduction of location-based services on mobile/cell phones, as described in Chapter 2 and above, that use GPS and satellite navigation technology, means that organisations, and indeed hackers, have the capabilities to locate users. The use and security of this information is likely to be an important topic for consideration. Ofcom (2008b, p. 87) report that citizens' awareness of the 'access that is given to personal data (identity and location – despite active consent to that through click based 'opt-in') through mobile devices is relatively low and their concerns about identity theft and loss of personal details is rising'. Ofcom's research (2008b, p. 88) also highlighted citizens' increasing concern regarding identity theft and privacy concerns, which included the threat of spam, collection and storage of personal data. Respondents in this research also felt that the mobile/cell phone would increasingly be exploited by marketers, with a sense of being 'under siege'.

While many of the above concerns were raised in the Ofcom research more in relation to the internet as a platform, as internet access is a service also provided via mobile/cell phones, it will be necessary to consider their impact on mobile learners.

Txt Spk and New Literacies

Hartnell-Young and Vetere (2008, p. 283) have pointed out that allowing students to use tools such as mobile/cell phones within the learning process can encourage students to contribute to their own learning contexts; they also point out that such a practice 'raises issues of cultural differences between teachers and students, and the importance of developing critical literacy in conjunction with new communication forms and other new literacies'. These researchers expand on the term 'new literacies' by drawing on the work of Lankshear and Knobel (2006):

> With increasing use of computing technologies, Lankshear and Knobel take the view that these new technical tools help people participate in literacy practices that involve different kinds of values, emphases, priorities and perspectives, which they refer to as 'new ethos' (2006, 3). They use the term 'new literacies' and suggest that the extent to which practices are 'new' will depend on the extent to which they involve significant differences from conventional literacy that were established through the print and analogue era, and, importantly for this article, in some cases even earlier. They expand the well-known literacies of reading and writing to include the ability to communicate in multiple modes: written, visual, audio and gestural. A visually literate person, for example, is able to interpret visual messages and to compose meaningful visual communications (Hartnell-Young and Vetere, 2008, pp. 283–284).

Indeed, in relation to visual literacy, Kress and van Leeuwen (1996) have suggested that images may be used in genres which are akin to story-writing. Furthermore, Kress (2003) has observed that young people use new forms of communication, which appear to include layers of meaning not accessible by 'traditional' language skills alone. Young people are often skilled at interpreting meaning in different uses of sound, such as speech, soundtrack, music, still and moving images, and interact in ways that engage several communication pathways at the same. Given this broader context, and particularly the notion of new literacies, in the remainder of this section we examine the debate that has emerged around 'txt spk', the form of communicative interaction that has evolved around the use of texting between mobile/cell phones. However, one school of thought would have it that as smartphones with reasonably 'proper' keyboards become more commonplace, the issue of 'txt speech' will diminish in significance. Other input approaches, such as voice recognition may change interaction patterns. However, whether or not these alternatives to txt are adopted is an open question.

In his book 'Txtng: the gr8db8' (Crystal 2008), and in an interview with the Guardian newspaper (2008), David Crystal puts forward the, in our view convincing, argument that txt spk is responsible neither for bad spelling nor moral decay. Various technologies have brought about 'moral panics', as Crystal explains (Guardian 2008):

> The reality is that people have always had a tremendous fear about the impact of new technology on language. When the printing press was first invented, people thought it was an instrument of the devil that would spawn unauthorised versions of the bible. The telephone created fears of a breakdown in family life, with people no longer speaking directly to one another. And radio and television raised concerns about brain-washing. Text messaging is just the most recent focus of people's anxiety; what people are really worried about is a new generation gaining control of what they see as their language.

A recent example of the anxiety caused by texting happened in 2003 when a school teacher posted an exam essay he had been marking on the internet because it had been written in text speak (http://news.bbc.co.uk/1/hi/talking_point/2815461.stm). Within days, the issue had been picked up by the media and appeared in several tabloid newspapers:

> No matter that the essay was soon revealed to be a hoax. The myth was much more appealing than the truth and it gave... people, such as Lynne Truss and John Humphrys, carte blanche to cash in on everyone's fears by writing knee-jerk defences of standard English in the face of threats that only ever existed in their imaginations. In fact, texting was such a new phenomenon that there was no research-based evidence to prove anything very much (Guardian 2008).

Indeed, as recently 2007, Humphrys, who is a very well-respected presenter and interviewer for the BBC's Radio 4 Today programme, wrote an article called 'I h8 txt msgs: How texting is wrecking our language' (http://www.dailymail.co.uk/news/article-483511/I-h8-txt-msgs-How-texting-wrecking-language.html). In it he blames texting for the decline in our children's language skills in the context of the Oxford English Dictionary (OED) dropping the hyphen from 16,000 of its words. Humphrys ends his piece thus:

> But at least I have not succumbed to 'text-speak' and I wish the OED had not hoisted the white flag either. I recall a piece of doggerel which sums up my fears nicely: *Mary had a mobile. She texted day and night. But when it came to her exams. She'd forgotten how to write.*

We would agree with Crystal's assertion above, that what underpins people's anxiety is a fear of a new generation gaining control of what they see as 'their' language. We might also say that language has always been used as a metaphor of social matters: corruption, decline, generational or other social difference – 'threats' from below, for instance; power and control; in that context, texting is simply the instance currently most readily to hand. Crystal explains the research-based evidence on text speak (Guardian 2008):

> Almost every basic principle that people hold about texting turns out to be misconceived. Misspelling isn't universal: analysis shows that only 10% of words used in texts are misspelt. Nor are most texts sent by kids: 80% are sent by businesses and adults. Likewise, there is no evidence that texting teaches people to spell badly: rather, research shows that those kids who text frequently are more likely to be the most literate and the best spellers, because you have to know how to manipulate language... If you can't spell a word, then you don't really know whether it's cool to misspell it. Kids have a very precise idea of context – none of those I have spoken to would dream of using text abbreviations in their exams – they know they would be marked down for it.

In the context of the new literacies described above, we would think that in texting all these social factors come to the fore. In any case, in txting, one group's 'misspelling' is another group's 'cool', creative, innovative use of the resources of 'orthography'. It is motivated, among the many other social/cultural/aesthetic reasons, by reasons of economy. The limited number of 'keystrokes', which are available for one txt msg, you have to 'speak' in a txt (e.g. some providers limit a txt msg to a maximum 160 keystrokes; if I write 161 'letters+spaces', two txt msgs will be sent so I will be charged double. Money is a relevant issue, especially for teens...). Linguists suggest that economy is one of the principles of human language (together with redundancy, recursivity etc.). Essentially, what the interlocutor intends is to spend time in thinking how to put words in a txt so as to optimize the medium's affordances. It calls for a particular (and not at all useless) imagination in order to say the most that is possible in the best/most effective way, in the smallest space: much as some characterizations of poetry. Economy with such a new medium combines with community-specific issues of identity; that is to say you are perceived as cool if you adopt a certain 'anti-language' which is shared by your peers, which identifies yourself as an insider in your group, and which differentiates yourself and your group from others.

Whether txting can or should be called 'a new literacy' is a matter for debate. What seems beyond debate is that it has set in train what amounts to the most far reaching unsettling of orthography, which may produce a far-reaching spelling reform as well as what is in effect a new script system.

Txting, we suggest, is generally used for interpersonal communicative purposes; interlocutors have a new means, which allows the interchange of brief thoughts/notes/advices to others. Seen in this light, txting is part of a much wider movement, of which Twitter is one instance, but of which post-its were a similar manifestation involving a different medium. Both media and purposes have changed with modes and genres: or to put it differently, the social processes of fragmentation, provisionality and so, on are finding their realization in new genres with new media. Among teens, and indeed other groups, txting is a commonly used practice in intimate personal relations, where it becomes possible to write what would never have been spoken to a would-be lover, maybe. We can consider the genre of these 'love' txts as a contemporary form of love 'poetry' (both in their synthesis and in their 'pathos'). True 'illiterates' in txting – as in the use of all other modes and media – are those who do not have the resources to achieve their communicative purposes (affective, informative, rhetorical etc.) with their txt. This leads to aesthetics where a long and 'formal' txt by someone, leads to a judgement about the txter as rigid, not flexible, not up-to-date: not competent.

Perhaps a key point here is that the requirement that can be made of research is that it should develop ways of understanding and using the capacities and communicational potentials of theses new devices – always with an awareness of the social environments in which they are being used. This conception of full understanding of the social uses of the media that are available is achieved by 'exploiting' all their affordances, by using these media through a process of social and individual selection in a process of the creation of representational resources that are apt for the medium and suitable for the context. For instance, questions such as when do individuals prefer to *txt* rather than *call* someone for a voice-call or write a *msg* on their *facebook's* wall? These could be the basis of 'exercises' in which questions around the motivation for such choices are explored with students, in the light of their own understandings. Thinking in terms of 'gains and losses', the question of what a given technology – say, txting – enables the interlocutor to do, and what it hinders or backgrounds (for example, it hinders prolixity while fostering synthesis; it hinders 'live' feedback and confrontation with the interlocutor, while – being asynchronous – it fosters re-reading and planning). A central question is this: how do the semiotic practices, within which new media and practices surrounding these media are used, collocate within the media landscape and, through practices, redefine the media landscape itself?

Traditional functions and practices are 'appropriated' from other media and new practices are (re)assigned. In the approach taken throughout this book it is assumed that the social is generative of practices – whether with new (or old) media, with technology generally and with all semiotic processes. By 'socially' driven we mean driven by economical, political and cultural factors. So if we perceive social practices and features, which we regard as problematic, undesirable, socially and individually destructive (wars, individualization, excessive pace, social fragmentation, a wide sense of loss, profits sought with no regard to sustainability, an absence of any overarching sense of responsibility to individual or social well being, compulsive shopping), we assume that this affects practices involving specific technologies and other semiotic practices. However, there are, for the moment at least positive aspects: something that might, in very general terms be called 'democratisation', a levelling of power in relation to meaning-making and its dissemination. Never before in human history have so many had access to so many media and semiotic resources to make their own meaning and to communicate these.

We are not suggesting that txting should be taught in schools, or that there should be a simple teaching of the skills around digitally-based twenty-first century skills, i.e. skills involving the use of online social tools and networks. (For example see http://www.washingtonpost.com/wp-dyn/content/article/2009/01/04/AR2009010401532.html, and a response http://weblogg-ed.com/2009/response-to-jay-matthews-at-the-washington-post/) What we do suggest is the serious matter of *recognizing* what young people actually do: their dispositions towards and principles of meaning-making; and the changes of these in the light of the facilities made available by mobile technologies. Here as well as throughout the book we examine the socio-cultural practices employed by young people outside school and how these could and should change conceptions of the capacities of the same young people when they are in school as 'students'; and allow these capacities, principles and dispositions towards learning to be brought into the structures of the school. Such recognition might prove motivating – without encroaching on the life-world of children and young people outside school. In that way their capacities can be used by them for their purposes and for the purposes of the school and the things it proposes to be learned. The school can then more productively propose its purposes and foster characteristics of reflectiveness for its students.

Conclusions

As we have pointed out above, there are currently large changes taking place for children. We take the view that the case for including mobile/cell phones as part of the learning in the classroom is becoming persuasive:

> By October 2009, about half of the phones in the U.S. will have GPS and there are other emerging technologies that enable mobile devices to receive location-based data. The educational potential enabled by these applications—especially when used in combination with social networking applications—are significant. (Shuler 2009, p. 6).

Until recently, most educators and parents have been sceptical about the value that mobile devices as a resource for learning. If the trends and work reported in this chapter, and the views presented in the above quote, are anything to go by, this situation looks set to change. In the following chapters we will make a strong case for the incorporation of mobile/cell phones inside the classroom. Therefore, it seems to us that a key question to ask is this: can we use the skills and abilities that digitally literate learners have as a hook to get more citizens to engage in educational processes? We call this the 'outside in–inside out' challenge. Cultural practices involving new digital media can be brought into the educational institutions; these practices can be enhanced through educational processes inside schools and Further/Higher Education and in turn feed back into the digital world at large. Thus new digital technology and media can be regarded as cultural resources that can enable the bringing together of the informal learning contexts in the world outside educational institutions with those educational processes and contexts that are valued inside such organisations.

Chapter 4
Cases of Mobile Learning

Methodology of the Project Analysis

Selection and Description of Case Studies and Framework for Comparative Analysis

As discussed in Chapter 1, the analytical engagement with mobile learning within this book takes the shape of a theoretical and conceptual framework for mobile learning in which educational uses of mobile technologies are viewed in ecological terms as part of a socio-cultural and pedagogical context in transformation. Such an approach, in our view, has the power of providing a conceptual frame for analysis of the life-worlds of users/learners as they engage in interactive, practice-based meaning-making.

In order to be able to examine the interface between the different domains, which are part of the socio-cultural ecology, i.e. the place where agency, meaning-making and knowledge-building arise and evolve, adequately, a 'method mix' in our view is necessary. Among other things, such a method mix enables us to:

- analytically examine the interrelationship of (social) structures, learners' agency and the cultural practices attendant to learning and media use;
- explore media as cultural resources;
- discuss learners' participation in cultural production and in society;
- assimilate learning outside formal educational settings, the naïve and individualized expertise of students as well as the habitus of learning of different socio-cultural milieus.

In particular, we wish to:

- identify aspects of our notion of a socio-cultural ecology;
- gain an understanding of the dynamics around learning with mobile devices in the context of the conflicting demands of the component parts of socio-cultural practices of learning;
- identify how these practices are shaped by educational institutions on the one hand, and the nature of the link to everyday life practices of the learners, which might have relevance for learning in formal settings, on the other.

N. Pachler et al., *Mobile Learning*, DOI 10.1007/978-1-4419-0585-7_4,

The analysis framework we propose here draws on several methods, which are used in contemporary qualitative media research and which are also acknowledged methods in the field of cultural studies. We deem them as appropriate in order to consider:

- the activities of learners in the context of school/university and their life-worlds, as well as
- the resources, which learners are using (in terms of agentive and meaningful activities), and
- to ask for the potential inherent in these resources and activities.

This is particularly important as the research base and conceptual understanding in this area is currently relatively small.

Grounded theory (Strauss and Corbin 1990) was the basic approach used to generate a pool of mobile learning examples supplemented as appropriate by further methods. The research design, therefore, is based on triangulation in respect of methods, investigators and (interdisciplinary) theories (Treumann 2005, p. 210f). Concerning the latter, we refer to action theories (e.g. conversational framework; Laurillard 2007), social theories (e.g. socialisation, social interaction, identity building, social segmentation) and system theories (socio-cultural ecology). The research process was broadly guided by the following methods:

- Grounded theory and opportunity sampling (Brown and Dowling 1998, pp. 29–30) were used for the compilation and selection of the sample pool of cases; theories were chosen on the basis of their relevance for the analysis framework. Theories are used only to guide our selection and initial analysis; we remained open to the emergence of new concepts and meaning from our cases.
- The analysis focuses on individual case studies: selected mobile learning projects are chosen as typical cases for mobile learning in formal educational contexts. For the use of mobile/cell phones in conjunction with the internet as convergent medium, a case was chosen ('Cyrill'), which – in relation to school-based learning – represents a contrastive and unique example (Baur and Lamnek 2005, p. 245). It is meant to contrast learning in formal education contexts with agentive media use in everyday life and an understanding of learning as participation and appropriation.
- The mobile learning projects located in school contexts are reviewed using a discourse analysis approach in the broad sense (cf. Foucault 1972). Moreover, the idea of considering activities and conversations within learning in formal educational settings as discourses allows us to gain an understanding of the different (conceptual) bases, meanings and assumptions, on which a didactic/pedagogical design or learning with mobile devices is based. Thus, the analysis could be characterised more generally as analysis by means of action theories (see Diana Laurillard's (2007) discursive model of a 'conversational framework', which describes interrelationships between, and activities by teacher and learner in the meaning-making process) as they allow access to the individual's perspective,

situation, role and identity (Krotz 2005, p. 46), as well as social interactions and the communicative, discursive and participatory role of the leaner in the meaning-making and knowledge building process.

- The case study of Cyrill is taken from everyday life. We contend that it relates to the agentive use of (mobile) media in one specific context only, and that it also captures a specific episode pertaining to the practice depicted; in this sense the stance of interpretative ethnography (Winter 2005, p. 553) was adopted. Here, the observation of practice is carried out without the researchers appearing on the scene, but instead by researchers reverting to material, which is freely accessible on the internet. A reflexive approach is adopted insofar as the everyday life example has to be seen as being in tension with the examples from mobile learning in formal educational settings and – in terms of school/university and social integration – successful learning, and is thus in turn considered to be a representative example for 'at-risk learners' (i.e. learners who may be at a distance to education in formal settings and/or society).
- The final step of the analysis is a case comparison. The results of the analysis of the individual cases are compared with each other in order to gain a greater understanding of a socio-cultural ecology through a hermeneutic process, i.e. to find overall results (Baur and Lamnek 2005, p. 246) as well as to contrast points for further discussions.

For single case and cross-case analysis, a set of criteria was developed, which is based on our theoretical framework. In the following the process of generating these categories is described.

How, and on the Basis of What Data the Cases were Compiled

The cases, which are described and discussed in this chapter, were chosen after a review of mobile learning projects conducted in July and August 2007. As a baseline, reports from Futurelab, Kaleidoscope and Becta were viewed as well as programmes and proceedings of the main conferences in the field of mobile learning (in particular mLearn, Handheld Learning and IADIS; see Chapter 2). After this first overview it became evident that mobile learning projects in the UK are comparatively well documented and analysed, but that such systematic capturing, for example, is missing for German speaking countries (Germany, Austria and Switzerland). We carried out an internet search by using intuitive search strings[1] which we hoped would lead us to projects, which are rooted in natural educational settings rather than to projects requiring external financial and infrastructural support; the latter we deemed to be characteristic for many of the projects realised in the UK. As a result, a list originated, which contained 49 projects and applications

[1] For the internet search, the following search strings were used: einsatzmöglichkeiten handy unterricht; handy didaktisches hilfsmittel unterricht; Handy Unterricht; m-learning schule; m-learning-projekte; projekt handy im unterricht; Projekt Handy Schule; studie handy unterricht; unterrichtsprojekt handy; 'lernen mit dem handy'.

with relevance for learning. Emphasis was placed on examples of the use of mobile devices with school-aged children.

In a **first step** the projects were attributed to the categories 'in school' and 'outside school', and within these two categories to the following sub-categories:

- Projects in schools: mobile/cell phone as topic, mobile/cell phone in use, mobile/cell phone as topic as well as in use, mobile/cell phone for administration;
- Projects outside school: location awareness, software applications with interactive features, sound applications without interactive features (audio files), infrastructure.

In a **second step**, the projects were attributed to (1) their focus on teacher, learner and content, (2) school subjects in which they were conducted[2], (3) a functional framework[3] and (4) pedagogical underpinnings[4].

The quantification of these categories provides an overview, which is not representative (as we did not aim to assemble a comprehensive sample), but which allows the exploration of some assumptions: that mobile/cell phones are used as tool rather than discussed as a topic; that mobile learning is designed for students rather than for teachers; that there is a strong focus on the school subject and the curriculum; that mobile learning has a strong focus on pre-defined task/problem solving; that mobile learning is strongly represented in natural sciences and languages. We note that interdisciplinary projects are underrepresented and that mobile/cell phones are mainly used for interactivity purposes and information delivery. Furthermore, we note that instructional approaches to teaching and learning are more dominant than for example constructivist and collaborative approaches.

From the full set of examples, a subset was chosen in order to discuss mobile learning with reference to the framework of a socio-cultural ecology. Accordingly, those examples were chosen out of the pool, whose teaching focus is on a task-centred approach and, as far as possible, on the context of everyday life and its connection to school and the curriculum. Learners' physical activity and collaboration during the project, the use of the mobile device as learning tool as well as the location of the project, inside or outside school, were crucial for the selection. Finally, due to limited space being available, and in view of our aim of preparing a

---

[2]The projects can be seen to be associated with the following subjects: Interdisciplinary, Arts, Biology, Business IT, Economics, Ethics, General Studies, Geography, Journalism, Languages: misc., Languages: English as foreign language, Languages: French as foreign language, Languages: German as mother tongue, Maths, Music, Physics, Politics, Social Sciences, Technology.

[3]Administration, referential, interactive, microworld, data collection, location aware, collaborative. See Patten et al. 2006.

[4]Little pedagogy, instructional, behaviourist, constructionist, contextual, reflective, constructivist, collaborative. See Patten et al. 2006.

fairly detailed description and analysis of each case chosen, the number of relevant projects was limited to three. Each example featured exemplifies a specific combination of context, i.e. project situated in school, outside school or leisure time, and activity patterns envisaged by each project, e.g. instrumental or experimental use of the mobile device.

As result of the fact that one mobile learning project can cover more than one aspect, we examine the most salient aspects of each project only here; they form the focus of our analysis with other aspects being backgrounded. The list in Table 4.1, which is the result of the characterization of the projects, provides a basic overview of the learning and teaching related coverage by giving the central key words of each project, sorted by their relevance for the respective project (right hand side column). The left hand side column gives (1) the name of the project, (2) the country in which the project was conducted, (3) the subject and level of education as well as (4) the location (classroom, fieldtrip, leisure).

Table 4.1 Overview of the examples

Projects	Key words/coverage
(1) Handy (2) Switzerland (3) German, french, maths; secondary (4) Classroom	Multimodal content creation (transformative; knowledge building); microlearning; m-maturity/technical literacy; archive; sustainability; peer-teaching; languages; mathematics; everyday life; expert scheme; genres
(1) Learning Lab (2) India (3) Natural sciences; secondary (4) Field trip; classroom	Informal context (outside school); location awareness/GPS; data collection; life world (reflection); visualisation and knowledge building; natural sciences; pictures; media convergence; media literacy; combine analogue and digital media
(1) Cyrill (2) Germany (3) – (4) Leisure/city, without relation to school	'At-risk learner'; life world; everyday life; cultural practices; YouTube as convergent media platform; informal learning; literacy; modes of representation and design; critical reflection; identity

How, and on the Basis of What Data the Structure was Compiled

Drawing on a research tradition, which leans on phenomenology and hermeneutics, we developed an analytic framework, which is characterised by two levels: (1) common sense and accessible aspects and (2) latent – not immediately accessible – aspects. This hermeneutic analysis is based on the following questions:

(1) Level 1: the readily apparent, the core of an example of mobile learning. At this level considerations, concepts and lines of thinking about learners as experienced and culturally intelligent participants in school, mass communication or any other relevant cultural area are summarised.

- Leading question 1: What is obvious, accessible and readily readable 'on the face of the materials'?
- Leading question 2: What is (thematically) at the heart of the mobile learning example, what aspects are in focus?

(2) Level 2: the salient structures of the example, which have to be extracted by a theoretically informed analysis. At this level the theoretical framework is brought to bear: the model of a socio-cultural ecology for analysing the ongoing cultural transformation in society, media, school and everyday life.

- Leading question 1: What is covert, latent and not readily accessible to description and analysis?
- Leading question 2: In what way is the example different from 'main stream' mobile device use?

With our framework we aim to act in accordance with such an analytical approach, being aware of not being able to provide a completely comprehensive and exhaustive analysis, as well as having been able to take only a modest step towards the core of what is inherent in the data/materials. Although more cross-case analysis is needed, we feel our framework and analysis has already brought into view key issues related to the notions of mobility, mobility across contexts, as well as agency, cultural practices and approaches to teaching and learning. At the same time, we deem the analytic framework to be a novel and transferable frame for analysis of cases, which can be used independently from the cases which we haven chosen to include in our analysis.

Analysis Framework

The structure of the discussion of the examples has two parts; the first part consists of the project description (I), the second part of the analysis (II).

(I) Project Description

The data on which the project descriptions are based were compiled from information available from written project reports and/or from project presentations on the internet. In some cases the project coordinators or key persons involved in the project were contacted and provided additional information. To provide coherence in the description of the different projects, the following scheme was developed and applied as structure for the description to all cases:

1. context/rationale: background information (i.e. how many people, type of school, duration, devices used, technical support; learning and teaching aims and envisioned role of mobile devices)
2. approaches to teaching and learning: how are the devices used; key activities, key tasks, key pedagogical/'didactic' issues
3. technologies and requirements: interoperability, storage, usability etc.

4. project outcomes
5. lessons learnt/issues emerging: incl. replicability and transferability
6. recommendations and future possibilities
7. general project data: project name, url, country, year, contact, types of mobile devices, further media, number of persons, duration, location, educational establishment, phase of education, subject domain, teaching/learning focus, keywords

(II) Project Analysis

The criteria for the analysis relate to key concepts of our theoretical framework. During the analysis process the scheme was refined according to the progress of the London Mobile Learning Group in theory building, and resulted in the following list:

A agency, structure, cultural practice (educational 'script'): new habitus and social segmentation; 'at-risk learners'; literacy traditional vs. new; understanding media as cultural resources; participation in cultural practices
B approaches to teaching and learning (Didaktik) ('didaktik'/learning/teaching scripts): informal/informal/situated/collaborative/problem-based learning; bricolage; knowledge building; meaning-making
C notions of mobility: mobile device used as tool; mobile devices used in relation to meanings; mobility in contexts (place, time, concepts, social constellations, activities, curriculum, cultural resources, meanings)
D user-generated contents and contexts: transformation of mass communication; mobility; learning as meaning-making in context; ubiquity, choice, appropriation; context crossing
E replicability and transferability: replicability and transferability of the 'didaktik' script, using it in a new context; scalability

In a first attempt to analyse the examples, some redundant items emerged and we decided to merge and simplify the analysis framework according to the perceived usefulness of items for each single case. The key questions for the analysis derive from the foci as described above in step three of the case compilation, which might differ from one example to the next, but which can be kept under the five meta-categories A-E above. The following observations, for instance, emerged from the group thinking about leading categories for the Indian Learning Lab project (CKS 2005b):

C notions of mobility/D contents and contexts:

> mobile device used as tool because of their affordances; basis for mobility of contexts; mobility in contexts and across contexts (place, time, concepts, social constellations, activities, curriculum, cultural resources, meanings); bring mobility to students; physical: inside school, outside school; GPS and tools for data collection (picture taking, data logging); bring mobility to the curriculum; cross-over school and everyday life; mobility linked to convergence, convergent tool; interoperability, storage, usability; problem solving from one

context to an other; conceptual: transferring the concrete shape into mathematical constructs; sharing social situations with peers; mobile devices used in relation to meanings: the act of taking pictures is agency; meaning-making happens in the process of transfer of e.g. forms and shapes

A agency, structure, cultural practice/B approach to teaching and learning:

collaboration: new digital literacy: use images to represent our selective view to the world; cultural practices: the pictures which the learners took give an insight into different social contexts (incl. family members); transformation of agencies and individualised perspectives to common meanings and 'collaborative knowledge building'; shared understanding of each others' social contexts and view to the world; situated and active; negotiation of meaning-making/in the meaning-making process; collaborative knowledge building; location awareness: situated learning; appropriation; social status of the pupils involved in the project/social inclusion; notion of communication; global cultures and regional cultures

Discussion of the Process of Project Selection and the Criteria for Project Analysis

During our engagement with the selection process and development of an analysis framework we encountered some obstacles, which we want to share at this point in order to allow readers to assess the transferability of the analytic framework.

Resources with Mobile Learning Projects

Gaining an overview of mobile learning projects was the first hurdle with which we were confronted, as the number of mobile learning projects, which are realised inside and outside school/university, with explicit relevance for learning as well as for leisure purposes only, is large, but, unfortunately, only rarely available in a systematic form, e.g. on comprehensive databases. Resources were provided by the Kaleidoscope m-learning SIG (now: The International Association for Mobile Learning (IAMLearn); http://mlearning.noe-kaleidoscope.org/), on whose web pages an extensive list with links to mobile learning projects from all over the world is available, including a short editorial review of each project (http://mlearning.noe-kaleidoscope.org/projects/). Another helpful resource was the Futurelab mobile learning literature reviews and handbooks (http://www.futurelab.org.uk/resources/publications-reports-articles). Furthermore, abstracts and proceedings from mobile learning conferences contributed to the pool of resources to gain an overview of projects from the UK (amongst other countries). Deriving from the fact that mobile learning was, and still is, a topic of limited interest in Germany, Austria and Switzerland, a web search was necessary to find projects in these three countries which have relevance for mobile learning.

Categorisation of Projects for Selection

The categorisation of projects needed a basis with relevance for school learning, which we deemed to be essential for a first step towards a conceptual framework of mobile learning. The theoretical examination of mobile learning projects by e.g. Futurelab literature reviews, as well as key works – by e.g. Faux, McFarlane, Roche and Facer (2006); Kukulska-Hulme and Traxler (2005); Laurillard (2002); Metcalf (2006); Naismith, Lonsdale, Vavoula, Sharples, (2004); Sharples (2006) – informed our thinking. These project descriptions and analyses were critically engaging in the theoretical bases of the mobile learning discourse of that time, pointing at the question of what mobility means (in general as well as for learning in particular) as well as the critical reflection of mobile learning in the light of common and 'traditional' learning theories (i.e. behaviourist, constructivist, situated, collaborative and 'informal and lifelong learning' (Patten, Arnedillo-Sánchez and Tangney 2006, p. 296)). Even if comprehensive analyses of projects as well as theoretical frameworks were provided, and, thus, a taxonomic and quantifying classification of projects was potentially feasible (see step 1 of the methodology above), we realised that – because of their didactic concept and technological affordances – most of the projects could be assigned to most of the categories. For this reason, and in parallel to developing a more theoretical framework, we decided to develop an analysis frame, which potentially considers notions of mobility and different learning theories etc., but which are broadly based on a culturally determined, situative and dynamic understanding of learning in the framework of a socio-cultural ecology, which considers not only the individual, but also different contexts as well as cultural resources, as well as an understanding of learning and meaning-making as user-generated, dynamic, discursive, negotiated, and situative.

Selection of Projects

The projects, which we finally chose for inclusion in this book, are only a very small selection of the types of projects and practices to be found in the field of learning with mobile devices. Also, they focus on school and leisure rather than university or work. The cases we are showcasing here are included not as examples of good practice or as representative of the most salient aspects of mobile learning; rather, they have to be seen as illustrative and as a data set for our analysis, concepts and methodology building and testing. Thus, the analysis offered in this chapter is by no means comprehensive; in fact, the examples are referred to, and supplemented variously in other chapters of this book.

Also, it has to be noted that – even if we are aware of technological developments which took place during our engagement with the cases and will go on in the future – our focus is on pedagogical practices rather than on technological functionality. For this reason, we decided to not make any predictions on the future of mobile learning in relation to our cases. Some ideas about the future of mobile learning as we see it can be found in Part III of this book. However, the examples demonstrate that, with relatively standard functionality, some interesting work can be observed – a potential, which more sophisticated phones, such as smartphones, only amplify.

Analysis Framework

Viewed from this perspective, the analysis framework might best be described as a list of heuristics with relevance for mobile learning in the context of a notion of socio-cultural ecology, covered under meta-categories rather than a rigid analysis scheme. As the case of Cyrill shows, the analysis framework is open to examples from school contexts as well as for examples from everyday life. However, for the Cyrill case we opened the analysis to aspects of identity construction and social inclusion/exclusion in order to be able to access the most evident issues of this case. As for the categories used for the project description, more general or additional categories might be considered in order to describe cases from these two 'spheres'. As we haven't found categories yet, which are able to cover school as well as everyday life settings and activities, the Cyrill example is dealt with as a project in order to be able to use the same categories – at least most of them.

Replicability and Transferability

We deem our methodological approach to have wider generalisability and hope it is a useful tool for readers to devise and analyse cases of their own by using the categories for project description and analysis. We, therefore, provide our description and analysis grid in an online database for mobile learning project: MoLeaP – The Mobile Learning Project Database[5] (Seipold 2009). This database, which is accessible via http://www.moleap.net (Seipold and LMLG 2009), is conceptualized as a resource and tool for people who are interested in mobile learning, especially in sharing their experiences and projects with others, or in learning from already existing projects. The database, which is based on the idea of non-proprietary and collaborative knowledge building, aims to provide opportunities for the systematic gathering of practice,

- to distribute knowledge which was gained within such projects in order to make practice less ephemeral,
- to enable synergies,
- to contribute to sustainability in teaching, learning and research, as well as
- to enhance replicability of mobile learning projects.

[5] MoLeaP – The Mobile Learning Project Database (www.moleap.net) is part of the project *'And don't forget to bring your mobile' – Informing educational target groups about mobile learning opportunities* (project holder: Judith Seipold) funded by the Centre for Excellence in Work-Based Learning for Education Professionals (WLE Centre) at the Institute of Education (IoE), University of London.

Cases

Project 'Handy'

(I) Project Description

Context/Rationale

The 'Handy' project was realised by a teacher, Rolf Deubelbeiss, in a Swiss private secondary school (intermediate school [Realschule] and grammar school [Gymnasium]) with a specialism in sports (Nationale Elitesportschule Thurgau 2007). 60 pupils and one teacher were involved in this project. The envisaged project duration was 3 weeks, but had to be extended because the teacher was confronted with some minor obstacles such as lacking technological compatibility (see also lessons learnt/issues emerging). The teacher had no technical and infrastructural support: he installed the weblog and uploaded the learning units, which were produced by the students, at his own expense. The mobile/cell phones were the property of the students and the teacher.

Approaches to Teaching and Learning

The mobile/cell phone was used as learning tool as well as a topic of inquiry. The aim of the project was to demonstrate the value of mobile/cell phones for school, but to inform and to support pupils about and in the use of their mobile/cell phones, i.e. to help pupils to use the mobile/cell phones effectively and to amend the school's mobile/cell phone-rules. This included not only making students aware of the expenses they might incur by using their mobile/cell phones; the teacher also intended to show them how mobile/cell phones can be used in school contexts and thus for learning, as well as for broaching the issue of formal aspects of telephone conversations (e.g. with view to applying for jobs or to communicate in formalised environments).

The Mobile/Cell Phone as Topic

Regarding the mobile/cell phone as topic, the aims were as follows (Deubelbeiss 2007a):

- 'Handy-Knigge: Gebote, Verbote und Gesetzeslage in der Schweiz' (rules, prohibitions, legal situation in Switzerland)
- 'Handy als Schuldenfalle' (mobile/cell phone as 'debt trap')
- 'Handy als Lernhilfe und Lifestyle' (mobile/cell phone as learning help and lifestyle)
- 'Handy-Technik und Entwicklung der Kommunikationsformen' (mobile/cell phone technology and development of modes of communication)

The teacher provided these topics as well as the general aims to parents for information purposes in advance.

The teacher used the 'Dossier Handy' (Schweizer Fernsehen 2003) from the Swiss school TV, (which is about the 'debt trap' mobile/cell phone, radiation,

SMS-generation and communication, as well as information provided by the police of the Kanton Zürich about violence and porn on mobile/cell phones) (Kanton Zürich 2004). A freely accessible webquest (Vadas et al. 2007) was used to post questions about the content of the 'Dossier Handy' to the students after they watched the film on the websites of the Swiss school TV.

The Mobile/Cell Phone as Learning Tool

For the practical part of the project, pupils used their own mobile/cell phones. There was no external financial or technical support – except for the engagement of the teacher. Pupils were asked to work on a topic in German, French or Mathematics with a view to producing 'microlearning content'. Pupils were free to choose the school subject, as well as the media format (film, picture, sound or text); for the teacher, it was more important that pupils solve a task and produce 'microcontent' in keeping with curricular aims and objectives. The microcontent in the form of MMS (Multimedia Messaging Service) was saved as drafts and distributed via Bluetooth to the teacher's mobile/cell phone (Deubelbeiss 2007b). The teacher revised language and orthography, and uploaded the small units with his mobile/cell phone/USB to a public weblog[6].

According to the teacher, some of the pictures, which were used by the pupils, were already available on their phones, and thus not produced explicitly for the exercise (see e.g. the Limerick and the Syntax example below). Other pictures, such as the path-time-diagram, were taken from the textbook. In most cases the teacher had to take a leading role and direct pupils towards being 'creative' in composing the microcontent units (e.g. path-time-diagram).

Technologies and Requirements

The weblog, as public place to store pupils' learning units, was installed and hosted by the teacher. After the project was finished, pupils could access the material on the weblog, download it and use it as small learning units. Actually, the pupils produced more examples than provided on the weblog. The weblog contains only the 'best practice' examples, as the teacher stressed. The tendency was that 'good' and successful pupils liked to see their results on the internet; less good pupils, on the other hand, did not want to publish their artefacts. Besides the intention of the teacher to show exemplary results, this was another reason why the weblog contains 'best practice' examples only. Additionally, and due to the high expense of mobile blogging at the time of the project, the teacher was the only person, who uploaded the results of pupils' work on the weblog in order to minimise expense for pupils.

[6]See <http://metaportfolio-phsg.kaywa.ch>.

Project Outcomes

The following examples were produced by pupils, the teacher and a student teacher in the subjects of Mathematics, German and French. Further project outcomes, such as reading and orthography tests with reference to the webquest, the e-lesson of the Kanton Zürich police and the Dossier Handy, are not available on the internet because they were of relevance for the assessment of pupils.

Mathematics: The Path-Time Diagram (Fig. 4.1)

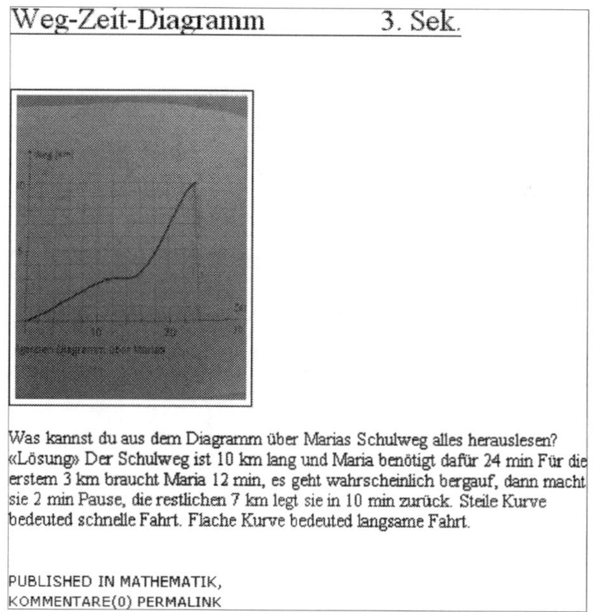

Weg-Zeit-Diagramm 3. Sek.

Was kannst du aus dem Diagramm über Marias Schulweg alles herauslesen?
«Lösung» Der Schulweg ist 10 km lang und Maria benötigt dafür 24 min Für die erstem 3 km braucht Maria 12 min, es geht wahrscheinlich bergauf, dann macht sie 2 min Pause, die restlichen 7 km legt sie in 10 min zurück. Steile Kurve bedeuted schnelle Fahrt. Flache Kurve bedeuted langsame Fahrt.

PUBLISHED IN MATHEMATIK,
KOMMENTARE(0) PERMALINK

Fig. 4.1 Path-time-diagram (Source: http://metaportfolio-phsg.kaywa.ch/mathematik/weg-zeit-diagramm-fabian-3-sek.html)

Description

The first part of the assignment is a photo of a diagram. Below it, the following question is posed:

'What can you read into the diagram about Maria's way to school?

«Answer» The way to school is 10 km and Maria needs 24 min for it. For the first 3 km Maria needs 12 min, the path might be uphill, then she rests for 2 min, she covers the remaining 7 km in 10 min. A steep curve represents a fast ride. A flat curve represents slow speed'. (Translated from Deubelbeiss 2007c).

German: Limerick (Fig. 4.2)

Fig. 4.2 Limerick (Source: http://metaportfolio-phsg.kaywa.ch/deutsch/elfchen-thamara-1-sek.html)

Description

At the beginning of the explanation there are two photos. The first shows the caption 'prince' and below it an illegible web address. The second photo shows the word 'LIMERICKS'. It is followed by the actual limerick and rules for composing limericks.

'I am the prince, it is hard to believe, I'm also nice to look at. Many hits on yellow ball. My name is prince, it is hard to believe.

Limerick rules: A limerick is a poem which consists of five lines. Lines 1, 2 and 5 have the same length and rhyme. Lines 3 and 4 are shorter and rhyme too. Short hand: a-a-b-b-a – The content is less important than the form; it can be absurd and does not have to be very serious. The main thing is that the format is correct!' (Translated from Deubelbeiss 2007d).

German: Syntax (Fig. 4.3)

Fig. 4.3 Satzglieder (Source: http://metaportfolio-phsg.kaywa.ch/deutsch/satzglieder-marco-3-sek.html)

Description

The first part of the assignment is a photo of a boy eating. Below the commentary says: 'Here is my picture of Fabian: and here a sentence to go with it, in which you have to determine the parts of the sentence': The pupil now posts the question: 'Can you determine the parts of the sentence?' and writes the following sentence, structured by the numbers 1–4: '1. Fabian 2. eats 3. a Hamburger 4. at the station'. At the bottom, in the final section, the solution is given:

'Solution:

1. Subject
2. Verb
3. Object
4. Prepositional object' (Translated from Deubelbeiss 2007e).

French: Passé Composé (Fig. 4.4)

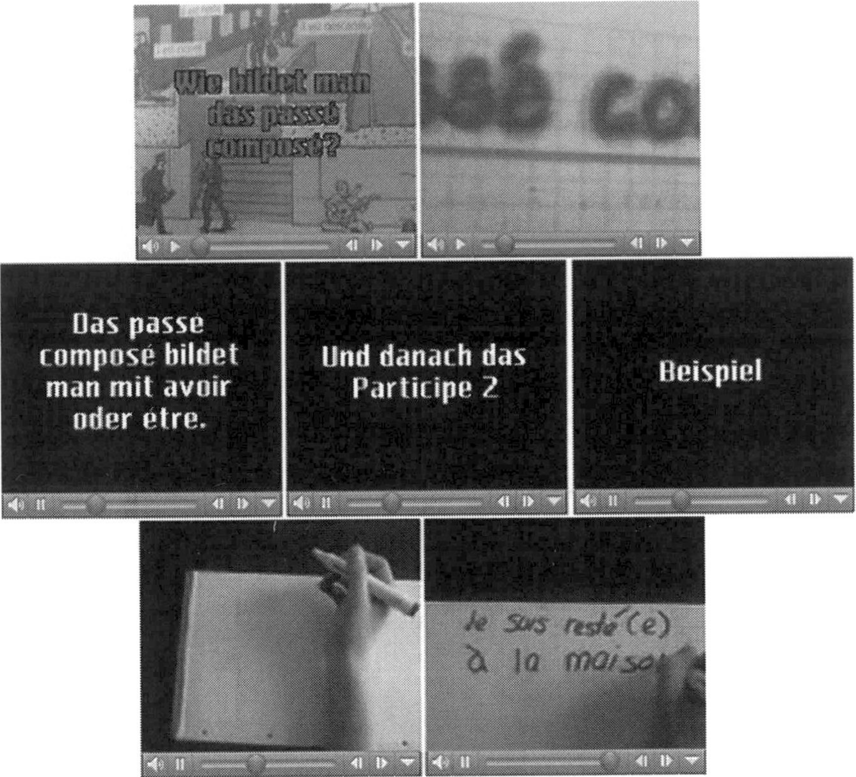

Fig. 4.4 Passé composé (Source: http://metaportfolio-phsg.kaywa.ch/files/VideoDJ.3gp, 29 Feb 2008)

Description

A boy produced a short film with his mobile/cell phone, in which he explains the passé composé. The first part of the film is a picture, maybe from his French book, including the title of the film 'How to form the passé composé'. As second part, the hand painted title 'passé composé' is displayed. Part 3 consists of three picture frames: Frame one: 'The passé composé is composed of avoir or étre'. Frame two: 'Followed by the past participle'. Frame three: 'Example'. Subsequent to the theoretical explanation, an example is given: the pupil welcomes the audience. Then he writes the sentence 'Je suis resté(e) à la maison'. (Translated from Deubelbeiss 2007f) By writing this sentence, the boy explains what he is doing with reference to the grammatical rule.

French: 'M. est plus grand que' (Fig. 4.5)

M. est plus grand que... 2. Sek.

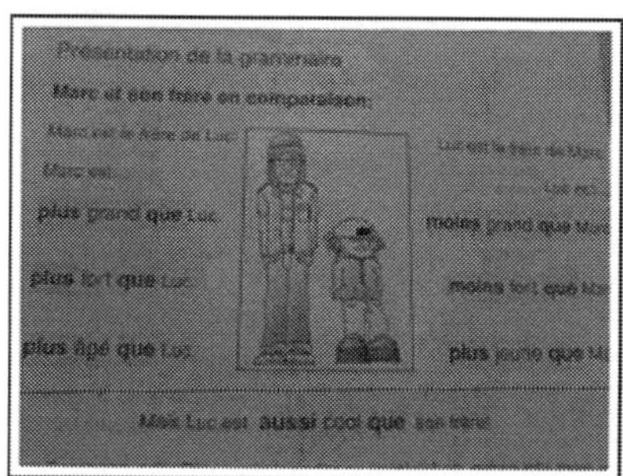

Memo.mp3

Marc est plus grand que Luc, plus fort que Luc, plus agé que Luc.

PUBLISHED IN FRANZÖSISCH ,
KOMMENTARE(0) PERMALINK

Fig. 4.5 M. est plus grand que (Source: http://metaportfolio-phsg.kaywa.ch/franzoesisch/m-est-plus-grand-que-adi-2-sek.html)

Description

The example (Deubelbeiss 2007 g) starts with a photo of a page from a French text book. Below this photo, an mp3 file with the title 'Memo' is available. In this sound file, a student recorded the spoken sentence 'Marc est plus grand que Luc, Marc est plus fort que Luc, Marc est plus agé que Luc'. It might have been taken from a professional audio tape in a language laboratory lesson. Below, the sentence 'Marc est plus grand que Luc, Marc est plus fort que Luc, Marc est plus agé que Luc'. is written which the pupil took from the book.

French: Objet (In)Direct (Fig. 4.6)

Französisch: Objet (in)direct
Praktikantin

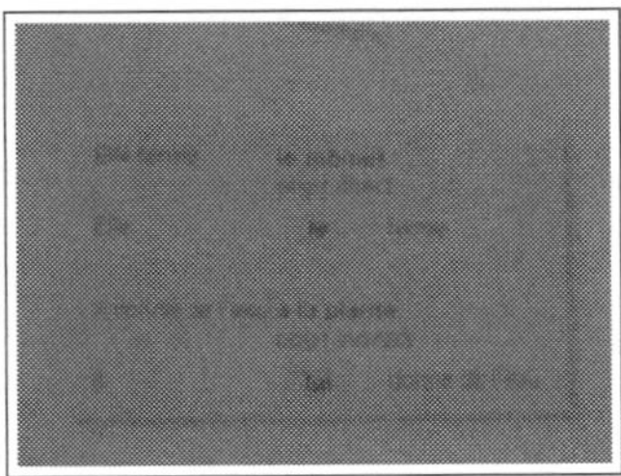

, Praktikantin, hat per Handy einen Beitrag zu den Objets produziert:

mms.mp3

Das objet direct: je-me, tu-te, il / elle-le / la, nous-nous, vous-vous, ils / elles-les. Das objet indirect hat nur in der 3. Person sing.und plu. eine andere Form: il / elle-lui, ils/elles-leur.

PUBLISHED IN FRANZÖSISCH ,
KOMMENTARE(0) PERMALINK

Fig. 4.6 Objet (in)direct (Source: http://metaportfolio-phsg.kaywa.ch/franzoesisch/franzoesisch-objet-indirect-von-ff.html)

Description

A photo of a page in a French text book is the first part of this lesson. A short description follows: 'Mrs. XY, student teacher, produced a contribution to Objets': This is followed by a short mp3 file. In this file, the student teacher says: 'Schaue Dir dazu die Theorie im envol 8 auf Seite 190 an'. ('Have a look at envol 8, page 190'). (Translated from Deubelbeiss 2007 h) The sound file is followed by the grammatical explanation: 'The objet direct: je-me, tu-te, il/elle-le/la, nous-nous, vous-vous. Ils/elles-les. Only in the third person sing. and plu. does the 'objet direct' have another form: il/elle-lui, ils/elles-leur'.

French: Le Comparative (Fig. 4.7)

le comparatif (S2)

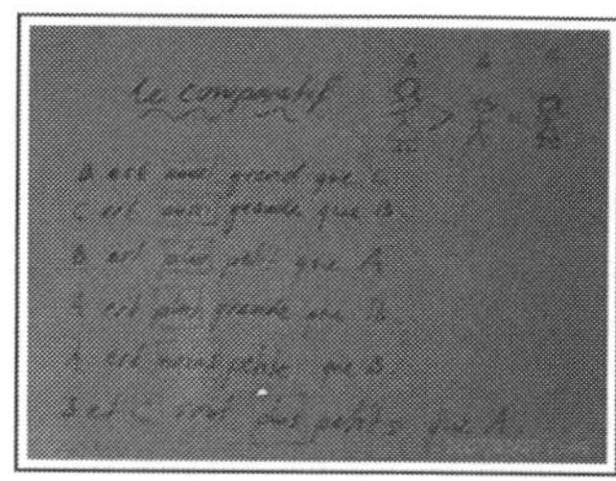

le comparatif

Diese Aufnahme habe ich im Unterricht mit dem Mobiltelefon gemacht und gleich per MMS ins Weblog überspielt - unsere Lernpartner können bspw. von zu Hause aus oder aus dem Trainingslager per Internet darauf zugreifen.

PUBLISHED IN FRANZÖSISCH , 27.2.2007, 17:22
KOMMENTARE(0) PERMALINK

Fig. 4.7 Le comparative (Source: http://metaportfolio-phsg.kaywa.ch/franzoesisch/le-comparatif-s2.html)

Description

A picture is shown, which consists of the headline 'le comparative', three stick-figures and six sentences. Two of the stick-figures have the same size, one is bigger than the other. The sentences describe which of the three stick-figures is bigger or smaller than the other. Below the picture is the text: 'le comparative'. The third part of this learning unit is an explanation of why this small lesson was produced: 'I have taken this picture in class with my mobile/cell phone and uploaded it to the weblog immediately by MMS – our learning partners are able to access it i.e. via internet from home or from the training camp'. (Translated from Deubelbeiss 2007i)

Lessons Learnt/Issues Emerging

The originally anticipated duration of the project, namely 3 weeks, was extended by the teacher. There are mainly three reasons for this:

One reason was that it was not as easy as assumed to deal with the different models of mobile/cell phones – in terms of compatibility and media convergence.

Second, the teacher misjudged the pupils' abilities to deal with all the required functions of the mobile/cell phones (e.g. being able to produce MMS or to know how to use Bluetooth). This, again, was partly due to the wide range of technologies, which the pupils had at their disposal: some students had the latest models of mobile/cell phones with a high quality camera, internet connectivity, and memory space. Other students only had old mobile/cell phones from their parents available, and were able to produce text messages only.

Third, the project was implemented in a school where mobile/cell phones are banned from the classroom as well as from the wider school area. However, students were free to choose one of their subjects to produce the microcontent. For this purpose, they had to ask teachers of the respective subject before or during the lesson if they were allowed to use the mobile/cell phone to e.g. take a picture or type a text. According to the teacher, this was not always easy because pupils might have interrupted the flow of the lesson, or other pupils got so interested in the mobile activities that the noise level disturbed the class.

Recommendations and Future Possibilities

The acceptance of mobile technologies for curricular learning in schools might be supported with projects like the 'Handy' project, which is referring to mobile/cell phones as topics and as tools for learning. The teacher did not only initiate a critical reflection of the pupils' usage habits, and discussed aspects, which indicate dangers for young people, but he also showed how to productively use the mobile/cell phone for learning. By referring to the idea of producing micro units, he adopted the concept of user-generated content through elementarisation of the learning material. On the other hand, and by posting these learning units on a public weblog, he made learning material accessible for others, who are free to use these materials for their own purposes.

With emerging technologies and lower costs for e.g. the access of internet and distribution of MMS technological interoperability might increase. This could be helpful for teachers and learners who are confronted with high costs for the distribution of their self-produced learning materials. Also, the ad-hoc access to and immediate distribution of information might be facilitated. However, such developments cannot hide the fact that the latest mobile technologies are available for a small group of users only, and that there will still be a group of learners which is not equipped with the latest models but with the parents' old and discarded devices.

General Project Data (Table 4.2)

Table 4.2 General project data project 'Handy'

Project name	Handy
URL	http://metaportfolio-phsg.kaywa.ch/
Country	Switzerland
Year	2007
Contact	Rolf Deubelbeiss, Nationale Elitesportschule Thurgau; Pädagogische Hochschule Zürich
Types of mobile devices	Mobile/cell phone
Further media	Weblog
Number of persons	61 (60 pupils, 1 teacher)
Duration	3 weeks +

Table 4.2 (continued)

Location	School/classroom
Educational establishment	Secondary school: intermediate school (Realschule) and grammar school (Gymnasium)
Phase of education	Year 7–9; 11/12–16/17 year old pupils
Subject domain	German, French, Mathematics; interdisciplinary
Teaching/learning focus	Support learning with mobile devices; reflect on usage habits and etiquette
Keywords	Multimodal content creation (transformative; knowledge building); microlearning; m-maturity/technical literacy; archive; sustainability; peer-teaching; languages; Mathematics; everyday life; expert scheme; genres

(II) Project Analysis

Approaches to Teaching and Learning

By having a first look at the project outcomes, the product orientation of this project is striking. The teacher gave his pupils a task, which required learners not only to reproduce knowledge, but to gather information, to reflect on the content and an adequate mode of representation, and to create a learning unit with which others are potentially able to learn. The idea to produce micro units is based on the concept of 'microlearning'. Microlearning can be described as miniaturisation, fragmentation and 'elementarisation' of learning material as well as short-term learning activities (see e.g. Hug 2007; Chapter 11). Learning takes place here through an assembly of modular learning units by the learner. The form of the material, in this case explicit learning material, was defined by the teacher in advance, who created – through his project design – a way of scaffolding the students' individualised experiences towards their own meaning-making process as well as towards meaning, which is central to school discourses (i.e. learning material) and which can be used as basis for a common and objectified meaning-making process.

A byproduct is peer-teaching in a wider sense, as the learning material, which the pupils produced, is available for others. Additionally, the teacher might have addressed the pupils as 'experts' for a specific subject area, or the pupils might have defined themselves as experts for certain tasks. However, the fact that the learning material, which others have to work with, has to be understandable and comprehensive presumes that the students producing the material are experts in the respective subject area.

Agency, Structure, Cultural Practice, Notions of Mobility and User-Generated Contents and Contexts

Even if mobile/cell phones were used as tool for the production of teaching units, the notions of mobility in this example refer mainly to mobility between contexts, i.e.

everyday life and school. Physical mobility seems to be of minor importance for the project as pupils are using the devices in the classroom only, without being obliged to be physically mobile in order to fulfil the learning task. In this regard, the cognitive achievement of the students, which we consider to be key rather than a glossy product, should not be underestimated because they successfully combined not only different modes, but also different contexts and different meanings. Students appear to be well versed in the production of learning material, in the organisation of discontinuous multimodal texts, as well as in particular literary genres. They demonstrate that they are able to generate and (re)produce knowledge, reflect on it, choose a teaching mode and a mode of representation of learning material, which they consider to be adequate or representative for specific teaching and learning purposes and contexts, or which best meets a specific affordance. This transformation process seems to be captured in the reflection and learning process, which is information retrieval with the purpose of information provision. Also, pupils reconfigure their everyday life knowledge according to existing conceptual frames with relevance for school-based learning. By doing so, they activate their agency in terms of their preferred media, genres and impression from everyday life. In this process, and the complex creation of multimodal products, the literacies of pupils are coming into effect: literacy in this case is not just the ability to produce a linear and written text, or to handle technologies; pupils are using genres and modes of representation, which are well known from textbooks (see e.g. the Path-Time-Diagram). On the other hand, pupils add modes to their units, which are not necessarily typical for school learning and teaching such as a film (e.g. the Passé composé film) or complementary spoken texts, but which might apply to the learners' media preferences from everyday life. None of these units seems to contain redundant parts; furthermore, the information provided is necessary to fully understand the individual units, and to contextualise the information, which is given in the examples, and thus to make pupils' intentions comprehensible for others.

By bringing together different texts, which are originally 'discontinuous' in relation to each other and, thus, linked to different meanings, the students structured their knowledge and transformed it into a coherent 'product'. This product has to conform to a number of conventions as it has the function of a learning object with which others subsequently have to work. By standardising representational modes to images and text the students' associative chains and 'streams of consciousness' are ordered, become shareable and can be engaged with by others. This applies to the 'Limerick' and the 'Syntax' examples rather than to the path-time-diagram, which refers to a mode that is well known from textbooks for school and which is constructed according to typical school conventions with a diagram and a question. The pictures, which are taken from everyday life situations (social relations: a friend from school eating on the train platform; commercials: the logo 'prince' from a sports equipment manufacturer), can be viewed as additional information, as contextualisation of the exercise or as reference framework.

Beside the link to social situations and to advertising, another informal dimension is marked by the choice of words. The word 'bierernst' (deadly serious) ironically juxtaposes the language use in the students' life-worlds with that in school.

Also, the emoticon in the Syntax example underpins the students' idea that school does not necessarily have to be 'serious' in order for success to be possible, and that connections to everyday life can be helpful. Therefore, everyday life could be seen as an associative and initial starting point for meaningful reflection in relation to school-based learning. In any case, by referring to social situations and adverts in their examples and by bringing supposedly irrelevant things such as adverts (which means consumption) and personal relations to a school friend to the attention of school, students close the gap between everyday life and school; they are mobile within and between contexts; the two contexts seem to be seamlessly connected.

Replicability and Transferability

Students with their mobile/cell phones and as experts succeed in making the connection between typical modes of representation of knowledge in terms of school and their everyday life. By doing so, they show what ideas they have about teaching methods and which might be their preferred teaching and learning methods, respecting the 'affordance' of the specific technology. Therefore, if teachers allow integrating mobile devices, such as children's mobile/cell phones, in the classroom and in open teaching and learning, they allow at the same time learner-generated contents and contexts (see Cook et al. 2007; Chapter 11). Those might be based on individual, and maybe less formal learning processes, and might include modes of representation, which are not originally coming from school contexts, thus not from formal settings for learning. As schemes for validating knowledge that is gained in informal contexts and processes, children can make use of their experiences, needs, demands, competencies etc. Such patterns, seen as frame for acquisition and estimation, are the link between children's everyday life and school. From this perspective, the Handy project seems to us to be a good showcase for the idea of supporting the learners in their status as experts, and to accept their expertise and interests – also of supposedly irrelevant things – as agentive and meaningful initial points for school learning.

The didactic setting, as well as the technological requirements, allows teachers to reproduce this project easily with only minor cost. The added value, which is given through the availability of the 'micro-units' on a weblog, might be an incentive to see such projects not only as temporary events, but as initiatives with a certain academic sustainability as well as a basis for modular learning and peer-teaching.

Project 'Learning Lab Initiative'

(I) Project Description

Context/Rationale

The 'Learning Lab' project was conducted in Bangalore, India, at a government school with 13–15 year old pupils. According to its website (CKS 2006), the overall aims of the Learning Lab initiative, which is an open standards initiative led by the Centre for Knowledge Societies (CKS), focuses on the use of mobile technologies for innovative teaching and learning, with a focus on learning through play. Furthermore, it aims to combine mobile technologies with already existing technologies, such as computer or television, for a distributed audience. (CKS 2005a) Besides these overall aims, and the curricular aims, which are described below, the Learning Lab initiative considers mobile technologies to be useful tools to improve education and the education system, i.e. in the administration sector, evaluation, teacher training and policy making:

> Handhelds have the potential of improving administrative processes and allow parents or other stakeholders to be involved in their child's education in a more proactive manner. For instance, handhelds can enable administrative officers track activities in remote rural schools in a more effective manner. GPRS enabled handhelds may also be included among ICTs used in distance teacher training programs. Moreover, Mobile Devices could be used by supervisory authorities to record data pertaining to individual school performance during field visits. Aggregating this data on a desktop resource can automate and ease the laborious process of evaluating school performance and aid policy making and educational planning. (CKS 2005a)

Within the project discussed here, 'students were encouraged to move out of the classroom and bring into play new ways of exploring and understanding their environment, and visualizing this new knowledge'. (CKS 2005a) Pupils were equipped with mobile devices, ranging from GPS devices to multi-media capable mobile/cell phones. At the beginning of the project, they were supported with workshops and training sessions.

The projects consisted of two assignments: 'Curricular Learning Outside the Classroom' and 'Exploring Locative Media'. The first assignment was related to a problem-oriented and problem-solving task from Mathematics and sciences, as well as to data collection, collaborative learning and location awareness. The second assignment, 'exploring locative media', was composed of different non-curricular activities.

Notions of Mobility, Aims of the Project and Research Design

The understanding of the use of mobile technologies in education settings is as follows, but no specification of the different aspects is given in the available material:

- Mobile-to-Desktop
- Mobile as Ready Reference
- In-Class Data Streaming
- Interactive Mobile Instruction
- Off-Grid Campus Connectivity
- Mobile as Modem
- Programming on Mobile
- Educational Gaming
- Child Security

'Vector One: Mobile-to-Desktop Synching', was realised in a Government High School in Bagalore/Domlur, namely the Karnataka State Government run Kannada English medium school. Aims of the project were to

- Synch data captured from a mobile device with a Desktop PC.
- Extend learning outside the classroom context.
- Enable project-based and peer-2-peer learning. (CKS 2005b)

Research questions underlying the research project were on technological requirements, the added value of mobile/cell phones and their applications, learning activities in terms of collaboration, as well as restrictions and limitations of the study:

- What use cases emerge from field experiments?
- What contexts of sharing and collective experiences emerge from this study?
- What educational attributes of a mobile/cell phone can be envisaged through this study?
- What new applications and content might be necessary to make the mobile/cell phone more useful for educational applications?
- What are the boundary conditions and limitations of this study? (CKS 2005b)

As theoretical approach, the analysis of the project (CKS 2005b) refers to Rieber's theory of playful learning (see below for a detailed description).

Altogether, 540 students, from grade 8 to 10, were involved in the project. Each grade was split into four groups. The pupil-teacher ration was 34:1, the girl-boy ratio 60:40. They had 15 computers available (Windows 98 & Office 2000, Pentium III processors), which leads to a pupil-computer ratio of 5:1. The subjects, with reference to the State Government Syllabus, in which the projects was realised, were English, Maths, Social Studies, Sciences, Kannada[7] and Computer Studies (CKS 2005b).

The research sample was composed of two boys and three girls from grade 9 (age group 13–15). They were from an urban area, and settled in the Socio Economic Class 'C' (SEC category C; 'mid' socioeconomic class)[8] (CKS 2005b).

[7] 'Kannada is one of the major Dravidian languages of India, spoken predominantly in the southern state of Karnataka. Kannada, whose native speakers are called Kannadigas (Kannadigaru), number roughly 35 million, making it the 27th most spoken language in the world. It is one of the official languages of India and the official and administrative language of the state of Karnataka'. (Wikipedia 2008).

[8] 'The socioeconomic classification (SEC) groups urban Indian households on the basis of education and occupation of the chief wage earner (CWE: the person who contributes the most to the household expenses) of the household into five segments (SEC A, SEC B, SEC C, SEC D and SEC E households in that order). This classification is more stable than one based on income alone and being reflective of lifestyle is more relevant to the examination of consumption behaviour. Here, "high" socioeconomic classes refers to SEC A&B, "mid" socioeconomic class refers to SEC C and "low" socioeconomic classes refers to SEC D&E. Data sourced from Indian Readership Survey (∗IRS 1998–1999) gives the education and occupation profile of the chief wage earner of households'. (IndiaRetailBiz 2006)

Education and Society in India and the Relevance of the Project for India

In India, education is a prerequisite for getting access to better societal opportunities, occupation and status, which is the reason for Indian families to invest in education. At the time of this project, about 1/3 of the people aged 25 or less (this age group is at about 50% of the total population in India) are the focus group for education (grades K to 8). However, governmental schools in India are missing infrastructural support, which leads to a lack in the availability of e.g. laboratories, computer centres, media centres and teaching and learning aids. This might be a reason why 'pedagogic techniques in India tend to be highly regimented, and emphasize textual learning and exam-taking skills'. One opportunity to support Indian's population in their education is seen in the use of mobile media, because compared to computers the penetration of mobiles phones is relatively high. Also available are 'applications, services and media capabilities at an ever decreasing cost'. (CKS 2005b)

Judging by the pupils' age (13–15) and the structure of the assignments, the project is situated in secondary education. Furthermore, judging by the pictures of the pupils' homes and families, they most probably do not belong to a Muslim minority but to a religious majority of Indian society.

In view of the national socio-economic context and the federal organisation of the education system in India, the site of the project has to be considered; it is unclear from the material available whether the projects was conducted in a rural or urban setting.

- Literacy rates of Karnataka in relation to India are just little above the average: overall: 66.6; male: 76.1; female 56.9
- In 2006, 59% of young males and 47% of young females entered secondary education. (The World Bank 2008a) The overall average for India is 51%. The ratio in urban areas is higher than in rural areas.
- Just 72% of children at primary school age enter school and just about 82% of them complete primary school.
- Just under half of the pupils complete the 'Secondary School Leaving Certificate'. (The World Bank 2002)

Education in India seems to be very dependent on socio-economic rather than religious factors. There is a gender gap that slightly privileges boys compared with girls.

Although the government of the region Karnataka is investing considerable effort in the issue of education in order to meet with the region's enormous economic growth, the risk for young people not being able to participate in secondary education is relevant here (Table 4.3).

Penetration of the Mobile/Cell Phone in India

The mobile/cell phone in India does not have the same penetration as in Germany and the UK, for example, where the percentage of mobile/cell phone owners is more

Table 4.3 Penetration of the mobile/cell phone in India (The World Bank 2008b)

	India 2006	Low-income group 2006
Mobile telephone subscribers (per 100 people)	15	14.3
Population covered by mobile telephony (%)	61	40
Internet users (per 100 people)	5.5	4.3
Personal computers (per 100 people)	1.6	1.4

than 100%, i.e. there are more phones than people. The differing figures for internet users and computer users indicate that there is a considerable number of users accessing the internet elsewhere. This has implications for wireless technologies and mobility as people have to go to specific locations to access the internet in order to engage with each other.

According to the Press Trust of India (September 11, 2007) the regional Karnataka government has decided to prohibit the sale of mobile/cell phones and handsets to children under the age of 16. School authorities were advised to confiscate mobile/cell phones and parents were advised to ensure that mobile/cell phones were not used at home. (PTI September 11, 2007)

Approaches to Teaching and Learning

The learning design of the project considers four categories, in which the project parts were settled: curricular, non curricular, activity based and project based. Within the **curricular and activity based** setting, students were encouraged to document, by using their Nokia 7610 devices,

- Ten living things and identify their biological names
- Parts of a plant and factors required for their growth
- Shapes and angles of various types
- Different communication devices. (CKS 2005b)

For the **non-curricular and activity based** part of the project, mobile devices with GPS function were used. The tasks for the pupils were:

- Create a route map from home to school
- Using the GPS device, track the above mentioned route
- Using the analogue camera, visually document family, friends & social circle
- Create an affective map of the community (CKS 2005b)

The **non-curricular and project-based** part included for students the tasks to

- Make a guidebook based on the map of a public place
- A public park was chosen by students
- Use all possible functions of the 7610 phone.

Assignment 1 'Curricular Learning Outside the Classroom'

Four groups of pupils, each consisting of three members, were provided a camera-enabled mobile/cell phone and were asked to engage in a maths or science task. The arrangement between pupils differed in terms of either sharing a device within the group or choosing one pupil as group leader, i.e. the one who holds the device (Figs. 4.8 and 4.9). (CKS 2005a)

Fig. 4.8 Pupils using image capture for science assignment (CKS 2005a)

> Some groups shared the device as a team whereas others chose to be led by a single student. Students were able to iteratively refine their photo capturing skills upon receiving feedback from their peers or by looking at the image in (sic) the phone. Finally, students collated their group project onto (sic) a desktop computer and shared findings with peers. Students were able to make a number of creative associations between the assignment and their environment. For example, students captured the images of 'roads, signboards, a celebrity poster' as examples of communication devices. (CKS 2005a)

Assignment 2 'Exploring Locative Media'

To explore the pupils' 'attitudes and approaches to visual expression', they were asked to engage in analogue tasks (i.e. painting images for a drawing assignment: 'Draw your way to and from home to school using pen and paper') before starting with using the GPS devices. Leading questions were 'What are the places you would show me in Bangalore? Which is you (sic) favourite festival? Present your idea of 'personal space' through a drawing' (CKS 2005a). Subsequently, three boys and two girls were chosen to participate in the second assignment.

The tasks for the pupils chosen to participate in this second assignment were as follows:

a. Draw your way to and from home to school using pen and paper.
b. Use GPS devices to create GPS tracks of the same route.
c. Synch this GPS data onto a digital map of Bangalore with a desktop computer.

Fig. 4.9 Examples of different shapes and angles from the first assignment (CKS 2005b)

d. Textually annotate landmarks of your choice by using the 'way point' function on the GPS device and layer this information on the digital map (Fig. 4.10). (CKS 2005a)

The second set of tasks combined GPS technology with analogue technology (analogue photo cameras). Pupils had to take pictures of different objects, places and persons whilst carrying the activated GPS devices with them.

e. Take pictures of your favourite things to familiarize yourself with the working of a camera.
f. Click images of landmarks or things that catch your attention enroute to school.
g. Capture images of things that make you happy, are forbidden to you or things you dislike.
h. Manually locate these photos and layer them on the digital map using the GPS data you have collected (CKS 2005a)

Within the second set of tasks, pupils produced pictures e.g. of their parents: (Fig. 4.11) The pictures taken within the second set of tasks, including the GPS data, which tracked the pupils' real paths and visited locations (called 'affective' maps), were merged with digital maps (Fig. 4.12).

The map in the middle of the image includes the pupil's path and visited locations. In the right-hand column and the bottom row, pictures are displayed, which pupils have taken for the second assignment.

The 'affective' maps that synthesized photographs and individual GPS tracks overlaid on digital maps were uploaded onto an internal website. This assignment was also paralleled by

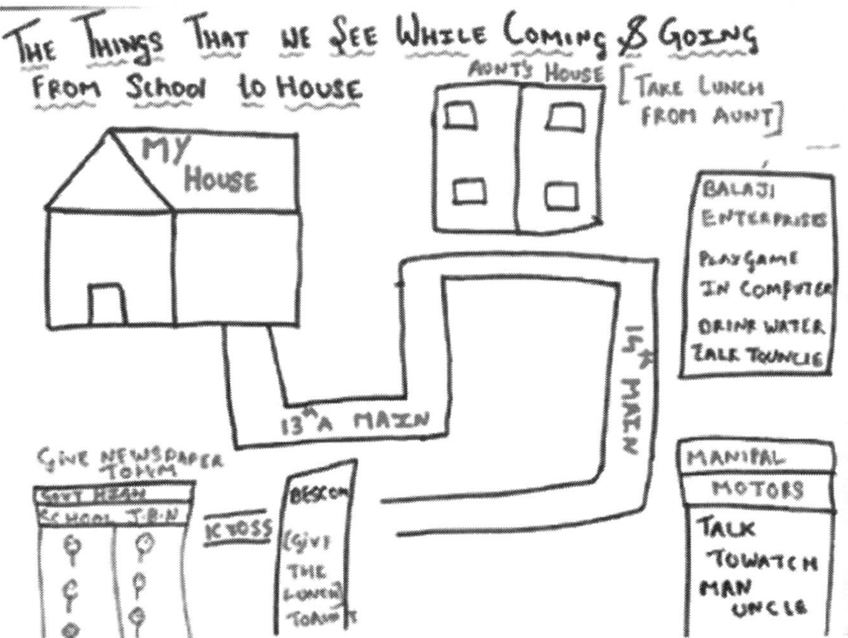

Fig. 4.10 A pupil creates a route map of his path from home to school (CKS 2005a)

Fig. 4.11 A pupil captures his parents at home to annotate his affective map (CKS 2005a)

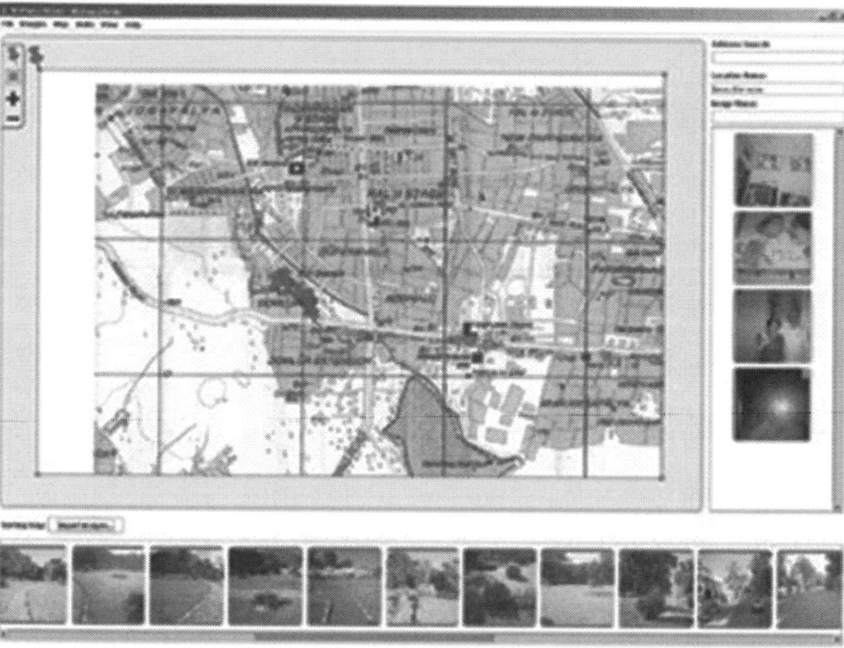

Fig. 4.12 An example of an affective map layered with GPS track data (CKS 2005a)

> a task that instructed students to create a physical map of resources in their neighbourhood to represent locations which had a personal connotative element.
> These exercises helped students develop a highly personalized and individualistic understanding of spaces around them. (CKS 2005a)

Technologies and Requirements

The Learning Lab initiative aims to combine mobile technologies with already existing technologies, such as computer or television:

> ... the project seeks to explore ways in which the Mobile Device maybe complemented by the T.V, radio or desktop. For instance, Mobile Devices maybe used in conjunction with a public broadcast system or a local cable T.V. network, thereby making educational lessons available to a distributed populace. (CKS 2005a)

Within the project framework, pupils were introduced to the use of the mobile devices and digital technologies at the beginning of the project. They were also asked to make themselves familiar with the analogue cameras before starting the assignment.

Project Outcomes

The results of the project refer to the use of (mobile) technologies as well as on learning activities and strategies: on the one hand pupils got familiar with mobile devices and the technologies provided; on the other hand, they worked and learned in more self-directed and responsible ways.

The pupils' started their assignments 'highly structured, directed and regimented' (CKS 2005b). However, during their engagement in the project, e.g. 'interactions with the field team and with the mobile devices they were given' their activities faded to a free behaviour, driven by 'curiosity, creativity, imagination, critical thinking and teamwork'. (CKS 2005a)

> During this course of interaction, students took greater initiative in planning and structuring activities and were able to devise creative strategies for the completion of projects. Their ability to collaborate productively and communicate within a group was also enhanced. These observations lead us to hope that students will continue to use such 'self directed' and 'participatory' approaches for learning even in the later stages of research. However, the key outcome of the research was that students were able to make connections between textbook based information and the world around them in new ways. (CKS 2005a)

This shift in the pupils' approaches to solve their tasks is described as a shift to 'playing and learning at the same time' (CKS 2005b). The theory underlying the CKS analysis is Rieber's theory of playful learning. (CKS 2005b) The researchers categorised the pupils' habitus of the use of mobile/cell phones in different group constellations during the field trip (e.g. how many pupils are touching the device at the same time) as well as their works/outcomes (i.e. the pictures taken in the course of their tasks) according to Rieber as related to play as fantasy, play as self, play as control and play as progress. Theories of play categorise 'play as progress, play as power, play as fantasy, and play as self'; 'challenge, curiosity, fantasy, and control' are 'characteristics common to all intrinsically motivating learning environments' (Rieber 1996, p. 50).

> Play as progress concerns the belief that the purpose of play is to learn something useful. Play is a means to improve or enable psychological or social needs. This type of play is almost always described as an important mechanism by which children become adults, thus strongly suggesting a clear distinction between children's play and adults' play (though many researchers dispute this by viewing such distinctions as artificial). Play as power refers to contests or competitions in which winners and losers are declared. Such examples center around players or participants involved in some source of conflict, whether that be a game of football or chess. Unlike play as progress, play as power belongs almost exclusively to adult forms of play. Play as fantasy refers to play's role in liberating the mind to engage in creative and imaginative thinking. There are some obvious connections here to play as progress, such as when one views creativity as an outcome to be pursued as opposed to a state to be intrinsically valued. Play as self is the most recent of themes. It places value on play's role as a way to achieve optimal life experiences. What is valued is the quality of the experience and not other secondary outcomes (such as learning). The main issue here is the intrinsic worth of an experience. (See Sutton-Smith 1995, for a critical analysis of these four themes.) (Rieber 1996, p. 44)

Learning through play in the project is specified as

- natural learning strategy
- socio-culturally influenced
- experience is the focus, not outcome
- effective platform for learning & instruction
- employs multiple learning approaches
- problem-solving & creation of new knowledge
- enhances Goal-orientation (CKS 2005b)

The pupils' according approaches are described as

- spontaneous
- motivated
- exploratory
- serendipitous discovery
- flexible
- iterative. (CKS 2005b)

The different kinds of play and their respective expressions are exemplified by using the pupils' pictures which they have taken during their curricular and non-curricular activities.

Fantasy: References to the Bollywood genre, a game which boys play in their leisure, and two quizzes are categorised under fantasy:

- Movie Zone
- Fancy Dress
- One Cow or Two?
- Coffee Powder on the Palm (CKS 2005b)

Self: References to the individuals in different group constellations, identity and self-perception (alone, with friends, in class, with family):

- Self Portrait
- Self Discovery
- Self Perception
- Social Support (CKS 2005b)

Control: References to different approaches to teaching (getting advice, teaching the teacher), learning (peer-to-peer), gender roles, ownership and appropriation:

- Facilitation
- Role Reversal
- Peer-to-Peer Exchange & Learning
- Gender Play
- Social Structuring
- Drive to Discovery (CKS 2005b)

Progress: References to technologies:

- Improved Photography Skills (CKS 2005b)

The learning outcomes were described as 'self directed' and 'participatory' learning, which includes 'planning and structuring activities' as well as 'devise creative strategies for the completion of projects'. At a technical level, pupil learned how to use mobile devices in terms of taking pictures and downloading them on a PC. They got familiar with the principle of GPS, too. At the curricular level, location awareness was strengthened, i.e. the question of individual perception of locations and places.

- Students synched and organized their data on a PC.
- Several students were able to use a single mobile/cell phone in collaboration with each other.
- The rich-media capabilities of the device enabled project-based learning through the playful extension of their senses.
- Parents encouraged students' explorations with the technology even though it was outside school work. (CKS 2005b)

Regarding the learning by play approach, which was introduced earlier, the key findings are as follows:

- Behavioural Change
  - Building Social Skills by Sharing & Negotiation
  - Peer-2-Peer Learning
  - Teaching and Collaborating
- Cognitive Development
  - Creative Construction & Deformation of Rules
  - Problem Solving/Self-Learning
- Skills Enhancement
  - Virtual Navigation
  - Visual Media Capture/Editing/Annotation
  - Spatial Literacy/Context Awareness (CKS 2005b)

Lessons Learnt/Issues Emerging

The perspective of learning with mobile devices evaluated by the Learning Lab team is, in general, optimistic with regard to pupils and parents: pupils use the mobile devices competently and organise their learning in a self-directed manner. Parents seem to support the use of mobile devices in curricular contexts and are prepared to 'invest in any promising educational technology' (CKS 2005b).

The teachers' role, as well as administrative aspects, is considered to contain challenges:

Teachers

- prefer hierarchical over p2p communications
- loss of authority and communicative control
- inability to keep up with technology

Administrators

- lack of control over the use of technology in the school (CKS 2005b)

Limitations of the project were discovered in different areas, covering the role of the school authorities, expenditure of time, 24/7 ownership of the devices, pedagogical approaches, the implementation of learning outcomes in the curriculum, the limited use of the mobile/cell phone functions, and the limited coverage related to the number of pupils involved and regional coverage.

- The project was an intervention by external agencies, and may have entailed a sense of loss of control for school authorities.
- Project assignments required students to work outside school hours. Nevertheless, students were prevented from taking the device home with them on account of its high cost.
- The study emphasized project-based learning, an approach that ran counter to the everyday pedagogic practices of the school. Learning outcomes could not integrated into the school syllabus or system of evaluation in any way.
- The phone was not used for any kind of communication. Its use was restricted to rich-media capture, synching and sharing.
- The project involved a very small segment of students in a single region and location type within India. (CKS 2005b)

Recommendations and Future Possibilities

The recommendations refer to the teaching concepts, the acceptance by the groups involved, infrastructural support and strategic support by stakeholders; these areas have to be addressed towards the use of mobile/cell phones in the teaching and learning process and their implementation in schools.

- Although this project emphasized project-based learning, most Indian school environments use more traditional 'transmissionist' educational strategies.
- Students and their parents were the most responsive and receptive segments of the sector.
- In order for any technology intervention to be successful in the educational context, however, it is essential for teachers and administrators to also buy in.
- We therefore advocate a multi-pronged strategy to address different stakeholders in the education sector and convert them to the idea of mobile learning. (CKS 2005b)

Possibilities and recommendations refer to product concepts and sales strategies, as CKS is a profit organisation as well. Envisaged are mobile devices for different target groups involved in the pupils' learning: pupils, teachers and parents, including different sales strategies (mobile devices to be purchased by families ('Family Learning Fone', 'Phone Learning Kit', 'Add-On Child Service'; CKS 2005b) or by institutions ('Teacher's Administrative Assistant', 'Student Non-Phone'); CKS 2005b). Accordingly, the adoption of the proposed concepts would be a win-win situation for all parties:

- Introduces Families to Mobile Learning
- Third Party Provides Credible Educational Value
- Service Provider Gains Add-On Subscribers
- Introduces Mobile Devices into the School
- Vast Numbers of Students Techno-Literate (CKS 2005b)

As phase 2 of the project, the conception of a 'Student NonPhone' is envisaged, including different technological and methodological improvements.

- Develop Rich Media Functions for Learning
  - Relationship to School Curriculum
  - Modalities of p2p Interaction
  - Compatibility with other Devices in Home and School
- Control for Variables
  - Urban/Peri Urban/Rural Locations
  - India/China/Brazil World Regions
  - Different Regions in each Country
  - School + Home + Other Contexts
- Refine Concepts for Student Products Only
  - Devices for Family-Purchase
  - Access Controls for Child Security and Protection (CKS 2005b)

General Project Data

Table 4.4 General project data 'learning lab initiative'

Project name	Learning lab initiative
URL	http://www.cks.in/html/ecology_htmls/cks_ecology_building01.html #section11
Country	India
Year	About 2004/2005
Contact	Learning Lab team at the Center for Knowledge Societies, Bangalore, India; cks@cks.in
Types of devices	Mobile/cell phones; GPS devices
Further media	Computer; analogue photo cameras
Number of persons	3–5 in each group
Duration	Unknown
Location	Outside school; inside school
Educational establishment	
Phase of education	Overall project: grade 8 to 10; research sample: grade 9 (age 13–15)
Subject domain	Maths, sciences; further on (but not described in the available reports): english, social studies, kannada and computer studies
Teaching/learning focus	Context and location awareness; new ways of exploring and understanding the environment; visualisation of knowledge
Keywords	Informal context (out of school); location awareness/GPS; data collection; life world (reflection); visualisation and knowledge building; natural sciences; pictures; media convergence; media literacy; combine analogue and digital media

(II) Analysis

The following analysis focuses on notions of mobility, mobility across contexts, as well as agency, cultural practices and approaches to teaching and learning.

Notions of Mobility, Contents and Contexts

Whilst mobile devices in this project were used because of their portability, i.e. image capturing, GPS functionality and synchronisation with personal computers, other affordances of mobile devices, e.g. for communication purposes (phone calls, email, messaging), or the option to audio-record oral descriptions of the observations instead of taking pictures, were not used (CKS 2005b). Accordingly, the mobile/cell phones are used here for their 'mobile' affordances rather than their most 'structural' and natural purpose, the communicative and interpersonal functions. The reasons for this are not known and may depend on restrictions on the use of mobile/cell phones in the Indian education system or on economic restrictions of the project; also, didactic[9] reasons or inadequate funding may have prevented the use of the communication functions. On the one hand, this points to the media convergence potential or multi-media use of these tools, which can be used instead of other devices such as, for example, cameras or GPS devices, which can be used according to one's own interests independently from the 'main' function for which they were designed. On the other hand, this may lead one to observe that educational settings can under-exploit the potential of these devices for learning and teaching, because of various restrictions including institutional ones.

As mobility is in the foreground, the question is about the different notions of mobility, which are deriving from their situative use: mobility is initiated by, and happens in terms of contexts. For notions of context to which we refer see Chapter 11, as well as e.g. Bakardjieva 2005; Dourish 2004; Cook et al. 2007; Luckin et al. 2005; Sharples 2007a; Sharples, Taylor and Vavoula 2007, 2008. In the following, different notions of context within the Learning Lab project are outlined:

First of all, and due to their affordances, the mobile devices used bring mobility to the pupils in terms of ***physical*** mobility; the school as place for teaching and learning is augmented by other public and private locations outside school. As the mobile/cell phone is used as a tool for data collection and data storage (picture taking, data logging), mobility also contains the notion of carrying ***contents/resources*** from one place to another. In this respect the aspect of time is relevant, because availability over ***places*** corresponds to availability over ***time***. The GPS e.g. provides such a structural convergence in terms of making data from outside school available for their use in school.

[9]The term 'didactic' is not used here in the English tradition implying excessive instructional direction and teacher-centredness, but in the German sense of referring to theoretical and practical considerations concerning teaching and learning.

These notions of mobility, which can be described as convergence in terms of technological interoperability and functionality, are strongly related to continuity in learning. Continuity in learning is on the one hand provided by the technological affordances of the mobile devices (availability of resources over time and places). On the other hand, these technological affordances have also consequences for activity-related and conceptual mobilities, which are considered to be prerequisites for continuity in learning:

The cross-over from school into everyday life entails a certain mobility of the ***curriculum***. In the process, theorising and abstracting, which are often dominant within the curriculum, are supported by a figural output-dimension in terms of pupils' activities (different forms of group learning; pictures as output) as well as by a practical dimension in terms of the real world being the context and initial point/reference for learning. For example, pupils are confronted with the task of problem-solving between conceptual contexts by way of transfer and transformation: they have to link impressions and objects from outside school, in this case everyday life, to school and the curriculum; furthermore, they transfer a concrete shape, for example a car wheel, into the mathematical construct, in this case a circle, within their natural sciences and maths lessons.

Continuity is also achieved by means of pupils' ***activities*** during their field studies: they harmonise their task-related activities in terms of individual agency, and find common and objective denominators, which we deem to be a prerequisite for collaborative and group learning; the pupils have to agree on either the group taking a picture or only one pupil of this group; they have to agree on a shape; and they have to agree on the picture which (presumably) they all had to consider as being adequate to fulfil the assignment.

Agency, Structure, Cultural Practice, Approaches to Teaching and Learning

As schools are places for learning (about) a shared understanding of the world, it is necessary to find modes and contents for teaching and learning, which provide evidence of subjective and objective issues. To enable pupils to make their knowledge, meanings and agencies available and traceable for others, collaborative learning is seen as a mode to link subjective meaning making and individual agency to objective discourses, as well as to a shareable basis of common knowledge and meanings. The mobile/cell phone, as it is used in this project, is a tool to capture cultural practices based on the agents and their personal life worlds. Images are used to represent the pupils' selective views on the world, on different sites, and in different social constellations (e.g. peers, families). Collaborative knowledge building is enabled by the use of accepted representational modes such as images, and is based on a shared understanding of each others' social contexts and view of the world. The general function of the images, which represent at surface level the objectivisation of an individualised view of the world (here: e.g. a shape), is to provide a basis for discussion. But it also allows, by focusing on the perspective and the motive, to access the pupil's motivation, agency and meaning behind taking the picture. The same applies to the GPS data; these objectified data contain traces from the pupils' individual life worlds; thus, personal data become public and sharable because of the mode through which they are represented and the connected media (maps on PCs), which provide a frame against which individual agencies can be discussed.

Collaboration by means of sharing social situations, negotiating situated activities within social situations with peers, as well as individual agencies, and thus individualised and subjective perspectives, is extended in relation to negotiated meaning. The objectified process of meaning-making, which takes place at the institutionalised and formalised school and curriculum level as well as outside in the field (i.e. who holds the device and is thus the one whose selective activities/view is represented in the collected data), provides patterns, which connect subjective agencies to objective norms, rules, activities etc. Leaning on the theory of playful learning (as described above), the four forms of play (play as fantasy, self, control and progress) might be able to give evidence to such a shift, which is characterised by the transfer of individual meanings to common meaning on the basis of negotiation – whereas negotiation is not necessarily an activity between two or more pupils, but also the reflection on the self in relation to pre-existing rules and values. For this process of reflection, the term 'discussion' is used below (see also description Part 4 above):

As for fantasy as play, pupils ***discuss their different agencies***: this is the film genre, which I like; this is what I am doing with my friends in my leisure; this is how I show you an ambiguous situation which needs interpretation.

By referring to play as self, ***identities are discussed***: I am adult, I am an expert and able to teach my teacher, I am socially active and accepted and always with peers, I am with my family – this all is part of my life.

The dimension 'play as control' refers to the ***discussion of rules***, such as which skills do I need to have to handle the technology, which is my role as boy or as girl, in specific social situations, my role as learner.

Progress as play refers to the ***discussion of skills***, here in terms of using technologies. Which ones do I need as prerequisite, and how can I improve them.

However, even if the mobile/cell phone as tool can provide continuity and convergence in relation to the availability and interoperability of certain resources, the locus for the transfer and transformation of meanings is still on the teacher, who has to moderate by providing frames and by linking these two spheres to enable pupils to make connections between different contexts and their resources with relevance for both, school learning and individual everyday life. In other words, there is evidence of assimilative or accommodative adjustment of cultural practices of meaning-making to the dominant mode of learning.

Replicability and Transferability

From a technological perspective, the first part of the project, Assignment 1 'Curricular Learning Outside the Classroom', can easily be adapted by teachers given the minimum of technological resources needed. Only mobile/cell phones with cameras and connectivity options for the transfer of the collected material from the mobile/cell phone to a personal computer or laptop are required. Related to the didactic concept, collecting shapes from everyday life and nature, the task can be transferred to other school subjects because it focuses on data collection, whereas the semiotic relevance of the mode might be adjusted to the specific school subject (e.g. record spoken language for foreign language lessons; make films about current events in social studies etc.).

The second assignment depends essentially on the technological equipment: GPS-enabled devices, software for an electronic map as well as for the arrangement of the collected data (GPS data and pictures from the pupils' everyday lives). This part might thus not be realised without financial and technological support from outside.

Cyrill

(I) Description

Context/Rationale

Cyrill is an 18 year old German with a migration background, presumably second generation from Turkey and living in the south of Germany. At the time of writing he was being prosecuted because of the alleged harassment of homeless drunken men in his home town and the capturing of related video footage; the men were not able to agree to being filmed, which could be an issue of human dignity (Fig. 4.13).[10]

Cyrill uses different usernames and platforms on the internet. They are, as far as it was possible to track his traces, described below:

Cyrill on MySpace

Cyrill has a MySpace webpage (Endzeit 2008) via which he provides access to his videos. The videos of the homeless had to be removed from his website, as well as from his *YouTube* account. These videos are self-produced music videos, enhanced with rap and techno music (not self-produced). Also pictures of Cyrill in different poses are available. They are displayed in a moving cube. Cyrill's profile image (on the left hand, next to his personal and login data) is changed on an irregular basis (Figs. 4.14 and 4.15).

The rest of the page consists of typical MySpace elements: the list of Cyrill's friends on MySpace and his guestbook, called 'comments'. The comments consist of greetings and messages, some refer to the aesthetics of the website (comments range from 'cool'[11] to 'creepy'[12]), questions about technical issues (e.g. how was

[10] A report about these videos is available on the local newspaper Augsburger Allgemeine Zeitung (2007)

[11] 'AAAAAAATTZZZEEEEE waaas geht haha xD dein profil is voll geil man. . .die 'atmosphäre' taugt mir hehe greez'. From: http://www.myspace.com/cypictures

[12] 'iwie wenn man ne längere zeit auf deiner seite is das gruselig:Ddein lied und dein layout xDund iwie das wass sich da so dreht xD'. Available at: http://www.myspace.com/cypictures.

Fig. 4.13 A young man is counting in front of a sleeping homeless man before he starts yelling at him (Downloaded from http://www.linktakas.net/video/95654/Augsburg_-_CYRILL_-_Die_Legende_kehrt_zur%FCck.html). The video is no longer available online, 9 Jan 2008

the background image implemented[13]) as well as on Cyrill's videos. Furthermore, short biographies of visitors can be found in the comments providing insights into the communities of the visitors as well as Cyrill according to music taste, migration background and life-style.

On the picture page of his MySpace page, Cyrill provides recent pictures and web design work to registered MySpace users. They include photos displaying himself in various contexts, both casual as well as carefully choreographed. They also contain pictures of t-shirts and footwear that he has probably designed with graphical artwork.

Cyrill on Youtube.de

On Youtube.de, Cyrill has a 'channel' (the user's homepage on YouTube) with the name 'The unemployed channel' ('Der Arbeitslosen-Channel' (direktindiefresse 2008a)). His channel is set as 'director', which is the highest status of YouTube channels; it means that Cyrill considers himself as an experienced video-maker. However, Cyrill's channel does not seem to be very popular – considering the six subscribers and 1,593 channel views by August 23, 2008.

With his names, as well as with his comments and tags on his video pages, he situates himself in the culture of HipHop, and more generally in the 'violence affine' segment. His videos are about activities with friends – at parties, in the street, at

[13] 'CYRILL wie hasT du dich selber als hinTERgruND gemaCHt? sag mal bitte peace'. Available at: http://www.myspace.com/cypictures

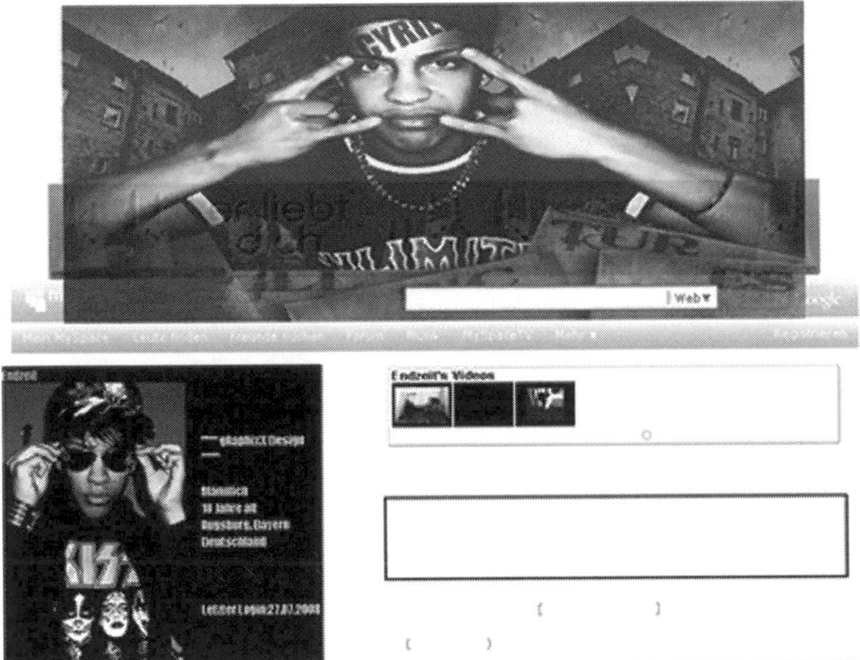

Fig. 4.14 Cyrill's MySpace page (Screenshot from http://www.myspace.com/cypictures), 28 Jun 2008

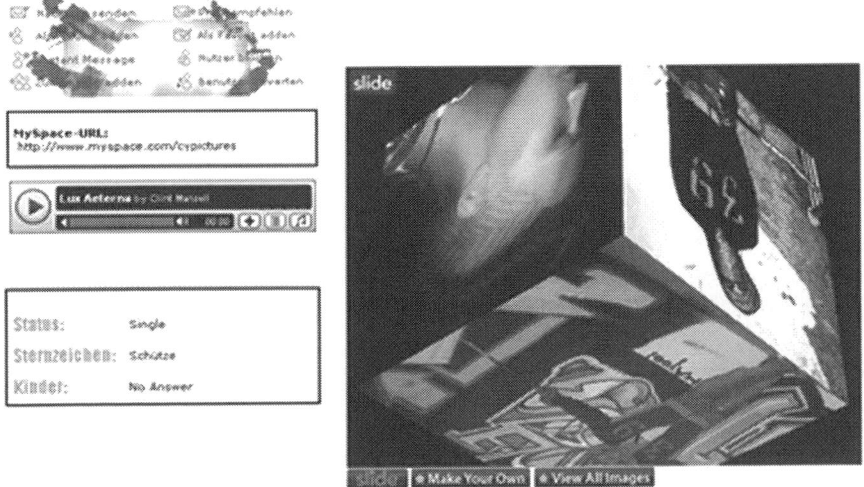

Fig. 4.15 Rotating cube with pictures of Cyrill in different poses (Screenshot from http://www.myspace.com/cypictures), 28 Jun 2008

home, as well as videos produced for local Rap musicians. The optional description of each video is used by Cyrill as commenting function rather than as description. For example, amongst other videos, there is one with two of his military colleagues during a march, behaving stupidly (title: 'That's how it is' ('So ist das halt' (direktindiefresse 2008b))). This video is categorised under 'education' and tagged with 'Dear god' ('lieber gott'). Also a video with three young men in a room is available, smoking an Arab water pipe and trying to solve a mathematical question: 'what is 3 plus 3 times 3?' ('Was ist 3 + 3 × 3?' (direktindiefresse 2008c)). This video is in the category 'comedy' and described as 'a Turk calculating' ('türke beim rechnen'). The video is tagged amongst others with 'mathematics, learning, school, special education, special education needs, psycho, bouncer, reportage' ('türke mathematik lernen bodyguard schule sonderschule zurückgeblieben psycho türsteher reportage'). As the video clearly evidences, the answer is not known by the person who was asked to solve this mathematical task; laughing loudly, his friends point to the rule of multiplication before addition ('Punkt-vor-Strich-Regel'), which they were taught in the fifth grade.

Mid-September 2008, Cyrill added new videos to his YouTube account, which are compilations of videos from the year 2007. Interestingly, the three new videos had titles, which indicated a kind of reflection, as well as a melancholic look back to the 'good old days'. This impression was underlined by background music, which features a slow and violin-dominated piece with a melancholic attitude by the famous ex-GDR band 'City' (song: Am Fenster (At the window)).

Since the beginning of October 2008, Cyrill's video account is empty, and no new content appears to have been added (Fig. 4.16).

In some postings Cyrill mentions that his computer and his video camera are still not available to him because the police had confiscated them, and it is not clear whether he will get his equipment back. So he is dependent on his mobile/cell phone and a low quality computer to make films about which he is unhappy.

Cyrill on GQ.com

Through a websearch a profile page of Cyrill could be found on GQ.com, a lifestyle magazine for men (GQ.com 2008a). There, Cyrill provides not only pictures of himself in different clothes (GQ.com 2008b, c), but is also mentioned in the GQ's online 'Style Diary' (GQ.com 2008d, e) (Fig. 4.17).

Cyrill on timeshot.de

On timeshot.com, a community website for the south of Germany, Cyrill is also present and with 69 posts by August 2008 quite active (bimbofighter 2008). On his profile page are pictures of parties and friends, including a picture of Cyrill and some other recruits in their military uniforms. This page is only accessible for registered users, and only for users who are not blocked by its owner. On this platform, Cyrill participates in discussions about films, music, girls, the military etc. His comments

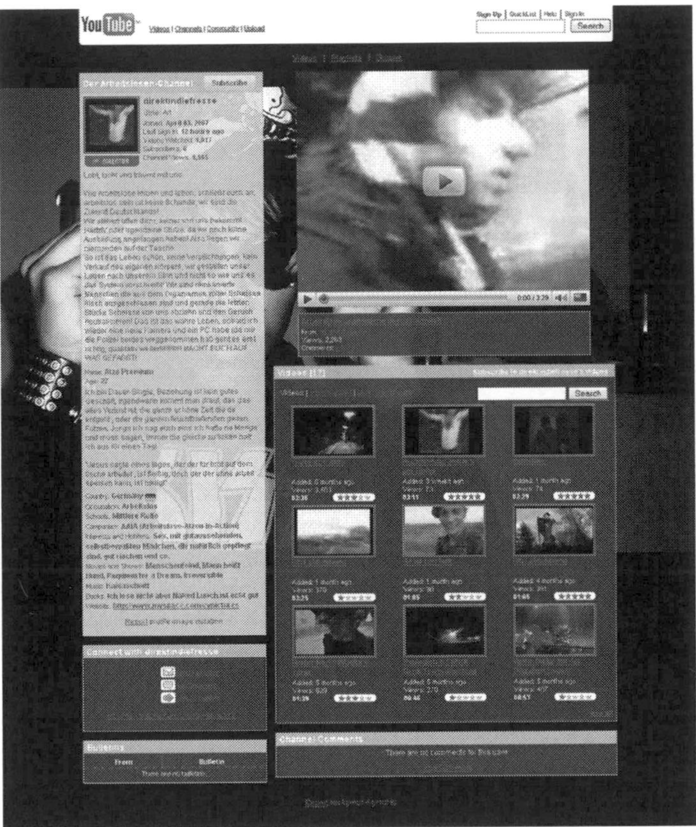

Fig. 4.16 Cyrill's profile page on YouTube.de (Screenshot from http://www.youtube.com/user/direktindiefresse), 20 Aug 2008

can be characterised as being critical, cynical and provocative. He also initiates a forum about the prettiest girl in town.[14] Because no girls answer, but some men, who say that their girl is the prettiest, Cyrill decides – one year after he started the discussion – to comment this with: 'I am the prettiest girl and end'.[15]

[14]'Wer das Gefühl hat, und denkt sie ist das schönste Mädchen bitte hier melden! Mit Foto!!!!!Schau ma mal, wer sich alles meldet!mfg—bImb0fIgHTeR_XxX'. Written on April 20th, 2005. Available at: http://www.timeshot.de/viewtopic.php?p=104367&sid=8f48fe3a67c26e8177c60921119b03d2 (Timeshot 2005).

[15]'ich bin das schönste mädchen und fertig'. Written on April 26th, 2006. Available at: http://www.timeshot.de/viewtopic.php?p=592849&sid=3038537f62eee24bd13592228c4052a0 (Timeshot 2006).

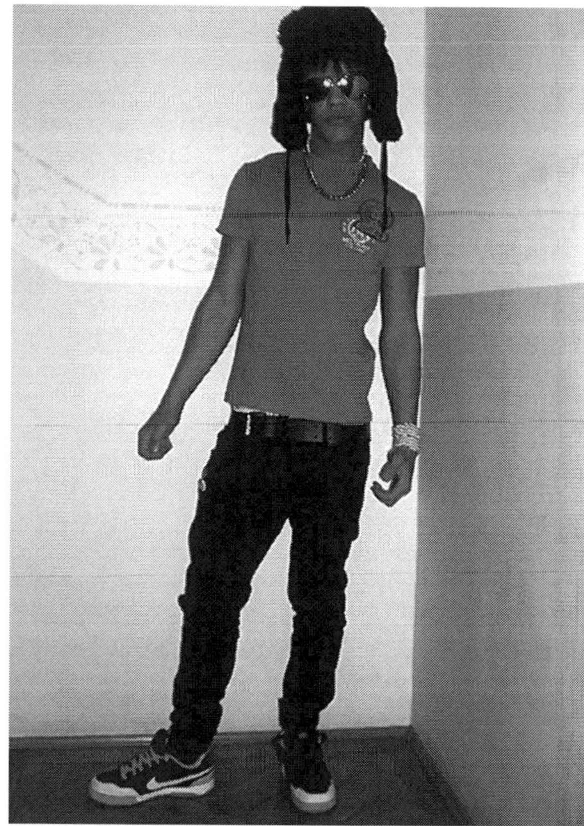

Fig. 4.17 Style Diary: Cyrill alias 'bimbofighter' (Screenshot from http://community.gq-magazin.de/blog/2008/03/13/cyrill-alias-bimbofighter/), 19 Aug 2008

Cyrill on spreadshirt.net/spreadtags.de

On a platform for non-professional shirt designers, Cyrill has a small market place area where he offers t-shirts with self-designed motives (cYRiLLPictures 2008). Some of the motives are also available on Cyrill's MySpace page.

Cyrill on Expert Platforms

Cyrill is also active in forums for digital video production and tutorials for graphic and video processing software (http://www.slashcam.de, http://www.pcwelt.de, http://www.psd-tutorials.de), posting questions on how to use a graphic or video programme or how to make cuts in grainy videos (Ashley 2007; bimbofighter 2006, 2007a, b).

Approaches to Teaching and Learning

On MySpace.de, Cyrill does not explicitly make reference to learning. However, some technical and web design related questions, which are directed to Cyrill by visitors of his page, have relevance for learning. Comments on forums suggest that Cyrill is self-taught in terms of video production and image processing.

On YouTube.de, Cyrill uploaded a video in which one of his friends has to solve an arithmetic problem. Because the young man is not able to find the solution, his friends point to a specific rule, which should enable him to find the right result. Cyrill tagged some of his videos with relevance to education, school and learning. He names some videos with reference to German TV documentary magazines as 'Stern TV' or 'Spiegel TV'. Also he tagged some videos as documentaries. This way he shows that he has a certain notion of learning with media and he shows his proximity to television.

On timeshot.de, Cyrill answers a comment by a girl who was at the time revising for an exam (Timeshot 2007). He writes using cynical language saying that there is 'nothing better than learning'.

Technologies and Requirements

Until his equipment, a video camera and a computer, were confiscated by the police, Cyrill appears to be using a Sony Dcr-Hc23E camcorder and Adobe After Effects 7 for video processing. Now he is dependent on his mobile/cell phone as tool for video-recording and a low quality computer, which do not allow him to produce the quality he would like. His comments show that he has a certain notion about the quality of videos and photos. Also the capability of a computer using dedicated software for video and photo manipulation has a certain meaning of quality to him. The mobile/cell phone on the other hand just provides the basic capability of taking photos and videos without the necessary quality.

Project Outcomes

As Cyrill's activities might be considered to be projects, the videos, pictures and pages on *MySpace.de, YouTube.de and timeshot.de* as well as his participation in activities on GQ.com can be seen as project outcomes. His 'projects' are in this perspective

- professional video, image and merchandising (t-shirts) production for local bands and musicians,
- fashion and clothing,
- leisure time with friends.

His projects provide a basis for follow-up communication for visitors in the form of comments on Cyrill's different outputs and sites. He addresses himself to different target groups and audiences by using different profiles and also different language on the different websites according to the respective community.

Lessons Learnt/Issues Emerging

From a technological perspective, Cyrill's 'projects' can be reproduced in everyday life as well as in school contexts, by using devices and resources, which are usually available at low cost, and accessible to a wide range of users. Generalising from Cyrill's notion of quality one could state that quality of outcome does matter and that when doing projects with video and photo in schools, pupils might not be satisfied with the quality and capability of the mobile/cell phones.

Recommendations and Future Possibilities

Cyrill is interested mainly in two topics: one is the political and societal issue of participation, in particular societal integration and exclusion. The other is related to leisure activities: creativity, fashion/style/body and friends. He deals with the topic of societal inclusion and exclusion in a way that brings him into conflict with the law by provoking homeless people. But, as his recent videos demonstrate, Cyrill has changed his attitude towards this group of people: more recent videos include scenes, in which the young men shown are attempting to approach the homeless in a conciliatory manner by offering them cigarettes and food. In addition, Cyril describes himself on his YouTube account as being unemployed. By doing so, he is placing himself in proximity to the homeless people, with the difference that he has a residence and is embedded in a social network of friends and peers on that he can rely. This topic could be used to discuss Cyrill's societal and political interests and not least his own situation and fears. The mode of video and the documentary genre could be links to enable Cyrill to express and reflect on these topics. But it seems to be necessary to allow Cyrill to bring creative and experimental elements into such video production in order not to limit him in his personal style and attitudes.

Another link between Cyrill's activities and preferences and a potential employment – besides his affinity to video production – could be his interest in fashion and (body) style. To offer him job opportunities where he has creative freedom could be a fruitful symbiosis and a strong basis for Cyrill to bring together his personal interests, his individuality and a solid basis to care about his income – instead of being reliant on social welfare.

General Project Data (Table 4.5)

(II) Analysis

Contents and Contexts/Agency, Structure, Cultural Practice

As outlined above, Cyrill uses different platforms on the internet to present himself in different contexts and with different facets of his identity. Rather than drawing

Table 4.5 General project data 'Cyrill'

Project name	Cyrill
URL	http://www.MySpace.com/cypictures
Country	Germany
Year	2007–2008
Contact	–
Types of mobile devices	Mobile/cell phone
Further media	Video camera, PC, internet platforms, video and image processing software
Number of persons	1
Duration	Observation period: September 2007–October 2008
Location	Outside school/city
Educational establishment	–
Phase of education	–
Subject domain	–
Teaching/learning focus	–
Keywords	'At-risk learner'; life world; everyday life; cultural practices; Youtube as convergent media platform; informal learning; literacy; modes of representation and design; critical reflection; identity

a comprehensive picture of this young man, his life-world and his agency in terms of identity construction, this case study is considered in terms of whether, and if so how, the cultural practices of a young man at the periphery of society and school, but with a rather well developed expertise within media convergence, can be brought into a fruitful relationship with formal education.

The Video

The video of homeless drunken men at the regional tram station was deemed by the public prosecutor to depict a situation of harassment. However, harassment is definitely not in the foreground of the video, but instead the observation of white German dropouts is. The intention of this video probably is to show who the real social underdogs are – in Cyrill's and his group's view the underdogs are not the young migrants, but local homeless people. The main attitude of the video is to observe and criticise a social situation, a kind of an unemotional description that avoids personal feelings.

The result of the analysis of Cyrill's video in terms of identity and attitudes can be summarised thus:

- expressing feelings as an underdog,
- depicting society's real underdogs,
- having fun with a peer group

- using the video capability of the mobile in a very simple way without post production, but with a soundtrack,
- publishing the video on a social networking site.

Media Structures Relating to the Mobile/Cell Phone

Cyrill acts within the structure of the ongoing transformation of mass communication, in which the mobile/cell phone is a very powerful agent. Cyrill does not act as a trend-setter but on the basis of expertise he has developed:

- outside an editorial system towards archives such as media platforms,
- away from a push to a pull system in media distribution,
- use of the mobile/cell phone with a variety of applications as ubiquitous person media tool,
- user-generated content and contexts,
- convergence with Web 2.0 options of the internet,
- within the structure of internet media platforms.

Cyrill's Media Expertise with the Mobile Video and on MySpace.com

Cyrill integrated his videos in his personal site on YouTube and MySpace. He names his space on MySpace 'cypictures', which refers to his user name on some internet pages. His video bears the logo 'Cyril pictures', which gives the impression of professional backing and corresponds to the institutional offers and adverts of video internet sites.

In the foreground of his site on MySpace are:

- the presentation of himself and
- the follow-up communication in guestbooks and through comments, which is typical for such sites.

He presents himself in a varied manner, from being hurt and vulnerable to being a gang fighter, but also as trend-setter in terms of fashion and style.

The modes of presentation, e.g. using a rotating cube, require an elaborate knowledge and handling of relevant software. This expertise finds expression in follow-up communication (Fig. 4.18).

Cyrill's Online and Mobile/Cell Phone Usage in the Context of German Usage Data from 2007

With his use of Web 2.0 and its community functions, Cyrill is characteristic of the mainstream amongst 12–19 year olds in 2007 in terms of usage of the internet, communication and social networking. This tendency seems to apply also to the use of

Fig. 4.18 derschatz (The treasure – or: the darling?) (Source: http://www.myspace.com/cypictures), 15 Jan 2008

mobile/cell phones, as the data below show. The only difference to the mainstream is that Cyrill is one of the few young people who are actively providing content on the internet instead of merely retrieving information. In general, reception is a more dominant usage pattern of the 12–19 years olds than production, and the internet is used as tool for information retrieval whilst the mobile/cell phone can be considered to be a tool for production in the widest sense.

For some years now, mobile media are ranging amongst the top 10 of young people's most preferred media. Especially the mobile/cell phone is playing a dominant role. In 2008, 96% females and 94% males between 12 and 19 years of age owned at least one mobile/cell phone. No other medium is owned as frequently as this device, and only television and the computer are used more often in leisure time. The functionality of mobile/cell phones for young people ranges between entertainment (using the phone as MP3-player or playing games on the mobile/cell phone) and regulation of emotions/interaction with others (contact to friends, expression of feelings by SMS). Also 'inspiration' by means of using the mobile/cell phone as style and prestige object or as trading platform for music, videos and pictures is an important issue for adolescents (Bauer Media 2007, p. 46).

Mobile/Cell Phones – Tools for Conversation, Production and Distribution

According to the JIM-Studie 2008 (Mpfs 2008) young people between 12 and 19 are using mobile/cell phones for conversation, entertainment, organisation and archiving:

- text based conversation: SMS (text messaging); e-mail
- voice based conversation: telephone
- entertainment: listen to music; gaming; listen to radio; watch mobile TV
- entertainment production/documentation: taking pictures; recording videos
- information retrieval: news services; surf the web
- archive/database: trade data via blue tooth and MMS (photos, films, music).

A closer look at the categorisation of mobile/cell phone functions reveals the following:

- Conversation is conducted by synchronous voice communication as well as via asynchronous text-based communication. Synchronous text-based communication such as chat is not common.
- As entertainment media, music and games are in evidence as is mobile TV; watching films or videos on the other hand is less in evidence. Picture taking and video recording is more prevalent than sound recording or production.
- Data exchange relates to the distribution of content and to archiving. The mobile/cell phone can be used as (transitory) data storage.
- The use of mobile/cell phones for organisation, which appeared still in 2007 with reference to the clock function of the phone, is not mentioned any longer in 2008.

For the 12–19 year olds communication is central as is entertainment. Up- and down-loading of data and P2P are practiced by engaging in communication, entertainment and information retrieval.

Internet – Space for Conversation, Information Retrieval and Entertainment

Examples of mobile learning practice also include the use of convergent media such as internet platforms or weblogs. This technological convergence, which seems to be central and has an important symbiotic function in the field of mobile learning practice, leads to questions about internet activities of 12–19 year olds in everyday life. Conversation, entertainment and archiving are at the centre of young people's internet activities just as they are of their activities with mobile/cell phones. Additionally, information retrieval and production (participation) as well as commerce apply to the usage patterns of 12–19 year olds:

- text based conversation: instant messaging; e-mail; chat
- voice based conversation: voice over IP
- entertainment: listening to music and sounds; watching films and videos, web TV; gaming; listening to web radio
- entertainment production/documentation: podcasting
- information retrieval: general information (not for school); news; information for school and job; newsgroups; regional events; sports live ticker; read Weblogs; use search engines and Wikipedia
- information production: writing in newsgroups and Weblogs
- social networking: online communities
- commerce: buying online
- archive/database: music, film and video download; uploading videos and pictures; uploading music/sounds.

Based on these data, the following conclusions for handling information or engaging in communication by using different functions and modes can be drawn:

- Conversation is text-based and uses different formats. Synchronous and asynchronous tools are used as well as formats, which are either short in length and specified language (such as chat language) or more formal letters. Voice-based communication as an equivalent to telephone conversation is not used very frequently.
- Entertainment ranges from listening to music, sounds and web radio to watching films, videos and web TV, and gaming. Young people are the receivers/consumers of these formats and rarely providers of e.g. podcasts.
- Young people retrieve information rather than produce information; information is either accessed via web pages, search engines, Wikipedia or received via news tickers and newsgroups; only a few make written contributions to newsgroups and weblogs.
- Commerce is related to buying something on the internet.
- Music, film and video download is presumably done with the purpose of storing music, to build a repository, a data base or an archive.
- Social networking is practiced by more than 50% of the 12–19 year olds.

Related to internet use, communication, participation and negotiation seem to be central activities for the 12–19 year olds – besides activities, which can be characterised as entertainment.

Cyrill can be deemed to be an advanced user of computers, photos and videos. His activities are not uncommon within this segment but he is certainly using digital technologies for production purposes to a greater extent than many peers.

Notions of Mobility

Cyrill's Wider Network – Different User Names, Different Platforms, Different Roles

Having a closer look at Cyrill's further web activities (as far as it was possible to track his traces) makes obvious that he uses different usernames and platforms to present different facets of his personality: from rude and self-excluding to participating and integrative. His pages and content provide a basis for follow-up communication for visitors. He addresses himself differently to different target groups and audiences. By doing so, Cyrill is showing a notion of mobility, which is related to mobility of concepts of the self. Considering these identities, which are characterised by different web spaces, user names and contents, as different facets of a greater whole rather than identities, which are separate and stand next to each other, provides a quite comprehensive image of his person and personality.

Cyrill's mobility is not limited to aspects of his identity, but also his practices and interests. Cyrill appears as producer of content, provider of information, searcher for information and participant in discussions. He uses written language, photos, images and films to communicate and to be active in different areas of interest. His interests range from a critical estimation of social situations (being an underdog by using the example of homeless people as well as written statements on his YouTube page or in timeshot.de-discussions), over self-representation (being a friend and integrated member of different peer groups – hip hopper, rapper, friend, military; being a dressman and 'gentleman'), to providing and receiving support and advice in specific issue-related fields (using technology and software). Different platforms and different user names are used by Cyrill to switch between extremes: his role as an outsider on the one hand and a trendsetter on the other. In between are his social relations, his friends and parties as well as teaching and learning about media production.

Cyrill seems to be very self-confident in terms of his style. His self-esteem is strongly related to design and aesthetics, as well as to his physical appearance and his body. The fact that he provides his pictures on GQ.com to a huge and critical community gives evidence of his self assurance concerning his taste for fashion. Also evident is the huge number of photos of himself on his sites. He often appears as a posturing model – be it as beaten victim, powerful culprit, or posh designer – showing his body with or without clothes.

His aim to be professionally creative is not explicitly verbalised by Cyrill. Nevertheless, he offers his t-shirt creations on an internet market place, and thus demonstrates his ambitions concerning his potential to be professionally active in this field.

Replicability and Transferability/Approaches to Teaching and Learning

Media convergence is a central feature in Cyrill's life. He is present on different internet platforms, which provide space for him to express different facets of his

concerned with the protection of minors in the media sector provide comprehensive websites with information and tips for young people, parents and teachers about how to avoid or how to deal with risky situations in terms of inappropriate use of mobile/cell phones (see for example http://www.handysektor.de, http://www.klicksafe.de, http://www.handywissen.at, http://www.internet-abc.ch, http://www.phonebrain.org.uk, http://www.outofyourhands.com, http://www.bull ying.co.uk). In schools, prevention was realised in the form of prohibition and critical reflection: mobile/cell phones were often banned from schools and classrooms. However, in schools, the discourse about inappropriate use of mobile/cell phones was one of the early motivations for the discursive and productive process of integration of mobile/cell phones in curricular activities – starting with using the mobile/cell phone as topic, i.e. to critically reflect on opportunities and risks which the use of mobile/cell phones brings along: some teachers and pupils initiated working groups to critically engage in the discourses around the mobile/cell phone in social contexts such as violence and debt (e.g. Alfred-Teves-Schule 2008). Referring to the discussion about debt, some teachers started to teach Maths by using contracts and rates for mobile/cell phones (e.g. the teaching unit 'Handy-Tarife'; Finck 2001). Linear functions and linear equations are explained by using rates for mobile/cell phones as an initial point and calculation basis. This idea – metaphorically speaking – killed two birds with one stone: pupils learned how to calculate linear functions and linear equations; at the same time, they had to reflect on their own behaviour as consumer in relation to mobile/cell phone usage: which rates are included in the contract with my mobile/cell phone provider? How many text messages do I send during a certain time span? How long do I talk with my friend on my phone? Is a prepaid card cheaper than a contract? Where are the advantages depending on my individual habits? As study from market research e.g. gives evidence to, there is uncertainty amongst young people in how to handle different provider options and technologies (Bauer Media 2004, p. 34). Thus, school has clear reasons to choose the debt question as a central issue and to critically reflect pupils' options and needs.

Mobile Learning Between Narrow and Teacher-Led Use and Constructivist and Open Settings

Mobile learning in the examples, which we are using in this chapter reverts to mobile/cell phones as tools. Mobile/cell phones are used with a view to a specific curricular task, which is defined by the teacher in advance. And they refer to a repository in the form of a platform or a weblog in order to store material and have it available for later recall. With reference to the activities, the learners are either led or they are free to choose how to use the mobile devices. The didactic design ranges between behaviourist approaches to learning on the one hand, and open education with elements of experimental and playful approaches to learning on the other. In more general terms, one can find mobile/cell phones conceptualised as tools in a quite narrow sense, with a focus on the transmission of information, or one can find a focus on the agency and cultural practices of the learners as well as on situated learning and the affordances of mobile/cell phones.

The Didactic Design is Determining the Way Mobile Learning is Realised

The use of mobile media for learning does not necessarily implement 'spontaneous, personal, informal, contextual, portable, ubiquitous (available everywhere) and pervasive (so integrated with daily activities that it is hardly noticed)' (Kukulska-Hulme 2005, p. 2), or even 'highly situated, personal, collaborative and long term; in other words, truly learner-centred learning' (Naismith et al. 2004). Furthermore, the didactic design is determining for the activities undertaken by the learner and the location where learning takes place. Mobile learning can also mean learning with portable devices without using or considering their most original functions such as the telephone or text messaging functions, including the option to learn across contexts or to refer to convergent media and structures.

Capturing Situations or Generating Contexts? From Ad-hoc Usage to 'Delayed' Use

Convergent media, such as platforms and weblogs, are used as repositories or archives; their relevance for information retrieval, which is one of the activities in which young people engage most often outside school, is not the dominant functionality in school. Instead, they host documents, which were produced with the mobile/cell phone, e.g. pictures, films or audio recordings etc. for reliability, sustainability and later recall. In view of the omission of conversation and information retrieval in many projects, one might assume that the meaning-making process, the building of common and negotiated meanings and knowledge, is 'outsourced' to a further medium[16], and as a consequence one could say that the immediacy and 'ad hoc' notions inherent in mobile devices are not maximised, as well as that mobile/cell phones serve as tools for capturing immediacy or situations rather than enabling pupils to access and generate situations and contexts in situ. Such specific uses – ad hoc or at a later stage in the learning process – might be intended by the teacher, who is setting the didactic design (e.g. with focus on content, context or affordances); or they might not be used by pupils because learners try to meet the requirements of school learning in terms of rules and regulations. However, an opportunity, which is included, is that all learners will have access to the learning material on a platform and are not dependent on a situative success or failure of their current task.

---

[16]For knowledge building and meaning making by using Weblogs see e.g. Shao et al. (2007), for archives e.g. Featherstone (2006).

Re-contextualisation and Situated Negotiation: Determined Use or Free Space?

A look at the functionalities (i.e. the affordances, which are envisaged by using a specific function) within the examples might yield some evidence for a 'break' between the two contexts of school and everyday life: the mobile/cell phone tends to be a communicative device in terms of conversation in everyday life contexts of young people, whereas it is 're-contextualised' and becomes e.g. a device for documentation in school. One could say that such a shift might be negotiated in use (by means of Bakardjeva's (2005) and Cook et al.'s (2007) notion of learner-generated contexts; see also Chapter 11). But one could also argue that the set of rules and regulations in school and for school learning might cause the children to act without allowing themselves to refer to their agency and cultural practices and to notions of mobile/cell phones, which are related to fun and conversation. Conversation is indeed not as often used in these mobile learning settings as one could assume. The exclusion of this typical everyday life use of the mobile/cell phone marks a break between everyday life and school, a notion of 'discontinuity'; it also points to the fact that communicative and discursive practices in the process of meaning-making, which are based on conversation, are not the core issues in all mobile learning projects. Viewed from this perspective, the question about convergence and the opportunity of mobile devices to provide structures in order to allow seamless transitions between different learning contexts has to be concretised here: even if technological convergence is available and used, notions of convergence, which point to the learners' habitus, agency and cultural practices are often left out. At this point, mobile learning concepts might be revised towards use rather than to settle for technological convergences.

Mobile Devices and Convergent Media Allow for Learners to Examine and Establish Structures to Construct Their Own and Individualised Learning Spaces

The variety of learning outcomes, which are available from the three cases, is broad. Mobile devices are used in connection with online platforms such as websites, fora, weblogs, discussion boards and PCs. The learners didn't reduce their activities to written and text message such as texts only, but used also images, videos and sound as modes in order to complete their tasks; they used all kinds of modes which they are considering as being adequate to make their meanings and understanding of learning available to others, and especially to the teacher, whose intention might be to assess the pupils' products in school terms. Here, it becomes obvious that, in the dynamics of changing mass communication, 'text' must not be interpreted in a narrow sense only, i.e. written text or spoken language. Pupils and young people are familiar with different modes of representation from their everyday life use of media and media formats, and are able to use different modes and media for conversation, communication and learning. However, it also became evident that it is still the teacher and his or her didactic concept that determines the scope in which learners can act. The more open the teacher leaves the space for learners to engage in learning material and school-related tasks in the way they deem it to be appropriate, the more space they are granting to learners to include their agency, structures and cultural practices into school learning, and the more space they are providing to learners to construct and realise their own learning habitus. By doing so, teachers enable learners to establish their own strategies for lifelong learning, but they also open school towards the learners. In this way, school can be a place where situated and contextual learning with notions of personalised learning and meaning-making can be scaffolded and moderated in order to provide a basis for common meaning-making and learning.

Chapter 5
Whither a Socio-Cultural Ecology of Learning with Mobile Devices

Introduction

In this chapter we attempt an overview, and critique of the dominant theoretical and conceptual frames currently used by researchers to explain and analyse learning with mobile devices. In particular, we discuss Activity Theory (Engeström) as well as, to a lesser extent, situated learning theory (Lave and Wenger), the Conversational Framework (Laurillard) and the Ecology of Resources Model (Luckin). We conclude that, whilst they are of merit, the dominant frame, Activity Theory (AT), is characterised by a number of features and weaknesses, which makes it unsuitable for our purposes.

The discussion of learner-generated contexts in Chapter 2 has brought to the fore the dynamic interdependence of numerous variables governing the processes of learning in general, and learning with mobile devices in particular. Winters (2007, pp. 9–10), for example, points out that a key characteristic of learning with mobile devices lies in it being contingent upon a number of aspects including emerging contexts (incl. environment, time, spaces, institutional support, infrastructure), curricula, cultures (of use), ethics, tools and their affordances, learning activities, access to, and relationship with, information and people, communication, communities, learning histories, and appropriation.

As already noted in Chapter 1, we view the emergence of learning with mobile devices not as a condition of learning per se, but as an educational response to complex cultural changes in socialisation, in particular individualisation in a risk society (Giddens 1999; Beck 1992), and in the structures of media organisation in society, in particular the shift in mass communication away from institutionally centralised editorial systems to an individualised 'mobile' system of generating content and contexts for learning. This structural change in the media and of the relationship of the subject and society is also characterised by new, portable and functionally convergent media tools and attendant patterns of appropriation around personally motivated use of media and knowledge within individual frames of everyday life as well as individualised developmental perspectives. We are particularly interested in their location within informal and across a diverse range of contexts, networks and resources for knowledge generation and meaning-making characterised by learner

N. Pachler et al., *Mobile Learning*, DOI 10.1007/978-1-4419-0585-7_5,

agency. And, we see learner agency in the context of learning as meaning-making not as an arbitrary pedagogic choice but as the logical response to socio-cultural individualisation and individualised mobile mass communication.

In our reading of the mobile and technology-enhanced learning literature we have failed to encounter a conceptual model, which – in our view – adequately explains and theorises the full complexity of learning with mobile devices as conceived of by us, in particular the need to rethink media as cultural resources in the process of the development of children into individual and responsible adults. As a consequence, we undertake the development of what we term a 'socio-cultural ecological approach' in this book. In this context we deem it necessary to discuss the most pertinent theoretical perspectives and explanatory conceptual frames to date with a view to exploring their respective characteristics, strengths and weaknesses.

In proposing an analytical frame in this book, our aim is to offer a scheme that is readily operationalisable and articulates with the professional 'lifeworlds' of teachers/educators. For reasons discussed in this chapter, we are not convinced that existing frames, in particular AT, meet such criteria. Yet, we devote significant space in this book to AT because of its prevalence in the emerging theoretical literature on the use of mobile devices for teaching and learning as well as on educational discourse more widely. And, we wish to substantiate the need, in our view, to look towards an alternative theoretical frame of reference, namely a socio-cultural ecological approach.

As already noted in Chapter 1 and by way of a brief contextualisation of the discussion of conceptual frames in this chapter, we are particularly interested in the appropriation of mobile technologies in the life-worlds of users. The notion of life-worlds has its roots in phenomenology and philosophy, is associated with the work of scholars such as Alfred Schütz (1967/1932), and denotes the world as experienced in the perceptual subjectivity of everyday life. The concept of life-world is a response to the changed agency of people in the industrial society in order to assimilate its structures. This assimilation can be seen to occur in relation to relevant structures of people's practices, who transform these structures within cultural practices into the realities of their lives. The basic dynamic relates to meaning-making in the context of personal actions. We are interested in the role of digital technologies, in particular mobile devices, in these processes as well as on how personal practices in everyday life, which are increasingly governed by individualised construction of what is 'real' within socio-cultural milieus in a risk society, relate to learning in formal and informal contexts.

In our understanding of it, the concept of appropriation focuses on the processes 'learners' engage in when using mobile media within existing or new cultural practices of everyday life or educational institutions (for a detailed discussion see Pachler et al. 2010). We see appropriation of mobile devices closely linked to learning with mobile devices understood as a process of meaning-making within social structures, cultural practices and agency. Agency for us manifests itself as the learner's social and semiotic capacity, i.e. their ability to form relationships with others (mediated by technology) as well as to make meaning and develop representations of the world using a range of sign systems such as language or images.

Within everyday life, mobile devices, especially the mobile/cell phone, have become embedded and taken for granted by being appropriated as part of a process of individualised agency and within the practices of everyday life. In general, we view meaning-making as the theoretical and practical link between the everyday life use of mobile/cell phones and learning as 'coming to know'. From our perspective mobile/cell phones can function as learning resources also within the cultural practices of educational institutions with their definitions of learning. And, we consider it very significant that learning as process of meaning-making occurs through acts of communication on the basis of a pre-given, objectified cultural world characterised by rapidly changing socio-cultural, mass communication and technological structures.

Activity Theory

There has been a particular interest in the literature in AT, most readily associated with Yrjö Engeström, as an explanatory theoretical frame for learning with mobile devices. AT can be seen as a heuristic device, which is rooted in Vygotsky's and cultural-historical psychology, Marxist theory (in particular the concepts of commodity, contradiction and use and exchange value) and Leont'ev's developmental psychology.

It has so-called 'activity systems' as its units of analysis comprising a subject acting on an object (i.e. purpose) with a view to transforming it using mediating artefacts, be they physical or conceptual (symbolic or embodied) and be they enabling or limiting, in order to achieve an outcome. The subject is in turn deemed to be influenced by the rules of the context (explicit and implicit norms, conventions and social relations), the community and division of labour (explicit and implicit organisation of a community in relation to the transformation of the object into an outcome) (see

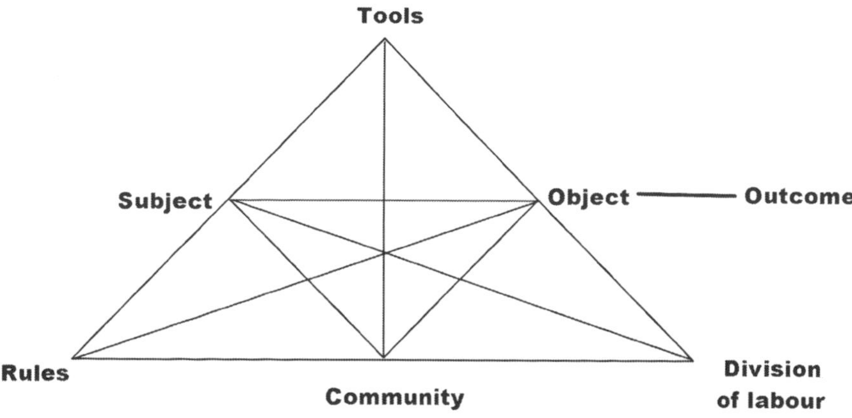

Fig. 5.1 Activity system (Engeström 1987) (Source: Taylor et al. 2006, p. 8)

Fig. 5.1). Some commentators stress the importance of the three-way interaction between subjects, objects and community. The 'object of activity' within individual activity systems is widely considered to be the key component of this heuristic, the so-called 'sense maker', which affords meaning and determines the values of various components (see Hardman 2007, p. 111; Kaptelinin 2005; Wali et al. 2008, pp. 45–48).

> The object of activity has a dual status; it is both a projection of human mind onto the objective world and a projection of the world onto human mind. Employing the object of activity as a conceptual lens means anchoring and contextualising subjective phenomena in the objective world, and changes one's perspective on both the mind and the world. Instead of being a collection of 'mental processes', the human mind emerges as biased, striving for meaning and value, suffering and rejoicing, failing and hoping, alive, real. On the other hand, the world is no longer just a collection of physical bodies, organizational structures, and so forth, but a place full of meaning and value, a place that can be comfortable or dangerous, restricting or supporting, beautiful or ugly, or (as is often the case) all of these at the same time. (Kaptelinin 2005, p. 5)

Activity theorists see the object-orientatedness of an activity system as a key characteristic and proponents of AT espouse different definitions of an object (see Hardman 2007; Kaptelinin 2005). Engeström (1987) views activities as collective phenomena and posits that 'individuals can carry out actions oriented towards goals only within the wider arena of a collective' (Hardman 2007, p. 116). He also relates the object of activity to production; and 'by highlighting the dual nature of the object as both material and ideal, what emerges is a notion of the object as containing within it both the "what" and the "why" of the activity' (Hardman 2007, p. 116).

With reference to Engeström (2001), Avis (2009, pp. 158–159) discusses five principles that underpin AT:

> 1. A collective, artefact-mediated and object orientated activity system, seen in its network relations to other activity systems, is the prime unit of analysis.
> 2. Activity systems are multi-voiced and the division of labour creates different positions for participants, who carry their own diverse histories, and the activity system itself carries multiple layers and strands of history.
> 3. Activity systems take shape and get transformed over lengthy periods of time (historicity).
> 4. Contradictions (historically accumulating structural tensions within and between activity systems) play a central role as sources of change and development.
> 5. There exists the possibility of expansive transformation (i.e. learning) in activity systems.

Transformation over time is linked for Engeström (2001, p. 152) to the questioning of current arrangements and can result in expansive learning and represented diagrammatically (Fig. 5.2).

More recently, Engeström (2008) puts forward the notion of 'knotworking and agency in fluid organisational fields'. Knotworking, according to Engeström et al. (1999), relates to dynamically changing and distributed collaborative processes attendant to work on tasks and emergent objects organized among actors who do not usually know each other beforehand and activity systems not previously connected.

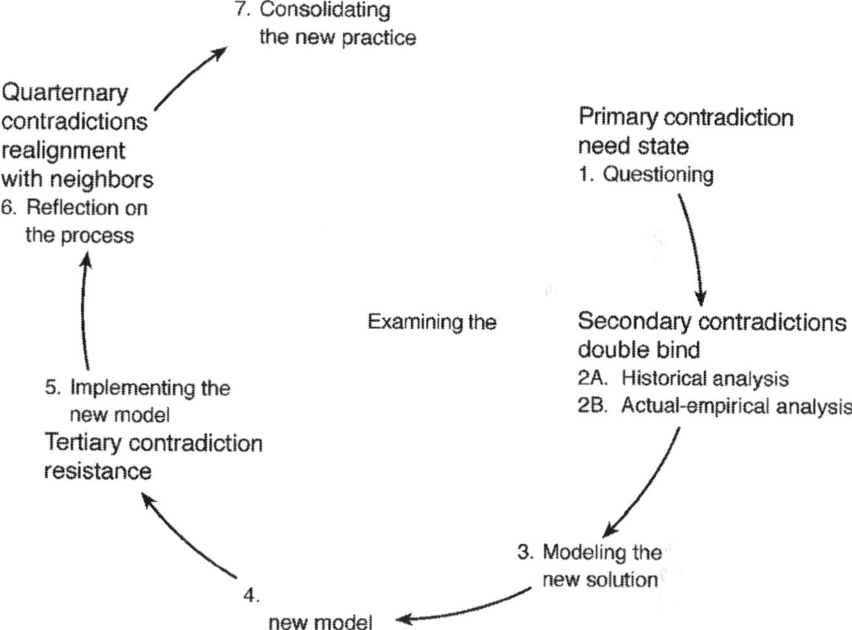

Fig. 5.2 Strategic learning actions and corresponding contradictions in the cycle of expansive learning (Engeström 2001, p. 152, Fig. 11)

> I make an attempt to hybridize three relatively separate fields of inquiry: 'theories and studies of collective intentionality and distributed agency… (2) theories and studies of social capital in organizations, and (3) cultural-historical activity theory' (p. 199). Engeström draws on a diverse range of literature to support what he calls the emerging notion of 'collaborative intentionality capital' (p. 200).

Although Engeström maintains that 'careful analysis of the activity systems involved [using his triangular model] is more important than ever' (p. 229), he also notes that 'negotiation is a central coordinating mechanism of the distributed agency required in knotworking within social production' (p. 230), and by using the example of the Open Source community, he notes that social production of systems like Linux is dependent on publically accessible critical commentary and peer review (p. 230).

We propose that reference to the structures of individualisation and risk society are more tangible than the metaphorical arguments involved in 'knotworking and agency in fluid organisational fields'. Indeed, we maintain that the structures of individualisation and risk society also provide a link to the agency of the learner in order to deal with meaning-making in different social environments (see also Pachler et al. 2010). In short, we favour a focus on the subject rather than the object. AT's notion of a division of labour can be seen to be part of a socio-cultural ecology. Yet, as our focus is on consumption and appropriation by the subject and as we are interested in questions such as why mobile/cell phones have become so prevalent in modern life, we consider agency of the subject to be a more powerful analytical tool.

We believe there to be difficulties in relation to defining (learning) objects as we consider them to be increasingly inseparable from learner-generated content and contexts, i.e. the agency of individual learners. Clearly, the (learning) object is not irrelevant but content and context are more important for us. We view learning objects as cultural products and in this function they are equivalent to generated contexts. Like all cultural products they operate through appropriation. Traditional media structures (editorial control, push etc) are breaking away, and we are moving towards mass archives, which are increasingly user-defined. In the context of life-worlds characterised by learner-generated contexts and by learners having to set reference points for themselves, we are more focussed on processes and not objects. Our rejection of AT is in part, therefore, motivated by not wishing to become side-tracked by explanations of how the world is constructed that are abstract and general (e.g. about objects and their relationship to the subject); instead, we are interested in dynamic and rather unpredictable activities and processes, in contexts of learning and their cultural history, the life-worlds of learners and ontology, i.e. the theory of being, which emphasises the importance of sociology, culture and media studies and only to a lesser extent philosophy and natural sciences.

Conversation and Discursive Appropriation as Contextual and Reflexive Activity

Mike Sharples, Josie Taylor, Giasemi Vavoula and colleagues (Taylor et al. 2006; Sharples et al. 2007), coming from a socio-cognitive engineering design perspective, have attempted to develop what they call ‘a theory of learning for the mobile age’ based on the synthesis of relevant theoretical approaches, in particular AT as well as Diana Laurillard’s Conversational Framework based on a dialectic cycle of theorising, design and evaluation. The Conversational Framework can be viewed as an appropriation model that locates communicative activities within teaching and learning frames.

Laurillard’s (2002, 2007) model is based on the notion of the learning process as a ‘conversation’ between the teacher and the student that operates at a discursive and interactive level linked by reflection and adaptation. Learning is viewed as a series of iterative conversations with the external world and its artefacts, with oneself, with other learners and, of course, teachers. Laurillard stresses the importance of the learner being in control of activities, able to test ideas by performing experiments, asking questions, collaborating with other people, seeking out new knowledge and planning new actions. We, too, draw on the Conversational Framework as an analytical tool later on in this book but not so much in terms of a theoretical framework but as a useful description of teaching and learning practices inside and outside of educational institutions (Fig. 5.3).

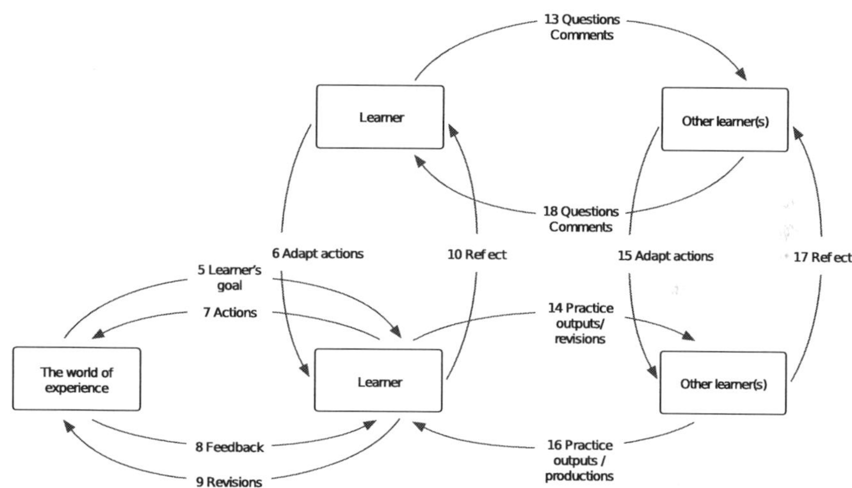

Fig. 5.3 The conversational framework for supporting the formal learning process (Source: Laurillard 2007, p. 160)

Taylor et al. (2006, p. 2) argue for 'a separation between the semiotics of a learning situation – in terms of knowledge, language and conceptual resources needed for effective learning – and the embodiment of these functionalities in specific devices or constellations of devices'. By that they mean that learners 'know what kind of functionalities (resources for learning) they would like around them to be effective, and will seek these out as and when they need them' (2006, p. 14). This process they view as 'appropriation' (2007, pp. 235–236). Our view of appropriation is more differentiated than that (see e.g. Pachler et al. 2010; Cook and Pachler 2010). We define appropriation as the processes attendant to the development of personal practices with mobile devices and we consider these processes in the main to be interaction, assimilation and accommodation as well as change. We find Piaget's (1955) take on learning and perception helpful in this context. With reference to him, assimilation for us refers to the integration of the mobile devices and their attendant socio-cultural practices into one's own practices drawing on one's semiotic and learning capacities. And we view accommodation as the complementary process of fitting practices into given structures and practices on the basis of the mobile user's agency. Therefore, assimilation in the context of learning means that a learner takes something unknown into her existing cognitive structures, whereas accommodation refers to the changing of cognitive structures to make sense of the environment. For us, the context of appropriation is emergent and not predetermined by events. And, we place centrality on practice, which can be viewed as a learner's engagement with particular settings, in which context becomes 'embodied interaction' (Dourish 2004).

In order to be of value, Taylor et al. (2006, p. 6) argue that a theory of mobile learning must be relevant for formal as well as informal settings, account for the dynamics of learning, physical mobility as well as changes in social environment and in access to resources.

> A relevant theory of learning must embrace contemporary accounts of the practices and ontogeny of learning. Learning is a constructive process, involving the active construction of knowledge. It is both a social and a cognitive activity, occurring within a rich milieu of physical and cultural tools, settings and social interactions. And it comprises not only a process of continual personal development and enrichment, but also the possibility of rapid and radical conceptual change. (Taylor et al. 2006, p. 6)

Taylor et al. also argue (2006, p. 9) that Engeström's model (see Fig. 5.1) insufficiently emphasises that learning is an internal and external conversation, that activities are contextual, that human activity systems have reflexive potential and that, therefore, AT needs to be consolidated with approaches taken from conversation theory (see Pask 1976; Laurillard 2002, 2007), which in turn is premised on a view of learning as conversations between different knowledge systems with technology providing support for modelling as well as an environment that enables conversation.

They see essential differences between mobile learning and other types of learning activity in terms of the mobility of learners across space, contexts, time (and transition points) and topics as well as in terms of learners moving in and out of engagement with personal and shared technology (2007, pp. 222–224). In addition, we see mobile learning as being structured by the 'mobile complex' (see Chapters 1, 6 and 8), which leads to new and individualised forms of mass communication as well as to new individualised socio-cultural stratification by milieus. In these new social structures mobility and available contexts are important. To move from one point to another with a mobile/cell phone in one's hand is just the visible part of a cultural transformation. One defining feature of the mobile complex is that it consists of contexts as available cultural products for personal disposal. Such contexts appear within media convergence and socio-cultural milieus (e.g. see the case of Cyrill in Chapters 4 and 10). They also note that a central concern must be 'to understand how people artfully engage with their surroundings to create impromptu sites of learning' (2007, p. 223).

On the basis of this, and premised on their definition of mobile learning as 'the process of coming to know through conversations across multiple contexts among people and personal interactive technologies' (2007, p. 225), Taylor et al. develop the framework for analysing mobile learning in Fig. 5.4, which – according to the authors – aims 'to provide a coherent account of how the activities are performed, the people involved, the contexts, the tools and technologies they employ, the structure of the tasks and an account of their cognitive processes, management of knowledge, and social interactions' (2006, p. 17).

The focus of this framework can be seen to be on the communicative interaction between the learning and technology with the aim of achieving an outcome of revised knowledge and skills. Learning and cognition in this model are distributed and meaning-making and knowledge generation, which evolve the state of knowing of the learning system, take place through exchange. For the authors, the agency for

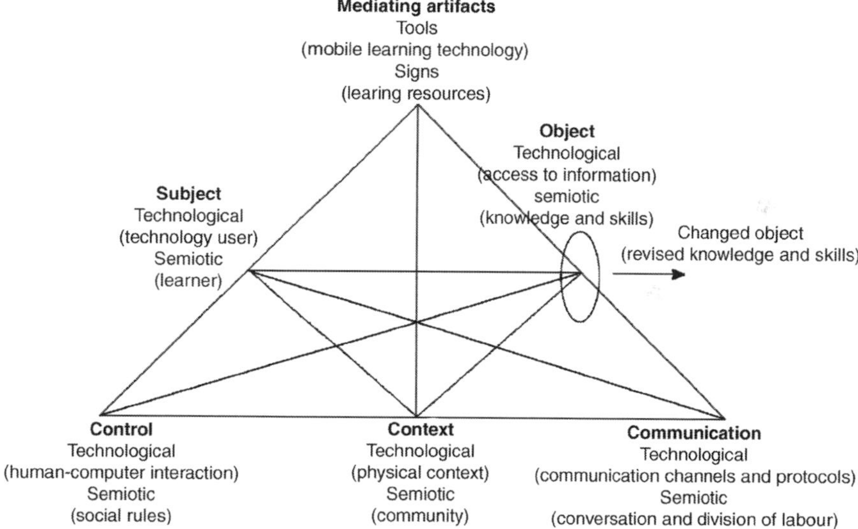

Fig. 5.4 A framework for analysing mobile learning (Taylor et al. 2006, p. 16 and in a slightly modified form also Sharples et al. 2007, p. 233)

learning is not with a single individual, nor with the technology but in the synergy between the different parts of the system (2007, p. 244).

The authors (Sharples et al. 2007, p. 243) note that their framework 'does not give sufficient importance to what it is that makes a learning activity valuable, to the role of teachers in promoting effective learning, to classrooms as well as organized locations for study, and to educational institutions in extending and validating learners' knowledge'. We would argue that as with Engeström's original model, the level of abstraction is too high for it to be readily operationalisable and, therefore, the model is arguably of limited value for policy makers and practitioners.

Continuity of Learning Activities Between and Across Contexts

In a recent paper, Wali et al. (2008) critique Sharples et al.'s framework. Whilst they, too, draw on AT, their focus is on the continuity of learning activities between and across contexts, physical and social settings, which they describe as 'context crossing' (p. 48). Whilst they consider Sharples et al.'s definition of mobile learning to have some merit, particularly in terms of conceptualising 'context as the physical environment and the community that interacts around shared objectives' (pp. 44–45), they posit that there is a need for a greater focus on learning as practice as well as on context, both in terms of 'that which surrounds us' and 'that which weaves together' (Cole 1996; see also Dourish 2004). They also argue that there is no need to introduce two layers to represent the semiotic and technological dimensions of

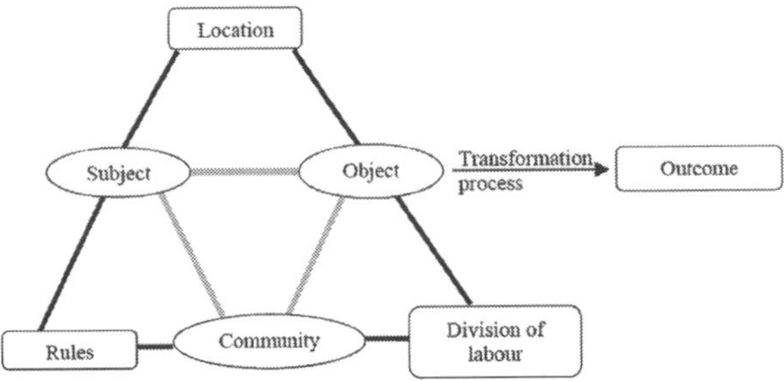

Fig. 5.5 Wali et al.'s framework for analysing mobile learning (2008, p. 55)

activity (p. 48). Their definition of mobile learning is: 'learning that occurs as a result of pursuing activities that are directed towards achieving the same objective across multiple contexts (physical and social)' (p. 55). They stress the importance of viewing context both in terms of the features of the environment in which learning takes place as well as the social setting of the learning activities (p. 47). Compared with Sharples et al., not the community dimension of the AT triangle changes to context, but the tool dimension becomes subsumed under the concept of 'location' (see Fig. 5.5). This, in our view, belittles the importance of the conceptual tools involved in learning, in particular language and other semiotic means.

According to their definition, it is the continuity of learning activities in different contexts that makes learning mobile (p. 56). We are not convinced that the visual representation in Fig. 5.5 captures this notion adequately.

Whilst we agree with their emphasis on learning and practice, which in our framework is captured by our focus on socio-cultural practices mainly concerning the appropriation of media resources for purposes of cultural participation and personal development as well as by our view of learning as meaning-making, we consider Wali et al.'s framework to remain too abstract. And, we feel the framework insufficiently connects with the fundamental changes currently taking place in everyday life, in particular the changing socio-cultural and mass communication structures within the context of an individual risk society.

Activity Theory: A Critical Perspective

AT is a highly sophisticated conceptual construct that has a multi-facetted philosophical and scientific underpinning. However, its complexity makes it very difficult to simplify. In our view, and that of some recent commentators (see for example the Special Issue on 'Critical perspectives on activity theory' published by the journal *Educational Review* in May 2009) a full understanding of AT, we believe, is predicated on an engagement inter alia with its philosophical and political roots. Yet, there is no, or at best little evidence in the current debates in the field of mobile learning of such an engagement with AT.

We consider AT lacking in the ontological breadth required to capture the cultural practices and social structures we consider to be of particular importance in relation to a full understanding of learning with mobile devices. Like Peim (2009, p. 170), we deem AT to be limited in scope to address macro-social and political processes.

We do not consider it to have the necessary simplicity to be of immediate appeal to practitioners and policy makers who tend not to be steeped in the attendant discourses.

We recognize that AT offers the potential of a shared language with which to discuss and analyse learning processes taking place around the use of mobile devices but we consider the philosophical and political baggage to constitute a historical barrier, which potentially obfuscates, rather than illuminates attendant issues. Yet categories of AT, in order to be properly understood, we would argue, have to be read in the context of historical discourses, which are not always readily understood and which can be argued to have lost at least some of their currency with the passage of time. Indeed, Peim (2009, p. 167) argues that AT was characterized by a desire to 'unmoor itself from any awkward political affiliations' and argues that 'it is an odd feature of this socio-cultural historical theory that it reduces all of those dimensions – the social, the cultural, the historical – to apolitical abstractions'.

The fact that the conceptual heritage is based on problematical translations of texts, in particular by Vygostky, from Russian into English, can be seen to be adding levels of complexity with which we too are having to grapple (see Chapter 1).

At a theoretical level, we find the notion of learning as the acquisition of objects, as well as the distinction between learning subjects and objects, problematic. For us the notion of context is defining. We do not see the pedagogical challenge lie in the creation of sets for learning but in how mobile devices can be used as cultural resources for learning. As such we consider AT to be reductionist in nature and focus on a description of what is, rather than on transformation.

Peim (2009, p. 173) raises the question of the analytical power of AT as well as the plausibility of the idea of activity as a fundamental unit of analysis in the context of the considerable scope, structure and significance of activities: where does an activity system begin and where does it end? (p. 174). For him (p. 176), as for us, one key question concerns 'what it is that binds the components of the activity system together?' He rightly notes in our view that goal orientation appears to drive the mobilization of the system but that there is no account of subjectivity, subjective experiences, subjective motivation or subjective differences.

Arguably also, AT insufficiently foregrounds the ideational dimension and inner contradictions and focuses mostly on the material.

Bakhurst (2009, p. 206) wonders whether AT is a theory at all and whether it is better conceived of as a model or a schema with 'minimal predictive power' but which can be 'a useful heuristic in reference to certain kinds of activity' (p. 207). He also notes that AT tends to work well where there exists 'a reasonably well-defined object, a pretty good sense of desirable outcomes, a self-identifying set of subjects, a good sense of what might count as an instrument or tool, etc' (p. 206). And, he questions the rationale for the triangular structure as opposed to, for example, a list of factors and points out that the model says almost nothing about the relation the various components bear to one another and how they are constitutive of each other (p. 207).

Gay et al. (2002) view AT as a possible 'framework and discursive (resource) with which to talk about and understand human activities, conceived as multilevel, multi-dimensional, dynamic, collective, context-sensitive, and mediated by cultural artefacts'. And Nardi (1996) argues that one important insight afforded by AT is the ontological difference between technology and people with the former mediating human activity, rather than being on an equal footing. We contend that these analytical functions of AT offer a rather formal frame and argue that AT backgrounds, if not altogether ignores, the process of appropriation, which we view as central to a full understanding of the use of mobile devices for learning. The notion of a 'division of labour' for us does not possess the constituting dynamic of social structures and cultural practices, which are central to our lateral understanding of mobility in the context of a society characterised by individualised risk and its implications for a differentiated habitus of learning.

Unlike other commentators (e.g. Hardcastle 2009), including the authors of this book, Bakhurst questions whether more theory is needed in relation to AT and he is not convinced that going back to philosophical foundations is going to be of much help because of the ambiguity of the term 'object of activity' in English (p. 208).

Learning and Meaning-Making as Subject-Centred and Context-Related Cultural Practice

Our view of AT at best as a heuristic underlines our scepticism concerning its potential as an analytic frame beyond structural description. The brief summary of the current discourse surrounding AT in the specialist literature on mobile learning suggests to us that there is actually a danger of it potentially obfuscating, rather than clarifying the issues involved. Notwithstanding the potential merits of AT, we offer an alternative approach to explaining and analysing mobile learning, namely one based on social semiotics and media pedagogy; an approach, which is tangentially metaphorical in nature and sees learning as meaning-making, as the making of signs and concepts closely linked to the context of the media-rich life-world of learners which, as we have already noted earlier, we see as representing a new habitus of learning, as both a challenge to as well as potential resource for learning (see Kress and Pachler 2007). By 'habitus' we mean dispositions and action patterns based on appropriated social structures within typical cultural practices. In particular, we are interested in the potential of mobile devices not just to provide, but also to enable the shaping of highly individualised, yet socially and physically connected, culturally differentiated and semiotically rich contexts for learning. For us the focus on context is important because of its centrality in meaning-making processes, as developers who have tried to approach the design of new devices from a 'gadget-centric' point of view will readily attest (see Nardi 2002, p. 529). And it is in relation to identifying and analysing the variables involved that we use the metaphorical notion of a socio-cultural ecology as our explanatory frame.

We take the decision to opt for a metaphorical approach deliberately. Whilst we are mindful of the potential dangers attendant to the notion of an 'ecology', which is used widely, and disparately in the literature, we believe that the benefits outweigh the disadvantages. Take the notion of 'stereotypes' in culture teaching and learning as an example: clearly there are dangers in using simplified conceptions about characteristics of other people and their ways of communicating and being. Yet, the limits of human perception and cognition require us to operate with shorthands in order to attempt categorisation to achieve understanding and clarity, i.e. there is a certain psychological inevitability about using stereotypes. We have a similar take on metaphors: clearly there are question marks over the quest for conceptual unification through the use of metaphors. As Sfard (1998, p. 5) rightly points out, the choice of metaphors can be 'highly consequential':

> Different metaphors may lead to different ways of thinking and to different activities. (Metaphors) are a double-edged sword: On the one hand, as a basic mechanism behind any conceptualization, they are what makes our abstract (and scientific) thinking possible; on the other hand, they keep human imagination within the confines of our former experience and conceptions.... (The) same figurative idea may engender several greatly varying conceptual frameworks.... (Too) great a devotion to one particular metaphor and rejection of all others can lead to theoretical distortion and to undesirable practical consequences.

In our view, the particular attraction of metaphors, also mentioned by Sfard (1998, p. 4), is that they enable 'conceptual osmosis between everyday and scientific discourses' which to us – in a field like mobile learning, which straddles many discourse boundaries – is particularly valuable.

Ecological Approaches to (Mobile) Learning

Our conceptual frame of a 'socio-cultural ecology' has links to AT, for example, in that it is premised on notions of learner agency, i.e. intent and motivation, which can manifest itself in object-orientated activity systems. And, we agree with Wali et al. (2008) who foreground the importance of location and context. With Gay et al. (2002) we consider one of the defining characteristics of learning with mobile devices to be the moving of 'computational power to the site in which the user is engaged' (p. 511) as well as the context-awareness of the devices and augmented physical spaces. This, in our view, opens up new possibilities for the relationship between learning in and across formal and informal contexts, between the classroom and other sites of learning.

> Rather than subverting 'direct experience' and communion with the field, mobile computers have the potential to move the learning experience from the artificial confines of the classroom and out to more naturalistic field settings. This is in sharp contrast with traditional schooling practices in which what is being taught is abstracted from its naturalistic (ecological) space where it has real function with the world and, instead, is told to learners in a classroom context, 'where the school-assigned meanings become the goal – complex problems are solved to get a good grade, completed for the purpose of satisfying a teacher or parent, not for the functional purposes for which these practices initially merged as important'. (Barab 2002, p. 535)

Barab goes on to coin the term 'content-culture incongruity' (p. 353) for school-based activity driven by pedagogic rather than student need. This is also one of our key concerns. Barab finds the notion of an 'ecology' appealing for it suggests to him that

> instruction implies mediating key elements of the larger context so as to facilitate the merging of learner and environment into a single system.... The role of the learning facilitator is no longer to play 'teacher expert' or 'didactic caretaker' of information. Rather, it is his or her responsibility to establish and support an environment that affords goals from which the individual develops intentions whose realization requires the appropriation of specific practices that bring about functional object transformations. (p. 535–536)

The metaphorical use of notions of 'ecologies' or 'ecosystems' in relation to the integration of information technologies into educational settings, processes and practices is by no means new. Indeed, in some of our earlier work on mobile learning (Kress and Pachler 2007), we referred to the work of Bruce and Hogan (1998), who conceptualised the integration of technology in the 'ecology' of everyday life as a 'disappearance'. We also want to mention a piece by Zhao and Frank (2003), which has come to note in the specialist literature, who used the notions of ecology and ecosystems to theoretically integrate and organise various factors affecting the implementation of ICT in school-based education. Whilst readers who are familiar with the history of the implementation of ICT in mainstream education, certainly in the UK, might rightly wonder about some of the assumptions made in the paper about non technology-enhanced approaches to pedagogy, their paper does demonstrate that an ecological perspective can offer a possible analytical framework for understanding issues attendant to the use of technologies in educational settings. We find the notion of the interdependence (requiring a state of internal equilibrium) of the various interacting abiotic (inorganic) and biotic (organic) factors and species interesting in Zhao and Frank's model and see it also applying to our model.

Barab et al. (1999) also propose an ecological approach to learning. They argue for what they call a 'relational ontology' ('ecologized, or self-organization, model'), which situates and couples the learner within the learning context and which sees 'knowing, meaning, and cognition... actualized through the dynamic between learner (self) and environment (nonself)' (p. 350).

> At one level this has involved the design of rich learning contexts through which the content is situated in rich contexts, supporting students in learning the 'whats' in a manner that allows them to appreciate the 'whys'. At another level this involves situating the student as part of a community. Rather than a focus on the situatedness of meaning or content, this perspective focuses on communities and what it means to learn as a function of being a part of a community. (http://inkido.indiana.edu/research/theory.html)

They advocate a type of learning that develops through dynamic activity, via participation, as part of a system as a whole and they view context as fundamental.

> It is central to the ecological model being advanced that the individual, the task, the intention, practices, meanings, and environmental particulars exist as part of an interrelated system – not as isolated components. (Barab et al. 1999, p. 354)

The authors view instruction as establishing the appropriate 'field conditions' or 'connecting the learner into a system in the service of an intention', i.e. they afford great importance to the notion of 'functional significance' of learning goals and activities in terms of 'actualization' of learning (p. 352) and 'potentiating' of learner-facilitator interaction (p. 353); this is a view we share.

> Instead of advocating for the systemic and didactic presentation of abstract content, a self-organizing model points to the importance of fully contextualized experience in which there is no artificial separation between the act of learning, of participation, and the context in which it arises. (Barab et al. 1999, p. 353)

Participative, Interactive, Situated and Contextual Learning

We deem mobile devices to have a significant contribution to make in respect of the 'actualization' of learning. Participation implies membership of a community, which in turn is premised on a process of socialisation, i.e. familiarity with the stated and tacit norms of that community. Using an ecological approach as an explanatory frame for the use of mobile devices in learning and foregrounding in it the importance of context, invariably poses the question around the relationship to the popular concept of 'communities of practice' (COP) and the duality of participation versus reification as well as zones of participation (peripheral versus central). It is inter alia with reference to COP that we have widened Giddens' (1984) binary model of structures and agency into a triangular one, which includes cultural practices.

Situated learning theory (SLT), like AT, focuses on the notion of practice and social practices in order to overcome the limitations inherent in cognitive and/or structuralist accounts of learning. Invariably, there exists an extensive literature exploring the definitional basis of practice and social practices. According to Arnseth (208, p. 290), Pickering (1995, p. 4), for example, distinguishes practices (patterned sequences of actions and activities) and practice (the work of cultural extension and transformation in time). Arnseth notes that both SLT and AT view practice as constitutive. AT, he notes (pp. 291 f.), views consciousness and material reality being transformed through object-orientated practical activity, mediated by semiotic and material artefacts within certain social and material conditions. Contexts, Engeström (1993, p. 67) argues, are activity systems. Lave and Wenger (1991), according to Arnseth (pp. 294 f.) see learning as constituted in the lived-in-world, i.e. the world as it is experienced in social practice, and as participation in COP with practice shaping and constitution knowledge and knowing and with learners gradually able to master procedures for talking and acting through participation. In our socio-cultural ecological model we focus on cultural practices that are constantly negotiated and re-negotiated and we question the applicability of the apprenticeship model in relation to learning with mobile devices in so far as it focuses on a certain historically developed repertoire of practices, whose meaning and significance is produced and reproduced in situ (Arnseth 2008, p. 297). We emphasise the ever evolving and changing nature of these cultural practices within social, technological and cultural structures. SLT, for us, places too much emphasis on social reproduction (Arnseth 2008, p. 299) and too little on interconnections and temporal emergence, i.e. 'how meanings and functions of actions and objects emerge in and through practical activity' (p. 300). Also, SLT, a theory, which emerged at the beginning 1990s, examined cultural practices of learning of the day, such as apprenticeship. Due to the historic context at the time, SLT critically questioned pervasive school-based learning at that time. It was not conceptualised as a critique of cultural practices and products of, and constituted by fluid context generation with and through mobile devices, which have since emerged and become prevalent.

Finally, we want to acknowledge one other model that has enjoyed some support of late as an explanatory framework, certainly in the UK. It is Luckin's notion of an 'ecology of resources of educational contexts' (Luckin et al. 2005; Luckin 2008). Seemingly following Vygotsky's socio-cultural psychology, Luckin views the development of the individual as the result of the internalisation of her interactions with her environment. Environment and context of learning, therefore, are viewed as highly significant. Summarising previous research, Luckin describes context as 'a situation defined through the relationship and interactions between the elements with that situation over time' (2008, p. 451) and as 'a situation defined through social interactions that are themselves historically situated and culturally idiosyncratic' (2008, p. 451). Based on these summaries she proposes a definition of learning context as 'an Ecology of Resources: a set of inter-related resource elements, including people and objects, the interactions between which provide a particular context' (2008, p. 451). Noteworthy about her model are also the notions of ZAA and ZPA through which she attempts to clarify the relationship between Vygotsky's Zone of Proximal Development (ZPD) and educational technology. The Zone of Available Assistance (ZAA) and the Zone of Proximal Adjustment (ZPA) are used to describe the types of resources available in particular contexts (ZAA) as well as the most appropriate resources (ZPA) for a given learner at a particular moment in time (see Luckin 2008, pp. 450–451). In a keynote at the 2008 JISC online innovating e-learning conference (http://www.jisc.ac.uk/whatwedo/programmes/elearningpedagogy/elpconference08/programme), Luckin distinguishes between context (knowledge, resources, environment) and filter (curriculum, administration, organisation) elements. Luckin describes her Ecology of Resources model as a way of characterising a learner, and the interactions that form that learner's context both statically, as a snapshot of the elements describing a learner's context, or dynamically, as a process of instigating and maintaining learning interactions in technology-rich environments. Implicitly, Luckin appears to understand resources as physical, rather than conceptual artefacts; that we view as a considerable constraint on her model.

Our perspective on the ecology metaphor is less directly related to natural scientific models such as that of Zhao and Frank (2003), which is basically premised on the idea that living entities and their environment constitute each other. We are much more interested in

- the socio-cultural processes – mainly increasing individualisation through mobility and context generation – that govern the relationship between learners and the tools they use for meaning-making and learning,
- the contexts for learning the interaction of the different variables in an ecosystem allow for and generate as well as
- the structural relationships embedded in cultural ecologies between informal (life-world) and formal (educational institution) sites for and of learning.

In such a view of learning, meaning-making through signs is situated in, and distributed across learning activities, their content and the contexts in which they occur. Important in the context of the notion of a socio-cultural ecological model of mobile learning for us is the fact that the actions of learners through which they are seeking to augment their conceptual resources, i.e. learn, are not directly on the world, but that they are mediated by social-semiotic tools, such as language, as well as by material artefacts incl. technology; by implication, learning is socio-culturally-bound or contingent, for example in terms of time, location as well as co-learners, pedagogical approaches and technical means available (see Thorne 2003, p. 40). In the socio-cultural dynamic of individualisation and individually constructed life-worlds cultural resources and artefacts function mainly by way of personal appropriation and not longer on the basis of socially guaranteed traditions (see e.g. Beck and Giddens 1991). Of course, these traditions offer an anthropologically and educationally valid baseline but in the dynamic of increasing individualisation brought about by mobility appropriation is less dependent on traditional frames of structures and traditional forms of habitus or traditional cultural practices such as learning in schools. Today appropriation depends mainly on personal agency and the availability of new contexts.

Summary and Outlook

In this chapter, we have attempted to provide an overview as well as a critical analysis of the most prevalent conceptual and theoretical models discussed in the mobile and technology-enhanced learning literature. We have tried to show that, and how these models have restricted analytical purchase and/or tangibility for us, which is why we deemed it necessary to develop an approach of our own. And it is to the operationlisation of this socio-cultural ecological approach to which we turn in Part II of this book. In the main, our approach focuses on the use of mobile devices as cultural resources as well as on the assimilation of learning in informal contexts into formal educational settings (a) through the recognition of the 'naïve' expertise of learners in relation to mobile device use and (b) through user-generated mobile contexts. We argue that assimilation can be fostered (a) through building on conversational threads from learners' life-worlds as well as (b) through the docking of formal educational learning situations onto contexts of personal development and learning around the use of mobile devices in learners' everyday lives.

Part II
Mobile Devices as Resources for Learning: A Socio-Cultural Ecological Analysis of the Mobile Complex

Chapter 6
Analysing the Mobile Complex for Education: Key Concepts

In order to be useful, a pedagogical approach to mobile learning has to engage critically with the 'mobile complex' (see Chapter 1 for an introduction to the term). It has to enable the identification of cultural resources that are relevant for the development of children, their participation in cultural practices and their meaning-making, i.e. learning. Until recently, schools have tended to react to the mobile complex mainly by banning mobile devices and by seeking to keep them off their premises. This kind of response is rooted in an educational tradition of protecting learning and the development of children from distracting influences, in this case of mobile device use in everyday life. However, such an approach fails to acknowledge the potential of newly emerging cultural resources within the mobile complex.

As already noted in Chapter 1, learning is a contested term and it is normally associated with planned activities carried out in, and sponsored by, educational institutions. We espouse a broader definition of learning, namely one that goes beyond the acquisition of pre-defined knowledge and skills, often on the basis of pedagogical interventions. We see learning as the result of the transformative engagement with (aspects of) the world, and we see meaning-making in everyday life as an integral part of learning.

In our work we promote the assimilation of new cultural resources into school-based learning and pedagogical practices (see Chapter 11 and 12). With reference to Piaget's concept of assimilation (1947/2001), we focus on the development of children through appropriation. Of course, our understanding of assimilation respects the established practices of teaching and learning of schools but it also advocates opening them up to learning in informal contexts, in particular within the cultural mobile practices of young people (see Chapter 11). These mobile practices range from listening to music downloaded onto MP3-player to spontaneously recording videos with a mobile/cell phone, which are then uploaded onto a video platform on the internet. What, we ask, are the characteristics of learning in these contexts and how could it be mapped onto learning taking place in schools?

This part of the book explores answers to these questions and analyses, among other things, in Chapter 10, the practices of an 18-year-old boy, who investigated homeless drunkards with the help of the video functionality on his mobile/cell phone. He uploaded the video he took onto an internet video platform, which ultimately resulted in the state attorney bringing harassment charges against him. By

N. Pachler et al., *Mobile Learning*, DOI 10.1007/978-1-4419-0585-7_6,

means of the conceptual model of a socio-cultural ecology, described in outline in Chapter 1 and in detail in Part II of this book, we recognise expertise within such complex mobile practices. We consider it as the 'naïve expertise' of everyday life (see Chapter 11), which in our view can benefit from the tried and tested learning experiences fostered by school by being developed into reflexive consciousness in order to become foundational for learning in formal contexts.

Our socio-cultural ecological approach allows us to identify new cultural resources of relevance for learning inside and outside of formal educational settings. In Chapter 7 we consider the social semiotic affordances, which mobile devices contribute as cultural resources. From our perspective, the cultural resources of the mobile complex comprise not only mobile devices and attendant practices but also new contexts, which emerge through these practices. The key notion for us is that of 'user-/learner-generated contexts' (see Chapter 11), and, as discussed in Chapter 1, we view mobile devices, contexts and content as cultural products within the mobile complex of structures, agency and cultural practices (see also Chapter 8).

A key educational challenge for us is to find a way of harnessing these mobile cultural products with their inherent agency of 'naïve expertise' for legitimised use within formal learning contexts. One of our proposals in this book, discussed in Chapter 11, is to take 'conversational threads' from everyday life and extend them into formal education as well as to identify points of convergence of school-based learning, formal education and user-generated contexts. We further propose to view contexts within the mobile complex as 'zones' of development and learning. The notion of zones aligns our socio-cultural ecology to Vygotsky's (1986/1934, 1978/1930) 'zones of proximal development' as well as the notion of 'scaffolding' (Wood et al. 1976) (see Chapter 9). In adapting Vygotsky's proposal for supporting the development of a child during a specific phase or 'zone of development' to the prevailing socio-political and cultural realities of today, we understand the new cultural contexts of milieus and user-generated contexts as formative and constitutive. And, we ask if these new contexts act supportively in relation to the developmental needs of a child.

We start from the premise that the school, and its pedagogy have to react in some way to all media innovations, from photography to television, the personal computer or the internet. School and pedagogy tend to follow the prevailing socio-cultural conditions and treat them as prerequisites for educational practices. Therefore, the school, as an institution and as a cultural practice, as well as pedagogy, as a theoretical discourse, have to react to the complex socio-cultural phenomena attendant to mobile devices. There exists a pedagogic tradition to analyse the development and education of children as a social phenomenon within given societal frames (see among others Vygotsky 1986/1934, 1978/1930). We follow this tradition and analyse the mobile complex, i.e. the physical devices as well as the structures and cultural practices around them, as a social phenomenon.

We argue in this book that the mobile complex with its devices such as multimedia mobile/cell phones (see Chapter 7), MP3-player, portable game consoles, etc. can be explained by the interplay of socio-cultural structures, agency and cultural practices (see Chapter 8). These socio-cultural structures, agency and cultural practices also frame child development and learning in informal settings. Self-evidently for us, they are highly relevant for education, school and pedagogy. We view the cultural practices of everyday life and child development as two central dynamics with which education and school have to engage and to which they have to respond, among other things with appropriate structures, curricula and approaches to teaching and learning. Pedagogy has to respond with theoretical interpretations and empirical analysis and in this second part of the book we attempt just such a response.

One important set of questions for us concerns socialisation (see Chapter 8). What does socialisation mean and how does it take place in the context of the mobile complex? We understand socialisation as the process of child development within the cultural practices of everyday life, which are increasingly governed by the structures of the mobile complex. Socialisation takes place through the appropriation of cultural products such as user-generated contexts or through the use of mobile devices within the broader context of media convergence. Socialisation occurs without a deliberate educational plan. Policy makers, the public, schools and parents all react to manifestations of 'mobile socialisation' such as, for example, 'happy slapping', a staging of violence between young people with the purpose of producing video recordings on a mobile/cell phone. Historically, schools have tended to be motivated in their reaction to mobile devices primarily by the perceived distraction to learning caused by them. Parents tend to react by buying phones for their children so they can be in constant touch with them.

On the one hand, mobile/cell phones impact on the processes of development as well as on the cultural practices of everyday life. This is the case because they function as, and result in cultural products (see Chapter 9). Mobile/Cell phones assist users, in this case children and young people, in negotiating their social and cultural world and its relationship with their inner, mental world. On the other hand, mobile/cell phones act as cultural products and resources for learning (see Chapter 9) and participation (see Chapter 10). The latter is a curricular and didactic perspective, which is rooted in how mobile devices function as cultural resources in everyday life for communicating in writing or speech, taking and sharing pictures or playing music, etc. Considering mobile devices as cultural resources brings the use of cultural products for education and pedagogy into focus. Indeed, our emphasis on the affordances and potentials of mobile resources for fostering learning in formal contexts and for participation in an increasingly fragmented society is one of the key arguments we advance in this book with reference to our socio-cultural ecological approach. We argue that mobile devices can serve as meaningful resources for learning in formal and informal contexts and that they can function as resources for generating content and contexts for learning (see Chapter 11). Also, we posit that in relation to socialization and learning mobile devices function as cultural products within a socio-culturally specific interrelationship between structures, agency and cultural practices (see Chapter 8).

Within the mobile complex, mobile devices reinforce individualization and mobility, which has the capacity to transform agency in the context of new individualized, mobile mass communication (see Chapter 8). The key term in the

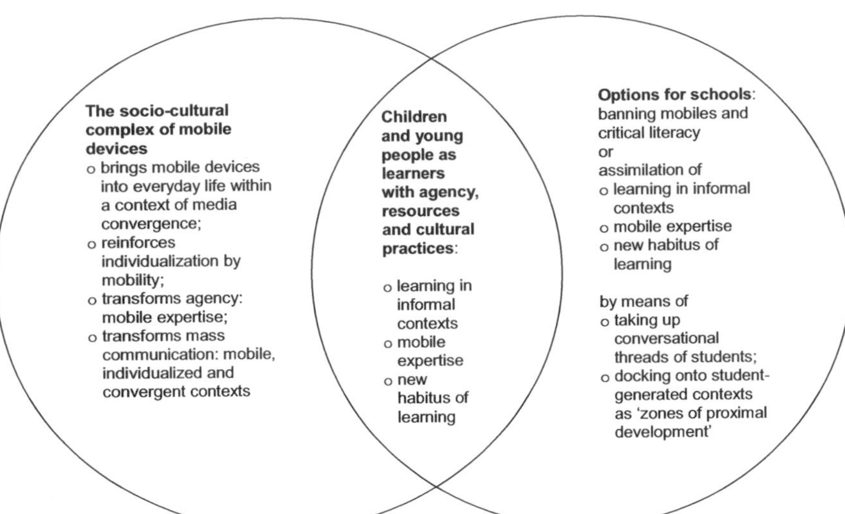

Fig. 6.1 Children and young people as learners at the intersection of the mobile complex and school

transformation of agency for us is *mobile expertise,* which relates to a new habitus of learning (see Chapter 7) and correlates with the socio-cultural segmentation of milieus (see Chapters 9 and 10). The key terms in the transformation of mass communication from an educational and pedagogical perspective are *mobile, individualised, convergent.*

The circle on the left in Fig. 6.1 illustrates the relevant features of the mobile complex within students' everyday life. The circle on the right depicts the basic options of educational institutions for responding to the mobile complex. The intersection of the two is inhabited by children and young people as learners in informal and formal contexts. The case study of a young man, Cyrill, in Chapter 10 visualises what constitutes this intersection between the mobile complex in everyday life and the school. Cyrill uses the video application of his mobile/cell phone for a provocative reportage and publishes his video on an internet media platform together with images of himself. A careful analysis of the artefacts on the internet platform evidences his mobile expertise within his social habitus. This social habitus is mainly governed by the segmentation of socio-cultural milieus, in which he can be seen to belong to the group of risk- and consumption-orientated 'hedonists' (for a detailed discussion see Chapter 10).

Mobile expertise is also a result of the young man's appropriation of mobile structures, e.g. the convergence of the mobile video application with an internet media platform, as a way of dealing with his social situation as a second generation migrant by means of his cultural practices. The school is not central to these cultural practices. In an individualised society, we argue, personal appropriation is the dominant way of dealing with socio-cultural conditions and of forming a personal life world. In today's individualised world, personal appropriation of cultural products is the main mechanism for dealing with the world. For us the focus is on the adjective 'personal', i.e. appropriation within a personal frame of relevance. This personal frame consists of the learner's life-world and her everyday life.

Learning is personally framed, which creates a tension with the object (and school-subject) orientation of learning in the school curriculum. In some of the socio-cultural milieus learning is closely related to media use within entertainment contexts (see section 'Conversational Threads in *Responsive*, User-Generated Contexts' in Chapter 10). Therefore, and in view of the dynamic of individualization, which is accelerated by mobile devices and their structures, it is no longer appropriate it seems to us to view learning as located mainly within narrow institutional boundaries of schools, colleges, universities etc. Instead, it needs to be recognised that learning takes place in abundance in everyday life and the learners' life-worlds and ways need to be found of valorising it. We take the view that there has always been learning outside of the school and that the main question is that of the legitimacy of, and relationship between both, learning in formal and informal contexts. For us an important educational challenge is that of finding ways of dealing with mobile devices as cultural resources for learning by recognising and validating learning taking place outside educational institutions and by decentring views of learning as school-bound (see Chapter 9 for a detailed discussion). How can schools respond to mobile devices and the practices around their use in everyday life? The circle on the right-hand side in Fig. 6.1 refers to the socialization function of mobile devices within everyday life and to the resource function, which is widened to learning (see Chapter 7).

How can we ground a pedagogy of the mobile complex theoretically and ensure schools, which are after all still society's leading learning institutions, adopt it? As we have already noted, in our view the theoretical key is to conceptualise mobile devices as cultural products that operate according to the conditions of the mobile complex and that can function as cultural resources for learning. In the following we briefly discuss key concepts relating to our socio-cultural ecological framework. The concept of appropriation, with which we discuss in detail in Chapter 9, for us opens up an educational perspective on children and young people and includes the learner's relationship with mobile devices as well as the objects, which the school is offering its students for learning.

Appropriation

Until now the dominant educational discourse has not really considered learning with media of everyday life as a prevalent mode of appropriation, although informal learning is becoming increasingly significant. Constant use of technological devices requires users to make choices and decisions and understand operations all of which can and, we argue, should be viewed as learning processes in informal contexts. Of course, cultural traditions influence our understanding of learning both in terms of its definition, i.e. in terms of whether it is promoted as a valid practice inside formal educational settings, and in terms of recognition, i.e. whether it is validated by educational institutions of learning. Therefore, we deem it helpful to seek theoretical distance to established learning concepts and practices. Traditionally, much media use within a context of mass communication has been defined as entertainment, not as learning. At a general theoretical level, media use and the use of mobile devices can be interpreted as appropriation of cultural products. Of course, there are obvious specificities relating to media used in school because of the different cultural frames that govern them. For example, user-generated ring tones (see Chapter 8) are not recognized as relevant for learning within the school, except in the context of a student trying to avoid engagement with learning by entertaining his/her friends with a ring tone. The ring tone represents entertainment and not learning but that need not necessarily be so: for example, it could be integrated meaningfully in Music education. This brings us back to the problem of recognition: what is recognised as learning by some authority?

Within a social framework of education and child development (see e.g. Vygotsky 1986/1934, 1978/1930) the appropriation of cultural products is a process by which the subjectivity or identity of a person is located within a frame for development. Within this frame, and with reference to school-based learning, Vygotsky (1978/1930, p. 84) interpreted the interplay between child development and school learning as a 'zone' of 'development'. This zone, in our view, corresponds to the emerging mode of user-generated contexts around mobile device use within the context of media convergence. We argue that because all personal development, including learning, depends on cultural products, the cultural specificity of mobile devices needs to be investigated in terms of its role as an educationally relevant zone of development and learning. If it is possible to clarify the relevant structures of appropriation, then learning with mobile devices can be deliberately planned for and implemented by schools. To this end, we outline a model of appropriation in the tradition of cultural idealism of the nineteenth century and the social frame of child development of the early twentieth century in Chapter 9 (for a summary of our proposal, see also Chapter 1, and Pachler et al. 2010).

One of the key tasks in the development of such a model of appropriation for us is the identification of common structures of media use and media reception with reference to learning (see Chapter 8). Appropriation of mobile devices within the socio-cultural structures governing them also leads us to an examination of socialization and a discussion of the habitus of learning around the notion of mobile expertise (see Chapter 8).

Learning Resources

Whilst schools have by-and-large responded decisively to mobile devices for learning, to date they have done so rather negatively. Around the world schools have tended to prohibit mobile devices such as mobile/cell phones, MP3-player and games consoles as tools for learning. Instead, they have tended to address them as objects for critical media education and media literacy. Only relatively few innovative teachers and schools have experimented with the use of mobile/cell phones but there number is growing (for examples see the case studies in Chapter 4). As already discussed in Chapter 2, organisations such as the European

Kaleidoscope network, (http://mlearning.noe-kaleidoscope) the Australian Flexible Learning Network (http://e-standards.flexiblelearning.net.au/topics/mlearn.htm) or the International Association for Mobile Learning (http://mlearning.noe-kaleidoscope.org/projects) are exploring the interrelationship of mobile devices and deliberate, intentional, 'formal' learning. The *Becta research report* 'Emerging technologies for learning' (Volume 3, 2008) (http://partners.becta.org.uk/upload-dir/downloads/page_documents/research/emerging_technologies08-2.pdf) discusses one way of considering mobile devices as curricular resources within network systems. In one of the contributions van't Hooft (2008) analyses how mobile, wireless, connected information clouds can become relevant for formally recognised learning. In order to be able to use mobile devices in this way, one has to recognise them as learning resources.

Such a perspective may give the impression that technology and functionality are defining the use of mobile devices for learning. Yet, this is only true in so far as internet connectivity greatly increases the affordances and educational potential of mobile devices. It is important for us to recognise that functionality remains but a means to an end. The potential of connectivity lies in the fact that it opens up mobile devices and those artefacts available on and through them as resources for learning, which are contingent upon participation in society and its culture(s). A view of mobile devices and associated artefacts as cultural resources (see Chapter 9) does not, however, segregate the mobile devices and attendant structures, agency and practices from existing and evolving forms of learning. Together with the overarching concept of appropriation, the concept of cultural resource supports an integrative view of children and young people and their media practices and life-worlds.

Redefinition and Recognition of Learning

Apart from trying to 'protect' learners from the dangers often associated with mobile devices in the media, which we discussed in Chapter 3, by banning them, schools also have the option of responding to their impact on socialization through an emphasis on 'critical literacy' and by offering compensatory experiences to ubiquitous mobility. An emphasis on 'critical mobile literacy' can still be seen to aim at protecting learners from the perceived inherent dangers of mobile devices. A rather different approach, and – as we have already noted – one we argue for, is to recognise mobile devices and associated artefacts as cultural resources for teaching and learning. A straightforward way of harnessing mobile devices in this way is to use them for out-of-school investigation.[1] In order to be able to delineate more complex

[1] For examples, see Chapter 11 Sean and Dan calculating speed outside the school (http://www.youtube.com/watch?v=DQ-4qg3D_W8) can be seen as one way of using mobile devices as learning resources linking everyday life and school-based learning. See also the boys taking photos of geometrical forms in everyday life (http://www.hhc.rca.ac.uk/archive/hhrc/programmes/include/2005/proceedings/pdf/soodadityadev.pdf; http://www.cks.in/html/cks_pdfs/learninglab_ppt.pdf)

pedagogical options, the use and functioning of mobile devices within everyday life structures have to be investigated (see Chapter 8). And, the notion of learning must no longer be equated merely with the traditional cultural practices of schools: firstly, we have to identify and value learning in informal contexts with the intention of connecting it to, and assimilating it into the school; secondly, the mobile complex, its socio-cultural structures, agency and cultural practices, have to be viewed as a stimulus for change not only in terms of the relationship of public and private but also in terms of the traditional relationship with mass communication, e.g. of users increasingly becoming producers of user-generated contexts and content. As the experience of *ubiquity* in everyday life becomes more and more taken for granted, user-generated content and contexts have to be deliberately uncovered and analysed, e.g. through case studies such as that of Cyrill. But also well-known procedures of learning are being re-negotiated around mobile devices and their functionality. Homework communities on an internet video platforms are a striking example. For a detailed discussion see Chapter 11.

Conversational Integration and Contextual Zones of Development

Learning as well as teaching are grounded in conversational activities such as communication about tasks, goals, the asking and answering of questions, the giving and receiving of comments and feedback, adaptive actions, reflection, etc (see e.g. Laurillard's Conversational Framework, 2007, p. 160). In Chapter 12 these conversational activities are the basis for our operationalization of 'didactic parameters' for planning and analysis of situations for mobile learning. The concrete 'dialogic processes' of learning within mediated situations (Laurillard 2007, p. 159) distinguish two different levels of conversation: the 'discursive level' (e.g. theories, concepts) and the 'experiential level' (practices, activity, procedures). These levels bring students, teachers, learning objects and learning situations into a complex interrelationship with each other and provide a frame for combining the learning activities of the school with the media activities of everyday life. Of course, media-related activities also are conversational activities framed by everyday life and the structures inherent in the media.

The pedagogic task, as we see it, is to identify conversational threads, which knot the media use of everyday life with school-based learning. Our case analysis of Cyrill in Chapter 4 and in Chapter 10 lays bare conversational threads such as the self-presentation of identity by means of media and software expertise. The contexts of such threads are not just media- and school-related but they are framed by user-generated contexts.

User-generated contexts are established through self-organisation by young people as in the example of a homework community on an internet media platform in Chapter 11. 'Conversation' in the case of a homework community can mean that students upload videos about their school homework to an internet community and thereby initiate a dialogic process. A teacher can take up a relevant conversational thread relating to the homework on the video platform and relate it to school-based activities, e.g. through feedback.

Such a context, in which content generated by students is linked with the pedagogical endeavours of a teacher, in our view meets the characteristics of a 'proximal zone' for development and learning in the sense of Vygotsky (1978/1930, p. 84) or, in Bruner's terminology (Wood et al. 1976), it works as supportive scaffolding. In espousing such a view we are deliberately widening Vygotsky's notion of the 'zones of development' with the notion of context. We understand the new social phenomena of (user-generated) contexts as highly relevant for the development of children and young people. Originally, as conceptualised in twentieth century thinking, the zones were seen mainly as age periods in the life course. We argue that they are now characterised by socio-cultural contexts. Such contexts, which influence child development, span from milieus to media contexts on the internet, which are interacted with by way of 'mobile' interventions, e.g. when young people upload and comment on mobile videos. By means of such conversational interventions user-generated contexts emerge. When these contexts influence or supportively shape the development of young people we can describe them as 'responsive' to young people's personal development (see Chapter 9).

Participation

The case study of Cyrill (see Chapters 4 and 10), which documents provocative mobile/cell phone use within the context of media convergence, helps us identify mobile devices and their artefacts as cultural resources not only for learning but also for participation.

An analysis of the socio-cultural structures, agency and cultural practices around school-based learning leads us to the conclusion that the participatory potential of media, including importantly that of mobile devices, is of great relevance for formal education. This participatory potential is not only relevant in view of the apparent deficits of school and other educational institutions in industrial societies in organizing learning successfully for *all* of its students. More broadly speaking, it is also relevant in view of social stratification in which success in school is only one variable with lifestyle segmentation being another (see Chapters 1 and 10 for details). A case such as Cyrill's makes visible that a lifestyle milieu segment with the motto 'more risk, more fun' requires a deliberate effort on the part of formal education for integration to become possible.

Integration in an individualized society requires active self-integration, which leads us to the important notion of participation by means of mobile devices. Participation through mobile devices, we argue, is not a fringe activity. Given its prevalence and ubiquity, mobile device use has acquired the significance of predecessor technologies such as television, which has functioned for more than one generation as a social tool for integration through news, big stories, anchormen, etc. Within the increasing fragmentation of consumer society, television worked as an integrative frame, for example by setting a common agenda. With the mobile individualization of mass communication this function is transferring to mobile devices and is, of course, realised in relation to their affordance (see Chapter 7) and specificity, i.e. user-generated contexts and content (see Chapter 11). We argue that the educational operationalisation of participation, therefore, has to be seen in the context of an analytical understanding of the mobile complex to which socio-cultural milieus with their different lifestyle and values belong.

The Culture Ecological Framework

We argue that a view of mobile devices as cultural products inevitably sharpens our perspective on the socio-cultural structures of increasing individualisation fostered by mobile devices. They are part of the context within which user-centred mass communication has to be understood. Furthermore, they are negotiated in users' life-worlds by personal appropriation, a process, which arguably has the potential to become a mode of learning.

All these features, we posit, interrelate to a flexible system, in which mobile devices function as resources. For a pedagogic recognition of these resources and their implementation into schools and their teaching and learning practices not only the systemic aspects of mobile devices are relevant. From an equality of access and opportunity perspective, questions around the distribution of these resources are equally essential. In education, the distribution of cultural resources has to be assessed in terms of children's and young people's participation with culture and for the purposes of their life accomplishment.

In Chapter 8 we attempt an analysis of the mobile complex and its structures and we try to explore mobile phenomena in their full complexity. Through the notion of the appropriation of cultural products (Chapter 9) we seek to understand the use of mobile devices from the point of view of how children and young people act within the social characteristics of the mobile complex. Through the case of Cyrill (Chapter 10) we explore the possible intersection between the dynamic of the mobile complex and possible responses by the school. His learning in informal contexts and his cultural habitus, including his habitus of learning and his mobile expertise, are discussed. The case of Cyrill underlines the need to focus on the participation patterns of children and young people in socio-cultural milieus, particularly those that are removed from the cultural practices of learning in schools. In Chapters 11 and 12 we attempt to identify possible 'docking points' for the mobile activities of children with school learning. First, however, in Chapter 7, we turn to a semiotic analysis of smartphones to explore the affordances of high-specification mobile devices and how they relate to wider, socio-cultural issues such as socialization and the development of specific forms of habitus.

Chapter 7
A Social Semiotic Analysis of Mobile Devices: Interrelations of Technology and Social Habitus

A Social Semiotic 'Take' on Technology

In this chapter we show the dense interconnections of social issues with the (technical) affordances of a specific media device; and show, in that, the connection with our wider interest in the phenomenon of 'mobile learning'. We regard the notion of 'mobility' as a response to a number of diverse yet convergent factors in contemporary 'western', 'developed' societies, variously named and characterized: as 'globalization'; as 'diversity' – more or less intense; as fragmentation, provisionality, instability. All point to the fragmentation and fraying of formerly stable social structures, of frames and conventions: whether of ideologies and values, of knowledge(s), of forms of (canonical) representations of knowledge, of sites of learning; of temporal framings; of means and forms of representations, of modes, genres, discourses as much as of media. A questioning of the legitimacy of any one of these is bound to lead to the questioning of legitimacy in all domains of communication, representation, knowledge. This undermining of *stability*, of social forms and structures, leads to *instability*; in turn, the absence of fixed anchorings leads to *mobility*. In this way, the conditions for the use of sets of technological potentials emerge: potentials for *mobility*, contrasted with conditions of *being fixed*, *static*, in any of the areas just mentioned.

Allied to this, and as one major effect of 'the market' – in Anglophone societies at least – is the move from notions of social responsibility to values of individual satisfaction. Where identity was formerly constructed through the achievement of social position and of position in work or profession, *identity* is now constructed through the exercise of *choice* in consumption in the market. *Choice* assumes agency in relation to ranges of options; this disposition is carried by the young from the market into the school (as into all of their life-world), where their assumptions meet the former structures of authority in relation to values, knowledge, and semiotic action in representation and communication.

Developments in contemporary media run in parallel to these social conditions: it is a conjunction, which provides an amplification, a further unsettling force of the social conditions. Current technologies of communication unsettle patterns of communication, which in their turn had developed in response to former social givens. In

N. Pachler et al., *Mobile Learning*, DOI 10.1007/978-1-4419-0585-7_7,

the theoretical conception underlying the book, 'the social' is the source of meaning; in that frame, the use of technologies provides instances of meaning-making and meaning. In our description and analysis of the features and affordances of one convergent media device, we emphasize *meaning-potentials* rather than technical specifications. We are not interested in an exploration, let alone a celebration of technical potentials or characteristics, but in the potentials for making meanings of many kinds, in line with the broader social features we have just mentioned.

Given the over-arching frame of meaning, the description and analysis provided here is *semiotic*: it is focussed on meaning. Meaning is produced in 'the social', so that our form of semiotics is 'social semiotics'. Put simply, as an example: a choice to take a photograph with a convergent device and to send that image, rather than writing an (admittedly small) txt about the bit of the world framed in the image, is a choice about meaning. It speaks of a decision about a particular kind of social relation between me and the recipient; a choice about ontology, as forms of *realism*, as the potential to 'capture' the world in the way I wish to; it speaks of a specific aesthetics; and similarly with all of the facilities of the device.

Social semiotics, like other forms of semiotics, takes the *sign* as the central, basic unit; a unit in which meaning is fused with a form in a single entity. In Social Semiotics the assumption is that signs are always newly *made* rather than *used*, on each occasion of meaning-making. Every act of choice, in representation as in communication, produces a sign: choosing to represent my meaning as image rather than as word is significant: the meaning potentials of images are different than the potentials of words in sequence; and the social valuations attaching to the use of image in communication are different to those attaching to speech – if I phone – or writing. Writing a short text rather than downloading an otherwise suitable piece of writing is significant: the effort I expend in making my meaning for another rather than – as it were – passing some meaning on to that other. The convergent media device we examine offers a multiplicity of choices in this way: in representation, in production, in communication; our aim here is to elucidate some of these potentials and make suggestions about their effects in shaping subjectivities, identities, *habitus*.

These are decisions resting on individual choice made in social environments: in another era or in another social group with a different individual as an addressee, a written text in a specific genre might have been preferred – affectively or aesthetically or socially. Such social choices are made at all times, specific to particular occasions: choices about meanings of various kinds. In other words, we treat the devices of contemporary communication as means for making meanings: and for that, Social Semiotics offers the apt theoretical frame.

The return to the questions of rhetoric over the last two decades or three is both consequence and symptom. When social conditions are unstable and provisional, each instance of communication requires, in principle at least, an assessment on each occasion of the communicational environment in terms of power, characteristics of participants, of their expectations, their tastes and style preferences. In the design of messages, the suitability of available cultural/semiotic resources has to be assessed newly and on each occasion. Hence there is a shift, alongside that to rhetoric, to *design*, as the attempt to realize rhetorical purposes in the shape of messages, which will be apt to the requirements of *this* situation and instance of communication. In that context, the device we analyze here can be seen as an instrument in the service of rhetorical purposes and in the service of the *design* of these purposes in instances of communication. The device offers its potentials to the user; in doing so it imposes its 'orientations' and its limitations, which interact with the orientations and limitations of the user.

That is the frame within which we attempt to understand one of these convergent media devices, to understand its specific affordances as well as its likely 'uptake' in communication; and more significantly still its likely effects in terms of the production of a habitus.

The Affordances of Smartphones: A Social Semiotic Analysis

The analysis focuses on the 'affordances'[1] (Kress and van Leeuwen 1996, 2006) of Smartphones. Every medium, every technology that we use to represent and to communicate – to make and to disseminate meaning – has affordances, both of material and social possibilities and constraints, that is, what it is materially and socially possible to do with it. If learning is a process of meaning-making about ourselves and of our 'life-world' (Kress and Pachler 2007), as in our view it is, then the media we use and their affordances – what they facilitate, what they hinder and inhibit – influence how we make meaning and hence the way we learn.

'Smartphones' – portable 'media convergence' devices which bring together the functionalities of several (formerly) separate digital devices, have recently been introduced into the media landscape; they are among the media we use in everyday life. Understanding their affordances casts light onto the processes and capacities that they foster, as well as on those, which they do not; they illuminate how we learn to make meaning of the world through their use. In using such devices we shape *habitus*[2] and with that the way we approach and conceive of our life-world. This promises a more grounded basis for their adoption in school than when adoption had been argued on the less clear sense of technology as a (positive or negative) phenomenon in itself.

Stemming from this assumption, we attempt a social semiotic analysis of these mobile devices, in order to understand their affordances and see what capacities and what *habitus* they foster or impede. Various types of Smartphone are available, in various shapes and with different functionalities; we have taken one of these (the Nokia N95) as an instance of these new devices and carried out an analysis to investigate its affordances. Without denying the specificity of the affordances that each models entails, the observations can be seen as indicative of general trends underpinning the affordances of the whole category of 'Smartphones'.

---

[1] The notion of affordances is being subject to a wide academic debate (for a critical review see Oliver 2005); here it is understood and used in social semiotics' terms.

[2] We use the term '*habitus*' as an extension of the notion of '*habitus* of learning' (Kress and Pachler 2007). Cf. the definition in Chapter 1 in the present work.

The analysis focuses, firstly, on the affordances of the device and its design and then on the software and the main functionalities. Some general observations are drawn in terms of capacities and *habitus* that these affordances foster (or hinder) and these are considered in terms of the implications, which might follow from the use of mobile devices in educational contexts.

Affordances of the Hardware

When the device is closed (Fig. 7.1), its shape and options differ significantly from former models of mobile/cell phones. It has a large, coloured screen with thumbnails, which occupies ¾ of the device, while a relatively small section is devoted to buttons. The touch input section has a central 5-way navigator, surrounded by other buttons of various dimensions arranged symmetrically around the navigator.

Fig. 7.1 Closed device with navigation keys (Source: http://www.flickr.com/photos/stevegarfield/369173209/sizes/o/)

The section devoted to the visual output is bigger than the one devoted to the kinaesthetic input, which is navigational rather than for textual input, so that the device resembles an advanced version of a *Gameboy* rather than of a mobile/cell phone.[3] Only when the device is 'open' (by sliding the front part vertically over the back, Fig. 7.2) can one relate its shape to that of a mobile/cell phone: a mobile/cell phone keyboard appears and the size of the screen becomes proportionally less significant, at about ½ of the size of the device.

[3] Some elements still give the clue of the phone functionality: the top row of the screen shows the network operator name in the centre; two inverted pyramids of little bars on the two sides refer to the connectivity signal and the battery level, analogously to other mobile/cell phones; on the left of the bottom row of the screen the label 'messaging' also indicates a typical functionality of mobile/cell phones. The left and right buttons have a green and red label respectively, the colours usually associated with the 'call' and 'end call' keys in 'traditional' mobile/cell phones. However, these elements of continuity with the mobile/cell phone are relatively few and small (one needs to look at them at a very close distance to see them) and thus less salient than the discontinuity in the overall shape of the device.

Fig. 7.2 Opened device (Source: http://www.flickr.com/photos/stevegarfield/369171027/sizes/o/

Although different models of this media convergence device vary in shape, with each having specific affordances, most share the priority given to visual output and navigational input over textual input. The radical change in the shape of these devices is significant as a clue of the designers' intentions about the affordances of types of representations fostered and the semiotic modes thereby foregrounded or backgrounded; not to mention the manual skills needed to use the device.

'Shape': Designers' Intentions and Social Implications

The latest 'media convergence devices' are bigger than traditional mobile/cell phones; the N95 for example, is as long as the average open hand and wider than the palm. 'Small-as-possible' no longer seems a positive feature. New priorities have brought design features other than reduced size to the fore; large size of the screen[4] is a more positively valued feature: the larger the screen, the better the output for the functionalities which rely on the visual mode, such as imaging, Web browsing and GPS positioning (but also selection of audio files). The still relatively small dimensions keep the device portable; though easy portability is now counterbalanced by the need for maximum usability of the different media functionalities, which, in their output, rely more and more on the visual.

The shift in shape – larger screen size, non-visible alphanumeric keyboard, touch input section devoted to navigation – make the phoning functionalities less prominent than others. You cannot 'txt' (one of the main functions now associated with mobile/cell phones) nor compose a phone number,[5] without sliding the device open.

In other words, shape is a clue to the designers' interest in functionalities of the device; those devoted to phoning are backgrounded. The organization of

[4]On the Nokia Website, the N95 specifications page advertises the large screen size as the first hardware feature of the device.

[5]Although you can answer incoming calls and select your contacts and call them, which is a frequent way to make calls with a mobile/cell phone.

the instruction manual echoes this point: the section devoted to messaging is eleventh and the 'Make calls' is twelfth in the list. Both chapters are preceded by functionalities such as Web browsing, imaging, GPS positioning and media applications.

In sum, the design of these devices emphasises their 'convergence' characteristics – the fact that they merge many traditional digital devices such as camera, video camera, laptop, GPS navigator, gaming mobile device, portable music player, with the mobile/cell phone function maybe a little last and least.

The shape changes how the device is handled. Because of their relatively large size, the devices are frequently not held to the ear; instead, they might be kept in a bag or pocket and used with earphones (wireless or not), and carried in the way an MP3 is. In several of their functionalities, they are held with both hands, horizontally,[6] with outstretched arms – when taking pictures or videos – or held horizontally or vertically in the lap, using the fingers of both hands to manipulate them (like handling a *Gameboy*).

The characteristic shape and how they are handled, makes them and their users recognizable, signifying a divide between the tech-savvy who own a high-tech media-convergence device and those who (merely) own a mobile/cell phone.

The Representational Affordances

Given that – with a screen as large as possible – visual output has become the priority, the alphanumeric keyboard had to be covered to keep the device reasonably small. The prioritizing of visual output goes at the expense of access to the alphanumeric keyboard of touch input in the textual mode; the touch input section still remains available for navigation, with the 5-way navigator below the screen. That is, in order to facilitate access to certain modes through immediate availability, others are backgrounded. Written production in particular is given lesser priority in favour of navigation and (internet) access to image and written text and the capture of images. As a result, 'content generation' and text creation is more likely to be done by means of representation-as-selection,[7] a 'framing' and copying of semiotic material available via, e.g. the internet. This changes the way we conceive representational means and meaning-making in the world, by favouring selection, 'capture' and transformation rather than 'production from scratch', transformation or 'transduction' (Bezemer and Kress 2008; Kress and van Leeuwen 1996, 2006, p. 39). That is, where before production might have been 'transduction' of ensembles of modes as texts from the written to the visual or from the visual to the verbal – for

[6]The device can also slide in the opposite direction (i.e., instead of moving the front up and the back down, as in Fig. 7.2, the front moves down and the back moves up). This uncovers a set of buttons typical of a music player and turns the screen graphics orientation horizontally. The screen graphics turned horizontal forces the user to turn the device horizontally. Again the visual output drives the way the device has to be handled.

[7]Cf. in this regard also the issues on authorship as a consequence of text production by means of 'downloading, mixing, cutting and pasting, sampling, re-contextualization' (Kress 2008).

instance in a review of an exhibition, a film or a video where something is written about a video to recommend it – now we can directly forward a 'link' or a 'file'. In this way action on or in the world is more likely (the kinaesthetic input) to happen through our selecting among options and forwarding these as (existing) 'links' rather than to use the affordances of writing to describe what we wanted to represent and communicate.

The Kinaesthetic Input Affordances

The navigational input section on the front of the device is composed of keys of different sizes, shapes and types of relief. It is composed of 13 different acting points distributed on 8 buttons, which cover an area of about 4 × 1.5 cm. Each of the buttons is of a different size; there is no blank – inactivity – space between them. The key-function associations of the navigational section are partially context-dependent, that is, some key functions vary according to the visual output of the screen.

With its restricted surface, the N95 navigation section requires different types of touch precision for different buttons, according to their varied size. Given that no blank space separates buttons, the 'cost' of using the wrong touch is higher for the N95 than for other devices, because it leads to pressing the button nearby and causing an undesired action rather than merely not the desired one.

In sum, mastering the N95 requires manual dexterity not only in the key-function associations – because of the partially context-dependent keys – but also in terms of varied touch precision, so that automating the function means associating the right touch precision to each key. Furthermore, if the device is used with both hands for some functionalities – such as Imaging, Web browsing and GPS positioning – this variable touch precision has to be achieved by both hands in coordination.

This coordinated adaptation, which is specific to the N95 model, requires acquiring a complex set of skills in order to use the device. Again, this is a more general consequence of the reduced amount of space given over to the touch input section in favour of greater prominence given to the visual output.

The Software Affordances

The options on the visual output are arranged in menus to whose logics we are already accustomed generally speaking, since a semiotics of interfaces based on menus is now widespread in the (Western) digital environment. This leads to a conception of semiotic (inter-)activity as a matter of 'navigation' and 'selection' among options. Combined with present hardware and software affordances it comes to make semiotic action – whether representation, production or communication – seen as selection-driven. This in turn might lead to notions of 'semiotic agency' more and more as a matter of selection from among predetermined templates; and a sense of (multimodal) text as *bricolage*.

The menus combine semiotic features of the mobile/cell phone (e.g. the 'settings' of the applications are in a separate menu) with those of mobile devices in general (e.g. the context-dependent functions associated with the keys appear on the screen) and with those of the computer (e.g. the use of thumbnails and a descriptive written caption which appears when one is selected). Some are features of the most up-to-date software tools (e.g. thumbnails that move on the screen). In other words, the design and the use of the Smartphone draws on previous knowledge of various digital devices. However, the multi-functionality of the device, the size of the screen and the touch input affordances also require adaptation of experience of other digital devices to the 'merged' semiotics of the media-convergence device. Remaking of knowledge of various previously encountered and used digital devices is thus a capacity fostered by the affordances of this device. Maybe this is fostered, demanded and naturalized in a world increasingly dominated by these technologies and devices in any case.

The Thumbnail 'Carousel' and the Interactive Aesthetics

By clicking the button to the right of the 5-way navigation key, thumbnails appear arranged in a circle, which moves around if one acts on the navigation keys to change the thumbnail selection (Fig. 7.3). At the level of meaning-making, two signifiers together signify 'selected item', not only, as in previous models, the foreground/background contrast (for example, in terms of a rectangle framing the selected thumbnail), but also the thumbnail's changed position.[8] The 'carousel'[9] is a dynamic way of visualizing the thumbnails and their selection; of itself it does not add much in terms of functionality. Yet usability is not the unique factor that drives the design of the visual output. Rather, adding mobility to the visual objects on the screen, has an 'affective' value in terms of a perceived enhanced interactive aesthetics.

The addition of moving visual entities is becoming more and more widespread in the design of digital devices, in MP3 devices for instance, in operating systems for computers, in Web page design and so on. The feature adds an aesthetics of motion-as-(inter)activity, since the idea of action is generally associated with movement. The movement of visual entities on the screen as an effect of a touch indicates action and more specifically is suggestive of physical handling and acting on the objects.

In this sense we can trace a development in software design. With earlier versions of mobile/cell phones there is neither *logical* nor *spatial proximity/continuity* of *action* and *effect*: a touch on the keyboard results in a foregrounding effect of an element on the screen – e.g., a rectangle framing the thumbnail. With devices such as the N95, there is *logical* proximity and continuity of action and effect – a touch

[8] Also the text label appears only for the selected thumbnail (as with pc software tools), so that it also signifies 'selection'; yet the text label has a descriptive function as well (it verbally transduces the thumbnail).

[9] The same mobility of objects is in the so-called 'Gallery' section of the device, which displays the thumbnails of the representational artefacts (e.g., pictures and videos) that are stored in the device.

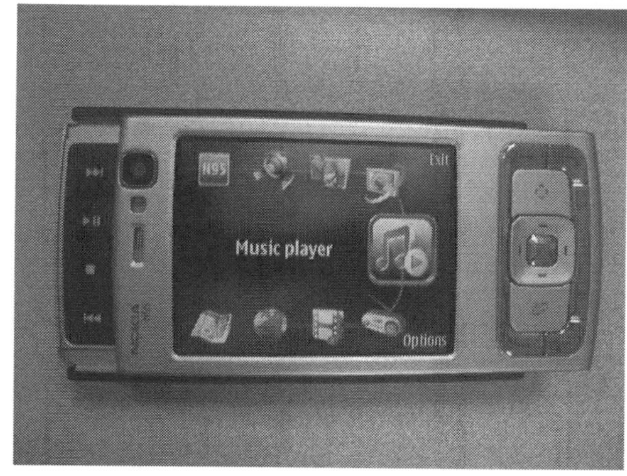

Fig. 7.3 Rotating thumbnails display (Source: http://www.flickr.com/photos/c_x/2544566184/sizes/o/)

moves the object – but there is still no *spatial* proximity/continuity – the touch is on the keys, while the object moves on the screen. With touch-screen devices like the *iPhone*, for example there is both *logical and spatial* proximity/continuity of action and effect – a touch *on* the object moves it – so that the perceived gap between virtual and real handling of objects is narrowed.

In sum, by means of a software programme, which simulates the laws of physics, interactivity with icons mirrors the aesthetics of interactivity with 'physical' objects; and so the perceptual boundaries between virtual and real are blurred. In this regard see Roschelle and Pea (2002) and their discussion of computers favouring topological representations over typological ones (for a distinction between typological and topological meaning, cf. Lemke 1999). Topological systems tend to represent reality in relational terms while typological ones tend to represent reality in specific terms and foster categorisation. Software design, it seems, may favour the former over the latter. If the distinction is seen in modal terms, the difference can be seen as ontological due to the affordances and logics of different modes, where each favours distinct forms of realism; the device's favoured topological systems represent (and conceive) reality as a matter of degrees, of continuity, rather than as a discrete distinction of *true* or *false*.

The Functionalities

Imaging

The device has two camera lenses, one on its back (so that you can see on the screen what happens in front of you and photograph it) and one on its front (so that you can see yourself on the screen while handling the device and photograph yourself). As soon as the camera lens at the back has been opened by sliding down its frame, the screen shows what is in focus of the lens and taking a picture is just one click away.

The definition of the lens (up to 5 mega pixels) is comparable to that of digital (video) cameras; while the cost of taking pictures or making a video is very low, both in terms of technological costs – one-click capturing and high-storage capacity – and, even more, of social costs. Taking a picture with a device which still remains a mobile/cell phone avoids the negative label of 'tourist'[10] for its user – something a digital camera usually signifies – while it confers on its user the status of a tech-savvy owner of an (expensive) high-tech device.

This material and social attribute of the imaging functionality makes it highly usable, so that the user of the device is easily 'seduced' into the photographic capturing of reality and as a consequence becoming motivated to understand this function, and beginning to see the world around as portions of reality to be selected and captured.

As a result, many more images of everyday life are captured with this device rather than with a digital camera; representing reality by selecting and 'capturing' becomes a 'naturalized' activity. In this way, present reality is conceived in terms of one's future needs of representation of past event, in terms of usability as representation and artefact, rather than of living experience. On the one hand, every representation can achieve further significance and, as representation has little cost, many more events and objects may seem worth being represented. Once represented they are framed (Bateson 1972) and achieve a new meaning. On the other hand, the environment may be being lived so as to represent it; and life-world may be turned into an artefact[11] to be (re)used. That can be done on the spot, by uploading the artefact on the Web or sending it to friends, for example. As a consequence, life lived offline is directly connected to online life, for instance to one's YouTube or MySpace profiles, which are 'literally' lived and enacted by means of representations. Life lived offline may provide material to life lived online (and vice versa, as in the case of the Web browsing functionality discussed here below).

Web Browsing

The mobile device makes Web browsing easy, with real consequences in one's life and social *habitus*, without necessarily being more usable.

[10]A tourist means an outsider and a mass-consumer. Tourists see touristic places, they do touristic things, they eat touristic food. They experience a predetermined aspect of a place, the one detailed in tourist guides. In taking photos of the places they visit, tourists take 'representational souvenirs' of their visit already projecting themselves as 'back home'. While this is of course a stereotyped idea of a tourist, stereotypes are the cultural homologues of socially constructed roles.

[11]This takes a stage further what has been discussed by Sharples et al. (2007, citing Banks 2004) 'Personal technology now offers people the opportunity to preserve and organise digital records of their learning over a lifetime'.

Mobile Web Access and Changes in Social *Habitus*

Mobile Web browsing reduces the need for planning ahead for activities, which happen away from non-mobile sources of information; and it reduces the need for organizing the information needed to carry out activities ahead of time. In effect this makes strategic (global) planning redundant.

The introduction of the mobile/cell phone had already made social networks more 'mobile' and meetings more contingent. Already it seems like some remote past when one had to arrange times and place of meetings well ahead of time: a time when things became really complex and difficult if any changes to previously made plans were contemplated. With mobile web browsing, the interpersonal mobility and connectivity conveyed by the mobile/cell phone joins the mobility of ubiquitous information access, so that planning of either is becoming less necessary. This may make the everyday seem or be more densely packed and at the same time make planning for future events seem an unnecessary imposition – for instance, with events, which require booking in advance. Planning may come to be felt as a constraint on the freedom to follow the desires of the moment in real-time. Where timetables and activities are predetermined, in the context of the school for instance as in many forms of work, this may produce tensions and have consequences in terms of affect.

It is inevitable that different kinds of human social dispositions, subjectivities, identities correspond to these different scenarios. It seems evident already that a generation, which is fully used to the immediacy and ubiquity of access finds it increasingly difficult to cope with social institutions and regulations of the previous kind. 'The school' is the most obvious of these institutions and it is 'the school' which is most in the firing-line in this respect.

If ubiquitous access to the web obviates much planning (cf. also Fischer and Konomi 2007), it also eliminates the need of moving signs from one medium to another or of transducting signs from one mode to another. Taking notes on post-its – themselves in their time signs of a then new fragmentation and mobility of information – printing ticket confirmations or receipts become virtually unnecessary and pointless when they are accessible via these devices. This radically changes the media and semiotic landscapes of everyday life-worlds. More and more, representations are selected and re-used in different contexts rather than transducted or produced for each new context; *recontextualization* of signifiers (form) becomes more usual than the production of new content and form in each context. It is a fore-grounding of the function of frame over content.

Since information is accessible on the spot, detailed information about the environment is now provided online (cf. the notion of 'digital augmentation' in Price 2007; and that of 'augmentation of physical space' in Roschelle and Pea 2002), so one is less likely to end up, inadvertently, in unknown places. Accessibility of information reduces risks of certain kinds. This produces changed attitude to life, time, relations and world: being informed to optimize time and experiences avoids 'time-wasting', when time is felt as a highly valued commodity. Rather than an exploration of the unknown, discovery becomes information-driven experiencing. Experiencing life becomes an activity shaped and framed by information; and 'learning' may well get confused with grabbing (reliable?) information about the environment.

Furthermore, if the environment is supplemented with detailed online information, the 'reality' of the environment is made offline and online at the same time and in the same place. This blurs the boundaries of virtual and real even more because the so-called 'virtual' no longer has a pre-assigned place and time – for instance, at home or in the office on the PC or laptop. The 'virtual' can now be accessed on the spot to check on the 'real'. The online is an extension of the offline and vice versa.

Mobile Web Usability and Changes in *Habitus*

Mobile Web browsing is easy, at least potentially, and as we have suggested, it can change how social life is conceived. However, using the facility is not necessarily easy. Web browsing on a mobile device is very different from Web browsing on the PC or laptop, both in touch input and in visual output. Because of its size, the screen of the mobile device shows a limited portion of the Web page only. The complete page can be viewed but due to its small size it is unreadable. Keying in information about searches is more cumbersome than on a PC, given the reduced affordances of the mobile keyboard.

Time spent Web browsing has a different social value on the mobile device. Indeed, in the likely conditions of use (i.e., outdoor with specific and pragmatic aims), online information must be accessed as fast as possible. These constraints of mobile Web browsing lead to a planning in advance in different form, namely for the most effective search path, with the highest possible accuracy. As a result, search strategies distinctive for this device are likely to be developed: for example, typing the Website address rather than 'googling' it to save at least one expensive passage. This may have effects on habits of search activity also with other devices (for instance, more attention might be paid to memorizing URLs of Websites, irrespective of where they are being accessed). Where the URL is unknown, specialized rather than generic search engines are more likely to be used, to save effort both in typing and in time for browsing.

The N95 predictive text database for Web browsing does not rely on online service text prediction (e.g. the one provided by browsers such as *Firefox*), but relies on the phone predictive text database – the base used for text messaging. In other words, the functionality is ahead of the semiotics of the device: the latter is oriented to the former processes of text-production, in particular through writing. This proves, for the moment at any rate to be a further difficulty in touch input. In terms of use, when mobile web browsing, it is most likely that proper names are searched – of places or of Websites. For these, the mobile's predictive text facility is useless. However since social-pragmatic purposes generally drive technologies of communication – in this case (outdoor) mobile browsing, it is likely that the device and the software will be developed in this direction.

As a consequence, at present there is a need for planning ahead for possible *short* and *effective* search strings. So while on the one hand there is a decreasing need for long term/global planning/strategy, short term local and operational planning do come into play, to access with least effort and time, the most effective path for getting the information needed.

E-mailing

Mobile email amounts to a form of mobile Web browsing in as much as sites and times of interaction are merged with activities and environments online and offline. An email can be read online while the sender is talking face-to-face to the addressee about the contents of that email. The textual input affordances of the device make reading *incoming* emails and forwarding them easier than writing emails. This is another instance of the affordance of representation-as-selection: it is more likely that selected artefacts are emailed – by forwarding incoming emails or by sending photos or Web links – rather than writing texts.

There are some textual features which allow one to tell whether an email is from a mobile device – briefer texts, very little or no introductory or closing elements, implicit reference, (lack of) punctuation and capitalization, spelling and spacing; sometimes just pictures or web links are sent with no – or small – written captions with them. The widespread use of these devices seems to be fostering a new genre, the 'mobile email', characterized by representation-as-selection more than by representation-as-new-production, compared to emails from PCs or laptops. This fits with the trend we have mentioned already.

'Positioning'

The GPS positioning function enables users to situate themselves via a representation of geography. Here a typed input, say an address, results in a visual topological output, say a geographical representation.

A paper road map, framed and selective, shows an area and its locations as both context and content; its user can focus on location and route from a given point of view. Conversely, the GPS dynamically visualizes a given position and the desired route on the screen in relation to the user's actual position. The reference point as the point of view – focus vs. context – is automatically framed on the screen; as the former changes, the context is reframed as well. By doing this with the mobile device, geographical representations of one's actual situation are recorded while being experienced. Again, life-world becomes representation/artefact, and movement becomes visual output.

Moreover, the *self* is positioned in the representation on the screen.[12] This displacement of the self, geographically represented in real time, adds to the capturing/representing of experiences of the imaging function and to the blurring of boundaries between online and offline reality.

[12]Cf. 'literally *represented in* the information structure that supports the instructional discourse, rather than *outside of it* as an information consumer' (Roschelle and Pea 2002).

Phoning and Messaging

Many options of the phoning/messaging functionality of the device are new, compared to former models of mobile/cell phones; these mainly deal with combining phoning and messaging with the other functionalities so that you can show the artefacts you are documenting/recording to the person called, for example. The addressee's device needs to be suited for real-time sharing of the 'semiotic entities' afforded by the N95. Hence the spread of such devices is likely to be fostered by social networks. This is likely to give rise to new uses of these devices, in which representations are collectively transformed in multi-'authored' chains of semiosis.

Lifeblog

The device records the whole activity done by its user, by producing a chronological multimodal representation of the user's activity. It is a multimodal diary, automatically recorded and assembled while using the device. All of life turns into a visual artefact, which is then (re-)usable, since each artefact can be edited and transferred to other devices (cf. the notion of 'act as artefact' in Roschelle and Pea 2002 and their admitted risks of '"big brothers" overtones of continuous surveillance' when applied to formal learning environments).

In a Life-blog, the ephemera of existence are captured and recorded automatically, with all the related consequences of fulfilled existential needs of 'leaving a trace' of your existence in the world (cf. among others, LeJeune 1975 and all literature dealing with 'life-writing'). The device automatically records/documents, there is, on the one hand a new question about what 'selection' might mean while on the other hand there is no need for the effort of transducing one's experiences: that is, to select them according to the interest of a specific moment and purpose, hence to frame them subjectively, and to transduct them in writing in a specific genre, as happens in writing a journal. A *trace* is automatically left; self-reflection can be left out or at any rate, can be left to later.

Barcode Reader

This is a functionality which works with the camera of the device by reading the information associated to a barcode in the offline environment. When the barcode on the offline item is associated by its designer to online information, the barcode reader can help overcoming the textual input limitations and the connection time costs for accessing online information. Here again content generation is selection, access, linkage and *bricolage*.

'Entertaining' Functionalities: Music Player, Gaming, Video Player

Portable music players are widespread and are often used to fill 'a gap of meaning' of 'non-places' and 'non-times', for instance, the unavoidable, at times frequent and long time spent in commuting, transferring, and so on. On the one hand, this is a form of isolation by ruling out one of the senses – hearing – from the perception of the environment. On the other hand, lived experience is provided with a personalized soundtrack; meaning in the form of music is added to lived experience, so that the meanings of both are transformed.

Again, with a media-convergence device, digital and (outdoor) physical environment merge, overlap and influence one another. Indeed, by merging the music player and the gaming functionalities or the video player one can entertain oneself with the device by cutting off hearing/seeing/touching from the environment (cf. also, Stald 2008). In a society which produces the sense that there is never enough time (despite the 'non-times' just mentioned), nothing must be left to chance, every moment must be optimized, so that 'life' is filled with personalized interests. In this way chance encounters and activities are also ruled out.

The Affordances of the Multifunctionality Feature

At its best, 'mobility' is foregrounded in the use of each functionality; the 'live' aspect – as 'immediacy' – is preferred over a concern with 'quality' of the artefact, which can always be edited later or once it is uploaded on to another device. This advances by a further step a *habitus* fostered by the introduction of the digital, in which editing and post-production has little cost.

In a multifunctional device, customizing each functionality is an activity which falls at a deeper conceptual level than in digital devices with one function, which have only one (main) functional destination. So, for example, in order to capture an image with the Smartphone, one must first of all select the imaging functionality out of the many others of the device, then, possibly, from there, one can customize the imaging settings (i.e., zoom, colour effects, flash etc.). In turn, a traditional digital camera is already, by default, set so as to capture images (i.e., it only needs to be switched on for the imagining functionality to be readily available), so that the imaging customization comes at a more surface level of semiotic action (just after switching on the device) than in multifunctional devices. In other words, with a multifunctional device, refining the use (i.e., personalizing the settings) of each functionality involves greater semiotic/conceptual work.

The result of the availability of multiple functions is that real-time mobility, connectivity and synergetic use of all the potentialities are prioritized over a fine-grained use of each of them. This affordance of media-convergence devices is homologous with social trends of contemporary life to change our *habitus* in terms of favouring immediacy, quantity and 'multitasking' instead of accuracy and focus. Since each functionality is more likely to be used in its default settings rather than by being 'personalized' through using its advanced options, it mirrors contemporary social trends, by facilitating a *habitus* where agency is first of all a matter of selection among template-based options, from software tools to commodities and services. In each case, 'personalization' entails greater – semiotic – costs and is therefore left to the realm of expert, that is, to highly interested and competent users. Choosing from among (pre-)given templates the one which (most) aptly fulfils immediate needs becomes normal. In turn this means that users adapt their 'needs' to fit the range of preset templates. Here too, selection and text-making as *bricolage* becomes the signifier of a contemporary notion of creativity, in which personalization as choice of the immediately available is most favoured and the semiotic work of more elaborated design are less favoured.

The multifunctionality of the device brings other material constraints, which require capacities of estimating and balancing their use for optimising resources in line with personal needs. For example, if the battery runs out in a digital camera, this limits the possibility of taking further videos or pictures. If the battery of the media convergence device runs out, it limits all connectivity: you can no longer take photos; you can neither phone nor text nor browse the Web. Since the extent of the use of one functionality leads to a possible compromising of other uses – a compromise between my interest in that use and my interest in having the device available for other functionalities – it is the user's interest which establishes a priority among uses. So real-time and just-in-time use of its affordances might be the greater priority, though it might not. Maximization of use is a signifier of what the user sees as optimization of resources.

Implications

Foregrounded and Backgrounded Capacities

The semiotic analysis here is framed with several questions in mind. From a social and economic perspective: 'what kinds of capacities are likely to be needed and in what environments?' or, from an educational one: 'what kinds of capacities are foregrounded by the affordances of media-convergence devices and how can they be used for educational purposes?' We might ask the question which has been posed several times already: 'what forms of habitus are most facilitated by this device and what forms are less or least facilitated?' And we might ask questions about gains and losses, socially, culturally, economically and communicationally: 'what cultural resources are least facilitated and most likely to be lost, what cultural products are most facilitated?'

We have answered some of these questions, implicitly and explicitly. It is difficult to sort these into positive and negative features: depending on social environments, on life-worlds and their demands, on uses and social valuations, they will be evaluated as either or both. Here are some features of the device that may be seen positively – always depending on wider social circumstances. They are nonetheless changing trends which are fostered not only by Smartphones but by all other media which we combine more and more to select, assemble and distribute our representations (i.e., to communicate). The capacities required, and thus developed, in the use of Smartphones (and many other contemporary media) are:

- flexibility of sensory engagement with the environment and adaptation of previous knowledge drawn from heterogeneous phenomena;
- real-time mobility, multi-tasking and synergetic optimized use over fine-grained focus and accuracy;

- learning '*how to* (processes)', rather than the *what* of 'content accumulation'; analogously, they foreground the function of framing (i.e., (re)contextualization of given signs) than of contents;
- a relational (topological) ontology of reality than a descrete (typological) one;
- real-time selection of apt options according to micro – individualized – interests; with more semiotic work needed for considering meso- or macro-design;
- local and operational tactics more than strategic – global – planning.

Mobile learning environments are now (more) constituted through: *how to access, select, capture, use, recontextualize* and *transform* global/collective information and events for local/individual aims, relations and activities in real-time. It remains to think about how learning as such may be affected in this.

Affordances for a Changed Social Habitus

The affordances of these convergent devices run in parallel with contemporary social trends – they are the dominant ones in our media landscape and within our cultural, economic and political environments – in fostering a *habitus* which conceives of action – and agency – as matters of navigating and selecting among options and sees content generation in the form of representation-as-selection. Through the facilities they offer, the devices contribute to a continuing and increasing blurring of the boundaries between virtual and real, offline and online; between times and sites of leisure and work; where information about activities and relations about the self, life and life-world and the environment – social and cultural more widely – can be documented/recorded/'captured' – as representation and artefact; to be selected, edited and (re-)used later and as needed as contemporary means of recording, storing, recollecting and shaping experience.

As a result, semiotic production is selection, assemblage and transformation of pre-given signs and entities (templates); in these terms it may be said that more and more production is achieved through a (newly-shaped) type of consumption (of transformation and assemblage of pre-produced components and templates); it is indeed the recording and transformation of experience (of the existing ephemeral) into a tangible representation to be (re)used.

When a life-world becomes mobile in this sense, there is a tendency to lose tolerance of any 'fixing', of planning of life; these are now perceived as limitations of freedom of agency and choice: trivial yet telling examples are 'pre-booking' or 'time and content scheduling' such as school timetables and the curricula of formal and informal learning.

When the environment is ubiquitously augmented with information, any possibility of exploration of 'the unknown' becomes difficult to recognize: when all of the world is treated as known, knowable and instantly accessible, the horizons of the new, the unknown have receded beyond visibility. Risk taking is avoidable; 'learning' is seen as grabbing all possible kinds of (reliable?) information about the environment at issue. Experiencing life is conceived of as 'being in motion', fully supplied with on-the-spot information, 'delivered' in real time. Usability, selection (choice within given possibilities), *bricolage* and mobility are values that (have) come to signify a contemporary notion of 'freedom' and 'creation'.

Over time, the introduction of a new technology with its specific (and sharp-edged) affordances/facilities into a life-world generates new (newly-shaped) needs and, hence, new purposes. Prior to a change in terms of the use you make of it according to the purposes brought from the most immediate past, appropriating[13] the device means that your purposes change as well. It is a cyclic process: you draw on the devices you know and on your purposes for which you use them to learn the possibilities of the new device; you explore what it can make; you think of what you can make of it; you use it to your (newly shaped) purposes; you shape its functionalities in use. With enhanced mobility, connectivity and means for capturing/representing reality, you are likely to aim at being more mobile, more connected and at capturing/representing more of your life/reality.

Open Questions: Gains and Losses

Technologies are cultural resources. They are taken up or not, and inserted or not by social agents according to felt social requirements, and in that they follow and foster contemporary social transformations and are shaped by them.

More and more entrenched in our media landscape – in itself characterized by a convergence of various media for the dissemination of semiotic activity produced through selection transformation and recontextualization – these mobile devices and their affordances instantiate far-reaching global trends. Large questions arise; they cannot be answered straightforwardly; yet it is necessary to try at least to formulate some of them. As a first step it is not helpful either to stigmatize mobile technology or to worship it as a panacea to any problems. As a first step we think it is wise to describe the affordances and the limitations. We might then evaluate descriptively as far as possible what is gained and what is lost in the change, in the far-reaching shift between foregrounded and backgrounded capacities, dispositions and social *habitus*. Even though the social effects of the technologies reach across many social domains, in trying to estimate gains and losses, it will be essential to do so by focussing on specific domains, on their requirements and demands. Given the aims of this book, we could, for instance, reflect on the rationale of curricular practices, which might respond to and be affected both by the technologies and by the habitus they engender in young people.

---

[13] 'We define appropriation as exploration, accommodation, assimilation and change for and in context-governed meaning-making with users/learners negotiating and evolving practices and meanings in their interaction with other users/learners, technologies and information' (Cook et al. 2008).

We do not think that at this point it is wise for us to make policy recommendations. That is a different step, to be taken in the light of needs in specific social environments. So while we would not make recommendations of the kind 'schools should introduce (rather than ban) mobile devices in formal learning practices so as to use their affordances to prepare individuals for the demands required by contemporary societies (newly-shaped consumers)', we do think that schools must engage in a serious, searching investigation of the pedagogic affordances of such devices and make decisions in the light of the perceived need of specific social aims for education. Our study is meant as a resource in such an aim.

So, by way of summing up the implications deriving from the analysis, it will be essential to ask about the desirability of capacities such as in the list below for young people and the School's perceived responsibility to present these in a seriously reflective manner:

1. The ability to act flexibly in representation, communication, text-making and knowledge creation with a disposition to adaptability;
2. To understand principles of learning as the effect of sustained engagement by a learner with aspects of a learning environment, for instance through selection as framing and as transformation;
3. To have the capacities and required disposition towards production with contemporary media in the creation of semiotic artefacts, namely those of selecting and recontextualizing;
4. To be at ease with real-time decision-making and multitasking.

There is more, of course. Given these developed capacities (i.e., required in the use of mobile tools), schools will need to provide 'navigational aids' which enable individuals to be reflective in their use of these skills, specifically in terms of 'awareness' in selection, of full understanding and creative and transformative use of templates and of a willingness to challenge seeming boundaries of what is provided, for instance in the 'personalization' of templates provided in convergent technologies.

Finally, once acknowledged and ascertained what is in the foreground in the use of these tools, schools will need to be aware of and prepared to take the initiative to fill gaps of what is not afforded, or of what is backgrounded; especially in relation to

1. fostering a reflective use of resources in 'critical thinking' so-called;
2. fostering a disposition towards agency which sees representation-as-content creation and to make full and confident use of the creative potentials of representation-as-transduction;
3. fostering dispositions which are positive toward self-reflection, risk-taking and exploration of the unknown;
4. encouraging fully 'involved' attitudes to the students' life-world, as 'experiencing';

5. encouraging the foregrounding of strategic dispositions and of design as prospective and participation in the shaping of the social world: a disposition towards 'architecture building' rather than one of mere navigation and selection among given options;
6. fostering a settled ethical view of communication as the question about benefit or disbenefit to members of the designer's community.

Chapter 8
The Mobile Complex, Socialization and Learning Resources

Introduction

Mobile devices, such as mobile/cell phones, portable gaming consoles or GPS tools, are the visible objects, the metaphorical 'tip of the iceberg' that is the mobile complex. This complex is structured in the inherent logic of ongoing socio-cultural developments. These developments lead, among other things, to a new, and highly individualised form of mobile mass communication as well as to a new social stratification with specific life style milieus and attendant value orientations. There are also socialisation effects, such as individualised expertise instead of a traditional knowledge canon defined by curricula, and there are general, as well milieu-specific habitus of learning. These features, we argue, can be explained analytically with reference to our socio-cultural ecological approach and the interrelationship between socio-cultural structures, agency and cultural practices, such as school-based learning or media use in everyday life.

Everyday Life with Mobile Devices, Socialization and Critical Mobile Literacy

The mobile complex has reached the everyday life of children and young people. If socio-cultural development does take place within everyday life, then by implication socialisation and, in turn, education are effected. The impact of new social and cultural structures on personal development is indeed affecting socialization (see Giddens 2006, pp. 160 ff.). We understand socialisation as the dynamic of a child's development as a subject in relation to a given social, cultural, factual environment and to a person's subjective, inner world of experiences, emotions, knowledge, etc. Personal development takes the form of appropriation of everyday life objects such as mobile devices. This basic argument derives from Elias (1979), who analysed socio-cultural development at the end of the European middle ages and the modernity of the Renaissance, for example by looking at the new tools of the nobility, such knifes and forks, and what habits, feelings, etc. were potentially 'inscribed' in these objects. The inscribed potential, Elias argued, could be appropriated through the use of these tools. All relevant cultural products can be

N. Pachler et al., *Mobile Learning*, DOI 10.1007/978-1-4419-0585-7_8,

seen to work in this way through appropriation. The fork, for example, provides a distance to the food on the table and requires training for toddlers on how to handle it. When socio-cultural development is at play in everyday life, education has to respond. Depending on its guiding values, education can try to gain influence, for example, through providing skills training, assessment opportunities, regulations, restrictions or making certain devices available. In the recent discussion about new technologies, the idea of the inscribed capacity of new technical cultural products was summarised by Selwyn (2008). The use of technology in everyday life, also its educative framing, contributes to the 'social construction of technology'. These technologically and socially constructed environments contain deliberately or coincidentally objectified social ideas and practices, e.g. feeling mobile, individual, integrated, autonomous, accessible, in contact, and/or wanting to be seen with a particular multimedia device in one's hand/pocket. This 'social construction of technology' takes place also in the interrelationship between generations. The adult generation produces the 'real' world through its objectified intentions, structures, competences, practices; the younger generation appropriates these complex social constructions by engaging with cultural products and their inscribed heritage. Internalisation of the objectified social construct by a user is an essential part of socialisation. Externalisation, for example by expressing, practising etc., is another way by which young people enter into a constructive relationship with their world. The integrated process of the internalisation of mobile devices as social constructions and their communicative, practical use is covered by the concept of appropriation, which we view as the basic dynamic of socialization.

Normalisation in Everyday Life

Watching children and young people wander around with earphones attached to MP3-players, making telephone calls, sending text messages, talking about their photos and videos on their mobile/cell phones, concentrating whilst operating a Nintendo play station etc., it quickly becomes obvious that mobile devices have penetrated everyday life. They have become normalised and are taken for granted across social stratifications. As we have already noted, when media or other technological devices with their specific structures and practices have reached, and amalgamate with everyday life, the educational field has to respond; but how and who?

German research data (JIM 2008), which we consider to be broadly representative for Western industrialised contexts, confirm that in 2008 95% of the over 14 year-olds owned a personal mobile/cell phone. The percentage was a bit smaller for 12 and 13 year-olds. There are no significant differences between boys and girls in higher and lower social segments. The criterion used for the discrimination between social strata by the study is the level of formal education. Just 10 years earlier, in 1998, the figure was under 10%. Since 2004 the percentage has reached the level of 95% and has remained steady. The mobile/cell phone is not at all restricted to telephony: it is a mobile multimedia device. Eighty-nine percent of the multimedia mobile/cell phones used by the 12- to 19-year-old Germans have a digital camera, around 80% have access to the internet, almost the same number can connect via Bluetooth and 58% via infrared. Seventy-four percent have access to music through an integrated MP3-player, 6% have a radio receiver. As many as 13% can access television through their mobile/cell phone.

There are social stratification differences in the breadth of applications available. Young people with a lower level of school education spend more money on their mobile/cell phones and have more applications available, although the differences are not great.

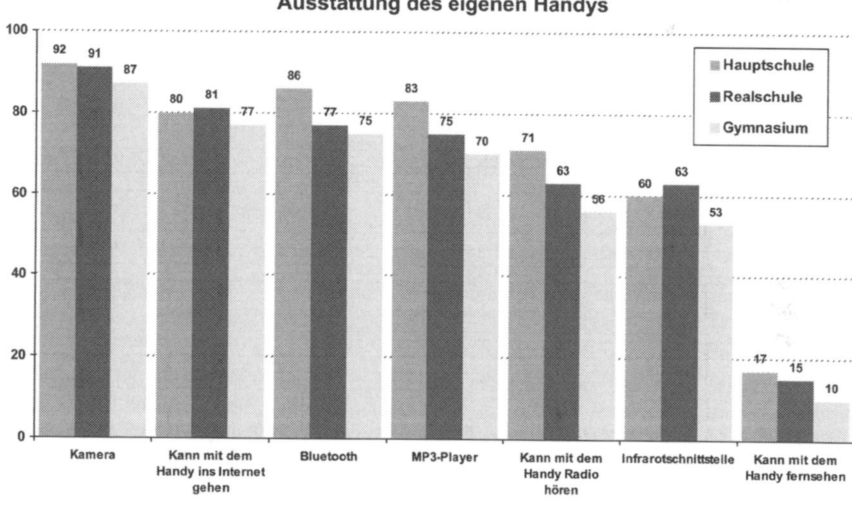

Quelle: JIM 2008, Angaben in Prozent

Basis: Handy-Besitzer, n=1.149

Fig. 8.1 Applications on mobile/cell phones in relation to level of school education (JIM 2008, p. 62)

Figure 8.2 shows the high relevance of telephony, text messaging, picture taking and listening to music. Telephony has the highest relevance (84%), followed by text messaging (79%), picture taking (45%) and listening to music (41%). The other multimedia features of the mobile/cell phone rank rather low in terms their relevance, which are the clock (8%), games (7%), listening to radio programmes (5%), exchanging data (4%), sending pictures (4%) or taking videos (3%)

Socialisation Effects of Multimedia and Multimodal Communication

Very early on in the debate about specific socialisation effects of mobile devices, Nyíri (2002) drew attention to the range of mobile applications with their mixture of representational modes within an interactive flow of communication. Writing against the background of Dewey's pedagogical perspective, Nyíri (2002, p. 2) evaluated this development rather optimistically:

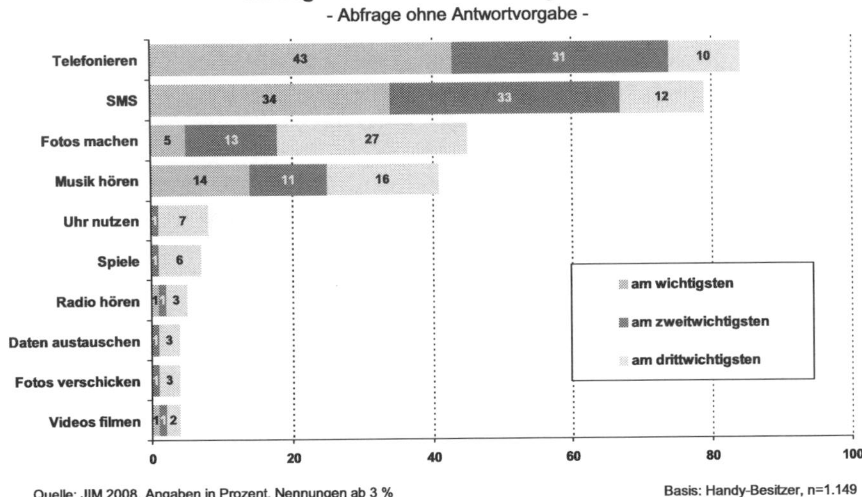

Fig. 8.2 Relevance of different mobile applications (JIM 2008, p. 64)

> Modern mobile multimedia communications devices combine voice, text, and live pictures – just think of the promise of MMS. Dewey would no doubt have found mobile telephony a medium with a great potential for the fostering of social cohesion. Also, Dewey's belief in the intrinsic connection between communication and community is fully corroborated by the insights of contemporary cognitive science.

This optimism of 'fostering social cohesion' was based on an unstable foundation already during the first phase of the introduction of the mobile/cell phone, when it was still closely linked in functionality and cultural practices to the landline. Around 2004/2005 mobile/cell phone users started to develop a real interest in personalized ring tones, which were heavily promoted by advertising. In the wake of this interest in ring tones, personalised background images for telephone displays also became available. The television adverts for these products were mainly in the form of freeze frames but required an interaction with the ring tone provider. But the interaction with the provider was based on a traditional television model and was impersonal. Horton and Wohl (1956) described this pretend social interaction as para-social. The viewer had to dial a particular telephone number with his/her mobile/cell phone in order to receive the ring tone or display background. This kind of interaction is anonymous and para-social in adhering to the logic of the old passive medium television. On the part of the provider, there is no person, just a computer, which pretends to respond interactively like a person. This para-social interaction of the adverts was based on the representation modes of the internet with images and sound and featured also some written text. Without dealing with, and making sense of, the complex, multimodal messages of the adverts one could not set up a contract for a ring tone package. Of course one possible work-around was to seek, and follow the advice of one's peer group, a strategy, which relates

Fig. 8.3 Examples of television-based adverts for ring tones and display images for mobile/cell phones by 'Jamba', which were broadcasted in Germany in March 2005 by several TV channels

to Nyíri's optimism of 'fostering of social cohesion'. The condensed nature of a ring tone contract, which is featured in subtitles, is part of literacy, which in turn relates to social stratification. The written text in the adverts is minimalist but carries important meaning: it contains the contractual conditions and obligations that are an integral part of acquiring the ring tone (Fig. 8.3). The text banner contains images of national flags with telephone numbers, web addresses and two lines of written text:

> 10 Farblogos für € 4,99/ Monat als Guthaben in diesem Sparabo (+Transport), Jederzeit Kündigung: Stoplogo an 33333.

The reading of such a condensed contract requires a high level of reading competence, and the complexity of the composition threatens social cohesion because it may deter some young people from downloading ringtones due to their inability to read the multimodal text or a lack of belief in their own ability to do so because of perceived and/or actual weaknesses in literacy competence. Reading competence is linked to social stratification and depends on the variable of gender as well as level of formal education and family background. The results of PISA on reading competence suggest a fragmenting function of written texts in terms of social cohesion. Only at a first glance, and only in the early stages of its introduction was the mobile/cell phone outside of the sphere of social stratification, namely when it was used more-or-less exclusively for telephoning whilst on the move.

> The social background of all students in a school is strongly associated with reading performance.... (The) social background of an individual student is the strongest single factor associated with performance in PISA. However, it is not just the characteristics of an individual's family but also the characteristics of the families of other students in the school that are closely associated with how well individuals performed in PISA. On average, students who attend schools with a more advantaged 'social profile' are likely to show considerably higher levels of literacy than those at less advantaged schools – and this superior performance is greater than can be accounted for by the sum of their own individual advantages (OECD 2004, p. 14).

The genre of ring tone adverts is characterised by a mixture of discontinuous images and diagrams, which have a social bias in the same way coherently written texts do. Except for in a few countries, for example in Finland, around 20% of 15 year old students tend to be unable to read texts in the sense of finding information in them, interpreting the information and reflecting on, or evaluating it; yet, as we have seen, this is a prerequisite, for example, for understanding contracts for ring tones. Multimedia and multimodal devices such as mobile/cell phones also require formal reading competence, for example to access the services offered for them.

The complexity of discontinuous texts within a communicative, para-social flow of several representation modes is rather high. But even static texts with diagrams, pictures and written elements within familiar textual genres normally used in the school context provide socio-cultural obstacles inhibiting understanding; the same is true for traditional book-based texts according to the PISA-results (OECD 2004; see also Thorpe 2006).

> Most students (80% across OECD countries) were capable of basic reading tasks at Level 2 – locating straightforward information, making low-level inferences of various types, working out what a well-defined part of a text means and using some outside knowledge to understand it. Longitudinal follow-up studies in Australia, Canada and Denmark suggest that the minority of students not capable of these tasks, those classified either at Level 1 or below, are likely to face difficulty using reading materials to fulfil their goals and to acquire knowledge (OECD 2007, p. 46).

Broadly speaking, it can be said that normally boys from low income and migrant families are less successful in school-based learning. This deficit is extended into the multimodal sphere of mobile/cell phones. Reading in the mobile context, e.g. for downloading ring tones, requires communicative and text-based practices, for example to deal with financial risks. But these communicative, text-based practices correlate with social status and do not provide for equal participation.

Nyíri (2002, p. 2) also underlined the 'informal learning' associated with mobile devices. He asserts that it has the capacity to change participation in democracy. Returning to ring tones as one of the first 'hypes' in relation to the appropriation of mobile/cell phones in everyday life, it is likely that those young people who did badly in the context of PISA, which measures learning in formal contexts, also lost money for downloading ring tones by getting trapped in long-term contracts. As already noted, one mechanism to mitigate the risks of not understanding ring tone contracts probably is recourse to social learning in peer groups. Learning outside the school, one of the defining features of informal learning, may indeed be one of the crucial socialisation effects of mobile devices.

Socialisation Effects of Ubiquity and Mobile Identity

'Always' and 'anywhere' are cultural features, which were reinforced by the internet and the cultural transformation it brought about. Ubiquity of 'conversation, participation and community' (Haythornthwaite 2008) is characteristic of this transformation, and is reinforced by mobile devices. We wonder whether the long-standing educational optimism inherent in Nyiri's quote (2002) is valid. Do mobile devices emphasise participation within the context of media convergence? Haythornthwaite expresses a certain scepticism in relation to the 'meaning of participation in an age of wiki wars, saboteurs, and information vandalism' (p. 559) but does recognise the transfer from 'traditional information gatekeepers – professional editors and librarians' (p. 559) – to new ones, such as search engines, especially Google. These developments influence what children perceive as learning and the relationship between learning in formal and informal settings. The mobility inherent in mobile devices provides significant, and deep changes by redefining the traditional relationship between children's inner and outer worlds. Stald (2008) summarises these in her examination of the social aspect of a 'mobile identity' and her exploration of mobiles as 'new tools for citizenship' (p. 146).

> First, there is (the mobile/cell phone's) immediate and ubiquitous use for social coordination and updating. Secondly, and related to this, the mobile – combined in some cases with the laptop – is a personal medium which liberates the user from the constraints of physical proximity and spatial immobility (Stald 2008, p. 147).

In other words, individualisation is increasing in the sense of availability and disposition of social activities and space. Stald (2008, p. 147) exemplifies this development by way of the following statement of a 20-year-old man:

> It is incredibly good to be mobile – when I put my mobile in my pocket and my laptop under my arm I have my office, my life, my work and my education with me – I carry everything I need with me, and the flexibility of that is totally fantastic.

This individual disposition afforded by mobile technology comprises the following key elements:

- being socially available and accessible with 'no free moments' (Stald 2008, p. 152);
- being 'simultaneously present' in a 'shared space' (Stald 2008, p. 154) as well as in 'several spaces' (Stald 2008, p. 156).

Mobile devices within a networked system can be seen to accelerate the trend towards individual disposition. This acceleration is part of a historical trajectory that arguably started as a physical experience with the invention of the car and which is now extended into the virtual world of media and communication. Viewed from the perspective of cultural history, this development is extremely new. The effect of key elements such as mobility plus individualisation plus a global system on personal development brings agency into view. Learning is clearly influenced by the increase of opportunities of technology-enhanced meaning-making outside formal settings. Furthermore, the availability of shared spaces for communication impacts on learning and its established practices. Traditional schooling is predicated on the appropriation of the objectified world and these objects dominate the processes of learning. In the mobile complex, content is generated within user-generated contexts. This trend has started with the internet and has intensified with mobile devices, applications and services. The inherent increase in individualisation accelerates individual dispositions not just in the social world but anywhere in space and time.

Educational Responses and Answers

These significant cultural changes and their effects on socialisation and everyday life are often hardly visible but at the same time profound. The first reaction of schools was to close their doors to everyday mobile life. Soon, though, schools started to engage with mobile devices in terms of critical literacy. This was motivated by violence and pornography on and around mobile/cell phones and their use and in line with its response to the emergence of previous media. Some schools, often on a project and trial-and-error basis, tried to engage with the new spaces. Following the terminology established in the context of internet theory, new spaces derive from contexts and their generation by the users (see Dourish 2004).

This educational response to harmful content has a long tradition. At the time of writing, the issue of 'sexting' (http://www.spiegel.de/netzwelt/web/0,1518,601399,00.html) was on the public agenda of mass communication. Apparently masses of American teenagers photographed themselves naked and distributed the pictures by MMS. Related accusations of child pornography were on the increase.

The German data on bullying and pornography and mobile/cell phones among 12 to 19 year-olds are ambiguous (JIM 2008, pp. 65 f.). More than 80% of boys and girls from all socio-cultural strata know about such content, but just around a third claim to know a person in their social environment, who has received violent or pornographic videos. Only 11% of boys and girls within a lower socio-cultural school context have personally received bullying or pornography-related content. These results suggest that the issue is on the public agenda, but is not very concrete. A relatively small group of 10% or fewer do have real experiences with harmful content

The data in Fig. 8.4 show a gender and social bias towards boys from a lower social class stratification. Figure 8.5 shows a dramatic bias in terms of social stratification but also in terms of age (14–17 year olds). Not so much the age factor but the correlation between gender (boys) and lower class stratification has to be taken into consideration by school as it correlates with success in school-based reading literacy (see the discussion of the PISA results above). Other German data (see Mößle et al. 2007, p. 99) on media use by migrant boys point in the same direction of a risk of this group in relation to the use of mobile devices.

For us a question about the social meaning of these difference arises from this data. We deem it necessary for schools to recognise these social differences and to make them visible as well as to respond to these different attitudes. The analysis of the case of the migrant boy Cyrill (Chapters 4 and 10), as well as the examination of new socio-cultural milieus, signal a trend for us, which points to

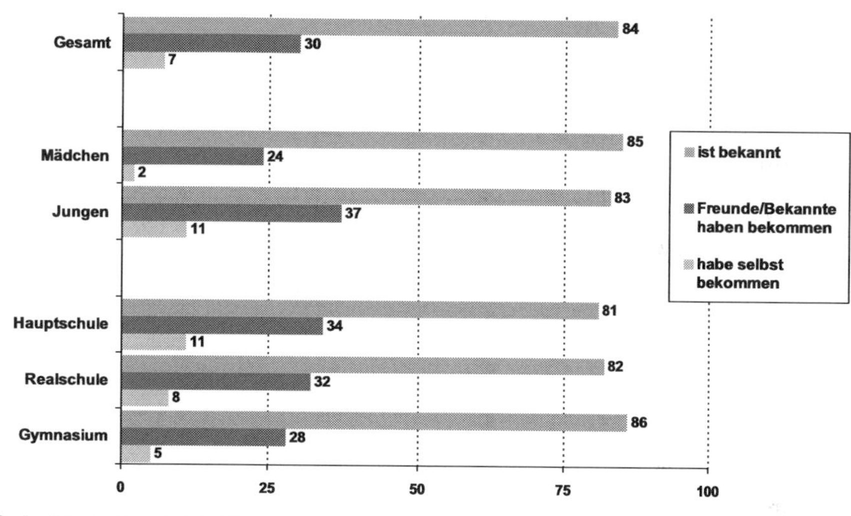

Fig. 8.4 Knowledge/receipt of harmful content on mobile/cell phones (from abstract to personal) (JIM 2008, p. 65)

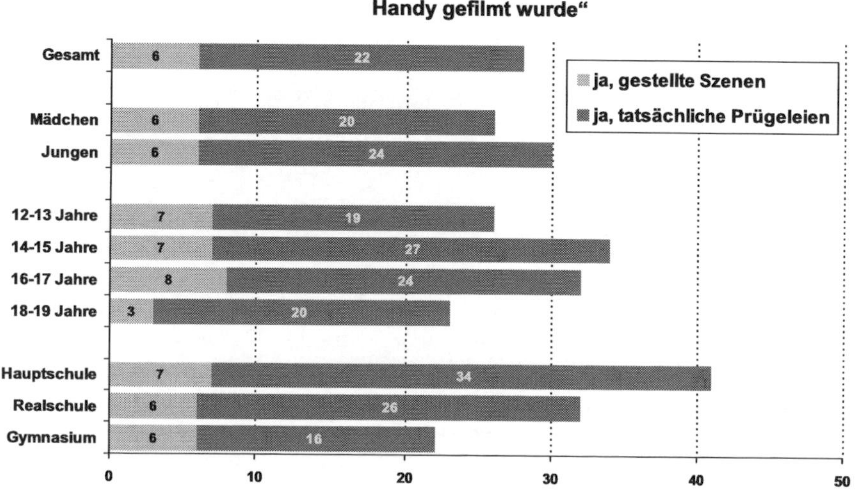

Fig. 8.5 Knowledge of a fight being filmed on a mobile/cell phone (from enacted to real) (Source: JIM 2008, p. 66)

a purposeful ‘disintegration’ and to the attempt by the individuals concerned to demonstrate their own cultural identity. Doing risky things belongs to this habitus. And it is because of this trend that participation needs to be on the educational agenda.

The German media education agency Medienpädagogischer Forschungsverbund Südwest, which provided the data on mobile media use above, also offers material on critical mobile literacy. These material are characterised by a multimedia approach and accessible on the internet. Downloads include advice on a range of topics such as respect and dignity, cyberbullying and avoiding costs. No evaluation data are available about the use and effectiveness of these resources, but the multimedia and multimodal approach seems to appeal even to the boys who are looking for fun and risks.

Another approach to critical literacy is to following the students to different cultural sites. The mobile/cell phone can accompany students into their life-worlds and help to objectify their perceptions and experiences. The example of the Indian school in Domlur (see Chapter 4 and 11) demonstrates the reflexivity, which provides a simple, but typical mobile investigation: boys exploring the city to find geometrical forms such as circles in the form of car tyres or cubes in architecture. They take photos of these objects and discuss them in the school within mathematics. Beside a reflection on aspects of everyday life that are taken for granted, an unexpected ambiguity becomes part of the Maths lesson in this way. Pictures from everyday life are being compared with the idealised images from the text book. Furthermore, the teacher has to deal with the differences between everyday life and science. In the Domlur example, the different settings are pre-given; the new challenge comes from the interrelationship of ‘natural’ with school settings as well from the new user-generated contexts, which appear within the frame of multimedia convergence. As noted above, Stald describes this development as being ‘simultaneously present’ in a ‘shared space’ (Stald 2008, p. 154) as well as in ‘several spaces’ (Stald 2008, p. 156). Fostering reflexivity in this way can be viewed as an act of critical mobile literacy.

The Mobile Complex Within Socio-Cultural Developments

In the specialist literature (e.g. Haythornthwaite 2008; Beale 2007b; Nyiri 2002), the reference to the importance of the notion of ‘ubiquity’ can frequently be found; we deem it necessary to provide a fruitful cultural perspective on the increase of individualisation by means of a variety of mobile devices within media convergence. Web 2.0 and social networking exemplify this convergence. Portable mobile devices in everyday life can be seen to contribute extensively to individualisation and the ubiquity that results from it. Another significant aspect of recent socio-cultural developments is the connection between different media and their convergence, which have become characteristic for everyday life.

The Triangle Model of Socio-Cultural Development

What basic structures govern ubiquity and mobile individualisation? There are of course the mobile devices themselves, their manufacturers and lots of applications made available for them, often by third party providers. The devices belong to, and are manifestations of, fundamental changes in mass communication in which increasing emphasis is on user-generated content and contexts. School, as an important locus for learning, remains characterised by relatively stabile cultural practices, which are governed by clear structures, such as guidance by a teacher and an objectified curriculum. And, to some extent school also exerts a certain influence on media use and socio-cultural development. Yet, the changes in everyday (media) culture, the (social) structures that facilitate and constrain them and the informal learning embedded in them, have a bearing on schools, for example, in terms of

- the ongoing de-trationaliszation inherent in globalisation with its individualisation of social risks;
- a new social stratification by milieus and lifestyle; and
- a transformation of mass communication characterised by user-generated contexts and content.

One important aspect of socio-cultural developments relates to the formation of identity and subjectivity, which in turn is the result of socialisation. The formation of identity and subjectivity leads to agency, which is the capacity to deal with, and to act upon, socio-cultural structures and prevailing cultural practices. In addition, agency includes the capacity to construct one's own life-world as well as one's own curriculum vitae but also to deal with media and to make meaning of, and in the world. The established cultural practices of media use in everyday life – in particular those around the use of mobile devices – as well as the cultural practices of school in our view both dominate children's lives and are, at the same time, formative and influential as socio-cultural structures in terms of children's development and their agency.

We see our socio-cultural frame for mobile learning based on the interrelationship of socio-cultural structures, agency (see Giddens 1984) and cultural practices (see e.g. Lefebvre 1972 and Wenger 1998, p. 5 as well as, in media and cultural studies, Hall 1997, p. 36). For a diagrammatic representation, see Fig. 1.4 in Chapter 1. Socio-cultural structures, agency and cultural practices reflect the change in mass communication from professionally edited content, transmitted on the basis of a fixed schedule, to Web 2.0 with its social networking tools and the rise of ubiquitous, individualised mobile content and context generation. The convergent mobile devices foster and shape the agency of users, who appropriate them not only in the way that is 'designed-in' by prevailing structures. Users act within existing cultural practices and they develop new ones.

Educationally Relevant Features Within the Mobile Complex

In the following we discuss key features of structures, agency and cultural practices for mobile devices as learning resources with educational relevance. Figure 8.6 provides a diagrammatic overview.

Socio-Cultural Structures, Including Technological sTRUCTURES, Within the Context of Individualized Risk

One key element in the discussion of mobile learning for us is the socio-cultural segmentation by milieus and lifestyles with their related attitudes to learning and media literacy. Another relates to some fundamental changes in mass communication from editorial push to individualized pull systems in social networks within the convergence of media as well as the convergence of physical and virtual spaces. At the same time, school is losing its influence as the dominant power in defining what counts as learning and we diagnose an increase in learning in informal contexts. The field of learning is expanding significantly beyond the school and factors such as socio-cultural milieus, family support and personalisation increasingly come into play. Curriculum-based learning in school is partially failing specific learners (see e.g. the discussion of PISA results above) and knowledge is no longer only defined by the learning processes and practices of the school, but also by the social structures of globalization.

Milieus as Main Socio-Cultural Structure

In the process of individualization new socio-cultural milieus appear; they can be viewed as collective frames of reference and consist of two constitutive variables: lifestyle, with its orientation towards traditions or modernity, and formal education, together with professional status. Socio-cultural milieus support specific attitudes and a certain habitus of media use as well as learning and they lead to a specific socio-cultural habitus and social stratification (see Fig. 8.7). The new, and by now stable social stratification is characterised by two variables: (a) social status, which contains formal education and professional success, and (b) lifestyle with an orientation towards modernity as a value. Most children and young people live within segments B and C at level 3 and 2: 'Sensation oriented'/'Consumer-Materialistic'/'Modern Mainstream' (see also Fig. 1.3).

In everyday life the 'designed-in' structures of the applications of mobile devices and their attendant media literacy coincide with the new horizontal social lifestyle segmentation as well as the hierarchical segmentation, which includes income, professional status and formal education.

Mobile, Individualised Mass Communication as a Socio-Cultural and Technological Structure

Mobile devices and their applications operate within the context of media convergence – the increasing interconnectedness of different media, tools, applications,

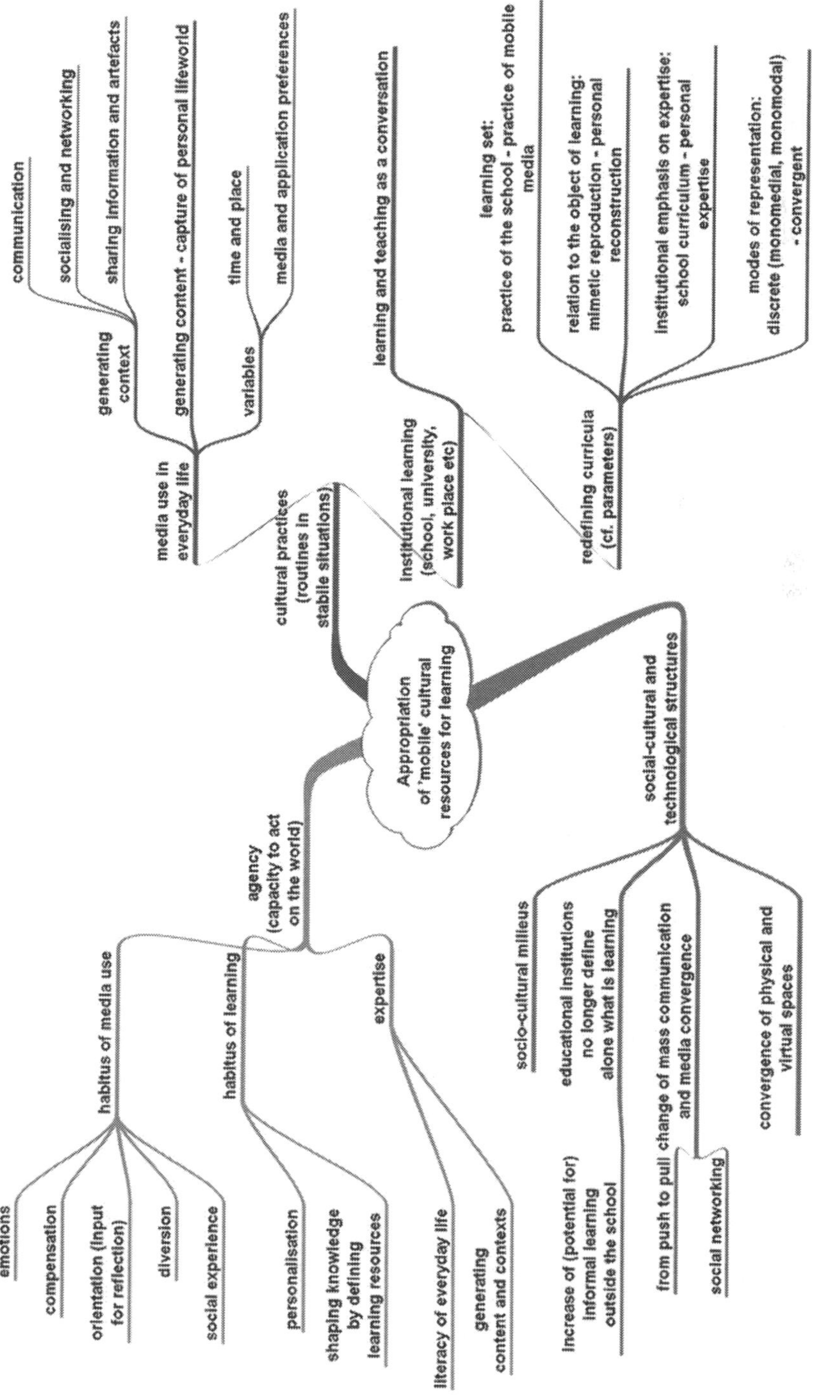

Fig. 8.6 Socio-cultural structures, agency and cultural practices in relation to mobile devices and learning

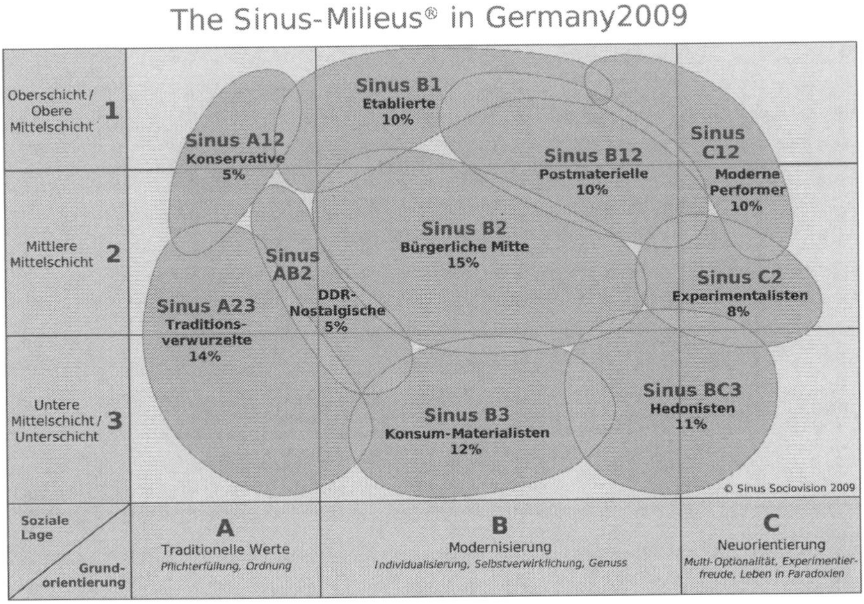

Fig. 8.7 Percentage of the German population per socio-cultural milieus (Sinus Sociovision 2009, p. 13)

programs, etc. mainly, but by no means exclusively around ubiquitous internet connectivity – and are a driving force behind individualisation in mass communication because of user-generated contexts. User-generated content and contexts are powerful and competitive alternatives to traditional mass communication, which is transmission-based and operates on the basis of editorial control. User-generated content and contexts are fast becoming an integral part of everyday life, for example in the form of Web 2.0 social networking with the following features:

- integration into everyday life activities such as shopping, banking, searching knowledge archives;
- social role, e.g. chats, online communities, blogs, telephony, learning platforms;
- shift of mass communication away from the traditional push-model to a pull-model with publicly accessible programme repositories;
- shift away from programme consumption to user-generated content;
- shift away from default contexts of media reception to individualised user-generated contexts, often within structures such as video platforms.

The new structure of mass communication is taken for granted by the majority of young people, for example when they engage with a Maths homework community on YouTube or when they use other Web 2.0 services such as Bebo for community building, self-expression and entertainment. The use of mobile video applications for capturing and editing footage and uploading it to web-based video repositories such as YouTube or MySpace has also become common (see e.g. the case study of Cyrill in Chapters 4 and 10) and is accelerating with the release of new technologies such as the iPhone 3Gs (http://www.techcrunch.com/2009/06/25/youtube-mobile-uploads-up-400-since-iphone-3gs-launch/). This mass media structure is a prerequisite for user agency. It is also on track to regulate new cultural practices. To give a specific example, a video platform contains the following structural elements (see Adami 2009):

- dual media access (computer and video recorder/mobile device) with multimodal representation;
- communicative order mainly through written texts and conversational chains;
- international communication underpinned by common codes of global English and international culture;
- regional communication through video characterised by an amateur style which integrates the personal (thematic) perspective of the user coupled with global publication;
- priority of the representational modes above content.

These milieu and cultural media contexts are not neutral for the development of children. Viewed in terms of Vygotsky's model of child development within 'zones of proximal development' (Vygotsky 1978/1930, pp. 84), these contexts can serve as scaffolding for the development of children. 'Scaffolding' is Bruner's educational response to render learning objects accessible for appropriation by children (Wood, Bruner, Ross 1976) by bringing learning objects and contexts into a meaningful relationship with each other.

Agency

Agency is the capacity to act on the world within its socio-cultural, technological structures and its cultural practices. It is the capacity to develop life-worlds and a personal life trajectory, among other things, by means of media use and meaning-making. Important factors in the context of agency are the prevalent learning habitus as well as the habitus for media use in personalised life-worlds. The societal trend towards individualised risk promotes individual expertise with which to act on one's personalised life-world. Within the variety of life-worlds and activity patterns available, everybody has to cope with her/his segment and pattern. There is no longer a general model for success and what can be seen as a fulfilled life. Everybody tries to make the best possible sense of the world around them by attending to specific features according to their social milieu and its activity patterns. This fragmentation enforces individualised expertise in seeking to avoid failure, because there is no longer a general and overarching 'insurance system', i.e. doing well in school as a guarantee for getting a good job, etc. (see Beck 1986). The rationale of individualisation of social risks promotes agency and individual expertise. For us, an understanding of agency as a process in the context of personal development through appropriation of cultural and social products from the real world, such as media, is crucial for access of education to the interrelationship of *mobile* structures, agency and cultural practices. Furthermore, we argue that within the process of individualisation the transfer of risks from the state to individuals is impacting on learning as a social risk. The risks for learning through the appropriation of cultural objects are different to the risks associated with nativistic, fixed views of intelligence as a determinant factor in learning. Because of the fragmentation of life-worlds and activity patterns, learning is losing its general validity, which was traditionally safeguarded for everybody by the institution of the school. School-based learning as appropriation of 'the' world is now co-regulated by life-worlds; it still appears to fit into three quarters of – increasingly fragmented – life-worlds and their respective patterns of appropriation. But the remaining 25% of people, the match of the structures and practices of school-based learning and the activity patterns of everyday life is less good; young people in this category are potential 'at-risk' learners because their way of appropriation does not match that of school. At this point, we argue, it is incumbent upon schools to assimilate the characteristics of these life-worlds and attendant patterns of appropriation. For a detailed discussion of some key factors see e.g. Bernstein and Henderson (1973), who focus on the variables of social class, language socialisation and school assessment. We would add to this the new socio-cultural milieus with their specific lifestyles. Negotiated by milieus and lifestyle, the management of learning risks is now an important issue for children and young people. They develop their habitus of action and learning within certain milieus and associated lifestyles, to which specific cultural products such as media, incl. mobile devices, belong. The case of Cyrill substantiates these assertions.

Agency Structures for Learning

Learning is one mode of meaning-making, which only partially coincides with the curricular traditions of schools. Within personalized life-worlds, certainly those of young people, a new habitus of learning has developed, and continues to develop, that is in tension with traditional learning, which is still governed by learning objects and school subjects and objectified learning outcomes. The process of individualization outlined above supports personalized expertise, which is individually appropriated on the basis of personal definitions of relevance within life-worlds. Furthermore, learning is individualized within divergent socio-cultural milieus, which leads to informal learning practices within milieus that are at a distance to the school.

Agency Structures for Media Use

The personal function of media use is one important variable in the context of agency. Media use can be understood to be based on five agency dimensions (Dehm and Storll 2003, p. 429), which apply to the television in the same way they do to the internet, and probably also to mobile devices as stand-alone devices or as part of a complex media set (cf. media convergence):

(1) emotions (e.g. to have fun, to laugh, to relax);
(2) orientation (e.g. input for reflection, stimulus for learning);
(3) balance, compensation (e.g. distraction from everyday life problems);
(4) diversion, to pass the time (e.g. meaningful use of time, habit); and
(5) social experience (e.g. to have the feeling of belonging, to participate in the life of others).

Cultural Practices with Relevance for Learning and the Use of Mobile Devices

Cultural practices are routines, which are typical for a particular culture and type of situation. Students operate across different types of cultural practices characterized by different kinds of media use. These cultural practices and related types of media use afford, and have inherent in them, different types of learning and they differ across everyday life and school. In everyday life, learning is often problem-solving orientated, subconscious, subliminal and tacit, experience-based, non-routine and serendipitous. School regulates learning strictly through curricula and assessment. Furthermore, the school, as institution, does have the means and wherewithal to design curricula, which are able to foster naïve learning at the appropriate level of reflection and complexity. One can expect a mobile device or application to have more chance of success to bring about learning that is formally recognised if the media use and the attendant learning complement each other across everyday life and school or, even better, if they reinforce each other through assimilation and accommodation. Therefore, an understanding of the underlying common structures is of high relevance, especially a perspective on curricular learning as situated (Lave and Wenger 1991) and a commitment by schools to explicitly link formal learning to content and context generation in everyday life. The decreasing power of the school to be able to define what successful learning is and should look like for all socio-cultural milieus, is mirrored by an increasing social self-definition of knowledge bases globally (see Dunning 2000). This social definition of a global knowledge society and its tension with canonical school knowledge and teaching and learning practices lead to an ambiguous function of media-based learning in everyday life as a resource for school-based learning. The ambiguity is compounded by differing definitions and roles of learning in socio-cultural milieus.

The redefining of curricula and pedagogical approaches with particular reference to the design of situations for learning is the main task of Chapter 11 and 12 where we propose four parameters for creating situations for mobile learning (see in particular Chapter 12):

- *learning set:* practice of the school – practices of mobile devices,
- *relation to the object of learning*: mimetic reproduction – personal reconstruction,
- *institutional emphasis on expertise*: school curriculum – personal expertise,
- *modes of representation*: discrete (mono medial, mono modal) – convergent.

Our discussion in this chapter shows that a key task relating to the planning of purposeful and effective learning situations within the mobile complex is to assimilate children's and young people's interest in the following for learning:

- meaning-making in everyday life,
- the generation of individualized contexts and the context- and milieu-defined relevance of meaning, and
- media use in everyday life with its overlapping regional and global cultural traditions of youth and entertainment.

Schools need to foster cultural participation within the mobile complex. In order to do so, they need to recognise the individualised, naïve expertise of young people for learning and to use their didactic knowledge to develop in students the capacity for critical reflection and critical literacy.

Chapter 9
Appropriation and Learning

Introduction

One key challenge for us relates to how we get from the phenomenology of the mobile complex, discussed in Chapter 8, to a workable educational response. In addressing this challenge, we turn our attention to a learner perspective and examine how they deal with everyday life and school. In this book we propose that the interrelationship of everyday life and school can be supported by

(a) *conversational threads* between the children's everyday lives and the school and
(b) docking the school as a developmental context onto contexts generated by students in and through their mobile practices in everyday life.

Our proposal is grounded in the relationship of children to pre-given cultural products, which they appropriate. In the process of appropriation children develop and grow up. Appropriation, in this view, is the process of internalisation and externalisation of the objectified world and it is the dynamic behind the development of children. The objectified world consists of cultural products of everyday life, such as media, as well as of objects for learning in school, such as foreign language vocabulary or grammar rules. In a society characterised by individualised risk, appropriation is losing one of its traditional frames, namely the common school curriculum, which is diminishing in importance. In some of the socio-cultural milieu, learning is already no longer primarily defined by the school curriculum and no longer afforded a higher value than predominately entertainment-orientated media use.

In this period of social transition, the notion of appropriation functions as an *umbrella* term for us, which captures children's activities in the world. We believe that it is a powerful concept for education in the context of the mobile complex.

Firstly, it fits in with the educational tradition going back to Vygotsky of understanding the development of children on the basis of their appropriation of cultural objects. At the beginning of the 20th century, a period of de-traditionalization and increasing industrialisation, the development of a child could no longer be taken for granted; a social frame for child development was needed. More than a century

N. Pachler et al., *Mobile Learning*, DOI 10.1007/978-1-4419-0585-7_9,

earlier, and also against the background of a dramatic social and cultural crisis – the end of feudalism – , Humboldt introduced the notion of 'Bildung' (formation) into education. 'Bildung' is based on the appropriation of cultural products. Both cultural approaches on education, that of Vygotsky and that of Humboldt, are helpful for our pedagogical deliberations in the context of the mobile complex. One key element of our thinking is the need for the deliberate assimilation of mobile devices into the school.

Of course, Habermas' social theory, in particular the theory of communicative reason or rationality, reinforces the general educational approach by way of appropriation, and helps to understand the ambiguity of the rationale from which mobile devices emerge as new resources. Mobile learning is not just an 'internal colonisation of the life-world' (Habermas 1995, Vol. 2, p. 489), 'a destruction of tradition which threatens the very continuance of the reproduction of society as a whole' (Giddens 1982, p. 328), but also a meaningful communicative activity and it constitutes a reflexive relationship with the world (Habermas 1995, Vol. 1, p. 148).

Secondly, socio-cultural development reinforces individualisation, which is why the mobile complex mainly works by way of appropriation. Individualisation becomes immediately visible, for example through the headphones young people wear as they listen to their personal music selection on their mobile device. The specific emphasis on individual use is one of the reasons why appropriation for us is at the centre of the socio-cultural and technological structures, agency and cultural practices of the mobile complex (see Fig. 8.7).

Furthermore, appropriation is a theoretical response to a society of individualised risks, which no longer has school learning as its preferred process of appropriation. Education has to engage with learning and media use at a meta-level in order to find assimilative components and parameters (see the four didactic parameters in Chapter 12).

From the perspective of children and young people at the intersection of everyday life and school (see Fig. 6.1), the components and parameters have to deal with the specificities of the ongoing cultural transformation caused by mobility. If one tried to condense the mobile complex for educational purposes, user-generated contexts and content would stand out. The reason for their high educational relevance is the inherent extension of the principles of individualised social risks for meaning-making. Meaning-making, which encompasses learning and media use, constitutively depends on situations, which are also one of the basic elements of situated learning (Lave and Wenger 1991, see also Chapter 11). One defining feature of situated meaning-making, which was not considered by Lave and Wenger, is the integration of situations within the social and cultural trend towards individualisation. Meaning-making, in the context of socio-cultural transformation, is fragmented and individualised within different cultural situations, which reach from media use to learning in formal contexts. What connects meaning-making across these contexts are the notions of user-generated contexts and content. The task for educators, as we see it, is to integrate these phenomena into an educational model of learning by means of appropriation (see also Luckin et al. 2005, p. 5, 2009, p. 5).

Appropriation: Personal Development and the Internalization of Cultural Products

How best to conceptualise learning in a mobile world? For us, learning is not about wandering through the spatial world in a self-determined way and picking up knowledge. First of all, mobility is not narrowly spatial but also importantly consists of the capacity to define situations and contexts in the pre-given world. Mobile devices provide new opportunities to define situations and contexts for learning. Outside the school such a definition of mobility in terms of situations and contexts highlights the risks and challenges for learners in the mobile complex. Through the focus on situational activities at the intersection of culture and child development the learning landscape is dramatically widened beyond stabile learning objects. These new contexts for learning necessitate an extension of the ideas of Vygotsky, whose influential work, we posit, must be understood in the context of the technologically and socially driven transformation of industrialization in the first third of the 20th century and who defined the characteristics of human development in contrast to a development based on the instrumental conditioning of reflexes or on the extension of the body by tools for mastering nature (Vygotsky 1978/1930, p. 19 ff.).

Internalization, Environment and Development

According to Vygotsky (1978/1930), 'higher psychological processes' result from a relationship 'between human beings and their environment, both physical and social' (p. 19). In the context of the early 21st century, these higher psychological processes are probably best thought of as *culturally defined activities and meaning-making*. Vygotsky considered social interactions, for example speaking and transformations of practical activities such as using a tool. In these processes of transformation children appropriate complex action modes, such as scientific concepts, within situations (Vygotsky 1986/1934, p. 146 ff.). The key process is internalization, for example of the instrumental use of a tool: 'An operation that initially represents an external activity is reconstructed and begins to occur internally' (Vygotsky 1978/1930, p 56 f.). Furthermore, the social situation of the external activity, for example the conditions for the use of tools, is internalized: 'An interpersonal process is transformed into an intrapersonal one' (Vygotsky 1978/1930, p 57). A child's development depends on these processes of internalization: 'The transformation of an interpersonal process into an intrapersonal one is the result of a long series of developmental events' (Vygotsky 1978/1930, p 57). Vygotsky characterises this interrelationship of internalization and development as culturally depended: 'The internalization of cultural forms of behavior involves the reconstruction of psychological activities on the basis of sign operations' (1978/1930, p 57).

How is learning to be understood in this interrelationship between internalization, cultural forms of activities and child development? Vygotsky (1978/1930, p. 84 ff.) makes a clear difference between forms of learning separating pre-school from school learning. A child, according to Vygotsky, is only able to proceed from 'non-systematic' preschool learning to school learning if s/he has reached an adequate level of development. The child's history of internalization and his/her development in terms of 'higher psychological processes' has to correlate with the tasks of internalization, which school learning demands.

The implication of Vygotsky's line of argument on internalization and child development was, and continues to be, important in terms of school-based learning: not the learning object rules learning, but child development, i.e. the phases within a child's development, the so-called 'zones of proximal development', in which children are susceptible to internalizing learning objects. Like his contemporary, Piaget (1947/2001, p. 8, 52, 110), Vygotsky (1978/1930, p. 84)[1] also speaks of learning as assimilation, which importantly has to respect a child's development as a process in its own right.

'Zones' Revisited: **Responsive** *Contexts for Development*

The aim behind our attempt to update Vygotsky's theoretical argument around the 'zone of proximal development' is to understand the user-generated contexts of mobile, individualized mass communication as personally relevant contexts for development. As we have already discussed in Chapter 1, in Vygotsky's terminology such a developmental context is a 'zone'. This includes a shift from time as developmental axis, which is in line with Piaget's work, to contextual zones of development. Today child development is no longer primarily theorized with reference to the variable of time, that is to growing up by internalization within phases of one's life course. Vygotsky's educational response to the challenges of phases of child development and formal learning was to teach according to a child's 'zone of proximal development' (Vygotsky 1978/1930, p. 84).

This response is still highly relevant but, in our view, requires re-interpretation in terms of the process of development. Today developmental phases and cultural environments shape child development. It is probably a coincidence of translation that the notion of 'the internalization of cultural forms of behavior' (Vygotsky 1978/1930, p 57) matches with that of Williams (1974) who, in the early years of Cultural Studies, wrote about communication and media, such as television, in similar terms. He argued that media, such as television, contribute to our social construction of reality and that they are part of our historical material processes and subject to change over time. Recent cultural forms of individualized mobile mass communication are primarily based on environmental contexts and not on time periods. This represents a significant difference to the conditions in the industrial society of Vygotsky. The notion of time periods in relation to cognitive development was introduced by Piaget in the form of his idea of a developmental age. Vygotsky's (1978/1930, pp. 85 ff.) corresponding notion is that of the 'mental age' (p. 87) of children. But the shift of cultural forms from the 1920s and 30s to today's media-dominated culture requires a rethinking in relation to notions of internalization,

[1] For explicit references to Piaget's ideas, see e.g. Vygotsky 1978/1930, p. 27; 1986/1934, p. 12 ff.

environment and development. Already mass communication between sender and receiver was not organized mainly temporarily, but as a situational environment consisting of programme provider, media with a programme offering and audience. The video recorder diminished the relevance of time flow within television-dominated environments. The ongoing shift away from a push system with a dominant program provider to a user-dominated pull system reduces the relevance of time structures further and makes to situational context structures even more important.

Why do we propose a shift away from 'proximal development', a term readily associated with Vygotsky, to a notion of 'responsive contexts'? One reason is to free ourselves from the constraints inherent in the almost stifling presence of Vygotsky's terminology and to open up the dynamic of child development again in view of the conditions of the new prevailing contexts. Of high relevance for us is the focus on the quality of contexts, which we seek to capture with the term 'responsive'. In so doing we aim to relate the importance of quality of context to child development: from our educational perspective, a context has to respond supportively to, and act as a challenge for a child.

One of the connotations of the English translation 'proximate' for Vygotsky's notion is closeness to a child's personal centre. The personal centre of a child can be educationally influenced through themes, which structure their activities and serve as personally meaningful guidance. The thematic approach to communication and learning was explored, among others, by Freire (1970/2007) with his concept of generative themes. Freire found in his work on the alphabetization of adult farmers that they deal with written text, if the rationale for reading and writing fits into their activity frame and align with the aims and objectives of their activities. The importance of personal themes was also empirically confirmed for media reception (see Charlton and Bachmair 1990). From the perspective of our educational rationale, a context constitutes a supportive framing for child development if it responds to the child by taking up themes that are relevant for him/her. For these reasons we understand new cultural contexts as *responsive* if they offer thematic conversational potential, which supports the development of a child.

Cultural Products and Child Development

We consider child development to be a reflexive relationship with the cultural environment and to work on the basis of the internalization of cultural products. This reflexive relationship includes the intra-personal world as well as the world around us, or the mediated world. This idea is central for Mead's idealistic version of child development (Mead 1934), to which the dialectic of 'I' and 'Me' belong: the I, the bodily identity, and the Me, the negotiated, appropriated and symbolic identity, which is situated in the internal world of a person. Of course, *cultural product* is a modern term, which derives from Cultural Studies. As we already explained in Chapter 1, the original term *manifestations of the human mind* derives from Hegel (1807/1986) and intends to summarize all cultural objectifications of mankind. Its educational application derives from Humboldt (1767–1835; 2002a–d), who tried to understand child development as a cultural phenomenon. Not to consider the development of children as a result of drill or in terms of the growing of plants (see e.g. Rousseau's metaphor of gardening) without any educational support was an approach rooted in the Enlightenment, where child development was related to relevant cultural objects.

Bildung (formation) can be understood as a person's agency to deal reflexively with oneself and the world. *Formation* results from two dialectic poles, one is child development, the other, and opposite pole, is constituted by objectified knowledge. Objectified knowledge comprises cultural products, such as a language and its literature, which incorporate, for example, the human values of the speaker and authors. Through the cultural products and artefacts of a society, individual and collective experiences are objectified and *archived* in texts, tools, words, buildings etc. It is obvious that each generation has to integrate these pre-given cultural objects into their life accomplishments. The modes of internalizing reach from the simple use of tools to complex work or learning activities. This appropriation through internalisation has, at least until recently, been constitutive for the inter-generational relationship between adults and young people. The adult generation 'produces' the world, which carries their objectified experiences, competencies, values, constraints, ideologies, visions etc. The personal development of children, their growing up, depends on the appropriation of the cultural products.

From such a theoretical perspective of appropriation of cultural products and their objectified knowledge or values etc. an empirical operationalization is possible. The theoretical field of Cultural Studies inter alia contains a view of mass communication as a cultural form, which is based on objectified cultural products and their appropriation, e.g. by way of modes of reading (Hall 1980, p. 136). The old mass communicative push system is an expression of producing media in the centralised form of industry; this is a process of encoding. Appropriation is decoding with different modes of reading (Hall 1980, Fig. 9.1).

Du Gay (1997, Fig. 9.2) provides a model of appropriation in the context of mass communication shifting to an open pull systems.

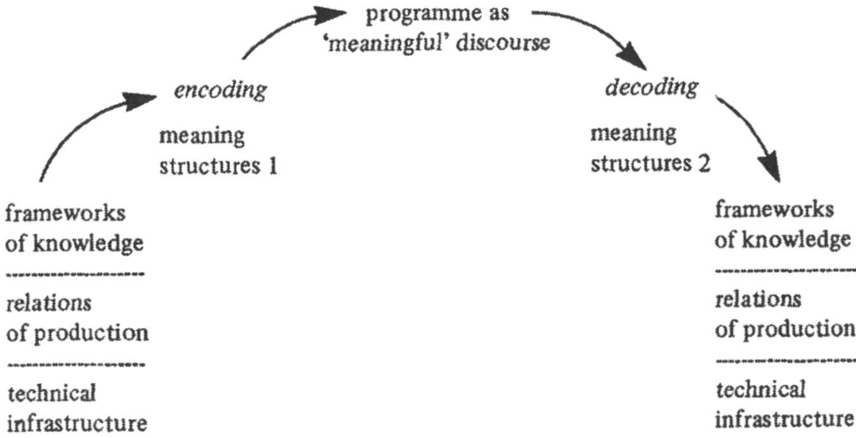

Fig. 9.1 Appropriation in the old push system of mass communication (Hall 1980, p. 131)

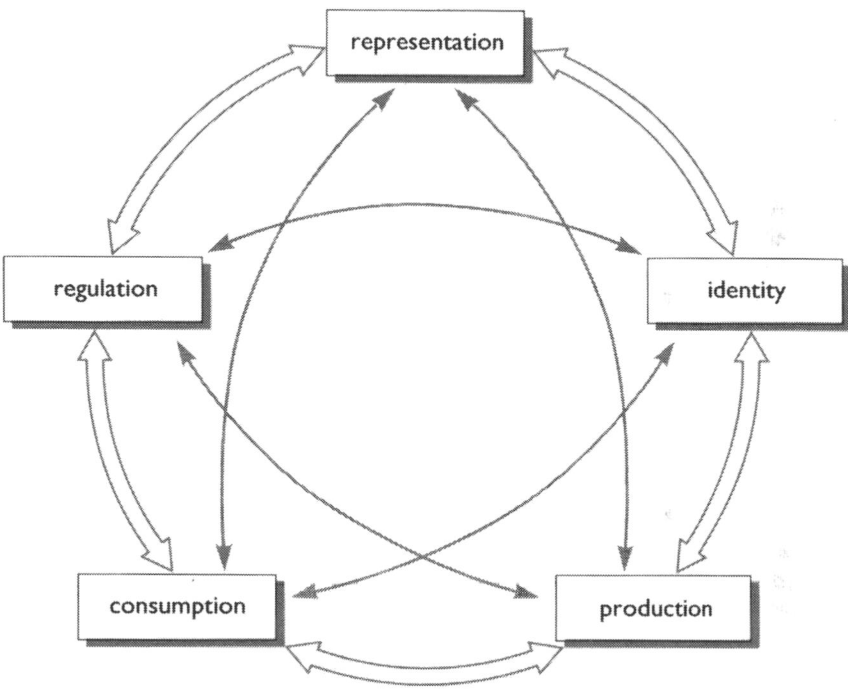

Fig. 9.2 Appropriation in a mass communication system on the way to a pull system (du Gay 1997, p. 1)

Hall (1997) makes the following important point, which summarises the function of cultural products within the context of mass communication in transition: 'since all cultural objects convey meaning, and all cultural practices depend on meaning, they must make use of signs; and in so far as they do, they must work like language works' (p. 36). In the case of user-generated contexts, cultural products do not just 'depend on meaning', they work as cultural products because they are objectifications and transcend the here-and-now. Our focus in discussing the mobile complex is on user-generated context. We are certain that there is a functional equivalence between a discrete cultural object in the sense of Hall and a user-generated context. We see user-generated and mobile contexts as situative cultural products because they are objectifications of human activities, which can be appropriated by others. They have the social function of traditional media such as books or movies. In such a line of argumentation, appropriation of user-generated content is a reaction to situative environments as cultural products. In our view, user-generated content has reached a state of normalisation in everyday life and it works as cultural products but with a specific representational mode.

Another important notion in the context of appropriation is that of alienation, which emerged in the context of philosophical Idealism at the end of the 18th and the beginning of the 19th century (see Humboldt 2002b, c, d). Learning is fundamentally a personal process of development, which entails, and to some extent is predicated on, alienation in relation to the cultural products of the objectified world. The cultural products of the objectified world provide the stimulus in relation to which people develop their identity. In the modern world of consumption, the risks of alienation through unreflective appropriation of cultural products are real but can be mitigated by education. The mitigation of risks is an important educational task also in relation to the use of mobile devices. The mobile/cell phone is a cultural product that gives access to cultural resources and thereby carries the potential for personal development. But there is the obvious risk of getting lost in the overwhelming world of mobile, individualized consumption and mass communication. With reference to Vygotsky (1978/ 1930, p. 84) and his concept of 'zones of proximal development' we argue that child development needs *sensitive* and *responsive* contexts to enable reflective appropriation, for the provision of which education and the school are responsible.

Humboldt integrated appropriation of cultural products within cultural forms and the resulting development into an education model, which sees appropriation embedded in the creative shaping of the world. This creative shaping and forming is mainly a transformation of a personally experienced, unstructured, overwhelming world into a holistic, coherent rich unity (Humboldt 1797/2002d, p. 346). In modern terminology this idea leads to a life-world, the creation of which is a formative task for people; and, it is a risky task with high complexity. One feature of this complexity derives from the option, and need for, the generation of contexts with mobile devices within a context of media convergence. In Humboldt's view, the abundance of opportunities for appropriation contains potential and the complex cultural offer in today's life world implies the potential for creative formation (see Humboldt 2002c/1797, p. 346).

Formation (*Bildung*) can succeed only with freedom as a prerequisite for appropriation and development (Humboldt 2002d/1792, p. 64). Furthermore, the hope of the Enlightenment, critical reflection ('Vernunft'), is a condition for appropriation. Critical reflection must be seen as being more than common sense and everyday life rationality (2002d/1792, p. 64), the development of which is, or at least should be, a key task for schools.

Humboldt argued, correctly in our view, that culture consists not only of the traditions, which were appropriated over generations and transformed into valid but polished objects. Culture arises also within the actual cultural forms of mobile individualisation through ubiquitous use of mobile/cell phones inside and outside of school, for example small talk or mobile video production. These mass systems of user-generated content and contexts are the results of the appropriation of new mass communicative and socio-cultural structures, which have become integrated in everyday life practices and initiate appropriation practices.

Humboldt (2002b, who wrote in the 1790s, p 235 f.) supported his educational aim with a general anthropological argument:

> Die letzte Aufgabe unsres Daseyns: dem Begriff der Menschheit in unserer Person, sowohl während der Zeit unseres Lebens, als auch noch über dasselbe hinaus, durch die Spuren des lebendigen Wirkens, die wir zurücklassen, einen so grossen Inhalt, als möglich, zu

verschaffen, diese Aufgabe löst sich allein durch die Verknüpfung unseres Ichs mit der Welt zu der allgemeinsten, regesten und freiesten Wechselwirkung.

The elements of an educational model of appropriation we have discussed so far in this chapter can be summarized as follows:

- child development is based on the appropriation of cultural products and their inherent, objectified cultural meaning;
- intentional, formal learning can become part of child development as appropriation of cultural products, if the responsive contexts, which work as 'zones of proximal development', are assimilated or adapted;
- internalization of diversity and abundance of opportunity require formative structuring;
- freedom is a pre-requisite for appropriation and critical reflexivity is a required condition;
- appropriation as child development is based on the alienating effects of the culturally unknown, which contains the risk of distracting more or less profoundly from cultural and personal identity; and
- mobile *colonialisation* through individualization and ubiquity presents high risk in the context of recent and current cultural forms.

The first five points in this list emerge from our discussion of a dialectic strand of educational theory as conceptualized by Vygotsky and Humboldt. But for us the discussion is not complete without the additional focus on mobile *colonialisation*. A look at recent newspaper stories about mobile/cell phones and their misuse reveals this gap. Habermas' (1995, Vol. 2, pp. 489 ff.) broad discussion of communicative actions, i.e. cooperative action undertaken by individuals based upon mutual deliberation and argumentation (See e.g. http://en.wikipedia.org/wiki/Communicative_action), reveals limitations, which can lead to a colonialisation of communication when 'the system' invades the life-world and interferes with the processes of meaning-making. The transfer of everyday life violence onto the mobile/cell phone, for example in the form of *happy slapping* alone is not convincing enough an example; but, together with Google maps plus GPS-functionality, the mobile enables practices, which can pose a fundamental threat to democracy. A case in California demonstrates this potential developmental trajectory: voters in a public poll who supported gay weddings were publicly put onto the pillory by having their homes tagged on Goggle maps by opposers. The rationale behind the mobile/cell phone, individualized mass communication, also individualizes the field of control and increases the potential for despotism. Therefore, even the benign colonialisation of everyday life by a convergent mobile system requires critical practice, which builds on reflexivity in the sense of Habermas' 'reflexive relationship with the world through communicative actions' ('reflexive Weltbezüge im kommunikativen Handeln') (1995, Vol. 1, p. 143 ff.). This reflexivity was intended by the traditional concept of appropriation and formation (*Bildung*). Education urgently has to develop critical practices in response to potential mobile colonialisation caused by individualization and ubiquitous media use.

Mobile Devices, Media and Mass Communication

Media use and media reception – these are the terms normally used in the context of media appropriation. Their meaning has changed from the emergence of television to it becoming the leading medium of everyday life, and again as it has evolved into just one important element in a landscape of media convergence since the inception of the internet and the increasing use of mobile devices. Figs. 8.1 and 8.2 offer a window on aspects of mobile/cell phones usage. Above we discussed mass communication and cultural products with reference to relevant technological structures for appropriation, such as media production, programmes and audience. In the following we widen our perspective with a summary of patterns of individualization within media use. These patters, whilst drawn from empirical research on television and the internet, in our view are relevant for our discussion of the appropriation of mobile devices in users' life-worlds.

Models of Mass Communication

Appropriation of mobile devices is integral to everyday life, to which, of course, all media use belongs. Indeed, media use is a taken-for-granted dimension of everyday life. In the ongoing process of cultural transformation, mobile devices can be viewed as successors to well-established media peripherals such as, for example, the remote control for the television. Mobile devices result from a preference for smaller and smaller media devices at one's individual disposal. New technical media are appropriated on the basis of cultural experiences with older technologies, including predecessor technologies such as landline telephones, radio, television or the personal computer. They are also linked to other cultural products such as the car, with its cultural heritage of individual mobility (see Bachmair 1991).

A brief look at our recent cultural history in relation to the television affords us an insight into the fundamentals of appropriation of relatively new media such as the mobile/cell phone. The appropriation of mass media, especially of the television, has been theorized and empirically well investigated; it can, to some extent at least, serve as a model for our understanding of the appropriation of mobile devices.

In the context of mass communication, the appropriation of the medium television is *reception*. Broadly speaking, there were three stages of theorising about television use (see also Jenkins 2006):

1. During the first phase of television in the 1940s, the conception was that of radio and television information being transferred form a sender to a receiver. This transportation model was canonized by Lasswell's question (1948, p. 37;

Lasswell et al. 1952, p. 12): 'Who, says what, how, to whom, with what effect?' Beside the ideological function of legitimating propaganda media, reception was seen as a uni-directional flow from a sender to a receiver who simply has to decode the objectified message.

2. During the 1960s, television became an integral part of everyday life. Of course, a television viewer does not simply respond to a programme's message as intended by the programme makers, for example to a commercial by buying the advertised commodities. Therefore, theories such as the uses- and gratifications-approach (Blumler and Katz 1974) were developed to explain media users as selectors, who follow their pursuits and seek gratification by watching specific programmes. Media reception was viewed as a structured processing of programmes from the perspective of personal themes (see also Freire's concept of generative themes) within referential frames of a meaningful everyday life (see among others Charlton and Bachmair 1990). The notion of 'consumption of commodities' through watching television functioned as referential social activity pattern within everyday life (see among others Silverstone 1994).

What users do with media, how they use them and what perspectives they bring to the programmes they watch and listen to, can be viewed as the integration of the media offering into how users shape and manage their own lives. Through media consumption, we personalise our life-worlds as frames for individual life skills. This individualisation through mass communication is dramatically increased by mobility. And, the accelerating individualisation increasingly takes place in a context of media convergence, which has led to a vast programme offering that can only be managed through individual, personal processing and selection. In fact, programme producers look for an individualised audience, they seek to appeal to an audience according to the characteristics of its socio-cultural milieu.

The pursuit of personally relevant and meaningful activities provides thematically focused motivation in the development of life skills by individuals. As already mentioned above, in this we follow Freire (1970/2007) and his concept of 'generative themes', which he used as a structural element for the organisation of adult literacy programmes. Writing and reading cannot be conceptualised as a mimetic reproduction of a given text by means of the memorised alphabet. It is also not just an application of personal themes for meaning-making with the help of a text and its constitutive elements. Freire used single words or phrases that were very relevant to learners' lives as generative themes to start conversations about the implications of the theme for the community. In this way meaning of lexical items was connected to the socio-political context in which learning took place. The principle behind this approach is that thematic motivation for reading and writing is enhanced by references to the individual life-worlds of learners and also by the transfer of social risks into individualised life-worlds, which in turn interact within the context of ubiquitous mass communication. With respect to individualisation, we are adding the term 'personal' to the aspect of 'generative'. Through the term 'generative, personal' themes we try to stress that 'generative' does not refer to a general, pre-given mental capacity residing inside human beings. Themes are always personally constructed in the life course and in cultural relevant circumstances such as individualised life-worlds.

We consider generative, personal themes and attendant conversational activities within, or mediated by media to have a bridging function between everyday life contexts and school learning. Identifying generative, personal themes and related conversational threads inside and outside formal education, we argue, helps to support the bridging of conversations by threads. This, we are certain, represents a practical pedagogical option for education. Outside the school, in their everyday lives, children and young people stake out *conversational threads*, which can be taken up by the school. For a detailed discussion see Chapter 11.

3. Multimedia programmes, such as the *Teletubbies* (1997–2001), became the norm some 20 years ago. They are multimedia in the sense that television functions as the lead medium, which is enriched by a complex arrangement of additional commodities such as toys, merchandise, websites etc. These media-based or media-orientated media arrangements led to the idea of media as environments (see e.g. Bovill and Livingstone 2001). These media environments we view as semiotic spaces and in them mass communication is shifting from linear to new discontinuous complex forms, forms which we term 'mobile and individualised'. The emphasis is no longer on a user-media relationship within the stream of everyday life activities; instead, children, young people and adults act within prefabricated, mediated environments. Furthermore, the multimodal interrelation of media, commodities and events, such as road shows, are generating semiotic spaces for individualised life-worlds (see Bachmair 2006). The mobile/cell phone is likely to become the main tool for access, expression and entertainment within such environments characterised by media convergence. They are contexts in Dourish's sense (2004) to which we already referred earlier. We propose to consider the use of the principles behind such mobile and individualised environments as contexts for learning as a second practical pedagogical option for education. The school as a standardised learning context can and should connect to user/student-generated contexts.

Such media environments and semiotic spaces differentiate everyday life into individually defined contexts and they bridge different and divergent cultural practices, such as entertainment outside school and learning in formal contexts. In the context of recent and ongoing socio-cultural developments we can observe that these semiotic spaces are absorbing the media and related tools. In due course, we argue, a differentiation between media for learning inside and outside institutional contexts is no longer going to be easily possible. Arguably, with the maturation of ubiquitous connectivity and the increasing convergence of mobile devices, this point of development is near. Learning from educational media (Fisch 2004) will occur in open or closed semiotic spaces, which are set up at the interface of users and how they generate contexts. This transformation uses the amalgamation of entertainment and a global programme offer (see Buckingham and Willet 2006; Buckingham and Scanlon 2003). The debate outside the field of media studies deals with this development under the theme of 'informal learning' (see e.g. Sefton-Green 2004).

Complex Patterns of Media Activities and Increasing Individualisation

The ongoing process of individualisation and social fragmentation is negotiated and enforced by the media of everyday life. In this dynamic, media are cultural products among various commodities with relevance for everyday life. They function as symbolic material within a standardised offer, which is open for consumption, and for the building of personal life-worlds. The shift from linear to discontinuous principles of mass communication fits into the process of individualisation, which potentially enables students to construct personally relevant knowledge within their life-worlds. In the scholarly debate about mobile learning an affinity with constructivist curricular approaches can be detected (see e.g. Naismith et al. 2004, pp. 12 f.). This corresponds to the construction of personal life-worlds, which have become taken for granted. Personal life-worlds include the individualisation of collective risks (see Giddens 1991, pp. 109 ff.) and a self-referential frame of personalised experiences of reality (see Schulze 1992, pp. 34 ff.).

These two drivers in support of personalized life-worlds have found their way into schools in the form of constructivist curricular approaches. In view of these developments, the educational dimension of the introduction of mobile devices into learning in formal contexts has to be considered critically between the poles of enhancing meaningful and situated learning (constructivist learning) and of individualising cultural and social risks through personalised and self-referential experiences.

As well as the necessary theoretical considerations, data on media consumption are relevant in this context and discussed below. We include this debate here because we see mobile learning framed by features of socio-cultural milieus as well as already habitualized patterns of media use.

In addition, a short summary of research findings on television and the internet will be provided.

Media Preferences of Socio-cultural Milieus

First and foremost, socio-cultural milieus can be identified as frames for media patterns. The milieu-related organisation of our society has emerged during the past two or three decades. Following the cultural sociology of Giddens (1991) or Schulze (1992), and looking at the results of respective empirical research, it can be noted that industrialized European societies are segmented into the milieus featured in Figs. 1.3 and 8.7. Their construction follows two dimensions (Dannhardt and Nowak 2007):

(a) Social Status: high, middle, lower. The social status is a result of profession, income and formal education.
(b) Basic Values: traditional (sense of duty and order), modernisation (individualisation, self-actualisation, pleasure), re-orientation (multi options, experimentation, paradoxes). This dimension is formed by life style and is eligible for the people.

Media trendsetters, for example, belong to the higher scorers on the dimension *Basic Values* and *Social Status*. They are probably part of the milieu *Modern Performer* or of the *Modern Mainstream* as well as of the milieu *Consumer-Materialistic*. The spatial personal environment, i.e. the living room or the bedroom, of the milieu *Modern Performer* is likely to be similar to that of the media trendsetter. They usually do not belong to a tradition-orientated milieu. Because the life style values are not only represented in media use but also in the physical environment, with living rooms and bedrooms representing the value variable of socio-cultural milieus. Of course media use and the physical space of a living room/bedroom correlate with the variable of social status (profession, formal education, income).

If a teacher invites students to use mobile devices in a constructivist learning environment, the value orientation of the *Modern Performers* are closer to such a project than that of young people from a traditional cultural environment. Certain projects will require a quite strong motivation for students from a traditional background with higher or lower social status and income. But it is likely that the traditionally orientated groups appreciate mobile calendars or organizer (what Patten et al. (2006, p. 296) call 'administrative function'), dictionaries ('referential function') or basic learning input like *drill and test* ('interactive function'). These kinds of learning tools are accepted by milieus with a more traditional orientation. One can assume that the three different basic values have different preferences in relation to school, teaching and learning. The basic values are: 'A: Traditional, sense of duty and order', 'B: Modernisation, individualisation, self-actualisation, pleasure' and 'C: Re-orientation, multiple options, experimentation, paradoxes'. A traditional values orientation goes hand in hand with traditional methods of schooling.

Also, genre preferences are pre-structured by socio-cultural milieu. For example, the podcast 'How to measure the width of a river' belongs to a well know children's TV series *Die Sendung mit der Maus* ('Programme with the mouse') (See http://www.wdrmaus.de) German children from innovative milieus with higher social status are likely to watch this series more, but children with a traditional orientation prefer information programmes outside the children's context. By looking at the socio-cultural milieus of their pupils, teachers can tailor specific inputs to activate specific media habits and media preferences for mobile learning.

Activity Patterns Within the Media Set and Within the Family Life of Children

Within the context of the cultural transformation of mass communication from linear to discontinuous modes of representation, and the relevance of cultural practices in terms of the segmentation of society, children are appropriating specific patterns of activities by using certain media sets in their family lives. The children's television channel SuperRTL investigated these patterns at the end of 1990s and at the beginning of the year 2000 (2000, 2002), when television was still the dominant medium of the media set of children.

The research project focused on four kinds of patterns:

(a) activity patterns in leisure time: different levels of activity and external orientation; level of activities: low/high,
(b) patterns of emotions and feelings;
(c) patterns of social and self experiences;
(d) patterns of the social and organised worlds of children;
(e) parental style of education.

The activity patterns ranged from casual watching of television to complex patterns of integration of television programmes to mundane and individual action patterns with different levels of activity and external orientation, as well as 'emotional patterns'.

Ad a: Activity patterns of children in leisure time (Medienforschung Super RTL 2000, pp. 58 ff.)

There are two main dimension of activities:

- orientation towards the outer world or to the inner world,
- level of activities.

Identified activity patterns are:

- 'passive children' with few activities of their own, however with a great deal of action-rich television consumption (22% of children);
- 'play-children' with many toys and fairy tales (22% of children);
- 'intellectuals' who concentrate on 'more knowledge, in order to receive an achievement-orientated advantage' (15% of children);
- 'game players' with their plethora of 'games, fun, and excitement' (16% of children);
- 'unnoticables' with their love for animals and openness to new things (11% of children);
- 'fun and action kids' who are 'young, dynamic, and rarely alone' (7% of children); and
- 'allrounder' with a 'need for leadership' and 'corners and edges' (7% of children) (see Fig. 9.3).

The keywords for summarising these differences, such as *play-children* or *fun and action kids*, are rather superficial but indicate the differences between groups of children in- and outside a classroom. If mobile devices are to be integrated into learning activities, teachers need to re-think these different patterns of activities on different levels and in relation to different orientations to the inner or outer world of children.

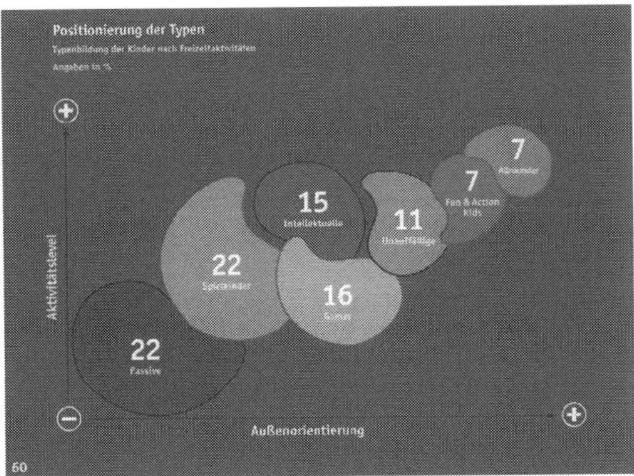

Fig. 9.3 Children's activity patterns in leisure time (Source: Medienforschung Super RTL 2000, p. 60)

These activity patterns map patterns of emotions and feelings and patterns of social and self experiences, which regulate the integration of media use in everyday life.

Ad b: Media/television are elements in patterns of emotions

- boredom;
- relaxation;
- regulation through anger;
- mood of sadness;
- mood of separation and retreat; and
- getting comfort.

Ad c: Patterns of social and personal experiences
The dimensions of these patterns are:

- comfort and attention in the family;
- self-determined retreat;
- friends;
- excitement and surprise;
- learning and desire for knowledge;
- curiosity for others;
- retreat, disinterest and boredom and
- dramatic search for suspense.

Ad d: Modes of organising children's worlds

There are other patterns, which regulate the social worlds of children especially in the way parents organise family life and educate their child or children (Medienforschung Super RTL 2002, pp. 74 ff.).

Clusters of educative styles of parents inclusive of TV

- Over-educative and regulative style
  - controller 7%
  - (over)protective 16%
  - contradictory 11%
- Engaged and communicative style
  - open minded 17%
  - generous, liberal 18%
- Distant
  - weak orientation towards family 12%
  - indifferent 19%

The 35% of children who benefit from an engaged and communicative style of education are likely to respond positively to teachers offering the use of mobile/cell phones and tools such as camera phones for *collaborative* investigations of *real world domains* like the museum or to work within the *micro world of models* offered by mobile devices (see Patten eet al. 2006, p. 296). This group of children is familiar with working autonomously, which is essential for successful constructivist learning. These positive experiences are also important for *collaborative* investigations of *real world domains* or creative use of the world of mobile games etc. But there exists also a large proportion of students who expect clear rules (23% with controlling and overprotective parents) or who do not have positive experiences in terms of support from their parents.

In Germany, 37% of children live in an *organised world*, 23% in an *open-minded world*, 24% in a *world of fantasies*. But 5% of children live in a world, which can be described as challenging. Correlating the activity styles of children with the mode of organising the world's children live in, one can see differences in the way or degree to which children can contribute to, or influence and form their world. It can be assumed that the ability to influence, and form their own world to a greater or lesser extent correlates closely with learning modes. Almost half the children expect a low degree of opportunity for forming, influencing and creating. They probably lack experiences, which they could use as positive learning frames for creative media use (see Fig. 9.4).

These children need positive experiences in school through meaningful and constructivist learning. Their organisation of everyday life suggests starting with calendars and organisers ('administrative function'), drill and test-software ('interactive function'), or dictionaries ('referential function').

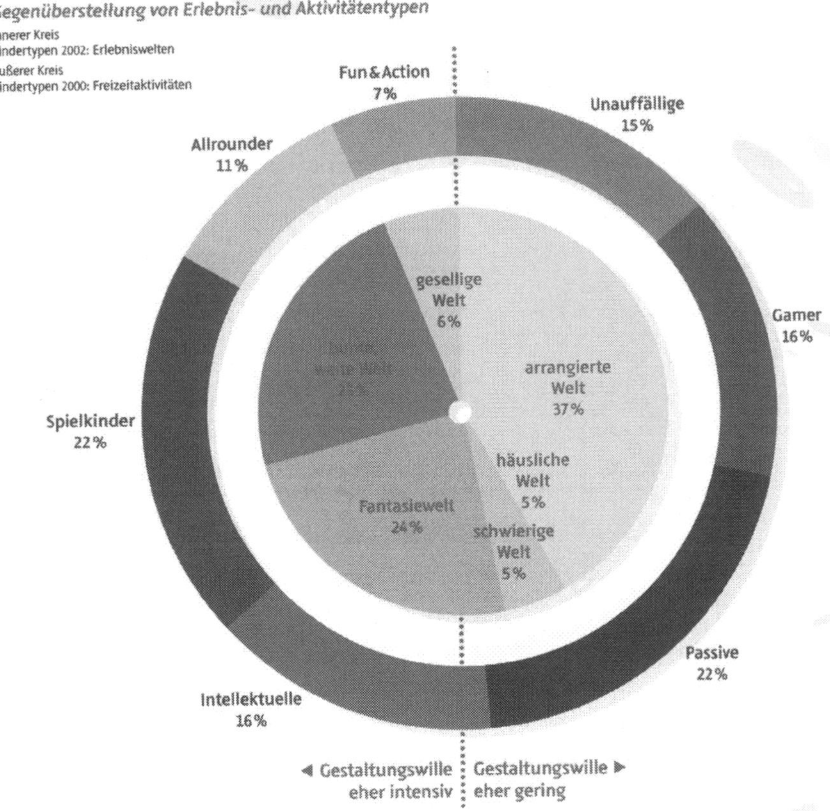

Fig. 9.4 Correlation between activity styles of the children (*outer circle*), the organisation of their everyday life world (*inner circle*) and the children's capability in relation to formation and organisation (*left sphere*: more intensive, to the *right*: limited) (Medienforschung Super RTL 2002, p. 77)

Typology for Television, Internet and Media Convergence

Empirical data concerning activity and engagement patterns within the media set as well as the educational dispositions within families can help to identify at-risk learners and their ways of coping with everyday life as a prerequisite for curricular organization and learning. Also, the research on typologies of media users affords relevant information on media habits, which have the potential to support successful mobile learning even for at-risk learners.

German public broadcasting developed user typologies for television and the internet. Dehm and Storll's (2003) five factors of involvement with television and also with the internet we already introduced in Chapter 8.

On the basis of these five factors of involvement with television, Dehm et al. (2004, pp. 217 ff.) found seven distinct profiles of television viewing:

- involved enthusiasm 11%
- emotionally involved connoisseurship 15%
- knowledge acquisition with pleasure 16%
- habitualised orientation seeking 12%
- habitualised participation 21%
- undemanding coping with stress 14%
- sceptical distance 10%.

These seven types of television viewers are now using mobile/cell phones and other mobile devices. Usually teachers do not have much of an idea which profile of television viewing is associated with a successful or a weak student. As schools move towards the integration of mobile technologies, these issues and considerations are becoming increasingly relevant, though.

In addition, internet users can be described by Dehm and Stroll's (2003) five factors of media involvement: emotions, orientation, balance and compensation, diversion (passing the time), social experience. On the basis of these five factors, four distinct types of internet user were identified (Dehm et al. 2006, p. 96):

- hedonistic participation 18%
- habitualised surfer for knowledge acquisition 31%
- curious surfer seeking compensation 26%
- browser 25%.

Patterns for Dealing with Convergence:

Since these studies were carried out, media convergence challenges also specific patterns of appropriation. Older children and young people use media convergent spaces for their activities or they build their own paths through the complex media offering. This leads, for example, to the following individualized patterns:

Integration of media as a space for specialisation: preferred sports or special interests such as science homework are the basis for media use. The development of knowledge or competences are in the foreground. Enhancing a stabile identity and social integration are important (Wagner et al. 2006, pp. 85 ff.).

Guided by the world of consumption: these children or young people prefer organized and default media settings. They look for advertised website, books or merchandising commodities accompanying a TV programme or a game (Wagner et al. 2006, p. 91 ff.) and extend their space of prefabricated activities by means of a wide range of media products and programmes.

Expanding the personal life-world: for this group the expansive offering of the media is used for augmenting life experiences. Users spend a lot of time dedicated to a particular kind of social life, e.g. within *Star Wars*, which becomes a cult world with chats, fan activities etc. (Wagner et al. 2006, pp. 99 ff.).

Media as a space for self-presentation and missionary work: this group carries their specialisation and expertise, e.g. of computer games such as *Counter-Strike,* from the media world into their 'real' social life. Users present themselves as Counter-Strike characters to other young people. They try to convince others of the value of the program and support others to improve playing it (Wagner et al. 2006, pp. 99 ff.).

The creative media producers: this group integrates the media offering productively, e.g. by producing videos with elements of their preferred computer game, pop music etc. They invest time and energy to get the right software to adapt a computer game to their special interests (Wagner et al. 2006, pp. 119 ff.).

Learning in Contexts and Supported by Conversations

One of the dominant features of the ongoing transformation of mass media is the individual disposition of situations of media use enabled by mobile devices. The main feature characterising these ubiquitous, personally determined situations, is the fragmentation of meaning-making and appropriation. The new *pull* principles of mass communication with user-generated contexts and content are the means for this transformation. But also the new activity patterns relating to media convergence or the differentiated types of internet use on the basis of the five factors of media involvement identified by Dehm and Storll (2003) – emotions, orientation, balance and compensation, diversion, social experience – together within differentiated family education and socio-cultural milieus, reinforce the individualisation of situations as contexts. Does, can or should schools and their established cultural practices as well as their powerful structures resist this trend towards individualisation and fragmented meaning-making and appropriation? The PISA-results on the competence levels reached by students in OECD-countries indicate that schools have lost the definitional power over what learning is about, certainly for boys from lower social strata and from migrant families.

This long-term trend affects learning by decreasing the relevance of institutional learning and increasing that of learning in informal contexts and widens situational contexts for learning.

Culturally Situated Learning Towards User-Generated Contexts

The above summary of milieus and activity patterns demonstrates how far developed and, at the same time, how normalised individualization has become. It leads to a widening of the situational contexts for learning, which cover the learning practices of school as well as learning within contexts of media use for entertainment or learning how to handle new software etc. This aspect of individualisation leads to a fragmentation of meaning-making. This fragmentation in the context of individualisation is possible because learning, like any other form of meaning-making, depends on situations. The situatedness (Lave and Wegner 1991, p. 31) of meaning-making, as we have already noted, is the central thesis of the model and it is related to Vygotsky's theory of appropriation. One of the basics of Vygotsky's theory is the idea of internalising the pre-given world. In their critique of Vygotsky, Lave and Wenger (1991, pp. 47, 51) point out that the notion of 'learning as internalising' is problematic because of its inherent misunderstanding that pre-given knowledge has to be memorised and stored, i.e. a reductionist view of learning. One example of a reductionist approach would be the alphabet if its internalization is regarded just as a memorising of clearly defined, elementarized knowledge. From such a perspective, elementary/primary school children would have to memorise all of the characters of the alphabet and apply them as a pre-given and memorized set of building blocks for reading and writing. One could argue that this memorised matching of characters and texts only works because the children do make meaning in such standardised, curricular situation, albeit without them being elicited. In traditional, stable situations of teaching and learning it is possible to overlook the fact that meaning-making, as the learning task, was transferred to the children. Within the de-traditionalization of typical learning situations, the situatedness of learning as meaning-making has to be considered and newly applied to deliberate learning:

> The attempt to clarify the concept of situated learning led to critical concerns about the theory and to further revisions that result in the move to our present view that learning is an integral and inseparable aspect of social practices (Lave and Wenger 1991, p. 31).

The social context as practice is defining 'learning as increasing participation in communities of practice', which 'concerns the whole person acting in the world' (Lave and Wenger 1991, p. 49). Practice and communities of practice for learning are fundamental within our ecological triangle (see Fig. 1.4) and for development in the context of socio-cultural and technologic structures, agency and cultural practices. For us, learning is appropriation within social practices. Lave and Wenger (1991, p. 59 ff.) discuss learning as 'peripheral participation' in the context of social practices such as apprenticeships and vocational groups such as midwives, tailors or butchers. We would add learning in contexts such as the use of internet-based media platforms and mobile devices where there arguably also exists a 'relational interdependency of agent, and world, activity, meaning cognition, learning, and knowing' (Lave and Wenger 1991, p. 50). In the context of the ongoing socio-cultural shift towards mobile individualization this interdependency remains but it requires of participants also the capacity to generate contexts for learning.

What are the implications of this basic definition of learning as being situated in social and culturally different practices?

First of all, it is predicated on an understanding of mobile devices within their specific structures, agency and practices as a recent cultural form (see Williams 1974). The specific role of mobile devices within the new, pull-orientated mass communication needs to be considered as context for learning. For example, what kind of learning is inherent in a Maths homework community that is imitating the cultural practices of school but is definitely a separate context? This user-generated Maths context functions as a practice with communicative threads, a clearly defined web-structure, creative photos, face-to-face and technology-mediated communication with peers etc. (see Chapter 11 for a detailed discussion). We propose to work with the notion of user-generated contexts of mobile and individualised mass communication and conversational thematic threads as a pedagogical frame. Our aim is to integrate learning in informal contexts into learning in formal contexts, in particular schools. The practical educational challenge, therefore, is to identify relevant contexts and communicative, conversational threads outside the school in order to connect them to the learning practices of the school. Identified threads can be extended from everyday life into the school. This extension helps connect user-generated contexts of mobile individualised mass communication to standardised learning practices in school contexts. (see Chapters 11 and 12)

Secondly, the correlation with formally recognised learning has to be explored if it is to be assimilated into pedagogical modes of scaffolding as, from the perspective of school-based learning, it has different characteristics for example in terms of structure, orientation, explicitness etc. Identifying and connecting conversational threads is such an assimilative approach.

Thirdly, the curricular shift from the dominance of learning objects to situational contexts needs to be considered. Lave and Wenger (1991) criticized internalisation as learning-by-heart and removed from meaning-making within social practices. A passive mentality can be seen as a result of formally legitimised curricular learning objects such as the alphabet, the vocabulary of a foreign language or mathematical formulas. What are the constraints of user-generated contexts, how do they 'colonise' learning (Habermas 1995, Vol. 2, p. 489)? The recent discussion of learner-generated contexts (Luckin et al. 2009, 2005) looks to participation as the main feature for avoiding an alienation of the learning agent that has become common in relation to curriculum-defined learning objects. Luckin et al. (2009, p. 3) define learner-generated contexts as follows:

> created by people interacting together with a common, self-defined learning goal. . . . the key aspect of Learner Generated Contexts is that they are generated through the enterprise of those who would previously have been consumers in a context created for them. (The concern is) to ensure that learning is a participatory experience that is about: participative technology, participative education and participative democracy. The current popularity amongst learners for the creation and publication of their own material, combined with the open content and open source initiatives offer the tools for increased educational democracy. These tools support the potential for the boundaries to be redrawn between learners and teachers, formal and informal education and the producers and consumers of knowledge.

In addition to participation, Luckin et al foreground 'educational democracy' and suggest that an alignment with open content and open source initiatives as broader contexts will help overcome the limitations of the boundaries of the local situations. In this model, by means of media convergence and ubiquitous mobile devices, a 'context is the combination of interactions a learner experiences across multiple physical spaces and times' (Luckin et al. 2009, p. 4).

Learning Resources and Conversational Integration

The debate about user-generated contexts reflects the whole complexity of the structural transformation of media convergence and mobile device use in everyday life and its contribution to new learning practices. We argue that the school, as the dominant learning practice of our society, can widen its repertoire of teaching and learning resources by taking mobile devices from everyday life seriously. The crucial point for us is to integrate them deliberately as cultural resources in school-based approaches to teaching and learning. The current educational debate views teaching and learning as conversational in nature (Laurillard 2002; Sharples 2005; Sharples et al. 2007). How can mobile devices be assimilated through conversation?

The idea of media as resources for learning is an old one and started with the transfer of film into school in the context of a positivist pedagogical frame from the 1940s onwards, i.e. the matching of media to learning requirements for the purposes of innovating approaches to teaching an learning without engaging in questions around the value they added. But this need not be so. The current discourse centres on a model of teaching and learning as conversation and on media as one of its conversational resources. Sharples et al. (2007) depict educational access to mobile devices as a 'resource' (though not in the sense of a cultural resource as we do) for the 'mobile age' and refer explicitly to Laurillard's 'Conversational Framework' (2002) as a didactic concept for learning:

> Learning is a continual conversation with the external world and its artefacts, with oneself, and also with other learners and teachers. (p. 227)

We understand the new, highly individualized technologies and media as part of the wider frame of communication. Communication is also a typical process in school, where it focuses on learning and knowledge as part of conversation, reflection, interaction, commentaries etc. Media and mobile devices of everyday life can also be conceptualised as being part of conversation, reflection, interaction, commentaries etc. within the cultural practices of young people outside the school.

As already noted, media practices – like all other cultural practices – are processes of meaning-making. Also, learning is grounded in meaning-making but always in culturally specific formal and/or informal structures and a specific learning habitus. In formal learning environments the mobile/cell phone is often just seen as a motivational tool, not as a defining part of a successful learning design. By interpreting teaching and learning as conversational discourses (see Laurillard 2002, 2007) we gain the option of setting up curricular conversational chains or threads, such as recognising follow-up communication to mass media practices on internet-based media platforms, for example, hip-hop channels on YouTube for migrant boys. Mobile videos on video platforms can work as 'openers' in a curricular learning design for mobile/cell phone use inside the school. This is the case in the example of Cyrill, which we discuss in Chapter 10, who produced an investigative and provocative mobile video outside of school-based learning.

This kind of curricular design requires critical questions; in Habermas' terms questions about the 'colonalisation' of learning to explore the relationship between system and lifeworld, i.e. how cultural practices are permeated by the logic of the structures governing them. Combining informal learning outside the school with formal learning inside the school on the basis of the mobile/cell phone's capability for knowledge management within the paradigm of the developing characteristics of non-editorial and convergent mass communication has to be considered critically, for example, in terms of its inherent literacy practices as well as potential tensions with the knowledge management systems promoted by school. An additional set of questions is to be asked in relation to students as active agents of learning within the new structures of mass communication.

With reference to the concrete dialogic processes of learning within mediated situations, Laurillard (2007, p. 159) proposes to distinguish two different levels of conversation:

- the 'discursive level, where the focus is theory, concepts, description-building' and
- the 'experiential level, where the focus is on practices, activity, procedure-building'.

What happens at the *discursive level*, e.g. in the case of the Domlur field research (see Chapters 4 and 12)? Pupils investigate the world outside the school. Their task is to find basic geometrical forms such as cubes, parallelograms, trapezes. They don't need a theory for identifying these mathematical concepts but an idea on description-building, which bears in mind the discrepancy between the ideal mathematical form and its variation and approximation in everyday life. At the experimental level, the issue is taking photos within a school project etc (see Fig. 9.5).

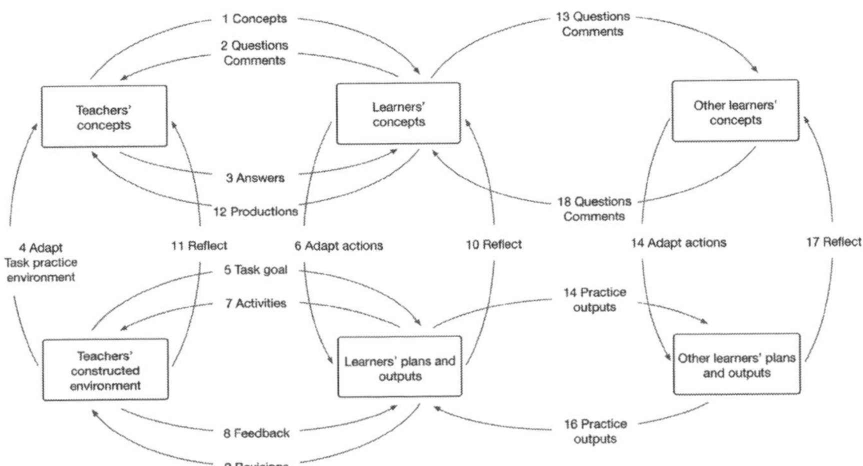

Fig. 9.5 Laurillard's 'Conversational Framework' for supporting the formal learning process (2007, p. 160)

The above questions about mobile expertise and about accepting user-generated contexts are not in the foreground at the experiential level of the teacher but, instead, relate to the environment constructed by the teacher. If a teacher is aware of the possible dilemma students might face in transferring media use in everyday life to their learning in school, then the educational consideration at the teacher's discursive level of the dialogic process should be covered by socio-cultural structures, agency and cultural practices for mobile devices and learning. In terms of the interference of mobile compared with traditional learning contexts at the discursive level, *reflexive context awareness* is required (see Chapter 12 for details). Reflexive context awareness was an implicit issue for the pupils in the Domulur school project, for example, where GPS was used by pupils walking from school to their homes taking photos of essential reference points on their way as well as at home (see Chapters 4 and 12). The traditional cultural contexts (school, at home) are overlapping with a new geographical structure, which supports the notion of moving in between cultural spheres by using the mobile's/cell's GPS and photo applications. Dealing with this movement, e.g. by producing a map with the GPS coordinates and personal photos, a simple form of situational reflection, namely reflexive context awareness, is made possible.

The result of a similar investigation, Jacucci et al. (2007), show that 'active construction of experiences' (p. 1) offers pointers on how to operationalize the concept of reflexive context awareness. Specifically, the mobile/cell phone was used at a car race, the FIA World Rally Championship in Finland, with no links to learning in formal contexts. Adult visitors recorded the rally by taking pictures on their mobile/cell phones. Among other things, the photos made visible the 'temporal frame' of the experienced event. Time appeared in the photos in the following way (Jacucci et al. 2007, p. 13):

'Type A. Time as a horizon. In the situations where the members enjoyed the moment, the group was waiting or resting and there was time and resources to actively stage entertaining situations and to engage in interactions with other spectators'.

'Type B. Time as a task. While driving, one member was absorbed in the task. Other members were taking the time to make calls and rest'.

'Type C. Time as a mixture of task and horizon. The group spent two or more hours each day in walking to or from the stages. While fewer media items were created in this case, members were constantly looking for ways to create entertaining situations, joking with other spectators, commenting about them inside the group, dancing or singing'.

'Type D. Time as cyclic events'. This was relevant for 'brief and intense moments that stood out significantly, e.g. ambushing a rally car between stages'.

Reflexive context awareness manifests itself mainly at the basic level of reflection and is integrated at the experiential level, using Laurillard's terminology. At the experimental level the social situation is constructed by the following photo-related 'practices, activities, procedure-building': 'staging, competing, documenting, portraying ad-hoc friends, storytelling, joking, hunting, and communicating presence' (Jacucci et al. 2007, p. 20). The staging example is rather simple, e.g. group members are portraying themselves or documenting some activity such as putting an artefact such as a cigarette into a hole in a tree and take pictures of this mis-en-scène. This mis-en-scène can be viewed as reflection at a basic level of practical experiences. The reflexive components of the other recorded activities in this example are similarly simple, but offer starting points for further as well as meta-level reflection. The discussion on curricular, 'didactic' parameters to assimilate mobile devices into schoolwork refers to other situational features, for example different cultural fames in everyday life such as milieus or regional religious traditions versus global entertainment (see Chapters 11 and 12).

This sporting event appears at a first glance just as banal entertainment and a simple leisure time activity. Yet, from a conversational perspective one can discover basic forms of reflexivity even in this context. If a pedagogic analysis removes the veil of banality from everyday life, then conversational possibilities for reflexivity come into view. Mobile applications used in the context of a sporting event are at such a great distance to forms of learning and reflection taking place at school that no successful connection seems to be possible. We argue that the pedagogic models of conversation and situated learning offer support for practice in schools.

Having described and analysed mobile device use and learning as different forms of situated meaning-making, we can now try to identify conversational threads in the mobile practices of children and young people who are at a great distance, often in opposition, to school. We view them as at-risk learners. In a discussion of the 'mobile' practices of a young man, Cyrill, we attempt to explore conversational elements with potential links to teaching and learning in schools.

Chapter 10
At-Risk Learners: Their Contextual and Conversational Options

Introduction

Mobile and individualised mass communication has reached all social strata and milieus. One educational challenge for schools is to deliberately identify the thematic conversational threads of those milieus that are at a distance to schooling. There exists a real risk that some milieus are unable to benefit from the resources society has to offer but which are essential for responsible and successful living in modern, individualised life-worlds.

Mobile devices possess an inherent potential for cultural participation as they are integrated into two main socio-cultural structures: media convergence and social-cultural stratification. A complex expertise is necessary in order to be able to act within these structures.

As a phenomenon of everyday life, the mobile complex is clearly segregated from schools, but schools contribute important competences, among others the ability to read and write. At the moment schools seem to seek a technological segregation between themselves and learners' life-worlds deliberately. Banning mobile devices from schools is an indicator for such deliberate segregation. In this chapter we discuss how Cyrill, a young man from the so-called hedonist milieu, does not have the intention to match his life-world expertise to that required in school. Looking at internet video platforms (see Chapter 11) we can see that a lot of homework is produced with the help of mobile/cell phones (see e.g. http://de.youtube.com/group/MathTutor). This indicates that Cyrill's personal, and school's prevailing institutional practice of technological segregation around mobile devices is not the only possibility.

To overcome the segregation of the mobile complex and the cultural practices of schools, our proposal is to adjust schools to the practices, agency and structures of the mobile complex. We already mentioned the proposed assimilative procedure of docking schools onto *responsive* mobile und user-generated contexts. One important reason for doing so is that these contexts work as 'zone of proximal development' in a Vygotskian sense. Furthermore, schools can take up conversational thematic threads, which are laid out by students in their personal media use (see also Chapters 11 and 12).

N. Pachler et al., *Mobile Learning*, DOI 10.1007/978-1-4419-0585-7_10,

In our socio-cultural ecology, we define mobile devices as cultural resources. In this chapter we discuss mobile resources in the hands of 'at-risk' learners. By 'at-risk' learners we mean young people who are underachieving in terms of the *Programme for International Student Assessment* (PISA) in the area of literacy, i.e. reading and writing. We clearly do not infer any lack of intelligence or competence but simply draw attention to the question of their resources not being validated by school and society or them not wanting to utilise the resources valorised by society. There is not scope in this book to offer a detailed discussion of at-risk learners. Suffice it not note that we are convinced, inter alia by our analysis of the case of Cyrill, that our notion of at-risk learners is not only valid but extremely important, for example in terms of social cohesion. In Germany these underachievers are mainly boys from lower socio-economic backgrounds and from migrant families.

We analyse the example of an 18 year-old young man here, who uploaded a provocative mobile video onto an internet-based media platform, as a case of a user-generated context of personal development. Also we try to identify conversational threads of identity and expertise, which the school can take up in order to assimilate the competences evidenced by the young man in the process of taking and uploading the video into the school.

In Chapter 6 we delineated two dominant fields underpinning a pedagogy of mobile learning: the mobile complex in everyday life and the learning practices of schools. In the following we focus on a young man at the intersection of these two powerful social areas and analyse a case of conflicting appropriation of the mobile complex (see Fig. 6.1).

Case Analysis of a Provocative Mobile Video

The main perspective of this case study analysis is on contexts of development and conversational threads, which allow the school an assimilation of mobile competence into formal learning contexts.

At one level, Cyrill, the young man in question (see Chapter 4 for a detailed description of his 'case'), can be viewed as *misbehaving* and as someone who adopts a provocative stance against the mainstream of society. He came to the attention of the public because he recorded with his mobile/cell phone, and uploaded to an internet-based media portal, drunken homeless people. He presented this video as part of his personal web presence, which represents a complex act of communication with peers in his geographic region as well as in his field of entertainment. At the time of taking the video, Cyrill, who comes from a migrant family background, was 17 or 18 years old, i.e. at the end of compulsory schooling.

The main analytic task for our purposes is to understand Cyrill's expertise in using mobile devices as a cultural resource that can support learning in formal contexts. At a first glance, this is not an easy undertaking, because he, together with his peers, was deemed to have harassed drunken homeless people, recorded themselves in the process on their mobile/cell phones and uploaded this short film onto the video platform YouTube. The police required Cyrill to delete this video as well as another video, in which he used the Nazi-salute. The video about homeless people was considered to violate their dignity as they were portrayed in public in a state of helplessness. At the time of writing Cyrill was being prosecuted under German law. The Nazi-salute is banned and legally prosecuted in Germany without fail.

The video could be downloaded freely from YouTube before Cyrill withdrew it as a result of the police intervention. The second video had already been deleted and was not available for download during the period of data collection for this book. Therefore, it cannot be discussed here.

From an educational perspective his case inter alia throws up the question of Cyrill's 'zone of proximal development', to use Vygostky's terminology. In our terminology it is to identify *responsive* user-generated contexts and their thematic conversational threads, which support Cyrill's development, i.e. to find adequate cultural situations for his development. We do not have information about Cyrill's media use in school. Cyrill defines his *responsive* developmental context by the way in which he generates, with his peers at the station, a mobile video and uploads it onto an internet video platform. He is an expert in mobile and convergent media. He builds his context, of which his peers, but not the school, are part, and in which his provocative reportage becomes visible for a global public. This context is not only an expression of his generative, personal themes, but he acts in line with his habitus as a second-generation migrant male. His habitus also reinforces his mode of appropriation, which increases his own demands on his standards of self-presentation in the world of social networking. This makes school frustrating for him because he probably feels under-challenged and that he can only contribute his expertise in a negative way, i.e. through disruption of the traditional cultural practices of school.

One very important structural feature is his milieu as a migrant boy, which probably furnishes him with the motivation to protest against the social mainstream by drawing attention to who, according to him, the real social outcasts are: not Cyrill and his friends, but drunken and drooling Germans. Cyrill is German but from a migrant family, 2nd generation Turkish, which is a highly relevant structure for his media use. Also, his habitus is mainly grounded in his socio-cultural milieu and status. His milieu is typical for someone with a self-centred, 'hedonistic' orientation who engages in risky activities in order to provoke.

How can school respond to such learners? First of all, it needs to recognise mobile devices within the structures and agency of the mobile complex described above, i.e. to recognise them as cultural resources. The frame for the context, which Cyrill generated on the basis of media convergence, is formed by socio-cultural structures and practices. He developed his agency within, or against these structures and practices. His agency is characterised by expertise with relevance mainly for learning in informal contexts. Within the structures of media convergence, the 18 year-old Cyrill developed his practice of using the mobile/cell phone on the basis of his agency, among other things to deal with media. For example, he addresses a self-generated public, something he could not do by watching television. In terms of Wagner et al.'s activity patterns of media convergence (2006, pp. 99 ff.), Cyrill uses the video application of his mobile/cell phone in conjunction with an internet media platform as a 'space for self presentation and missionary work' (see

Figs. 10.4–10.9). The structure of internet video platforms such as MySpace and YouTube shapes his way of taking videos as does the regional context in which he takes mobile videos.

Cyrill's visible *responsive* context for development is the self-referential and self-directed context of peers, media use in the regional context (e.g. the railway station, his town), and global internet media platforms, all framed by his 'hedonistic' and risk-orientated socio-cultural milieu. In relation to learning, Cyrill's *responsive* developmental contexts can be analysed and discussed from the following perspectives:

- mobile and media expertise as cultural resources, in Cyrill's case mainly for informal learning, for self-presentation but also for participation and for dealing with new media in the context of media convergence,
- the habitus of learning as an element of Cyrill's agency, and
- the conversational elements for assimilating mobile expertise into school-based learning.

The Mobile Video, Responsive *Contexts of Development and Conversational Threads*

The video functions as context for Cyrill's development, in which he lays out the following conversational threads:

- investigation/reportage,
- provocation, and
- professional distance.

The video production context consists of the regional station with drunken, homeless men, who were not able to consent to being video-recorded. His peers are also constitutive of the context as is the public space of the internet video platform. The video consists of 11 episodes and the picture and sound quality of the video are rather poor, but typical for their genre. The voices are very difficult, and partly impossible to understand. A techno sound, added after the recording was made, accompanies the video. The main part of the video shows short episodes of how the homeless men live at the station. In some episodes members of Cyrill's peer group are visible. Sometimes the boys comment on an episode during the recording. Occasionally the boys ask the drunken men short questions such as: 'Your life philosophy?' Answer of the drunken man: 'What kind of s*** is this?' Another question is: 'George Bush?'; no answer. Two video episodes deal with people, who don't belong to the group of old, drunken homeless men. In one episode one of the boys asks politely if he can help a drunken man, who is lying on the floor. A long video episode of around 1 min depicts, without a commentary, a verbal conflict between two drunken men.

Fig. 10.1 Frightening (Still pictures from Cyrill's mobile video on YouTube, downloaded from http://www.linktakas.net/video/95654/Augsburg_-_CYRILL_-_Die_Legende_kehrt_zur%FCck.html, 9 Jan 2008)

Still pictures from Cyrill's mobile video on YouTube.

One video episode (Fig. 10.1) presents a situation of harassment. A young man frightens a sleeping drunkard. But harassment is definitely not in the foreground of the video; instead it can be seen as a reflection on German society's white drop-outs. The long video episode about the verbal conflict between two drunken men is taken from a distant perspective of observation (Fig. 10.2). But there are also rather empathetic gestures of communication (Fig. 10.3) between the old men and Cyrill's peer group.

Fig. 10.2 Observing from a distance (Still pictures from Cyrill's mobile video on YouTube, downloaded from http://www.linktakas.net/video/95654/Augsburg_-_CYRILL_-_Die_Legende_kehrt_zur%FCck.html, 9 Jan 2008)

The intention of this video is probably to show who the real social underdogs are, i.e. not the young migrants. The main attitude of the video is one of observing a social situation by way of an unemotional description, which avoids personal feelings. The logo 'Cyrill pictures', in English, and the subtitle 'Atzen compilation', give the production a professional appearance. The word 'Atzen' is not standard German but a rare German slang word.

Fig. 10.3 Communicating (Still pictures from Cyrill's mobile video on YouTube, downloaded from http://www.linktakas.net/video/95654/Augsburg_-_CYRILL_-_Die_Legende_kehrt_zur%FCck.html, 9 Jan 2008)

Fig. 10.4 Self-presentation with a vague connotation of a thoughtful Ghetto child and hip hopper (Source: http://www.myspace.com/cypictures)

By way of summary: the personal issue, which serves as motivation for producing such a social situation, is to act out superiority in the mode of observation and through a social experiment on manipulation and on exercising control. Following

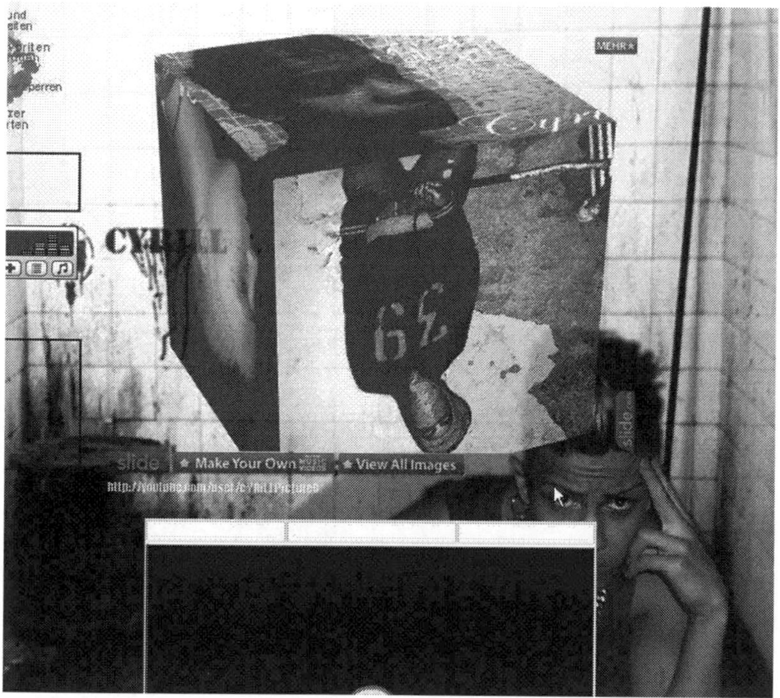

Fig. 10.5 Rotating cube as representational mode for personal images (Source: http://www.myspace.com/cypictures)

Freire's concept of generative, personal themes, which we already mentioned above, the video is mainly about control, distance and superiority, located in the context of late puberty of boys, as well as in the specific situation of 2nd generation migrants and it is part of their socio-cultural milieu. The video is probably best understood as a product of Cyrill's *responsive* developmental context, in which he uses the mobile/cell phone as a cultural resource for investigating a social situation with the unconscious intention of addressing his inferior social self-esteem. His mobile video expertise is rather basic but typical for similar videos on video internet platforms. In the main he records a variety of social situations from the stance of a distant observer and he signals this distance to the social situation by means of a professional frame in the form of a logo. It is not at all unlikely that this distance seeks to protect his vulnerability. Some of the images, in which Cyrill depicts himself, confirm this impression of vulnerability (see Figs. 10.7 and 10.8)

Cyrill uses the cultural offer of a mobile documentary for his personal expression. In the literature this is sometime referred to as citizen journalism (See e.g. http://en.wikipedia.org/wiki/Citizen_journalism). It is fully in line with the model of appropriation of cultural products discussed in Chapter 9 with reference to Vygotsky and Humboldt. But the mobile/cell phone is not only a restricted presentation medium

Fig. 10.6 Self-presentation in front of a graffiti wall (Source: http://www.myspace.com/cypictures)

like a photo album or private video show. Cyrill leaves his private, experimental space by using the affordance of media convergence and uploads the video onto YouTube. In so doing he provokes follow-up communication: a conversational thread is opened (see Fig. 10.10). This thread connects Cyrill's *responsive* developmental context with the regional values and the control mechanisms of the police. Addressing the public is part of the convergence of the mobile/cell phone with the internet. Within this convergence comes potential for conflict based on a conversational relationship, which Cyrill probably did not intend.

In a conversational model, this follow-up communication or thread could also be an assimilative tool for another regional cultural institution, school. How could a school engage with a conversational thread in relation to mobile/cell phone use such as Cyrill's? In terms of Laurillard's Conversational Framework (2007), which we outlined in Chapter 9 (Fig. 9.5), Cyrill acts at the level of learner's plans and outputs, which is close to the Domlur investigation of basic geometrical forms (see Chapters 4 and 11). In the context of Maths, distance is not only accepted but an intended curricular target. The investigation of the Indian students' way from school to their homes with mobile GPS and photography, which bridges different cultural areas, demonstrates a curricular possibility for a conversational thread. In the Indian school example it was clearly not the teacher's intention to depict different everyday life cultures, the traditional religious culture and the culture of global youth entertainment. But this happened when mobile/cell phones came onto the curricular horizon.

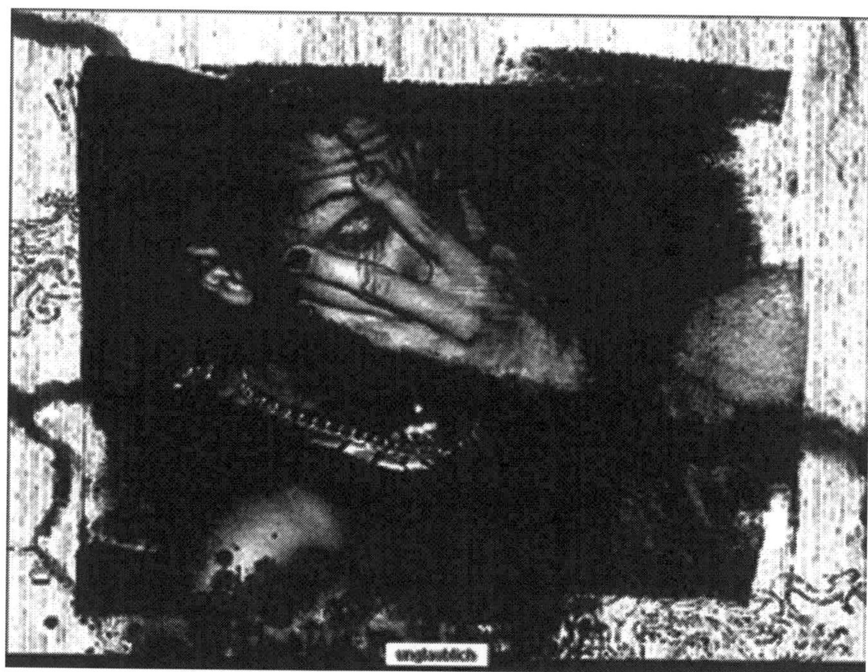

Fig. 10.7 Presentation as subdued and threatened person
(Source: http://www.myspace.com/cypictures)

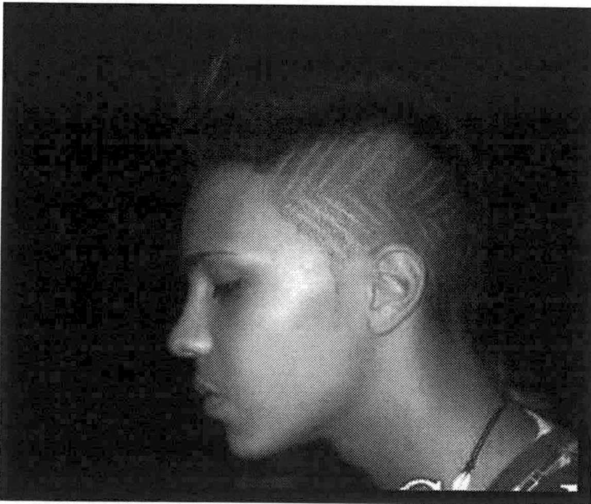

Fig. 10.8 Cyrill as vulnerable, introverted but stylish young man
(Source: http://www.myspace.com/cypictures)

Fig. 10.9 Cyrill as a street fighter
(Source: http://www.myspace.com/cypictures)

Onto which curricular area can Cyrill's observations of, and reflections on cultural lifestyles at the lower levels of society be mapped? Lifestyle issues are not usually part of the school curriculum, but the observational and investigative modes are. Cyrill's mobile practice of observation and reportage present a conversational link to formal learning practices in school. Observation and investigation/reportage also belong to the domain of professional expertise. Both characteristics are part of Cyrill's habitus. In school such a conversational link of observational distance and investigational professionalism would probably clash with the prevailing learning environment, which teachers have constructed carefully for their students (see Fig. 9.5, the 'experimental level' of school conversations, Laurillard 2007, p. 160). Because of the inscribed hierarchical power relationship of active, responsible teacher and passive, obedient student learners like Cyrill are likely to react by refusing to engage in 'childish' school learning. This is likely to cause tensions between pedagogically proscribed didactic engagement with media of the school and the lifestyle orientated media production of learners. A critical analysis of Cyrill's video in the classroom would probably provoke open conflict.

So what choices does school have? Perhaps the music teacher could address Cyrill's video expertise with questions about the choice of sound track: why Techno and not Rap? Also, the teacher could appeal to the mobile expertise of Cyrill on technical aspects of the video production process, for example how he got the sound track onto the mobile video. But this still lies at the periphery of the core curriculum. The mobile videos of Sean and Dan, who show how to calculate speed outside the school, seem to offer more potential in this respect (see Chapter 11).

Fig. 10.10 Screen shot of 'CYRILL PICTURES' on MySpace with a text written by a hip-hop supporter, his photo and a photo of Cyrill
(Source: http://www.myspace.com/cypictures)

All these preliminary curricular ideas are predicated on the acceptance of mobile devices as cultural resources for investigation. The use of mobile devices in this example takes place in the context of the user's attempt to find expression for his social feelings within his personal *responsive* context of development. Attitudes such as 'to be at a distance' are at the discursive level of conversation and media expertise. Acting as a professional is at the experimental level (Laurillard 2007). Both are conversational bridges or threads to the school.

Uploaded Content and Its Conversational Options

Uploading mobile videos to an internet platform forms a wider *responsive* developmental context and offers conversational threads such as getting a public following, self-presentation and identity work (see Fig. 10.10). The world of internet video platforms appears to be full of young, and not so young people desperate to get a public following.

Cyrill's media expertise is grounded in this mass communicative structural transformation, in which he develops his expertise as result of his cultural practices and his agency. By means of an internet video platform Cyrill widens his regional context, to which the video reportage with his peers at the railway station belongs. By using an internet platform he enters a mass communicative context with his personal issues characterised by structural convergence. With respect to the mobile/cell phone, Cyrill acts within the structures of the ongoing transformation of mass communication, in which the mobile/cell phone carries the most powerful dynamic. In this structure Cyrill does not act as a trendsetter but on the basis of developed expertise. The structure can be in opposition to the school, if the basic principles of the situatedness of learning are not reflected by the school.

Transmission-based information flow from the teacher and his/her media to the students is in conflict with Cyrill's practices of observation and investigation and his expectations of learning and media use in informal contexts. Cyrill acts within the frame of a media professional and according to the ongoing transformations of the media landscape:

- outside editorial systems but within archives such as media platforms,
- outside a push system but within a pull system of media distribution,
- within the mobile/cell phone and its wide-ranging applications as an ubiquitous person media tool,
- within user-generated content and contexts,
- within media convergence and social networking options of the internet.

The integrity of the cultural resources attendant to both, the personal context of the learner as well as those of schools, require careful educational handling when seeking to cater for the *responsive* developmental context of individual learners by assimilating their conversational threads into the cultural practices of the school. On the one hand, it is important to foster, and not to impede the individual developmental context of at-risk learners; on the other hand, user-generated contexts and media convergence can represent a considerable intrusion in a school's institutional autonomous realm.

The agency dimension of the socio-cultural ecology as well young people's cultural practices are also in flux, which challenges schools to react. Experienced in media convergence, Cyrill probably belongs to the 18% of internet users, who can be characterised as 'hedonistic' participants (Dehm et al. 2006, p. 96). This coincides with his lifestyle habitus in the context of his socio-cultural milieu, a counter-culture to the German mainstream. It is also likely, as already mentioned, that Cyrill considers the convergent media as a space for self-presentation and missionary work (see Wagner et al. 2006, pp. 99 ff.) and as an opportunity for creative media production (see Wagner et al. 2006, pp. 119 ff.). He can be seen to act within the structure of online-communities around video platforms discussed in Chapter 8 with references to Adami (2009).

Which conversational options are inherent in this structure? Which conversational threads exist between Cyrill's *responsive* developmental context and schools' institutionalised learning practices? Which conversational threads can schools establish, in particular to deal with Cyrill's milieu habitus and his patterns of media use? First of all, there is regional integration, which leads to a conversational thread to the police and the state attorney. It is about values and sanctions. The police react by investigating Cyrill in relation to this mobile video activity at the station. The regional culture and related activities, e.g. drunken men hanging around at the station, fit into this structure. Another relevant element is the use of a kind of international language, to which the video's label belongs: 'Cyrill pictures', 'Atzen compilation'. The verbal statements on a video platform such as YouTube or Myspace are globalised, in this case they are made up of a mixture of non-standard German and a kind of global English (see example below). Furthermore, a range of representational modes such as written statements, pictures, music added to the video, photos on a rotating cube etc. is used (see Figs. 10.4 and 10.5). Cyrill's self-presentation on his website reveals competence in media-processing software use.

Conversational Threads in *Responsive*, User-Generated Contexts

An analytic examination of Cyrill's websites reveals threads, which relate to the themes of publicity, identity and expertise within personally relevant contexts for development. For Cyrill the internet works as a *responsive* space, responsive in the sense of relating the young man's actual development needs and processes. (See also our discussion of Vygotsky's term 'zone of proximal development', Vygotsky 1930/1978, pp. 84 ff. in Chapter 9.)

In contrast to the technically rather unsophisticated video discussed above, Cyrill's web-offering is elaborate. Through it, Cyrill positions himself in his regional, as well as in a global context and he evidences his skills of dealing with software and representational modes within media-specific standards. The mobile/cell phone does not require planning, just to make decisions when and how to record an ongoing event. In contrast to the mobile video, a website is much more complex, particularly if its function is self-presentation. Cyrill's self-presentation on the internet media platform is a dialectic enlargement of his developmental context: the objective, but simple reportage receives its counterpart in the form of a personal and ambiguous self-presentation. Both media-related activities take place in, or relate to regional contexts. But the mode of publicity is different for self-presentation at the station; it lacks a public stage. The public coverage in the regional newspaper appears as result of Cyrill uploading the video to an internet media platform. It is a kind of regional, value-related response to the result of Cyrill's reportage. The public nature of a webpage is an essential feature of Cyrill's personal *responsive* context of development. The public domain is a key element of a developmental context, which is not typical for a school, but which is also not inherently excluded from the school, e.g. stage performances.

Self-presentation, and the presentation of an investigation are ordinary activities, to which convergence is a prerequisite as it widens the regional, self-generated context. The links between the conversational thread of investigation/reportage, in this case at the station, and the school curriculum are easily made. But, the conversational thread 'provocation' does not usually fit neatly and constructively with school-based learning.

Is this thematically based conversational thread of identity a possible bridge to school-based learning? From an educational perspective, teaching is inherently about supporting identity development, but it tends not to be a relevant issue in curricular terms. Probably only Cyrill's software expertise could be linked explicitly to curricular requirements. The screenshots in Figs. 10.4 and 10.5 from Cyrill's website consists of written texts and (rotating) photos, which require a rather sophisticated and creative competence in software handling.

Cyrill integrates his videos into his personal website on YouTube and MySpace. He names his site on MySpace with a clear professional touch: 'cypictures'. The syllabus 'cy' also gives him a personal identity by referring to the name, which he uses on the internet. Also his videos carry the logo: 'Cyrill pictures', which implies a relationship to a professional institution and corresponds to the practices commonly adopted in professional contexts.

During the police investigation Cyrill deleted the incriminating videos, abandoned his site on YouTube and moved to MySpace and other platforms. The focus of his site on MySpace is self-presentation and follow-up communication, both typical for internet media platforms.

He presents himself in different ways and poses ranging from being hurt and vulnerable to being a gang fighter (see Figs. 10.6–10.9). As already noted, the presentation by way of a rotating cube requires an elaborate knowledge and handling of digital media software, which is predicated on a learning process mainly outside of the school context. Cyrill developed and applied this expertise within the structure of the chosen video platform, which he links to the video function of the mobile/cell phone to take basic situational images.

The 'identity thread' is of high relevance. A young man, who calls himself 'eMKa', obviously a peer of Cyrill's, takes part in a follow-up communication (see Figs. 10.10), even if the online interaction doesn't necessarily directly relate to the digital video, which Cyrill had uploaded. He, too, does not refer to the video itself. Instead, he uses Cyril's web space to frame his personal reflection.

eMKa writes about where he grew up, how he came in contact with 'Hip Hop'. He refers to playing his favourite song on a trip to Turkey. He also writes that since that time he loves what he calls 'Holy black music', a hobby, which gives him an alternative to daily routines. It allows him to switch off and change his state of mind. He also notes that paid work changes how many pieces he is able to produce. And he notes that being married is very time-consuming and impedes his ability to DJ himself.

The language used in this short text does not follow standard German orthography, but at the same time, it is also not written by someone who is unfamiliar with German vocabulary and grammar. Instead, some kind of new German dialect, a *sociolect*, seems to be evolving. The text is characterised by a level of reflexivity, which brings the author's life story or curriculum vitae in an interesting relationship with the songs or music groups of particular periods of his life. Music can be seen to provide a structure and to add a meta-reflective richness to the author's curriculum vitae and the circumstances governing particular life episodes.

These postings on Cyrills website, have considerable relevance for schools, which function on the basis of a model of literacy, which was appropriated in, and promoted by the school. The posts on Cyrill's website are also relevant in the context of convergence of mass communication and for the role of mobile devices in them (cf. tools such as Twitter or Shozu). Apart from facilitating the ability to post to, and to read on the internet, the mobile, of course, offers other options for written communication such as text messaging. We view all these written verbal activities as potential levers to adjusting the linguistic practices of school-based learning and align them with the existing verbal competences in the context of current media-rich cultural practices of young men such as those we introduced above. The postings demonstrate ways of appropriating the pre-given media structures on the basis of a formative agency by way of cultural practices that are visible, make use of media convergence and can be seen to be related to literacy practices prevalent in schools.

Conversational Thread: Expertise

Our brief examination of Cyrill's combined use of his mobile/cell phone and an internet video platform reveals expertise, which is emphasised by Cyrill himself in his use of the label 'cypictures'. He represents himself deliberately as an expert and, as the conversational threads on the website show, he is accepted as such by his peer group. Typical for the conversational thread on expertise is the question of a boy, Sven, who addresses Cyrill as expert on web-design: *CYRILL wie hasT du dich selber als hinTERgruND gemaCHt? Sag mal bitte peace.* (Translation: *Cyrill how did you put yourself as background? Please tell me peace.*) Svens's question is not typed orthographically correctly. He uses capital letters incorrectly, which does not enhance readability. The word 'peace' is used outside traditional German contexts, but probably in the context of youth culture.

The concept of the 'expert' captures the interrelationship between agency and practices, to which learning, competences and assessment incl. reflection belong. In contrast to the concept of expertise, the concept of literacy beside agency and cultural practices also contains mass communicative structures. Media literacy or mobile literacy refer to a specific interrelationship between agency, structures and practices, e.g. with reference to the predominance of a medium such as books in school or television, mobile/cell phones and the internet in the everyday lives of young people. (For a further discussion on expertise see Chapter 11.) The notion of expertise is a promising bridge to school because of its focus on the objects of communication. Expertise is a mode of dealing with the objectified world, yet from the personal perspective of one's life-world, which is entangled among other things with identity issues. Without an understanding of Cyrill's identity, which he displays on his website, his software expertise remains unclear and ambiguous. He is probing key elements of his identity, which range from a violation of juridical borders to learning. It is likely that he is motivated by a narcissistic desire to being the centre of attention.

Habitus, Socio-Cultural Milieu and Learning

Our main question is about widening cultural participation. On the one hand, Cyrill is using mobile and internet resources effectively. On the other hand, he operates in a rather restricted milieu with a habitus, which sits outside the mainsteam of school and society. The educational task, as we see it, is not to change Cyrill's habitus. That would just result in a permanent struggle in relation to his socialisation. For us bringing the school and Cyrill's *responsive* developmental context into contact by means of conversational threads seems much more promising.

The Hedonistic Milieu

Cyrill belongs to a 'hedonistic' milieu with a migration background, which enacts the habitus of the social underdog. Broadly speaking, the milieu comprises second-generation migrants, who are not adjusted to mainstream society, refuse to live according to its expectations, have certain deficits in relation to their identity and are motivated by having fun. In the terminology of Bourdieu (1984), habitus is a stabile interrelationship of agency and the structures of the field, in which social activities are performed. Through socialisation and appropriation of cultural products, long-lasting personality characteristics are developed, which are characteristic of particular milieus. The habitualised and appropriated social structures work as a unifying principle of agency and practices and at the same time contribute to social distinction. Cyrill's mobile reportage produces a barrier between the values of the societal mainstream and Cyrill as a young man belonging to a second generation of migrants. But also language used on the internet media platform is characterised by significant differences to the language of schools, which threatens to cut the conversation threads between school and media-based conversations of everyday life. The milieu habitus is characterised by certain features, which – in the case of Cyrill – leads to self-portrayal as an underdog whilst, at the same time, conveying a certain sense of superiority. The *Sinus Milieus* (Sinus Sociovision 2007, p. 65; see also Fig. 8.6) offer the following description for the segment to which Cyrill probably belongs:

> The fun-oriented, modern lower class/lower-middle class (Escapists): Disregard for convention and behavioural expectations of the achievement-oriented society. This milieu contains 11% of the German population. (http://appz.sevenonemedia.de/download/sinusmilieus_04.pdf)

Against this background, Cyrill's investigative video about the homeless can be interpreted as an attempt to look for the real underdog as well as, of course, to have fun, which is always important.

The basic orientation of the *hedonistic-subcultural milieu* (BC3, escapists) in the migration context (Sinus Sociovision 2007, p. 65; see also Fig. 8.6) can be described as follows:

- against the background of the social exclusion experienced (self image of being a 'Kanak') on the one hand the dream of a rich life in Germany with 'easy money', luxury, prestige; on the other hand resignation and a defiant 'underdog' mentality: being unemployed, without chances, discouraged;
- (partly aggressive) distance to the mainstream of society together with not being adjusted – for example, in the outfit, in behaviour and language –, conflicts with authority and authorities (parents, teachers, supervisor, police); on one hand disapproval of demands for integration and achievement, and on the other hand the desire for success, appreciation, a higher income and a better job;
- orientation towards the 'here and now', hardly any long-term and future planning, uncontrolled spending of money, financial problems, often no perspective for the future, insecurity, being passive.

Modern German society, like other European societies, is segmented into socio-cultural milieus, which are constructed within two dimensions: the dimension of 'social status' and the dimension of 'basic values'. Social status comprises formal school education, profession and income. Stratification in this dimension corresponds more or less with layers of social class. Empirically verified social-cultural segmentation is available in the form of the SINUS-milieus.

The 'hedonistic-subcultural milieu' (BC3, escapists; see also Fig. 8.6) of the second-generation migrants in Germany belongs to the 'sensation orientated' segment of society with low social status, low income, low formal education, but looking for multi-value options.

In the terminology of the Sinus research (see Fig. 8.7, Column C) people in this segment look for a 're-orientation' with 'multiple options' and experimentation. This is the social habitus of a large social group, which is at a distance to the core rationale of school-based learning. In traditional school-based learning, the learning object drives the process of appropriation. But the learning object, e.g. software skills for optimal media use, is reflected for the hedonistic-subcultural milieu only as expertise within the personal life-world, which 'disregards convention and behavioural expectations of the achievement-orientated society'. Habitus of learning is part of the learner's agency as well as the different ways of learning inside and outside of school and the practices of media use. Learning habitus in the different, personally constructed life-worlds and socio-cultural milieus correlate with media practices. There exist hard empirical data on the correlation between the formal educational status of families, school-relevant language competence, preferences for media programmes (e.g. violence, amount of time for media use), type of family climate and school success (see Mößle et al. 2007, p. 99).

Of course there is the issue of the social interests inherent in habitus distinctions: who profits socially, politically and culturally? For example, in the case of excessive television viewing or the playing of violent digital games, the cultural looser are the boys, who forego success in school and, as a result, in the labour market. There exist more subtle connections: Bernstein's discussion about symbolic control and identity (1996/2000, pp. 81 ff.) asks questions about the ideological function of the divorcing of knowledge and the knower, which is a key characteristic of school learning. What kind of habitus of learning and of media use deals more successfully with the separation of knowledge and the knower in school? In terms of general gender characteristics it is not that of boys at the moment.

Learning is one mode of appropriation and a central mode at that, which depends on the predominant notion of subjectivity. With reference to Bourdieu's concept of habitus, the children and young people of our society act on the basis of a specific habitus, which correlates with their way of learning. For example, learning as memorizing curricular objects within a teacher-centred lesson was successful against the background of a specific personal and learning habitus, e.g. being passive, having no identity as a critical citizen, no self-organised innovative labour. This changes, though, in a context in which subjectivity is focused on individualisation in a consumer-orientated society, in *a society of individualised risks* (Beck 1986; Giddens 1990, 1991). The idea of the *at-risk society* is entangled with the appearance of a specific new habitus, the habitus of personalised appropriation of the objectified world. One defining feature is the objectified world as a *personal life-world*. The German key term is 'Erlebnisgesellschaft', the 'world of personalised perception'. In contradiction to the mainstream of learning since the Renaissance, which defined the structures of an objective world, today the predominant learning dynamic comes from the learning agent within his/her frames of fragmented life-worlds and his/her habitus of personalised appropriation. Mobile devices fit perfectly into the habitus of personalised appropriation within fragmented life-worlds.

The ongoing transformation of the industrial society leads to an increase of services and combined cultural commodities such as convergent media. This coincides with personalised life-worlds and a habitus of personalised perception and appropriation. This transformation takes place in the context of a shift from industrial production of commodities to 'symbolic' cultural products as key part of the economy. One result of these developments is the growing significance of mobile/cell phones and other personal mobile devices in everyday life within a context of media convergence. This reinforces specific features of personal habitus and learning habitus. The mobile/cell phone as the leading medium of convergence seems to guarantee an endless consumption and, by virtue of its ubiquitous disposition and close proximity to one's body, becomes the centre of one's personal life world. This ubiquity in everyday life clearly has implications for learning.

The Socio-Cultural Background of At-Risk Learners

The development of groups of at-risk learners seems to be part of a trend across OECD countries and beyond. A sizeable group of young people consistently fails in traditional school contexts whilst at the same time they are successful in their meaning-making with media and in particular with mobile technology. How can we understand this group of at-risk learners as part of a life-style? How does it incorporate patterns of media use, approaches to education and learning as well as general decision-taking, value orientation, visible and audible style elements e.g. of clothing and tastes in music and what are the implications for school-based learning? As we already noted, their characteristics are a feature of socio-cultural milieus. Two German research institutes (SINUS Sociovision and SIGMA) offer data on social segmentation, which covers media usage, general consumption and education. According to the model of milieu segmentation, the segments *Precarious Consumers* and *Hedonists* are especially relevant for the at-risk learners. The studies we refer to here were conducted from the perspective of the SINUS milieus, use the same epistemological model and are comparable to each other for those two segments.[1]

Who Are the *Precarious Consumers*?

The Precarious Consumers' main mechanism of participation is consumption. For them consumption, e.g. the purchase of often expensive items, compensates for the lack of access to other cultural resources. Due to lack of financial strength and a high rate of unemployment, the uncontrolled purchase of goods promises closer proximity to mainstream society. But for Precarious Consumers consumption itself is already risky. They seek safety in society and try to get closer to the mainstream of society, e.g. through their taste in clothing and music by seeking well-known brands, music groups and song titles to avoid uncertainty. The main reason for buying fashionable and well-known brands comes from the hope to be acknowledged by others. The risk for them lies not in failing this acknowledgement but in ending up in an even weaker position in society particularly by running into worse financial difficulties.

Boys within the Precarious Consumer segment do not tend to own gaming consoles, they do not tend to play online games and they do not tend to buy printed or audio books. Very few have personal computers at home; their offline PC usage is just for gaming. These boys report to use an encyclopaedia on the PC more than once a week. There is little evidence of internet access and their households tend not have MP3-players. However, the vast majority of male Precarious Consumers between 14 and 24 own a mobile/cell phone, mostly with prepaid cards. Most of these boys (>90%) use the mobile/cell phone on a daily basis, but 8.4% use the mobile less than once a week. When being asked for the brand of the mobile/cell phone, interestingly the phones were of minor brands. This seems to suggest that mobile/cell phones have not reached a certain level of importance for this group (yet). Normally the male Precarious Consumers spend €20–€25 per month or less on mobile telephony and all read and write text messages. Fewer than 10% take, receive or send photos with or from the mobile/cell phones and fewer than 10% use the mobile/cell phone as an MP3-player.

[1] Based on Sinus Sociovision (2009). Information on the informal learning of 'Precarious Consumers' and 'Hedonists' can be found in studies about participation in further education (Barz 2000; Tippelt et al. 2003; Barz and Tippelt 2004).

Male Precarious Consumers aged 14–24 name biking as a preferred leisure time activity, presumably because this is their only means of transportation. All of them also engage in other, not specified sports probably fitness, bodybuilding, martial arts, although just very few mention playing football, skiing, running or swimming. By comparison, most of them visit sports events such as football matches and they like being together with friends. They like listening to music and watching television, although only very few (less than 10%) mention reading magazines, watching DVDs, visiting pop concerts, eating out, partying or going to pubs or discos. Their music preferences focus on German and international pop and rock music.

Male Precarious Consumers aged 14–24 mention the following things as being important in life: having many friends, family and partnership, financial independence, being successful in their job, being able to afford something, having a safe future, being or looking attractive. Most of them see themselves as open to new things, say that they live in a healthy environment, have a good job/education, have holidays, live in a nice home or apartment, are sportive and active, eat healthily. Just a few think having much leisure time, hanging around from time to time, having a lot of fun and action and having a good all-round education are important issue in life.

Who are the Hedonists?

In the case study of Cyrill we already discussed the activities of a young man from the hedonist milieu. The following frames his case study with available data on the media habits of this milieu segment.

Hedonists are the biggest youth segment comprising about one third of all adolescents. It is the mainstream of young people. Due to the size of this segment there are great intra-segmental differences and the segment includes youth styles and social scenes that deliberately attempt to distinguish themselves from each other. The main characteristic of this segment is being in opposition to all authority and mainstream society. This is attempted through active risk-taking and active risky consumption, e.g. spending money on partying, gaming, ring tone subscriptions and mobile/cell phone contracts, etc. Hedonists participate in society through media and portable gaming consoles. Their active risk-taking is also in evidence in school by positioning themselves actively in opposition to the authority of the school, its teachers and its curriculum. Active risk-taking is in tension with passive risks, for example not to finish school and to end up without qualifications.

Portable Gaming Consoles

The male Hedonists aged 14–24 make up one fifth (20.5%) of the whole German population aged 14–24. More than 60% of them own a gaming console and many have a second console. Half of the gaming console owners posses a portable gaming device.

Computer and Internet

About two thirds have internet access at home and only one fifth to a quarter of the male Hedonists aged 14–24 years has not used the internet in the last 12 months. More than two thirds with internet at home have a broadband connection. About a quarter of the male Hedonists, who use the internet, go elsewhere to get access. About half of the internet users play games online. Approximately one third has bought at least one book in the past 12 months and 10% have bought at least one audio book in the past 12 months, which is the second highest rate compared with all other social segments. This means that male Hedonists have quite a high affinity to audio books.

Their preferred computer activities (offline) are gaming, communicating with others, listening, watching or recording audio and video as well as editing audio and video, and using encyclopaedias. About 14% have their own homepages. They have the highest rate of watching television through their personal computer. Male Hedonists' prefer online activities including communicating with others via chat programmes, email as well as using online communities. They like to download free music and videos, to watch videos, to search for information about television programmes and music. They have the highest rate of using eroticism and sex-related material on the internet.

Mobile/Cell Phones

Around half of all male Hedonists own a separate MP3-player. 94.2% of 14–24 year-old male Hedonists own a mobile/cell phone, which means that a significant 6% of them do not. Two thirds of those who have a mobile/cell phone, have a pre-paid card, one third has a monthly subscription. Thirteen percent use the mobile/cell phone just once a week or less often. About half spend €10–€25 per month using the mobile/cell phone and about 7% are spending €40 to more than €50 per month. Their most preferred brand is Nokia (36%), followed by Sony Ericsson (21%), then BenQ (12%) and Samsung (10%). With reference to the gaming preferences discussed above it is worth mentioning in this context that Nokia offers the N-Gage platform, which – at the time of writing in the 2nd quartile of 2009 – is available for the top-end Nokia n-Series devices. N-Gage as gaming console has the second highest rate for male Hedonists compared with all other social segments: tendency rising. The preferred mobile applications are texting, gaming, taking photos/videos and sending them via MMS, surfing the internet, using the organizer functions, downloading ringtones and wallpapers. Hedonists have the highest rate in using GPS functions.

Leisure Time Activities

The male Hedonists aged 14–24 prefer the following leisure time activities (in order of importance): listening to music, being together with friends, watching television, watching DVDs, using the PC and internet, partying, going to the movies/cinema, playing computer/video games, going to the disco/club, swimming, biking, eating out, playing football, going to the pub. Their music preferences concentrate on Hardrock, Heavy Metal and especially Dance and Electronic as well as Hip Hop and Rap. The important issues for male Hedonists in the age group 14–24 are: having many friends, financial independence, being successful at work, being able to afford something, having a safe future, fun and action, having a fixed job and a good job/education. Many of them mention family and partnership, having a lot of leisure time, being open to new things, performing well for merit, individuality, being attractive, a good versatile education, security in the country, living in a nice home/apartment and hanging around from time to time. In contrast these items were just named by a few Precarious Consumers. In contrast to Precarious Consumers, male Hedonists value having children, going on holidays often and eating healthily less.

Attitudes of *Precarious Consumers* and *Hedonists* Towards Learning

The Precarious Consumers' attitude towards formal education is shaped by low expectations. They feel a strong dichotomy between power and having no power. On the one hand they claim to be part of an important working class, but on the other they see themselves as underprivileged and treated unequally. This finds expression in a depreciation of their own knowledge. The two social segments at the bottom of the social stratification map show a great distance and an objection to social segments with higher education. They strongly distinguish themselves from the people who have higher education than them and are generally well educated (Barz 2000; Tippelt et al. 2003; Barz and Tippelt 2004). For the Precarious Consumers and Hedonists it is not easy to keep their social status, because a broad general education serves to maintain the current social position (see Vester 2006). Furthermore, they do not tend to have ambitions to increase their socio-economic status as they are far away from accessing higher education.

Learning Strategies of the Precarious Consumers

On one hand Precarious Consumers are very reluctant towards further education and all kinds of learning in formal contexts. They tend to have had bad experiences in school and were often unsuccessful in learning in formal contexts. When asked about their learning in informal contexts, all participants stated to have learned informally. They read textbooks or specialised books, magazines or professional journals. They reported that friends, relatives or colleagues had taught them. They either learn by watching friends, relatives or colleagues and imitated them successfully or they learn by trial and error and discussing the results with others (Tippelt et al. 2003, pp. 116, 124).

Although the Precarious Consumers read books and magazines for information, they tend not to use media for self-directed learning. Just 18% of Precarious Consumers think that they learn in a self-directed way by using media (Pietrass et al. 2005, p. 419). However 28% of this population believe in their capacity to learn from the media (Tippelt et al. 2003, p. 155). These statements fit into the general picture that Precarious Consumers often are not aware of having learnt informally. One interviewee stressed that they never attended a computer course, but learned everything about computers informally. Quiz shows on television such as *Who Wants To Be A Millionaire* are also an integral part of their everyday life in order 'to keep the brain going'. This strategy is two-fold. On the one hand, Precarious Consumers would not acknowledge this kind of appropriation as learning in informal contexts. On the other hand this kind of learning is a very strict form of learning. The obvious informal strategy to learn about computers is self-directed and motivated by everyday life needs in order to be able to cope with daily situations. It is work-based learning, which focuses on simple jobs. Generally speaking, the appropriation of competences is motivated by everyday life-needs. In their information retrieval they want to cope with their troublesome daily life.

The Precarious Consumers do not invest enough self-discipline for explicit learning and do not care about the effectiveness of their learning. Generally speaking, objects, which do not provide enough fun, e.g. a foreign language learning CD, remain untouched. The Precarious Consumers' learning is selective with regard to everyday life situations. Their learning in informal contexts focuses on knowledge, which – from their perspective – has immediate applicability.

Learning Strategies of the Hedonists

The Hedonists have a strong attitude towards self-directed and learning in informal contexts. This fits into the general picture of being in opposition to mainstream society and to authorities such as teachers, to institutions such as schools and anything that is prescribed. From this perspective they appreciate the non-authoritative, non-binding, non-committal and unconstrained character of learning in informal contexts. There is a strong influence of peers, asking them for help/advice, being taught and encouraged by them. They try to adopt attitudes of self-chosen idols but try to avoid unpleasant consequences, keeping themselves updated and learn in a self-organized manner in the field of ICT by using online manuals, forums, etc. The internet is an easy source for information.

Attitude to learning, as a key cultural resource, differs across socio-cultural milieus; so does the allocation of mobile resources of everyday life. Children and young people from of the Hedonist and Precarious Consumer milieus tend to have low expectations and a low opinion of their own knowledge. But these young people do acquire expertise through their engagement with mobile, individualised mass communication and these contexts can *respond* sensitively and supportively to their generative, personal themes.

Outlook

The educational task, as we see it, is to integrate the naïve and native expertise of at-risk learners into school. One didactic option is to dock the *responsive* developmental contexts of mass communication onto the practices of teaching and learning of schools. As shown in the case analysis of Cyrill, this can be done successfully by identifying and extending *conversational threads* form everyday life into the school.

An important pedagogical task, we believe, is to find a curricular way of extending the school's cultural practices and open them up to Cyrill's media practice. We consider Piaget's work (1947/2001, 1955) on learning and perception to be helpful in adjusting the different acts of culturally situated meaning-making Cyrill engages in as a user of a mobile/cell phone and as student. Piaget explained learning and perception as appropriation by two modes: assimilation and adaptation. Assimilation refers to the process of a child taking something unknown into his/her cognitive structures. A child can also adjust his/her cognitive structure to unknown facts or events. To adjust one's cognitive structures to a new reality is accommodation. This dual process of adjustment we find helpful in describing activities of the school and its agents, teachers and students, in the process of responding to the mobile/cell phone as genuine part of everyday life and mass communication. We see an analogue dynamic for mobile learning in the interrelation of school and everyday life. Schools have to engage in a process of appropriation by way of assimilation and adaptation. The relationship of the discourses of school and everyday life can be discovered by looking for typical structures of mobile/cell phone use in everyday life as well as convergent media within mass communication on the one hand and for curricular school structures on the other. On the basis of this comparison the pedagogical challenge is the adjustment of school discourses around learning to allow for an alignment with the cultural practices of children and young people, their meaning-making in the context of media use in everyday life including their representational modes in the context of changing mass communication and socio-cultural stratification.

The final chapters of Part II of this book, Chapters 11 and 12, deal with the didactic options available to school to create situations for mobile learning by means of *conversational threads* and naïve expertise and present some didactic parameters for analysing and planning interventions around mobile learning in formal educational settings.

Chapter 11
User-Generated Content and Contexts: An Educational Perspective

Introduction

Our pedagogically-orientated discussion of mobile learning so far has led us to the conclusion that one viable educational response to the mobile complex is to take up thematic threads from young people's responsive contexts of development and link them to the school curriculum and its teaching and learning practices. In our pedagogical deliberations on the mobile complex and on ubiquitous mobility we considered the new, user-generated *mobile* and *convergent* contexts as responsive contexts, in which young people appropriate the new mobile and convergent cultural products, e.g. mobile devices, their applications and their services. The conceptual pairing of *mobility* and *convergence*, we noted, results from the increasing intertwining of mobile devices with the internet. Through their applications, mobile devices, many of them mini-computers, offer a multi-functional interface to web-based services that is always available. At the centre of our pedagogical considerations stands appropriation, by which we mean the reflexive relationship of a person to his/her outside world, which challenges mental development, including development by learning. A lot of the learning, which is afforded through the appropriation of the mobile complex and mobile devices, is informal because it is integral to everyday life. Two important characteristics of learning in informal contexts are (a) that there is mostly no intention to learn and (b) that the processes tend not to be considered as learning by those engaging in them. Young people act in the situative contexts of the mobile complex when making meaning in, and of the world. As noted in Chapters 1 and 6, we view meaning-making as the central characteristic of learning be it in informal situations of everyday life or in formal ones related to educational institutions.

We argue that there is an urgent need for schools, as institutions for planned and assessed learning, to integrate, through assimilation, young people's informal meaning-making within user-generated mobile and convergent contexts. And, we are confident that schools are capable of successfully facing up to this task. In addition to the situational context of learning, we also diagnosed differences in cultural practices concerning meaning-making in school and in everyday life. One urgent task for schools, in our view, is the assimilation of these practices. Meaning-making

N. Pachler et al., *Mobile Learning*, DOI 10.1007/978-1-4419-0585-7_11,

in everyday life within the affordances and constraints of the mobile complex is a cultural practice with specific agency features such as a habitus of learning and mobile expertise (see Fig. 6.1). Our pedagogic challenge is to make suggestions about how to bring into a fruitful relationship the informal learning practices of everyday life with formal, institutionalised and curricular ones. By using the notion of assimilation, one of the key processes proposed by Piaget (see also Chapter 10), we set out to develop an analytic and planning tool in the form of didactic parameters, in order to assist educators with the *didactic*[1] task of assimilating learning in informal contexts into school. We discuss and apply these in Chapter 12.

As a consequence of our theoretical perspective, we do not primarily argue the case for augmenting classrooms with mobile devices, i.e. to 'upgrade our existing educational models' (Laurillard 2008, p. 521). Instead, we advocate enriching the learning practices of schools by assimilation of meaning-making within mobile and convergent contexts of everyday life. Therefore, our pedagogic arguments do not revolve around replacing established media but, instead, around identifying the specific functions of mobile devices within contexts for, and of meaning-making. One significant difference to the affordances of traditional technologies, such as television or photography, lies in the ubiquitous and multifunctional character of personalisable mobile devices within a convergent media system.

The practical task lies in meaningfully relating the affordances of mobile devices to school curricula and cultural practices. As noted already, we seek to do so by proposing didactic parameters for analysing and planning curricular situations with reference to mobile devices. Our proposals centre specifically around the assimilation of user-generated content and contexts from learners' everyday lives into the cultural practices of schools. We discuss some pertinent issues concerning user-generated content and contexts in this chapter before moving on to a detailed discussion of the parameters in Chapter 12. Our proposals are not about revolution but evolution, not about replacing but about broadening existing cultural practices of schools by taking seriously, and developing bridges to, the meaning-making of learners in their everyday lives and attendant cultural practices and media use.

The Situated Character of Mobile Media and Learning Contexts

The recommendation to integrate mobile media, especially those from everyday life, mainly mobile/cell phones or MP3-players, follows our idea of a cultural ecology by assimilating students' learning practices into the school. One reason for fostering

[1] The term 'didactic' for us refers to an educational approach to teaching and learning, which is based on the premise that learning is a form of reflexive appropriation of the world around and inside a person. Viewed from this perspective, teaching is aimed at the learner's reflexive relationship to him- or herself (his/her inner world) as well as the social, cultural and factual world outside. The development of a person through a reflexive and appropriative relationship is an essential purpose of school. For a discussion of the concept of 'didactics' in an Anglophone context see e.g. Friesen (2006).

this assimilation relates to the consideration of mobile devices as cultural resources for learning. We see learning as embedded in situations within cultural practices, to which the school contributes. Mobility widens the availability of situations relevant for learning outside, but also inside the school. A common feature for both, learning and the use of mobile media, is the situated character of meaning-making. The homework examples discussed later in this Chapter make some of these situations and their structures visible. Mobile videos, linked to an internet media platform, combine video production in a local/regional context with the international youth culture of entertainment. Portable computers combine off-site with on-site learning. This different contextualisation affects learning. Mobility impacts on the situational context of learning, both in terms of location as well as in terms of the structure, i.e. how mobile devices and their applications are integrated. Convergent mobile and individualised mass communication is such a structure.

Socio-cultural development leads to a widening of what learning is understood to be, and to the recognition of meaning-making outside the school as a mode of learning. Our ecological approach with its idea of assimilating different modes of learning into the learning practices of the school is also motivated by the ongoing process of socio-cultural transformation. Although learning within the school is a rather stabile cultural practice, the recent socio-cultural developments around the proliferation of mobile devices and media convergence enforce flux on cultural practices. One instance of such flux are working 'anywhere' and 'any time' within the structures of media convergence and not, for example, inside an office, between 9 am and 5 pm. Another example is social segmentation by lifestyle milieus. These changes and the perpetual state of flux puts pressure on school learning to change. The mobile practices of everyday life function as change agents for school practices.

The integration of the personal computer into the school happened on a different basis. Under the banner of preparing young people for the world of work, among other things for reasons of employability, as well as within a certain productivity paradigm imposed by industry, the school was tasked with teaching young people computing skills, for example the use of word processors and spreadsheet applications as well as, to some degree, programming and database-related activities etc. The normalisation of mobile technologies in everyday life has so far mostly only been responded to by them being banned at the school gate and their practice being excluded. The school still mainly focuses on the aspect of entertainment when considering the new multimedia and multimodal spaces and activities. By banning mobile devices, schools draw a clear dividing line between their teaching and learning practices and the communicative entertainment practices of the students in their everyday lives. At face value, such a separation of practices can, at least to some extent, be understood in that it arguably prevents students from getting distracted. However, examined from the perspective of our socio-cultural ecology, it becomes evident that in so doing the school is not harnessing mobile devices as cultural resources with their inherent potential for learning. We readily acknowledge that it is not as easy to recognise the learning potential of mobile devices as it is with computers: in fact, mobile devices, due to their characteristics such as portability, small size etc. are arguably 'sub-optimal' (Beale 2007b, p. 64) in terms of traditional computer applications such as word-processing. We argue that in order to be able to activate the inherent learning potential the barriers between the different, but also in part conflicting cultural practices of everyday life and school have to be lowered and transgressed. From our perspective this process should be in the form of a deliberate assimilation of learning outside school into its cultural practice of teaching and learning.

Mobility clearly is fore-grounded in a didactic approach to mobile devices. Of course, the notion of mobility covers movement from place to place, such as walking in and between locations, without impeded technology use. However, at a societal and cultural level mobility also signifies a significant transformation in cultural practices and social structures, in particular around individualised mass communication and media use, which impact on learners and on the school.

Situatedness of mobile learning, a very important facet for us, is debated in the specialist literature inter alia in relation to context generation (see e.g. Luckin et al. 2009; Luckin et al. 2005; Dourish 2004; Cook et al. 2007). Of course, a cultural-historical view reveals user-generated contexts as a possibility for all media. User-generation is a necessary consequence of the situated character of meaning-making. For example, during the cultural changes of the 18th century and the beginning of the 19th century, a number of situations for reading books were developed from reading whilst walking in the garden to still reading in the library or reading in clubs or cafes in order to replace paternalistic reading patterns in which the most senior male would read the same devotional, religious text out aloud over and over again (Schön 1987). There are parallels here to the changes taking place in the learning domain: no longer does the transfer of standardised knowledge seem to be the main curricular model, a transfer which is organised and monitored by a teacher in rather paternalistically structured school situations. By means of mobile devices not only are contexts and content of mass communication breaking with traditional patterns and practices but learning itself is understood as more flexible. The increasing acceptance of learning as flexible is linked to the notion of situated learning (Lave and Wenger 1991), which posits that learning is meaning-making in contexts. The reduction in the dominance of the paternalistic teacher is also inherent in the concept of collaborative knowledge building (Scardamalia and Bereiter 1999).

The availability and flexibility of content and contexts are essential features of mobile devices within new, multimodal spaces, 'mobilised' cultural practices and fragmented meaning-making. These changes are reaching the school, among other things through the proliferation of mobile devices. Importantly, however, many schools have been developing an interest in (co)constructivist approaches to teaching and learning for some time and, in so doing, have become receptive to the logic of user-generated contexts. In this way mobile devices should be seen to provide welcome support for the developing trajectory towards individualised appropriation of content inter alia through user-generated contexts.

Making learning in schools more open to meaning-making practices of everyday life by creating new contexts for learning or by mobilising learning content and contexts seems to us to be a logical response to the ongoing cultural transformation. Of course, mobile devices could simply be considered as new learning tools and introduced into existing teaching and learning practices as versatile, portable, multimodal storage, representation and communication devices with good connectivity to augment or substitute previously existing technological aids. One example would be to listen to a podcast in foreign language learning on a portable device. From the perspective of our socio-cultural ecology such an augmentation of curricular functions is, of course, not wrong; however, it is restricted as it does not foreground mobility in the broader sense. Of course, even in this example a substitution of existing media or representation tools, such as the tape recorder or CD player, does not remain neutral to the relationship of teacher, student and learning object within a classroom situation. The effect is always an alternative context for teaching and learning to the one that existed previously.

The educational discourse around the use of mobile devices, certainly in the UK where a lot of the pioneering work took place, was influenced by publications such as the Futurelab literature review (see Naismith et al. 2004), in which new practices around mobile device use were examined in terms of their fit with existing theories. The emphasis lay on demonstrating that mobile learning practices could address all the principal tenets of all major models of learning mainly on the principle of augmentation (p. 10):

1. Behaviourist – activities that promote learning as a change in observable actions.
2. Constructivist – activities in which learners actively construct new ideas or concepts based on both their previous and current knowledge.
3. Situated – activities that promote learning within an authentic context and culture.
4. Collaborative – activities that promote learning through social interaction.
5. Informal and lifelong – activities that support learning outside a dedicated learning environment and formal curriculum.
6. Learning and teaching support – activities that assist in the co-ordination of learners and resources for learning activities.

As can be seen, a wide spectrum of learning activities, more or less central to curricular aims and objectives, can usefully be supported by mobile media and devices. However, such an approach appears rather eclectic and arbitrary and there is no clear sense how the activities add up to a coherent learning trajectory and how they relate to the ongoing cultural transformation that impacts on the development of learners. Mapping learning activities onto existing learning theories in this way allows teachers to make some inferences about desirable pedagogical practices but tells them little about how they relate to the fundamental changes in cultural structures, agency and practices, which critically impact on the development of learners.

From our perspective the inclusion of mobile devices and media into school practices makes the assimilative integration of cultural practices of everyday life, which we consider to be central in the developmental process of learners, into school-based learning possible. An important task for us is to show how learning activities with mobile devices can be operationalised in a principled and systematic way, and what practical value they can have in relation to the ongoing cultural transformation of structures, agency and cultural practices. To this end, we propose four didactic parameters in this book (see Chapter 12) as an analytical tool for demonstrating the practical value of mobile device use by showing how it can support the assimilation of learning in and from everyday life into learning in school.

Flexibility of Contexts, Specificity for Mobile Learning

The options for different learners as well as teachers in terms of their learning and teaching styles/preferences are widening. Learner- and teacher-generated contexts offer a new pedagogical dimension. Have we found a 'learning Cockaigne', a land of plenty, with self-constructed learning environments and easy access to content through the mobile's/cell phone's wide-ranging functionality, storage and multimedia applications? Beale (2007b, p. 64) captures this utopia with the provocative title: 'Ubiquitous learning or learning how to learn and you'll never have to learn anything again?' Has learning at last been freed from the shackles of school-based learning and does it now take place in informal domains free from the burdens of traditional cultural practices of learning in formal contexts? We very much feel that such a utopia is misplaced. Instead, we argue for an examination of the specific features of ubiquity of mobile devices in everyday life and for learning. Beale (2007b, p. 64) compares the specificity of mobile devices in a media historic perspective with other culturally dominant media and their specific contribution to learning practices as follows:

> Mobile learning has come into its own now that it better understands the nature of mobility (devices and users) and plays to the strengths of context, location, and immediate presentation of relevant and interesting information.

The reference to context and location is crucial, because it opens the curricular view to one important characteristic of mobile devices, namely flexibility within spatial contexts. Whilst we agree with Beale's conclusion that 'finding new ways of seeing things, being creative, providing new perspectives on the world and our place in it will become more important' (p. 65), we disagree with the notion that 'knowing anything will become irrelevant' if one knows 'how to access information, what information to trust and how to combine and present it' (p. 64). For us, knowledge is a complex construct and whilst the importance of content knowledge might indeed diminish over time, procedural and tacit knowledge remain crucial and are likely to increase in importance, as in fact Beale himself seems to acknowledge. And, we have already noted the importance of user-generated knowledge.

Beside the flexibility of spatial contexts, media convergence and social networking tools, which are becoming increasingly available for mobile devices, enable qualitative differences in context. The example of the use of personal computers for homework to be discussed in a plenary in school (Luckin et al. 2005) demonstrates geographical flexibility at a local level. The YouTube homework examples below, on the other hand, function within the virtual space of media convergence and are available globally. In addition to these differentiated spatial dimensions of context, reflexivity is of curricular relevance in relation to widening or generating contexts. Meaning-making occurs in contexts such as, for example, the library or socio-cultural milieus. The library is culturally a very familiar, traditional 'situated' context, which is dedicated to the medium of books. Socio-cultural milieus are brand new contexts for media use but they are only partially defined by them; other constituent features are clothes and other cultural products. In both contexts the process of reflexivity is a defining characteristic of meaning-making: in the case of the library there is the requirement to find the right book as a condition for an enjoyable reading experience; in relation to the socio-cultural milieu, we have already discussed the deliberate investigation of people on the social periphery by presenting the case of Cyrill. Reflexivity results from the situated character of meaning-making.

Changing contexts and developing new modes of reflexivity in relation to contexts is a well-known cultural-historical phenomenon. For example, the non-individualised mobility afforded by trains nearly 200 years ago made travellers sick. Today sickness is no longer an issue, not even on high-speed trains. Becoming sick can be understood as a basic and bodily form of reflexive relationship to an environment. Today's travellers are well adjusted, physically and mentally, to a flexible spatial context called a train ride. Of course, adjusting to locative mobility was also a process of meaning-making, e.g. to derive fun from a train journey or a car ride. The new mobile media and devices fit into, and result from locative motion by train or by car. But they introduce new mobile features, which on the one hand bring the world to the learner, for example through ubiquitous connectivity, and on the other the learner into the world, take them outside the classroom to make and document first-hand experiences (see the project of the Indian school at Domlur in Chapter 4 and below).

As already discussed, making meaning is only possible in relationship to situations, e.g. places passed on the train, a cultural situation of communication with the mobile/cell phone in a train, or combining school learning of Maths with the help of the video function of the mobile/cell phone with an online community on an internet media platform.

Learning depends on meaning, which cannot simply be transported by signs, images, words etc. And meaning is constituted by situations. Therefore, the relationship of a learner with a learning object within situations is crucial for learning (see Hanks 1991). Mobile/cell phones became taken for granted in public situations after a very short period of time, for example in the public space of a train compartment. The initial disorientation caused by having to listen in to private conversations in public places disappeared quickly and is no longer an issue. This is a result of meaning-making within the context of the mobilisation of old interactive but geographically-fixed landline telephony. The originally vague idea and practice of ubiquitous mobility became normal and was enlarged by a new interrelation between public and private. Now, the ubiquitous character of the mobile/cell phone comprises more than just individual mobility between public and private spheres or activities in and across locations. The relationship to situations and contexts is in the foreground. The situated character of mobile devices furthermore includes:

- convergent and individual mass communication,
- multimodal representation,
- production, sending, storage of texts, photos and videos and
- existing practices of learning.

User-Generated Content and Individualized Knowledge Building

The concept of active construction of content is an issue concerning the relationship of learners to the object of learning. Active construction of content does not depend on specific media, tools or applications. Of course, mobile devices such as MP3-players work in a repetitive manner and require only low-level decision-making concerning programme choice. The constructive impetus in terms of their use comes from the contexts to which an MP3-player contributes, e.g. to listen in an isolated manner shielding oneself against surrounding activities or to listen with a view to forming group identity etc. Big individualised portable storage repositories are part of different contexts, to which a user contributes. The complexity of these contexts occurs alongside the transformation of content into small units. Factorising content, breaking it up into small constituent parts, seems like a fitting development in the context of the emergence of small, portable and multifunctional mobile devices.

From the perspective of socio-cultural developments, the increasing minimalisation, currently in relation to mobile devices, is familiar and well known. Ritzer (1993) coined the phrase 'McDonaldization' to explain it. The question arises whether *McDonaldization* has now also affected the cultural resource *knowledge* – assuming we view content as one of the main constitutive parts of knowledge – with mobile tentacles (see Castells 2004) and personal mobility within individualised life-worlds? Are the basic structures shifting from the technological transformation of food and cuisine to communication and knowledge? In Ritzer's analysis, the basic structure of this economically-driven, cultural transition of food, for which the food chain McDonald provided the label, consists of:

- 'efficiency' (pp. 35ff): the optimal way to go from being hungry to be satisfied;
- 'calculability' (pp. 62ff.): to transform food, production and consumers into measurable units;
- 'predictability' (pp. 83ff.): predictable management of offering and eating food units;
- 'control' (pp. 100): workers and consumers are subdued into processes governed by predictability, e.g. by pre-organised choice, going through channels;
- 'the irrationality of rationality' (pp. 121ff), which includes among other things the 'demystification, deprofessionalisation, and assembly-line medicine' (pp. 139ff.).

Deprofessionalisation seems of particular relevance for us in the context of our discussion of knowledge and its generation. The ongoing and increasing process of individualization has led to a deprofessionalization with professional media producers, for example, no longer being the main players in determining the programme offer in the field of mass communication. With the emergence of media internet platforms, anyone can produce content by using skills from their life-worlds within the structures outlined by Ritzer, i.e. of efficiency, calculability, predictability and control, plus the specificity of their life-worlds and mass communicative entertainment. One result of this process is the breaking up of content into small units with high entertainment value.

A quick look at the Maths tutor channel on YouTube (See http://www.youtube.com/groups_layout?name=MathTutor) reveals minimal units of mathematical content but within a complex environment. For example, the video 'Calculating Accuracy' (see Figs. 11.1).

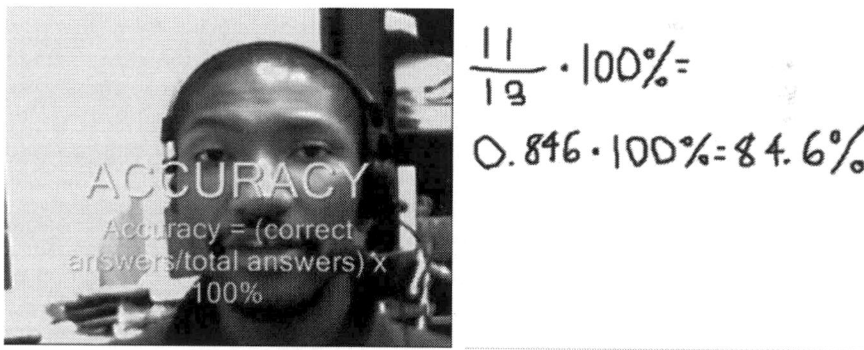

Fig. 11.1 'Calculating Accuracy' (Source: http://de.youtube.com/watch?v=DxS1BfTbA7k)

We can find similar examples in the case studies we introduced in Chapter 4, e.g. that of the Nationale Elitesportschule Thurgau. Here, within the school context and with the teacher as initiator, we can find mobile videos in which the students condense a language rule, in the Swiss example the Passé composé by using images, oral and written language into a short mobile video. The teacher's task was to put the videos onto the school website. In this example, Ritzer's categories meet traditional school practice (mimetic reproduction and the school curriculum). But, the focus on individualisation emphasises the learner's expertise under the supportive control of the teacher in the function as curricular programme professional (see Fig. 4.4).

This example demonstrates the trend to produce content and to construct knowledge in between cultural and economic resources. This trend results from the use of mobile devices. A student works competently and actively with several media (textbook + mobile/cell phone) and modes of representation (writing, video production, images). The aim is to make available a short and public summary for classmates.

Through this active and verbal production a student appropriates the functionality of the mobile/cell phone for his/her collaborative learning. At the same time s/he appropriates the basics of knowledge as an economic resource. Young (2006, pp. 737f.) describes how this aspect of content production and knowledge building maps onto the school. The traditional school curriculum works with insular knowledge ('insularity'), which is now shifting to 'hybridity'. Hybridity, according to Young (2006, p. 737), is characterised by:

1. the crossing of disciplinary boundaries,
2. the incorporation of everyday knowledge into curriculum design, and
3. the involvement of non-specialists in curriculum design.

Both examples obtain their hybridity from the mobile/cell phone, and its representational affordances, especially convergence, the easy and individual availability and the expectation of very short units and a native expertise. Additionally, two further structural elements for hybridity of curricula are at work in view of the mobile/cell phone's specificity, namely the requirement for small units. The small units are linked to the following two 'principles of hybridity' (Young 2006, p. 738): modular or unitized curricula and bite-sized chunks.

As can be seen, the trend towards 'bite-sized chunks' has not only taken hold in the area of food but, through the move towards individualized mass communication with the emergence of the video clip, the web-page that needs to structure content according to its display device (a computer or mobile/cell phone screen), also in the field of content (as constituent part of knowledge): miniaturisation of flexible and modular global and mass compatible resources is the order of the day (cf. reusable learning objects). The question arises not only how desirable this trend towards micro units of content is but also how the school can and should react to it. From a position of attempting to assimilate everyday life learning into school learning, this micro content and these small knowledge *chunks* are a didactic challenge. The reduction of learning objects into small knowledge *chunks* needs also to be critiqued. Does the downloadable application from the fast-food chain Subway Express for ordering customized sandwiches (See http://www.subwayexpress.co.nz/MobileIntro.aspx) show the way? Learners 'dialing in' for chunks of content according to (perceived need) selected from a wide menu of options? (see also the discussion about micro-learning by Hug et al. 2006 and Hug and Martin 2007). Needless to say modular content is at best part of the answer and only if accompanied by effective pedagogical interventions that enable learners to appropriate the content chunks into meaningful knowledge structures, not least as it is but an extension of transmission-based approaches to teaching and learning and only partially takes on board the complexity of the media cultural practices of young people in everyday life. In particular from an ecological perspective, the transformation of learning objects and the learning process into miniaturised elements follows the logic industrial production, e.g. for food, and subdues learning to this kind of rationale.

We are less concerned with what is new with regard to user-generated content, but what is specific to mobile learning. One important aspect of specificity is an inconsistency between the practices of everyday life and school. Many students are *natives* in the field of convergence and, therefore, well familiar with user-generated content within user- and otherwise generated contexts. The new repositories in the form of the storage capacity of mobile devices and on the Web are not new for young people. The important point is that all these developments are remote from the structures and practices of the school. Of course, the school can look back on a long cultural tradition of repositories, mainly those connected with the book, such as the library or the dictionary.

A crucial link between the different practices inside and outside the school comes from the concept of collaborative knowledge building (Scardamelia and Bereiter 1999), which recognises the learning object as essential for successful learning as it does its reconstruction by a group of learners. One important advantage the school has in relation to the transformation of knowledge into a global resource, instrumentalised for economic purposes, is that it stands at a distance to it and can discuss it critically. Learners' reconstructive activities within a knowledge building approach have to rely on the expertise of learners, which varies from individual to individual and across different socio-economic milieus. We find the notion of collaborative knowledge building helpful in considering mobile learning, not least as it is premised on the expertise of learners. As we have repeatedly noted already in relation to young people's cultural practices of media use, many of them possess high levels of 'native expertise'. Knowledge building, as developed by Scardamelia and Bereiter, relies on contexts, which have similarity to scientific discourse. One of the characteristics of such contexts is that knowledge does not require legitimation through practical application. What is important is to construct an understanding of the world as the students know it. But one has to bear in mind, that the focus on what has to be learnt is shifting away from the objective world, which is represented by science, towards the learner and his/her contexts.

Individualised Knowledge of Native Experts

Detraditionalization and flexibilization of contexts and frames of activity reinforce a fragmentation of meaning-making in situations, which is set up by individuals and their life worlds. A significant driver for this individualisation is the conversion of mass communication from a linear to an individualized, mobile 'pull' system and to public programme archives. Furthermore, the individualisation of social frames by socio-cultural milieus as new frames for personal life-worlds shifts the locus of responsibility onto the individual. This trend also fosters individual, personal forms and habitus of learning and moulds expert competence within the reference system of individualised life-worlds. What, we ask, are the consequences for schools? Compulsory schooling receives students, who are experts within their life-worlds and who appropriated knowledge within their relevant contexts. This expertise and this knowledge can be relevant, neutral or obstructive for school learning. Students arrive at the school as native experts within their life contexts. This native expertise can include competences in the area of new media, if they are relevant within the respective life context. One assimilative task for teachers is to look for the intersections of native expertise and curricular content and contexts.

Haythornthwaite (2008, p. 598) sees a significant impact on learning practices especially from the inclusive, participatory actions, which result from Web 2.0 and its

> cooperative conversations and contributions in listservs and discussion groups, recommender systems ..., cooperative classification systems ..., wiki-based encyclopaedia (Wikipedia) and dictionaries (Wiktionary), and citizen journalism in blogs and photoblogs. These new media lay the foundation for radical transformations in who learns from whom, where, under what circumstances, and for what and whose purpose. In short, they indicate a transformation to ubiquitous learning – a continuous anytime, anywhere, anyone contribution and retrieval of learning materials on and through the Internet and its technologies, communities, niches and social spaces.

In these cooperative, collaborative 'social spaces' of the new media and mass communication system the relationship between the teacher and students is changing:

> One result of the last 10 or more years of online learning has been the evolution and re-negotiation of what is required of teachers and learners, and thus of where authority lies. For example, where bulletin board contributions replace classroom participation, as they do in online learning courses, equal and sustained student participation becomes vital to a successful class. The role of students changes; they take on being more responsive to each other's questions and needs, changing their role and that of the teacher. It is common to speak of the teacher as 'sage on the stage' being replaced by the facilitating 'guide on the side'. Less often is it acknowledged that the student as 'empty vessel' is being replaced by a 'learnerleader' ..., who contributes to their own learning and the learning of others in the community. (Haythornthwaite 2008, p. 600)

These developments are augmented by the ongoing individual mobilisation of mass communication and its media convergence. The expert structure is becoming more relevant but as part of modern society's everyday life structures. In the life world theory of Berger and Luckmann (1966) concepts or mental representations become habituated and institutionalized, i.e. embedded in society, through interaction between people and groups and social reality is seen as socially constructed. In the context of the ongoing individualization, knowledge construction is up to the native expert of everyday life. Within the relevant structures and practices of their life-worlds, native experts develop and objectify concepts, explanations, legitimating reasons etc. This does not happen arbitrarily, because native expertise is the individualised version of cultural capital (see Bourdieu 1979). Therefore, it would be unwise to ignore the rather high level of contextually situated reflection of media natives of everyday life. Of course these media natives of everyday life operate by-and-large on a level of naïve consciousness, which is typical for everyday life. Everyday life relies on normality, routines and deals with what is taken for granted. One important option for the school is to offer reflexivity and critical awareness to native and naïve experts.

By establishing the native expert alongside the teacher as professional expert in and for the school the two versions of expertise are brought together. Students from some socio-cultural milieus as native experts do have a high level of relevant competences and knowledge. An increasing number of media users become experts (including teachers, of course), but they tend to do so within their relevance structures and their socio-cultural milieus. They come to school with different levels and types of expertise to the teacher and to each other. Beside these differences, the patterns of expertise offer contact points for co-operation and for integrating the patterns of learning in informal contexts and the resulting knowledge into school-based and school-related learning. The example of the Passé composé in the Swiss elite school (see Fig. 4.4) demonstrates the collaborative options for teachers and students. A pair of students summarise and verbalise the language rule by means of a mobile video, the teacher organises the 'connectivity' to the weblog to make available the summarised and objectified knowledge for the whole class. In the process the teacher is able to gain information about the degree of students' understanding and their progress. All this happens under the auspices of school-sponsored teaching and learning practices but with a strong emphasis on native media expertise.

The same dominance of the cultural practices of the school regulates the field research in the school in Domlur, India, but leads to cooperative forms of teaching and learning (see Center for Knowledge Societies 2005a, b and Chapter 4). Cooperation is targeted to identify, and to take photos of geometric forms outside of school, e.g. from the local environment. The naïve native experts are asked to recognize elements of everyday life deliberately and with a conscious vocabulary. Back at school, the Maths teacher asks them to discuss more or less specified objects by means of geometrical categories. This is an act of personal reconstruction, which develops the personal expertise of the life-world of naïve native experts and combines it with the professional expertise of the teacher. This offers to native experts an increase in awareness and supports the step from naïve to reflected expertise. In the process, mobile/cell phones are integrated into school to support the school curriculum in Maths, biology and computing (Fig. 11.2).

Fig. 11.2 Field research in Domlur: finding geometric forms (Source: CKS 2005a)

Bereiter and Scardamelia (1993) analysed the options of the socio-cultural development of native experts for learning within the knowledge society. For curricular planning we find the following analytic elements of expertise helpful:

- 'Fluid and crystallized expertise' (pp. 35f.)

In the two examples referred to above, the mobile video and photo application, the 'crystallizing' of insights around a language rule or geometrical forms is obvious. The very general function of media to objectify processes is part of the affordances of mobile/cell phones, as are the processes involved in taking photos and videos. The disadvantage of objectified knowledge is compensated by processes of watching, identifying, considering, evaluation etc. This leads to non-mimetic and active forms of appropriation.

- 'Hidden', 'informal' and 'self-regulatory knowledge' (pp. 43ff.)

The 'hidden knowledge of experts' (p. 46) of everyday life is characterised by being 'informal' and 'impressionistic' (p. 47). If one adds the episodic nature of today's contexts for meaning-making, the school should focus on objectifying for example through applications of the mobile/cell phone such as in the two examples above. This process of objectification leads to new archives of objectified knowledge in repositories.

An interesting feature of the expertise is its 'heroic element' (pp. 107ff.), which directly links to individualised expertise. An example is Cyrill's mobile and convergent media use by which he becomes the centre of attention of peers and society's institutions including the police.

The predecessors of mobile expertise are fan groups of media genres and specific media use like video groups (see e.g. Eckert et al. 1991 or Vogelsang 1991; promising research is also starting to emerge into structural features of blogs and online communities, e.g. White 2006). The specificity of mobile expertise comes from the fluidity of media convergence and user-generated contexts characterized by ubiquity. User-generated contexts were, and continue to be typical for media fan groups; media convergence is changing the conversational structures. For the moment, the following pattern seems to be valid:

(1) The social structure of expert groups is concentric with experts at the centre and novices at the periphery. The centre is defined by the media object of the expert group. Additionally, the structure is hierarchical with interaction taking place in relation to the competence of group members. There is also the possibility of specialisation and collaboration outside the concentric hierarchy. The learning processes follows this structure in terms of who passes knowledge to whom, learns from whom, evaluates or shares knowledge with whom etc.

(2) Verbalisation is a normal process for dealing with hidden and informal knowledge and to organise, regulate, legitimate and evaluate knowledge. The mobile/cell phone, with its interactive functions such as telephony or text messaging, supports these conversational activities. Typical in this context is the question

of a boy, Sven, who asks Cyril and addresses him as expert on websites. His question is framed by the appearance of the website (see Chapter 10).

The language used depends on the conversation to which a verbal statement belongs. Since at the moment the mobile/cell phone is mainly part of the personal life sphere as well as the regional and global entertainment culture, it is usually not the standard language used in school. This presents a real challenge for schools.

(3) Variety of forms of knowledge
Primary/elementary school children are often media experts. They use different types of knowledge, which cover, among others, content knowledge as well as procedural, tacit knowledge and know-how. Their content knowledge relates to things such as swapping elements of a media and programme set, e.g. Pokémon or reaching the final level of a game. It contains both, taxonomic elements such as the names of the 150 Pokémon characters, and holistic knowledge, e.g. about the story line of a game or a programme. This holistic knowledge can be also theoretical, for example explaining interrelations and levels or giving reasons. It appears usually in a follow-up communication to media use or media reception.

(4) Reflection and evaluation of their own media preferences and media use
Integrated in conversations, such as in the form of follow-up communication, children of primary/elementary age reflect on their own media preferences and media use. They compare them with those of others, such as peers or parents, and to those expected by others, for example teachers. Verbalisation, the variety of knowledge forms and reflection or evaluation around media use in everyday life are conversational elements which correspond to teaching and learning conversation within the school, but they belong to different, and conflicting cultural practices. An important assimilative task arises which challenges the conversational, communicative competence of school and its agents.

Assimilation of Mobile/Cell Phones and User-Generated Contexts

For us *user-generated context*s are a necessary response to the ongoing detraditionalization of culture. From the point of view of schools, understandably, the pressure to assimilate cultural change around mobilisation in the form of flexible contexts is not easy. It seems important to remind ourselves what we mean by context. In our explanation we follow Dourish (2004) who, without reference to the issue of mobilisation, considered context in relation to earlier phases of technological development in everyday activities, such as personal computers and the internet. Importantly for us, Dourish moves beyond viewing context as a representational problem and, instead, views it from an interactional perspective, i.e. he foregrounds human activities as being constitutive and describes context as an emergent property of interactions. (see also Chapter 2) We would at least add the need to recognise the ongoing convergence of media and representation through mobile devices, be it the mobile/cell phone or the MP3-player, as affecting the nature of context.

Whilst the idea of the changing nature of contexts might be disturbing, for example for the relatively stabile learning contexts in schools with fixed daily routines and practices, changes in media and mobility are well established features of context generation of which we are usually not aware. Space, in our modern understanding, was 'invented' at the beginning of the Renaissance, i.e. at the beginning of the 15th century. At that time, the so-called 'central perspective' emerged, a three-dimensional representation, which we take for granted today and which we consider as normal. The central perspective is characterized by all converging lines in a painting leading towards a single point at the centre of a composition, which creates an illusion of depth on two-dimensional surfaces. Although today we consider it as a natural way of depiction, the central perspective creates a virtual space, which is constructed as a context between a specific way of drawing, i.e. pictorial representation, and the perspective of the viewer. The viewer stands at a distance to the depicted object and constructs in his/her mind a virtual space between himself/herself and the viewed object. This distance through spatial relationship gave Leonardo da Vinci the possibility not only to depict the world in the modern sense but also to construct the world technologically as an ingenious engineer. The central perspective, with the inherent notion of the constructing subject, is one of the stabile cultural features of modernity, which defined contexts, for example as a space through which we travel deliberately and individually by car.

What kind of context is opened by mass communication and its technological media such as television? One of the spatial features is to offer access to the world far away, which is still inherent in the etymology of the word *tele*vision. Also it is a technologically constructed space, by senders, transmitters and receivers, to which everybody had access. The media of broadcasting emerged on the basis of this rationale of mass communication. It also defined mass communication as technological network. Today the network integrates a lot of social and conversational activities, which we can see within Web 2.0. Today's individualised, mobile mass communication is also based on a technological rationality. The new mass communication offers a technologically-based space for conversation, interaction, personal meaning-making etc. But this conversational space includes also control and alienation. It is fluid and flexible; it is not only open but also depends on individual and social contribution.

Mass communication is increasingly characterised by individualised meaning making by virtue of, and in individually generated context. Mobile devices such as the mobile/cell phone, PDA, iPod etc use the tradition of television, personal computing and the internet, but change their contexts of use. Television and personal computing had in common that the contexts were defined and pre-given, that is passively watching prefabricated television programmes or writing texts with the word processor in an office. By now, though, television is just one element in a complex programme system, which includes, for example casting events and/or accompanying internet sites. The personal computer became mobile as 'laptop' computer and through connectivity afforded by the internet. Media platforms such as Flickr or YouTube plus internet-capable mobile/cell phones both offer and require users to inhabit geographical as well as cultural spaces. For example, with the mobile/cell phones in their hands, the students of the Domlur school in India investigated their physical neighbourhood to identify right angles and circles. However, they also explored their cultural environment at home, which includes e.g. religious patterns and those associated with global youth culture and its artefacts.

The notion of generating contexts derives from individualised media use in standardised mass communication as well as from individualised movement within a transport system (see Bachmair 1986, 1991, Virilio 1990). Being blocked in traffic jams and restricted by diminishing fossile energy resources, mass mobility by fossile fuel powered cars is no longer the unquestioned future of individualized mass mobility. It is interesting to note that at the same time centralised mass communication through centrally broadcast television is being widened and replaced by the individualisation of contexts. The individualisation of contexts depends on new conversational and system-based technologies such as social networking. In a long line of structural changes and changes to agency throughout history, this development was logical and contexts generated by users with mobile media and the internet have become more or less ordinary for a lot of people in everyday life.

However, the normalisation of user-generation in everyday life and the new, convergent mobile media create a conflict in relation to the cultural practices of learning in school. Already Lave and Wenger (1991), with their seminal book on the situatedness of learning as a mode of meaning-making, unveiled the de-traditionalisation of learning. All meaning-making, we argue, depends on a situation as a condition sine qua non of learning.

In his discussion of contexts, Dourish (2004) clarifies some relevant features, which we consider to be helpful for creating situations for learning under the conditions of mobilised and individualised mass communication in everyday life. He bases his examination of context on 'the mundane details of lived experience', 'not as a stable description of the world, but as the outcome of embodied practice' (p. 15). In particular, Dourish discusses the relationship of practice – in terms of 'engaged action around artefacts and information that make those artifacts meaningful and relevant to people' (p. 11) – and technological structures (pp. 10ff.). He also talks about actions being 'embodied' in contexts (pp. 14ff.).

Although Dourish's discussion is about contexts induced by ubiquitous personal computing, rather than mobile devices, his ideas are relevant also for creating learning situations with mobile devices. Dourish posits (p. 11) that design opportunities do not lie in the use of predefined context within a ubiquitous computing system but, instead, in how ubiquitous computing can 'support the process by which context is continually manifest, defined, negotiated, and shared'. 'Ubiquitous computing technologies extend the reach of computation into the everyday world, and that world is one in which, through our everyday practice, we enact, sustain, and reproduce new forms of social meaning.' He offers the following design principles to show how social meaning can be fostered:

- by systems displaying their contexts: 'users of computer systems need to form interpretations of the state of the machine in order to determine appropriate courses of action' (pp. 11f.);

- to look deliberately for 'architectures for adaption': information systems are adapted to the different settings in which they are used (p. 12); and
- to set up information spaces: 'the meaningfulness of information for people's work is often encoded in the structures by which that information is organized' (pp. 12f.).

The flexibility of contexts is reaching a state of normality given the increased role of mobile devices in everyday life. This invariably influences situations for learning, which are also made flexible by the learners. In contrast to Douish's starting point, i.e. the impact of ubiquitous technology on contexts, Luckin et al. (2009 and 2005) explore learning contexts and the 'relationship and interaction between the elements within the situation over time' (2009, p. 5), which are relevant for learning. In a conceptualisation of context, which focuses on didactic questions around the resources used for learning in a static learning set, content, process of learning and teaching as well as places are given, defined by curricula and standardized institutionally. In a dynamic learning set the 'organizing activities that activate the resources' are at the learners' disposition (Luckin et al. 2005, pp. 5ff.). The way in which contexts deal with resources, therefore, ranges from augmenting the existing school context to widening the existing school by means of learner-generated contexts

In our discussion in Chapter 9 we already noted that children and young people set up their specific user-generated contexts (Wagner et al. 2006) in relation to media use. These contexts work like activity spaces, e.g. for

(a) specialization,
(b) consumption,
(c) expanding their own social field,
(d) space for presentation of their own favourites,
(e) creative production of media.

These five context-related patterns are part of local, regional and traditional culture and, at the same time, are linked to the global youth culture of entertainment (see Livingstone 2001, p. 331). The older children grow, the nearer they move to international youth culture. If a teacher intends to integrate mobile devices with their *convergence* into the classroom, these different context-related patterns become very important. An initial consequence of opening the school to the practices of mobile media is a high diversity between the students and their specific and habitualised patters. Given this diversity, any attempt to increase the degree of personal reconstruction will require a lot of effort and differentiation.

An Analysis of Reflexive Context Awareness

Generally speaking, reflexivity is the process of interacting with, and relating to the inner, personal world and the outside, social world. Reflexivity is activated by appropriating socio-cultural structures, dominant agency patterns and pre-given cultural practices. We discussed this in detail in Chapter 9. Because mobile devices are becoming normalized in everyday life, attendant practices are veiled by their situated character. Also, the generation of contexts tends to be hidden behind routines. The question arises how to support flexible contexts pedagogically. Dourish (2004. p. 14) takes a systems perspective and views the new, flexible contexts as 'embodied actions', which are inscribed into these contexts. Traditionally, the pedagogic response to media has been through fostering 'critical literacy', mainly in the form of media or programme analysis. But this is no longer sufficient.

User-generated contexts, we argue, should be viewed as a mode of appropriation. In the example of the Maths homework community, appropriation takes place essentially through the oral verbalisation of rules, which was recorded with the help of the video application of a mobile/cell phone. The mobile video delivers a mimetic reproduction of the teaching result. But verbalisation by means of the video for an internet audience shifts the student's learning outcome away from sheer mimetic reproduction to the pole of personal reconstruction.

If the relation of 'context and embodied action' (Dourish 2004, p. 14) is coming into the reflexive view of teacher and students, the opportunity for reflexive context awareness is opened.

Dourish, coming at the problem from a computational perspective, wonders how technology can be made sensitive and responsive to the setting in which it is used, e.g. through the adaptive functionality of the software and hardware such as sensor technologies. We view context awareness as being more than just 'the responsiveness of interactive technologies to predefined features of the times and places in which it is used' (Dourish 2004, p. 15). As noted already, in educational categories it is a mode of appropriation. The process of appropriation is situated and opens the opportunity to reflect the relation of action, media and context, which reaches from feelings and impressions to verbalisation.

Schools are facing a significant cultural transition in which contexts, which are situational constituents of meaning-making, are becoming far less stable and can no longer be taken for granted. Contexts need to be constructed and, in the logic of technological media, are flexible and disposable. This flexibility of contexts requires mobile context awareness on the part of the learner because meaning-making is embedded in convergent media spaces and practices. At the same time, children are taking their media contexts with their appropriated patterns of use for granted.

The field research inside the school practices of the Domlur School (Domlur School: http://udhyakumar.tripod.com/photos/computer_course/index.album/dsc00 651? i=8) in India illustrates how appropriation allows for reflexivity and how this naïve reflexivity can be widened in order to become more explicit. In this example reflexivity is embedded in pictures taken by students on their way from and to school and in their personal life-worlds and the cultural frames depicted. In this Indian school, the mobile/cell phone/cell phone, together with the computer, was used to open the school for new teaching and learning methods, from teacher-centred learning with text books and memorising facts to a more cooperative, self-organised style of learning, which included investigations outside the school. For mathematics (geometry) and biology work students went outside the school building to find relevant material, e.g. geometrical forms or plants. Students also used their way from school to home and back for becoming familiar with the GPS functionality of their phones to produce a map of their way between home and school. At home they would take photos for a display.

The teacher worked with the material, which the student brought into the school, in the lesson by storing it on a computer and using it for a display. At the bottom, the display shows the geographical context, which was set by the teacher. In the column at the right-hand side of Fig. 11.3, the students set their own context through the pictures they had gathered.

An analytical perspective reveals a particular attitude to the cultural setting. The depicted cultural setting is the regional religious context, which is visible in the form of the goddess in the background of the picture of a pupil's parents.

On the display (see Fig. 11.4), above the parents, is a photo, which depicts the student's bedroom with a television set and with posters that belong to the international youth culture . The school, as well as the regional geographical context are culturally extended by the students' own context. In a school with different socio-cultural milieus these regional and youth cultural context vary. This variation can lead to spontaneous and differing evaluations of the display and its represented contexts. In this way the cultural context of students is not taken for granted but opened for questioning and it supports Dourish's notion (2004, p. 14) of 'embodiment' of structures, regulations and activities.

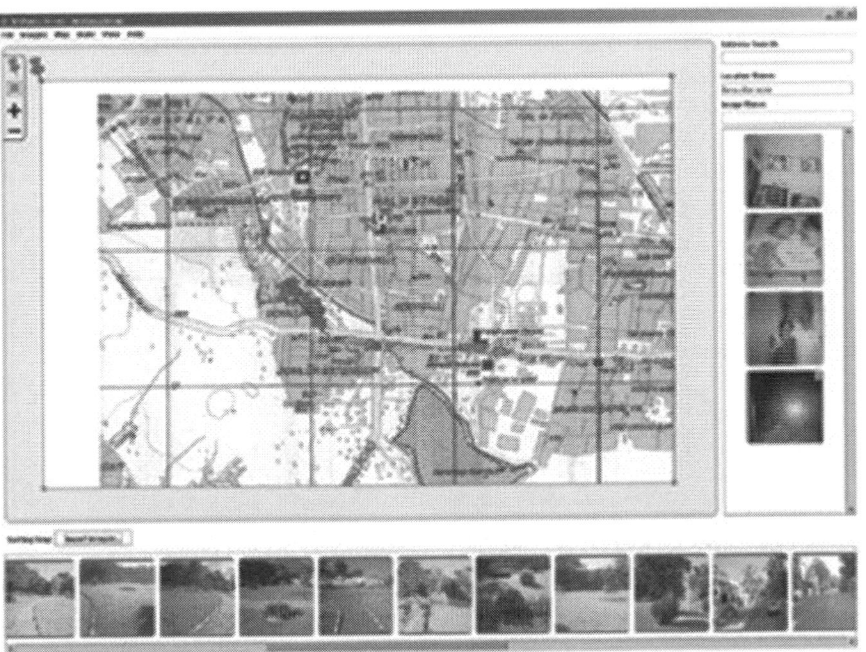

Fig. 11.3 Map with GPS track data (Source: CKS 2005a)

Fig. 11.4 Parents with goddess (Source: CKS 2005a)

Mobile/Cell Phones: From Everyday Life to School Learning

The mobile complex and individualized, mobile and fragmented mass communication have not yet entered schools and colleges in a big way, safe for some widely publicised projects[2]; instead, they characterise a wide range of learning processes outside of school.

The homework communities on YouTube are a nice example for such learning, yet not at all spectacular and not well integrated in youth culture. There are a lot of videos taken with mobile/cell phones that deal with a variety of Maths problems. They demonstrate that the ubiquitous mobile/cell phone can enhance learning processes through user-generated content and that it is capable of offering new contexts for learning within media convergence. In the case of the Maths community on YouTube, the new context is based on a repository as part of Web 2.0 social networking, which provides public communication within a specific structure. The mobile/cell phone itself is already a storage device for video files, pictures and texts. If augmented by social networking sites and connected to the internet, it provides access to an audience, links learner-generated content to a regional and global culture and creates new contexts for learning. In the example of homework communities on YouTube, the context centres on a small group of learners, who combine their video-recorded, school-related experiences with the affordances of an internet repository. The context is determined by the learner and his/her interests and is modelled on the cultural practices of the school, but students act autonomously without a teacher and – at least to some extent – on the basis of their own interests. These autonomous contexts, which are imitating school-related contexts, can be see as supplementary to school.

One example is offered by Sean and Dan, who calculate speed in their spare time. This video on YouTube summarizes their research on how to measure and calculate

[2]See e.g. the Wolverhampton Learning2Go project at http://www.learning2go.org/ or the Learning and Skills Council funded MoleNet project at http://www.molenet.org.uk/ (both UK).

'velocity'. The way to measure and calculate average speed is demonstrated in two case studies. In the first, one of the boys runs through a wood; in the second, the velocity of a miniature John Deed tractor, with one of the boys as driver, is measured. The method of measuring and calculating is shown in the video and related orally to Maths. The narration operates at a high level of abstraction, and requires significant cognitive processing. The clock function of the mobile/cell phone is used to take the time for calculating the average velocity (see Fig. 11.5).

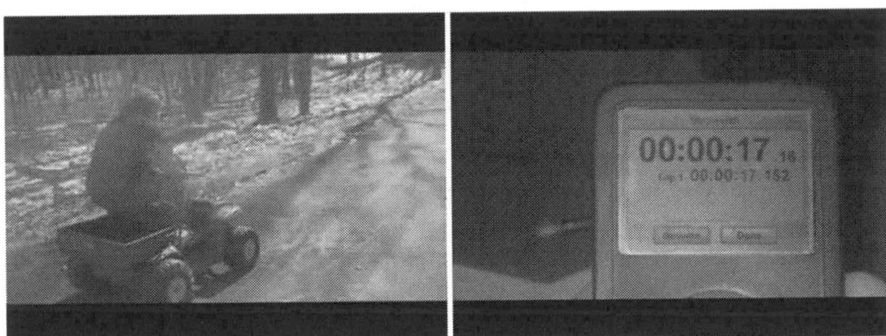

Fig. 11.5 Two boys calculate speed outside the school; screenshots from http://www.youtube.com/watch?v=DQ-4qg3D_W8

'Adding and Subtracting Polynomials' is another example out of a lot of others. It shows in detail how to deal with polynomials. The calculation are carried out in an exercise book, which is combined with the verbalisation of the procedure (see Fig. 11.6).

Fig. 11.6 Subtracting Polynomials; screenshot from http://www.youtube.com/watch?v=IDpnNnjFB1c

ZOPStudios – Math Tutor is an example of collaborative learning at home. The video tells the story of two boys who worry about Maths: 'Zach needs help with math'. Whilst the video provides some glimpses into an exercise book, the video is mainly about motivating each other for studying Maths, not about solving mathematical problems (Fig. 11.7)

Fig. 11.7 'Zach needs help with math'; screenshots from ZOPStudios – Math Tutor, http://www.youtube.com/watch?gl=DE&hl=de&v=-K01u6l0qNI

These three examples represent a tiny selection from a vast number of varied Maths videos on the video platform YouTube. Such videos represent user-generated content, which combines school with Web 2.0 through mobile video production. Of course, the related learning activities are not directly visible on the internet platform; the videos function as stimulus or resource. The videos are also elements of user-generated contexts, to which a community on the internet belongs. The use of mobile/cell phones is visible, for example in collaborative field study activities of Sean and Dan or as part of the collaborative Maths homework.

There are also other ways of setting up learning contexts. A case study on homework with tablet PCs and an interactive whiteboard in the classroom (Luckin et al. 2005, 9ff.) depicts a differently structured learning context. This project represents an extension of the institutional domain of schools that spans between the home and the classroom via portable tablet computers – not a mobile device in the strict sense of our definition in Chapter 1 – and the electronic whiteboard, which links individual work carried out at home to the public gaze of the classroom and its teacher-driven collaboration. The whiteboard screen doesn't work as a repository, merely as display technology and the homework artefacts remain stored on the computers of individual learners.

From these examples it becomes obvious that mobile electronic devices can help to utilise and create a variety of content as well as learning and activity contexts. Some of the contexts are linked more closely to traditional, classroom-based learning, others are rather farther away; some are more similar to school-based learning than others.

Following the idea of generating content and contexts it becomes possible to build a mobile bridge between purposeful learning in school and everyday life activities. This does not only change the activity context but also adds new contexts, such as interactive relations and internet representation and activities. Mobile devices augment learning and activity spaces through changes in agency and cultural practices, not necessarily through complex, specialist software. Mobile device use might meaningfully focus on turning everyday life into a 'learning precinct' of school. In this way, traditional and typical learning tasks can be enhanced by producing subject-related content or by widening or supplementing situations for learning.

Chapter 12
Four Didactic Parameters for Analysis and Planning

Four Didactic Parameters: An Introduction

The conceptual uncertainties underpinning mobile learning can be seen to have led to the use of mobile devices in a paradigm of replacement of other media, which were already part of the school's learning practices, within well-established theories of learning and attendant approaches to teaching. The augmentation of established approaches to teaching and learning is the main result of the integration of mobile devices in such a paradigm. However, as we have argued in previous chapters, mobile learning should be seen as an educational response to the ongoing socio-cultural transformation with an emphasis on assimilation of cultural practices and practices of media use in everyday life into schools and their cultural practices of teaching and learning.

We posit that from the perspective of flexibilization of content and contexts, learning can be modelled within a space, which is constructed among others by four parameters. These parameters offer purchase on:

- the features of media and of mobile devices,
- conversations teachers and students engage in inside and outside the school, and
- the overall educational and didactic discourse about learning.

Our four parameters span the poles 'static' and 'flexible'. They attempt to link opposing learning and media practices and address differences in learning habitus. If one applies these four parameters within the global space of learners' life-worlds, the scope and variability for analysing and planning learning situations becomes considerable. In line with our deliberations in Chapter 11, our discussion of the parameters here focuses in the main on content and context generation. We take the view that these didactic parameters provide a useful analytical tool for discussing and evaluating mobile learning, even if their focus is not per se on the role of technology but, instead, on general didactic considerations (see Table 12.1).

How can these four parameters be justified? For us they represent the operationalization of our socio-cultural ecological approach and they clarify the relevance

N. Pachler et al., *Mobile Learning*, DOI 10.1007/978-1-4419-0585-7_12,

Table 12.1 Didactic parameters for analysing and planning within the mobile space of convergence and learning

Parameter A: Learning sets
Pole: Practice of the school – Pole: Practices of mobile media
Parameter B: Relationship to the object of learning
Pole: Mimetic reproduction – Pole: Personal reconstruction
Parameter C: Institutional emphasis on expertise
Pole: School curriculum – Pole: Personal expertise
Parameter D: Modes of representation
Pole: Discrete (mono media, mono modal) – Pole: Convergent

of the following for the analysis and/or planning of approaches to teaching and learning:

- socio-cultural development (including individualisation, media convergence, milieus),
- action patterns/agency (including habitus of learning, native expertise) and
- cultural practices (including learning in formal and informal settings, media use in everyday life).

The parameters are intended as a tool to help educators respond to the key features of the socio-cultural triangle: cultural practices, agency and structures. The parameters identify points of contact between the cultural practices of learning sponsored by schools and the life-worlds and the habitus of learning of students in order to be able to bring them into a fruitful relationship. This link we conceptualise as assimilation, for example by schools making the results of individualisation through 'native expertise' and the fragmentation of learning practices within the context of life-worlds the subject of discussion and affording it curricular relevance. The parameters provide the interface for the connection between the school and the structures, action patterns, competences and learning practices aggregated in our socio-cultural ecological triangle (see Chapter 1, Fig. 1.4). Therefore, under the rubric 'learning set', the parameters encompass important didactic patterns, e.g. curriculum, mimetic learning, school-based approaches to teaching and learning. Also, they refer to current socio-cultural structures, to important forms of habitus and to learning in everyday life with mobile media.

The characteristics of the individual parameters relate to current social developments, by representing static and traditional forms of development on the left-hand pole and developmental trends on the right-hand pole. In this way, the horizontal axis also represents the ongoing socio-cultural de-traditionalization. It is important to note that the didactic principle of assimilation does not necessarily require teachers to opt for non-traditional forms of teaching and learning in the classroom. The crucial measure is whether or not pedagogical intervention is able to create 'zones of proximal development' (Vygotsky 1930/1978, p. 84ff.), in our terminology 'responsive contexts', i.e. to create learning situations as contexts for development, which respond in a sensitive and responsive manner to the activity themes of children and which are aimed at the perspective of meaning-making rooted in their life course. The parameters are intended as a planning and analysis tool to help teachers and other educators create sensitive and responsive contexts for learning and development for students.

How should the parameters be applied? They provide a structure for argumentation and intend to help in the process of planning to consider what a sensitive, responsive context for learning and development might look like. Educators can explore possible pedagogical options along each of the four dimensions as well as cumulatively across all four.

Using the Four Parameters as a Tool for Analysis

In the following, by way of exemplification, we apply the parameters as an analysis tool to existing projects to demonstrate that, and how they work, i.e. that they open up useful lines of enquiry.

Wireless Internet Learning Devices – WILD

In order to demonstrate the analytical value of the proposed four parameters we apply them here first of all to a prominent project within the Californian context entitled 'Wireless Internet Learning Devices – WILD' for computer-supported collaborative learning (Roschelle and Pea 2002; Roschelle 2003; Vahey et al. 2007). The curricular focus of the project was on Maths and it involved graphing calculators, Palm, or Pocket-PC handhelds, connected to a short-range wireless network.

The aim of WILD was to offer support for new modes of learning, in particular collaborative learning, with handheld devices. The handhelds, and their software were intended to enable the following:

(1) augmenting physical space;
(2) leveraging topological space . . .;
(3) aggregating coherently across all students' individual contributions;
(4) conducting classroom performances; and
(5) "act becomes artefact" (p. 24).

The WILD project developed the following three 'classroom applications' for mobile devices (Roschelle 2003, p. 262):

> *Classroom response systems:*
> "The system instantly collects and aggregates every student's response. Students hold individual handheld response units (which have variously been graphing calculators, WinCE handhelds, or specially purpose infrared beaming units) and send their response anonymously. The teacher's machine aggregates the students' responses and presents them in a coherent form, usually a histogram."

Participatory simulations:
These applications "use the availability of a separate device for each student and the capability of simple data exchanges among neighbouring students. They enable students to act as agents in simulations in which overall patterns emerge from local decisions and information exchanges. Such simulations enable students to model and learn about the many scientific phenomena relating to decentralised systems: swarming ants, traffic jams and flocking birds."

Collaborative data gathering:
This projects reflects the assumption that the ability to gather data, especially from live experiments, is a key affordance of mobile devices. Probes, for example, allowed "students to gather accurate data, and by graphing it quickly, allow students to focus on the interpretation of their data, rather than tedious processes of recording and plotting it. Thus, probes support the long-term pedagogical drive towards "inquiry centred" science classrooms, by making scientific experiments easier for students to perform and analyse." (p. 264)

Roschelle and Pea (2002, pp. 25f.) refer to the following archetypal computer-supported collaborative learning (CSCL) applications, which appear to have influenced the conceptualization of the WILD project:

- Distance Learning: participation in a shared, possibly immersive, virtual space that mimics some characteristics of real learning spaces . . .;
- Single Display GroupWare: side by side use of a shared, large display by a group of 2–4 students and (intermittently) a teacher . . .;
- Knowledge Spaces: contribution to a shared conceptual space that organizes individual knowledge elements . . .;
- Messaging: writing notes or messages to a partner or discussion forum . . .

With regard to the didactic parameter A: *learning set* a classroom response system changes the teacher's well-know function of being at the centre of the students' class room activities only in a modest way. Mainly, it can provide them with useful data for formative assessment. The school was opened up to mobile devices: at the time of the WILD project, mobile devices where not a normal part of young people's everyday life and they were not a part of entertainment in daily life. By now mobile devices are fully integrated into young people's everyday lives and their activities and from this perspective one might analyse the type of mobile device use differently. Therefore, today an opening of school practices to mobile practices of everyday life requires reference to variety of complex patterns of media activities, which we discussed in Chapter 9 and which are not in evidence here. The development of these structures and agency do have consequences for the interrelationship of practices of the school with mobile media, which we capture by parameter A: learning sets.

Also, participatory simulations and collaborative data gathering as used by the WILD project widen the established practices and the familiar role of the teacher with the intention of augmentation. One rationale behind the WILD project was to overcome the restrictions of special computer labs with a student-computer ratio of 5:1 and move to a 1:1 ratio. The intention was to enhance teaching practices and the quality of learning activities on the basis that handheld technology can make technology more integral to teaching and learning. There was no reference to integrating young people's practices of mobile media use in everyday life, however.

Applying parameter B: *relationship to the object of learning* to the WILD project we clearly see that the project avoids any simple mimetic reproduction of pre-given learning objects such as memorizing of rules or mathematical formula. Instead, the personal reconstruction of knowledge is supported by mobile devices.

> Given the continuing emphasis on collaborative and communicative processes in subject matter standards such as NCTM and the National Science Education Standards (in the US), many WILD classrooms should become classrooms more characterized by computer-supported collaborative learning. Students will work towards shared understanding in groups. Students will build joint representations of their knowledge. (Roschelle and Pea 2002, p. 5)

This didactic intention is also clearly visible if we look at the project design from the point of view of parameter C: *institutional emphasis on expertise.* The flexibility of mobile devices supports personal expertise and promotes group work. Collaborative data gathering and participatory simulations depend on mobile devices with their emphasis on personal reconstruction. Students can activate personal reconstruction by bringing their personal expertise to bear, which is one of the poles of parameter C. The integration of students' expertise into the pre-given Maths curriculum comes first of all from the classroom response system which 'collects and aggregates every student's response'. The classroom response system supports the centrality of the teacher in student learning (see parameter A with the pole *practice of the school*).

Discussing the approach to representation taken by the WILD project with reference to parameter D, we can see a clear tendency towards multimedia and multimodal representation. During the time of the project media convergence in the sense of mobile access to the internet and Web 2.0 was just emerging. A wide variety of representational modes becomes visible. But convergence is restricted to the handheld devices and an intranet. There is no explicit reference to everyday life media and their application.

But the functionality of the handheld devices clearly points beyond traditional learning by suggesting a new contextual frame for learning, which includes spaces as well as changing relationships between learner, teacher and learning object. The interrelationship was packed theoretically into an activity model of learning, which models teaching and learning in relation to 'agents' and 'objectives' mediated by 'tools', 'rules' and 'roles' (see also Chapter 5):

> *Tutor*: Computer is the agent, student problem-solving behavior is the objective (goal), model tracing is the tool
> *Tutee*: Student is the agent, a computer program written by the student is the objective, microworlds are the tools
> *Tool*: Student is the agent, computer is the semiotic tool, shared knowledge is the objective. (Roschelle and Pea 2002, pp. 30f)

This activity model does not make explicit reference to the concept of generating contexts, in particular those created by students as media users. The WILD project confined itself to a traditional classroom perspective, e.g. by discussing representational spaces and looking for potential to transform activities into objects ('act becomes artifact'). In relation to the *didactic* parameter D: media and modes of representation, an extension of traditional school approaches can be noted.

The didactic decision on representation is based on a discussion of mathematics and its specific representation in two strands: the 'interplay of language-based, taxonomic, categorical representations ("typological") and spatially based, visual, continuously varying representations ("topological")' (p. 13). We consider this to be a helpful approach to thinking about changes in representation in media and the internet together with the school curriculum and the specific requirements of particular subjects.

Raising Attainment in Literacy with Parental Involvement

The didactic parameter *institutional emphasis on expertise* is fore-grounded in a project about literacy development at elementary/primary school level discussed by Passey (2008). He is concerned with 'effective learning' through 'authentic' learning activities, 'where communication, social and societal interactions are involved' (p. 224), or which allow pupils to 'transfer their learning both within and across subjects' and which develop 'personal expertise', 'expert learners', 'deep learning' (p. 225). Passey is concerned with being able to identify what learning outcomes arise when learning with mobile technologies and he proposed six domains, which – according to him – offer a 'first level structure for the creation of a learning framework'. His first domain is the 'megacognitive'.

> Megacognitive (a term used here to describe those elements becoming recognised as fundamental to developing 'expert learners', deep learning, and wider learning, concerned with learning that goes beyond the ability to learn, that enables learners to transfer their learning both within and across subject or interest domains). The literature discusses the importance to expert learners of the gaining and using of 'big pictures', of working within a Zone of Proximal Development, and the practices of transferring learning from one situation to another. (p. 225)

Amongst the other domains in his framework are the 'cognitive', 'motivational' and 'societal'. They all focus on *personal reconstruction* within the didactic parameter B: *relationship to the object of learning*:

> Cognitive (aspects concerned with the impact of information or external stimuli on the internal mind, the forms of sensory stimuli used to engage learners, the ways in which information is handled within an existing internal information context, and the ways in which a learner can demonstrate or use the learning that has been acquired). The literature discusses the importance of learning processes such as conceptualisation, creativity and thinking skills, as well as the role of memory and the creation of learning outputs within the wider picture of learning....
>
> Motivational (aspects concerned with ways in which information is perceived, and the feedback a learner gains in order to recognise learning as worthwhile, or leading in directions of personal or appropriate choice).
>
> Societal (aspects concerned with the ways in which purposes of learning are perceived, the reason that certain information might be selected and recognised as being more fundamentally interesting or useful than other information, perhaps because it can be used within a particular societal, cultural or wider environmental context). (pp. 225–226)

Passey's 'social domain' supports 'digital natives' to turn them into 'learning natives' by linking learning sets from everyday life to the school but just in relation the prevalent learning set in school: 'ways in which a learner interacts with others, within classroom environments or in the home or other external environments'. Also forms of interaction are fostered 'that allow a learner to access or use information, as well as to share it, or to work co-operatively with others.' Furthermore, the school practices on the parameter *learning set* are widened by parental involvement (p. 227).

It is surprising to us that the 'modes of representation' remain discrete in the sense of being focused on one device rather than being linked to media use in everyday life. Passey describes the students of the Year 6 classes as having had 'no prior experience of PDA use'. This evidences a mono-media view of everyday life in so far as it is highly likely that the children in question were experienced users of several portable devices, such as CD-players or mobile/cell phones, which share a lot of functions with the PDA. Visual literacy related learning outcomes linked to photo-taking and storage, which are located on our parameter D, appear to have remained unexplored in this project by focusing on the definition of literacy promoted by school testing and not looking for the complex and convergent pole of representation in the life-worlds of the learners.

From Analysis to Planning

The concept of the four didactic parameters is our provisional response to the socio-cultural changes of mass communication and the cultural transformation of subjectivity, which goes hand in hand with a new emphasis on agency and ubiquitous learning. We say 'provisional' because we are, of course, aware that the parameters are conceptual at this stage, and have not been empirically tested and validated. As already noted, these developments lead to an enormous flexibility, which is already impacting on the very stabile cultural practices of the school. For example, there is the undeniable fact that schools and their teaching practices do not reach a significant minority of students; according to PISA results the figure is as high as 20–25%. As a result of such developments, but also other political, economic, technological, cultural and demographic trends, there are recurring calls for school modernization to which a seemingly endless stream of educational policies aimed at raising standards and promoting innovation in a context of increasing international comparison and competition in the OECD context in recent years are testimony.

We trust it will not come as a surprise for readers that our motivation for writing this book is not grounded specifically in a technologically-orientated motivation, rather in a cultural one: to support schools in achieving curricular aims such as helping young people live a fulfilling life and be able to help others to do so.

Our socio-cultural ecological approach is supportive of such curricular aims and argues that mobile learning should not just be about applying the functionality of mobile devices to existing practices of teaching and learning. Instead of viewing school-based learning as a way of increasing the effectiveness of knowledge transfer, mobile learning practices need to reflect learning as situated in cultural contexts of meaning-making. In a piece in *Educause Review*, a magazine that looks at current developments and trends in information technology and how they may affect (higher) education and society, Brown and Adler (2008) outline new kinds of open participatory learning ecosystems that support active, 'passion-based' learning. The leading educational and curricular discourses with their general models such as *situated* or *constructivist learning* provide the frame for considering what sort of approaches as well as media access are required in terms of prevailing socio-cultural structures, agency and cultural practices. For example, concepts such as *collaborative*, *constructivist* or *situated* learning emphasise the connection between context and learning (see Sharples et al. 2007, p. 230). From such a perspective, mobility is not the leading criterion for integrating mobile learning. To quote Sharples et al. (2007, p. 223): a 'central concern must be to understand how people artfully engage with their surroundings to create impromptu sites of learning'.

A further rationale for the integration of technologically-supported, mobile learning comes from a social-constructivist approach (Sharples et al. 2007, p. 223), which puts the learner and his/her appropriation of knowledge at the centre of school discourses of learning and teaching. Appropriation by learners is collaboratively framed and 'community-centred' (Sharples et al. 2007, p. 223). Scardamalia and Bereiter (1999) concretise the collaborative frame of appropriation as 'collaborative knowledge building'. They view learning as an internal process that results in changes of beliefs, attitudes or skills whereas knowledge building, for them, is about creating or modifying public knowledge that resides 'in the world', and is available to be 'worked on' and used by other people.

Our proposal of didactic parameters draws on considerations in the context of our general educational discussion on fostering teaching and learning in the school in a changing society (see Chapters 6 and 8 for details). Therefore, in particular in view of our socio-cultural ecological approach, we see the application of our parameters for planning and analysing teaching and learning with mobile devices always in an interrelationship with other cultural practices of teaching and learning. Because it is our intention to contribute to the broader debate about the future of schooling and new ways of teaching and learning, we tried to develop the parameters as an analytic interface between mobile structures, agency and practices and the school with its established approaches to media use, curriculum as well as teaching and learning. Therefore, the parameters do not primarily focus on technology but, instead, span from the established school practices, structures and agency (mimetic reproduction, curriculum, discrete modes of representation) to the *mobile* practices and agency (personal reconstruction, personal expertise) and structures (convergence). Because of our broader educational interests, the parameters foreground a didactic approach to analysis and planning with the leading categories of our socio-cultural ecological, its structures, agency and practices, in the background.

These concepts of educational change, seen in the light of mass communicative developments of individualised mobility, help to contextualise our four parameters.

Parameter A: Learning Set

Pole: Practices of the School – Pole: Practices of Mobile Devices

The concept of a *learning set* for us comprises all possible arrangements of constituent parts of learning such as teacher, learner, environment, media/tools, curriculum etc. This includes, for example, a teacher-centred lecture in a classroom, homework tasks completed with a laptop or an internet community for Maths etc. The dimension of learning set across the poles of school practices and mobile device practices captures the myriad possibilities of students from school to everyday life as well as in-between. Everyday life includes the use of mobile media and, of course, making meaning in and of the world, be it deliberate, intentional and planned or serendipidous and accidental, conscious or subconscious.

As our socio-cultural ecology focuses on resources, learning inside and outside the school should be assimilated as related discourses. To achieve this assimilation of discourses we use Laurillard's Conversational Framework (2002, 2007). In her model (2007, p. 171) the learners with their goals and the institution of the school are combined to a learning set by virtue of their conversational activities, namely: reflection, questions and comments, practice outputs/production, practice outputs/revision, adapt actions and feedback. The scheme in Fig. 12.1 depicts the learning set of the world of experience.

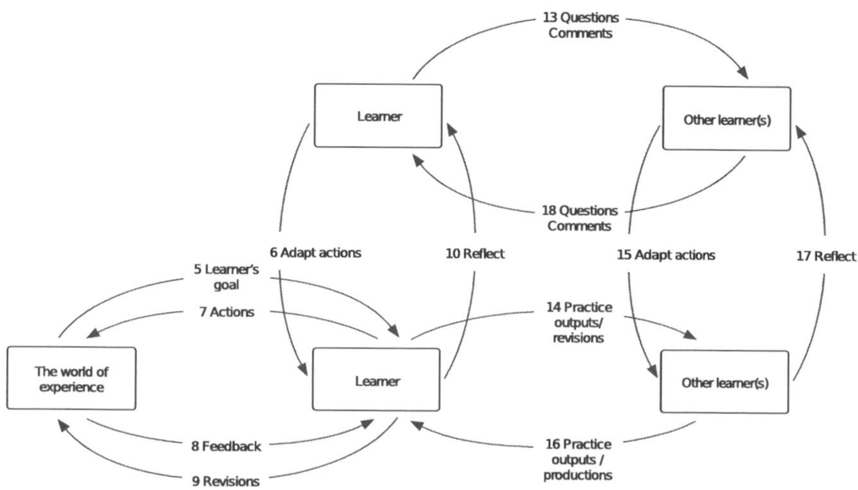

Fig. 12.1 The Conversational Framework for supporting learning in informal settings (Source: Laurillard 2007, p. 160)

Parameter B: Relationship to the Object of Learning

Pole: Mimetic Reproduction – Pole: Personal Reconstruction

Our intention is to facilitate a type of school-based learning, which does not only passively repeat and memorise objectified knowledge. We consider collaborative knowledge building to be a widely accepted, and practically tried-and-tested alternative. The examples of mobile homework on YouTube in Chapter 11 offer specific and workable suggestions about how to work with these mobile, convergent practices in the school. Collaborative knowledge building in our view can combine mimetic practices of learning and media use for personal reconstruction. As already noted, one important task of school is to move native, reconstructive learning onto a higher level of reflection. This is why the explicit concept of 'knowledge-building' is important to us. Scardamelia and Bereiter (1999, p. 278) view it as an 'approach to construct an understanding of the world as the students know it'. According to them, knowledge building is characterized by a positive research orientation: learning is not targeted at products, but at the development of common knowledge within a group of learners; students learn through their contributions to solving a problem; and learning is targeted at the knowledge relevant for the solving of a problem. Learning objects are believed to belong to different worlds, which Bereiter and Scardamelia (1996, p. 491) define with reference to Popper (1978) as World 1, the physical world, World 2, the subjective world inside our minds, and World 3, the world of objective knowledge. For the didactic parameter dealing with the relationship to the object of learning, it is highly relevant that all three worlds are based on objectifications. Worlds 1 and 3, from the perspective of educational knowledge building, are set for children as their given world. World 2 is the already appropriated, internalized world. Appropriation of facts and concepts across the pregiven world and the (objectified) experiences of one's personal life-world leads to knowledge.

Of course, everyday life provides other collaborative forms, which remain at a naïve level. We do consider Cyrill's native expertise in cooperation (see Chapter 10) as a practical focus for assimilation into the school. But there remains the theoretical task of better understanding the features of naïve and native expertise for further development.

Parameter C: Institutional Emphasis on Expertise

Pole: School Curriculum – Pole: Personal Expertise

Kollar and Fischer (2008) discuss a number of 'scripts', which contain a variety of options for relating the personal expertise of students to the given school curriculum, thereby opening up socio-culturally relevant directions for teachers:

- the four-component instructional design system (4C/ID-approach, van Merriënboer et al. 2002) with the components: (1) Learning Tasks, (2) Supportive Information, (3) Procedural Information and (4) Part-Task Practice (Kollar and Fischer 2008, p. 51);

- goal-based scenarios: students work on complex, authentic and personally relevant and, ideally, self-determined goals (p. 52);
- investigative learning (p. 52);
- learning-by-design: construction of real artefacts on the basis of scientific principles (p. 53);
- knowledge building: 'teaching-learning scripts' (p. 50) offer an assimilative view on instruction in the light of a 'culture of learning'.

Parameter D: Media and Modes of Representation

Pole: Discrete (Mono Medial, Mono Modal) – Pole: Convergent

Mobile media, in particular the mobile/cell phone, have became part of everyday life because they have affordances in relation to multimodal representation and enable near-ubiquitous access to convergent media for which the internet is the global network. Among others, mobile media offer the following applications for learning:

- interaction with peers by telephone, messaging, email;
- picture and video recording;
- storage for photos, data files, games, software etc.;
- access to the media world, internet, archives (media convergence);
- individual disposal of time and space through the formation of contexts and situations;
- multimodal representation.

In the context of the practical implementation of mobile/cell phones and other mobile devices by schools, curricular conceptual systems are emerging. An early example comes from Patten et al. (2006) who discuss media features in curricular terms within 'existing learning scenarios' (pp. 296ff.):

- *administrative:* e.g. calendar or *organiser* on the students' mobile/cell phone;
- *referential:* to store, access and annotate documents; information management and content delivery;
- *interactive:* e.g. a user responds to a task or receives feedback; 'drill and test' with multiple choice style quizzes; to create own simple animation;
- *microworld:* allows learners "to construct ... own knowledge through experimentation in constrained models of real world domains" (p. 298), e.g. exploring simple geometric concepts within the context of a billiard game;
- *data collection:* to record data and information and create learning experiences that would not otherwise be feasible or unproblematic; e.g. note taking, on 'the-spot analysis', recording of images or sound for observations and reflection;
- *location awareness:* to "contextualise learning activities by enabling the learners to interact appropriately with their environment" (p. 299); e.g. museum guides;
- *collaborative:* to share knowledge and create a learning environment "inspired by collaborative learning principles" (p. 299), e.g. using learning platforms.

In view of the affordances of mobile devices in relation to multimodality and media convergence, user-generated content and contexts are fast emerging as particularly relevant curricular application, which relate directly to individual mobile mass communication.

In order to be able to move from analysis to planning, the socio-cultural ecologic approach has to be concretised. We consider the example of Cyrill to be helpful in this context (see Chapters 4 and 10), who acts outside the school with mobile video linked to a media platform, as well as the example of the Indian students and their assignment of mobile photography on their way from school into their neighbourhood (see Chapters 4 and 11). By means of these examples the interrelationship of

- international youth culture with its media use and related meaning-making as well as
- the flexible learning practices of schools

can come into focus for the purposes of planning.

Parameter A: learning set

Pole: practice of the school – Pole: practices of mobile media

For Cyrill to engage, the school has to develop new practices to reach young people who are at a distance to the school. The main challenge is to find a meeting point for the practices of the school and the practices prevalent in the convergent media world. School has to develop a set of learning practices, which is open to the type of investigation by means of mobile devices young people like Cyrill routinely engage in outside of school. As we already proposed, the pedagogic agents of the school should identify and take up *conversational threads,* which students initiate outside of school.

Parameter B: relationship to the object of learning

Pole: mimetic reproduction – Pole: personal reconstruction

Both reproduction and reconstruction appear in the mobile practices of everyday life. Cyrill is very creative in terms of generating contexts (observing social activities at the station and creating his own website), generating contents (publishing images of himself on his website, carrying out a naïve ethnographic investigation). The Indian school uses mobile/cell phones because the teachers want to engage in non-mimetic learning. Therefore, they organise field research with reconstructive methods (to look for geometric patterns in everyday life).

Parameter C: institutional emphasis on expertise

Pole: school curriculum – Pole: personal expertise

In the case of Cyrill personal expertise could be brought inside the school by recognising his well developed expertise within the context of media convergence. In the case of the Indian students, the school curriculum is opening up to personal expertise investigating everyday life, which in turn draws on expertise in using mobile applications (taking photos) and brings GPS functionality within the realm of the school curriculum.

Parameter D: media and modes of representation
Pole: discrete (mono media, mono modal) – Pole: convergent

For Cyrill media convergence has reached a state of normalisation in his life-world. He works actively with multimedia and multimodal representation. However, the project on field research for geometry is partly mono media and mono modal (photos with the mobile/cell phone) and partly convergent (poster with mobile photos, linked to personal computers, use of GPS).

To summarize: the didactic parameters create didactic spaces for teaching and learning. They attempt to provide a map for possible ways of assimilating international youth culture, consisting of structures, agency and cultural practices with specific learning potentials, into school. The agents for its assimilation are mainly teachers and their emphases and preferences along the four didactic parameters.

Implications for Teacher Support and Development

What kind of obstacles can be expected, in particular those not made explicit by the four parameters? Laurillard's (2008) discussion of ICT innovation in the higher education sector seems to us to be instructive in this context. Schools are primarily under pressure from policy, students and technology (pp. 523–525). These areas of pressure correspond to our socio-cultural triangle of structures, agency and cultural practices. Laurillard (2008, p. 525) also views technology as a 'catalyst for change'. By catalyst she means the innovative function of technology, which she identifies in relation to a discussion of 'what it takes to learn'. For her, the common thread of research into this question is that learning is active (p. 527). An analysis of successful research proposals for ESCR-EPSRC Technology Enhanced Learning research in 2007 reveals a wide range of possible applications of digital technology:

> Games, tools, cultural tools, adaptive intelligent tutoring systems, avatars, embodied interaction, augmented cognition, personal learning environments, learner models, portable devices, conversation agents, editable digital artefacts, digital data tracking, haptic devices, virtual objects, online communities, adaptive support, simulation, collaborative technology. (p. 527)

In relation to this list of applications the challenge is to ensure that technology does adhere to the following principles of good teaching, which relate to our parameters B: relationship to the object of learning and C: institutional emphasis on expertise and which we know technology to be capable of doing:

- emulate small group tutorial discussions through virtual communications;
- provide realistic feedback on actions in a virtual environment;
- track learner performance to predict the optimal next task. (Laurillard 2008, p. 528)

Success seems to depend on the way in which teachers act within the cultural practices of the school, such as in 'peer-reviewed collaborative research' and the school as 'a learning system' (pp. 528f). Following this line of argument, innovations in schools' practices of learning and teaching require reflection at a didactic meta-level by teachers, which utilise parameters B and C as 'mechanisms' (Laurillard 2008, p. 532) for the innovation of student learning. At this meta-level teachers can be seen to expect

i. support for some personal development in how to teach,
ii. the means to build on the work of others to design their approach,
iii. the means to experiment and reflect on what the results imply for their design and their understanding, and
iv. the means to articulate and disseminate their contribution. (Laurillard 2008, p. 530)

Laurillard's conclusion focuses on the technology itself, which she considers to embody the means teachers require (p. 530). As such it complements our discussion of the four parameters so far. This conclusion aims at the convergence pole of didactic parameter D: media and modes of representation. It is a pity that the didactic parameter A: learning set with the poles inside and outside school are not taken into consideration by Laurillard. Therefore, convergent arrangements like mobile/cell phones plus YouTube don't feature in her discussion. The proposed Learning Activity Management System (LAMS) (p. 531) covers the didactic space on parameter A on the pole of the practices of the school with reference to the expertise of teachers, but not that of the students. If the didactic component of parameter A is used for assimilation of the students' everyday practices and if teachers' meta-level reflection is integrated into the school's learning practice, then the following support should be 'embodied' not only in technology, but also in the media convergence of everyday life including mobility:

> i. support for some personal development in how to teach – there are online learning design tools under development, which are explicitly designed to help teachers gradually bring learning technologies into their work, and link to repositories of existing digital resources in their field (See the JISC Design for Learning Programme, http://www.lkl.ac.uk/research/d4l/);
> ii. the means to build on the work of others to design their approach – online communities of practice can offer access to existing learning designs, case studies, lessons learned;
> iii. the means to experiment and reflect on what the results imply for their design and their understanding – an interactive learning activity management system can offer a simple authoring environment for the lecturer to sequence a set of learning activities, run it for student groups collaborating online, monitor student progress, offer a simple editing environment to improve it in the light of practice . . .;
> iv. the means to articulate and disseminate their contribution – creating a learning activity sequence is one form of articulation of what the lecturer thinks it takes to learn a particular topic, or achieve a particular learning outcome, and the online community is the means to disseminate that idea, once proven. (Laurillard 2008, pp. 530–531

Summary

Having tried to operationalize our parameters for creating a didactic space conducive for mobile learning within prevailing socio-cultural developments raises an important question: why should schools not resist the pressure to adapt? Our answer not only points to the increasing inability of schools to reach all of its pupils but also to the significant socio-cultural changes around what constitutes contexts for learning and meaning-making. As we have argued already, schools are losing the power to define such contexts for all children and young people.

Viewed from the perspective of our cultural ecology, the teaching and learning practices of schools can be augmented by mobile devices. We propose to investigate mobile practices of students with a view to assimilating their native, but naïve, expertise with mobile devices into school. For us, the notion of contexts is central to such a didactic endeavour. User-generated mobile and convergent contexts, we argue, should be recognised as *responsive* contexts for the extension of students' learning, an extension of naïve – a term clearly not meant pejoratively throughout our discussion – modes of meaning-making in everyday life. Specifically, we are proposing four didactic parameters for planning and analyzing: learning sets, the relationship of learners to the object of learning, the institutional emphasis on expertise and modes of representation.

Part III
Perspectives for Mobile Learning

Chapter 13
Setting the Scene

Equity of access to cultural resources through appropriation and learner generation of contexts for learning can be achieved by allowing all citizens to realise their potential through education. It is predicated on enabling and encouraging learners to bring the cultural practices they engage in outside formal education into schools, colleges and universities. Once inside these formal education organisations, learners can be supported, e.g. by scaffolding, into extending their cultural practices to incorporate educational processes that are valued by educational organisations. We would like to suggest that – loosely defined – criticality, creativity and reflective thinking are some of the key processes for education, learning and meaning-making generally. Democracy can be viewed as the possibility for equity of access to essential conceptual, cultural and social resources. Using emerging digital technologies to mediate these educational processes is a challenge for the future; there exists a real danger of creating a new digital divide.

Before attempting to look into the crystal ball to see where mobile learning is likely to be heading over the next few years, it is sensible to sound a cautionary note about the inherent problems of using mobile/cell phones for learning and critical questions need to be asked, for example: is there a lack of training for teachers or a dislocation from personal use of technologies? Is there a productivity paradigm inherent in the rationale for the inclusion of technologies in institutional education? Cuban (2001), in his book 'Oversold & Underused: Computers in the Classroom', drew on a range of sources to conclude that, with few exceptions, teachers have not made any serious changes in the way they teach as a result of the introduction of technologies for learning. As a consequence, he contentiously suggests that the experience of students in the typical classes had not been changed in any significant way. In a similar vein, Buckingham (2006) in his keynote presentation at Becta 2006 annual Research conference, provided a continuation of Cuban's challenging view, suggesting that the use of technology in schools has been misconceived and needs rethinking:

> I think a lot of use of technology in schools has been fundamentally misconceived and I would want to argue it needs to be fairly comprehensively rethought and in particular I want to argue that we need to think much harder about how children's use of technology in schools relates of their use of technology outside of schools. I think there has been along history of claims being made about the transformative potential of technology in education

N. Pachler et al., *Mobile Learning*, DOI 10.1007/978-1-4419-0585-7_13,

> which actually go back well before computers. The fantasy of the impending revolution in education goes back to Thomas Eddison talking about the cinema in the 1920s, people talking about radio and then television and so on, you can track that history. The idea that the school would be utterly changed, the teachers would be redundant and by and large those fantasies have failed to come true.

With Cuban's and Buckingham's warnings in mind, Part III of this book takes a critical perspective on what is being promised for mobile learning but with a view to navigating the space of what is possible. An overarching question that frames our discussion is whether emerging technologies, i.e. mobile and ubiquitous, will change attendant teaching and learning practice. Also, how can mobile devices be different as a transforming technology for schools? Is it because of personal ownership, functional convergence, impact on cultural practices of young people in everyday life?

In previous chapters we have proposed three curricular dimensions as a means of conceptualising teaching and learning practices that make use of emerging technologies, these were: media features; teacher's and students' discourses inside and outside the school; overall educational and curricular discourse. Other authors (e.g. Haythornthwaite et al. 2008. pp. 574) have similarly pointed to the transformative effects that new media can have on learning, reasoning that they provide the underpinning for a move to 'ubiquitous learning'. Haythornthwaite et al. propose that 'the affordances of the new media are transformations in the production process, with new media creating a need for multimodal literacy both in understanding and producing new texts'. Significantly, they also point out that 'changes also occur in the roles of reader and user, consumer and producer, learner and teacher.' Indeed, we are witnessing a trend where large sections of society are becoming digitally 'literate' learners:

> 21st century literacy is the set of abilities and skills where aural, visual and digital literacy overlap. These include the ability to understand the power of images and sounds, to recognize and use that power, to manipulate and transform digital media, to distribute them pervasively, and to easily adapt them to new forms (New Media Consortium 2005, p. 2).

Digitally literate learners are using new forms of communication, which appear to include layers of meaning not accessible by 'traditional' language skills alone (Kress 2003). They are using the internet and digital devices to make meaning in, and of the world as they engage in acts of communicating and content sharing. Media platforms such as YouTube and MySpace have witnessed phenomenal growth in recent years. Furthermore, in a recent inquiry of mobile learning from a primary/elementary school perspective, Shore (2008, p. 8) has acknowledged that although in the 21st century the traditional literacies of reading, writing and mathematics are crucial, they are not sufficient. In addition to the three Rs, today's primary/elementary school graduate needs to be able to: use digital tools effectively and safely, think critically, understand complex systems, know about other countries and cultures, participate in collaborative learning communities, invent, create, and design – alone and with others, and find wholeness in a 'remix' world.

A key future challenge, that mobile and related technologies present us with, is that, when appropriated in a cultural context for meaning-making, they are able to have an influence beyond formal learning contexts like the classroom. Through increased mobility learners are able to generate their own individualised contexts for learning. Outside the classroom learners are building up new rich media 'literacy' as they create their own habitus of learning in everyday life, where we have observed an integrated complex of attitudes and action patterns revolving around appropriated social structures within typical cultural practices. Furthermore, we have proposed that schools should recognise and embrace this change. However, we are aware that such a perspective provides a challenge to our conceptions of where the boundaries of education are positioned. This in turn gives rise to the following questions: are the emerging technologies transforming learning from a managed activity to a ubiquitous – anywhere, anytime, with anyone – form of learning? Do the new ways in which meaning is created, and data is stored, represented, delivered and/or accessed, influence what it means to participate in learning? Formal and informal learning inside and outside schools – is it still helpful to think in these terms?

This third part of the book is structured into two main chapters. In 'Emerging technologies and attendant practices' (Chapter 14) we survey emerging technologies and attendant learning and teaching practices from the perspective of media technology. It is followed by an exploration of 'Visions and suspicions' (Chapter 15) that emerge when we look at the future of mobile learning and attendant questions arising.

Chapter 14
Emerging Technologies and Attendant Practices

Introduction

At the end of Chapter 3 we noted that the co-construction of learning between teachers and students is regarded as a powerful vehicle for innovation. This argument was set in the context of children gaining ever-increasing access to functionally convergent digital media and mobile devices. We pointed to the emergence of anywhere, anytime, any device learning as relying on a combination of device affordances, appropriate pedagogical model plus fast context sensitive wireless networks. Below we extend our examination of emerging technologies and of practices that they may interact with in the future.

Some of the developments we describe here equally apply to other internet-capable devices; however, we do make specific reference to mobile/cell phones.

Adoption Horizons for Key Emerging Technologies

Although the Horizon reports (2008, 2009) aim to provide a Higher Education orientated perspective on what are seen as key emerging technologies, many of the issues raised are also relevant to schools; indeed, in 2009 Horizon also published a separate report for K-12 compulsory education (Horizon 2009). In 2008 an Australasian supplement was also published. The annual reports are a collaboration between The New Media Consortium and the influential EDUCAUSE Learning Initiative.

The reports place emerging technologies along three adoption horizons that represent likely time frames for entrance into mainstream use for teaching and learning. The higher education and K-12 editions do not differ in terms of the technologies featured but in terms of the adoption horizons anticipated with K-12 education lagging behind higher education. The first adoption horizon assumes the likelihood of entry within the next year (short-term); the second, within 2–3 years (medium-term); and the third, within 4–5 years (longer-term).

The reports identify the following key emerging technologies for learning: first is grassroots video and collaboration webs. These are already in use in many schools and on many campuses. Next is mobile broadband and data mashups, which appear more widely over the medium-term and are already evident in organisations at the

N. Pachler et al., *Mobile Learning*, DOI 10.1007/978-1-4419-0585-7_14,

leading edge of technology adoption. The third key issue is collective intelligence and social operating systems. This is predicted to happen in the longer-term and there are already examples in the worlds of commerce, industry and entertainment that hint at future use in academia. Curiously, the reports do not specifically mention context-sensitive learning (see Chapter 2 and also below), such an omission may be due to the fact that the report is US-based and the authors seem to prefer the term "social operating systems"; in any case they are not the same as context-sensitive learning systems.

Of particular interest to us are mobile broadband and social operating systems which we will examine below. The 2008 report notes that each year, more than a billion new mobile devices are manufactured; this is roughly a new phone for every six people on the planet. The 2008 report (p. 4) also notes that

> In this market, innovation is unfolding at an unprecedented pace. Capabilities are increasing rapidly, and prices are becoming ever more affordable. Indeed, mobiles are quickly becoming the most affordable portable platform for staying networked on the go. New displays and interfaces make it possible to use mobiles to access almost any Internet content – content that can be delivered over either a broadband cellular network or a local wireless network.

Specifically, in the short term we will see the deployment, in educational institutions, of such innovations as the next generation mobile devices, mobile broadband, cloud computing, collaborative webs, geo-everything and context aware learning. The 2009 K-12 supplement (pp. 6–7) identified the following trends and challenges as of particular relevance to primary and secondary education:

Trends:

- Technology continues to profoundly affect the way we work, collaborate communicate, and succeed.
- Technology is increasingly a means for empowering students, a method for communication and socializing, and a ubiquitous, transparent part of their lives.
- The web is an increasingly personal experience.
- The way we think of learning environments is changing. The "spaces" where students learn are becoming more community-driven, interdisciplinary, and supported by technologies that engage virtual communication and collaboration.
- The perceived value of innovation and creativity is increasing.

Critical challenges:

- There is a growing need for formal instruction in key new skills, including information literacy, visual literacy, and technological literacy.
- Students are different, but educational practice and the material that supports it is changing only slowly.
- Learning that incorporates real life experiences is not occurring enough and is undervalued when it does take place.

- There is a growing recognition that new technologies must be adopted and used as an everyday part of classroom activities, but effecting this change is difficult.
- A key challenge is the fundamental structure of the K-12 education establishment.

In Chapter 2 we highlighted some trends and patterns of adoption of mobile devices that support the notion of the growing ubiquity of this technology as appropriated in the life-worlds of school children. In this chapter we look at some of the emerging technologies identified in the Horizon reports, which are currently in the main still used in specialised contexts but which, we think, could be adopted for mainstream use for teaching and learning within 2–3 years.

First however, we discuss the trend for screens to get smaller and larger.

Computing Off the Desktop: Going Small, Large, Everywhere and Getting Interactive

There is an interesting trend relating to the integration of personal/private spaces and representations with public collaborative spaces. This typically takes the form of being able to share content held on personal devices, which have small screens, with a large audience on large screens. Furthermore, there is a trend towards the integration of traditional pen and new interactive digital display technologies:

> Multiple metaphors and interaction paradigms using pen, touch, and visual recognition are coming together with the other elements to create a new experience. In education, intuitive interfaces lower the barriers to using IT, allow for a better understanding of complex content and enhance opportunities for collaboration. In the near future it is likely that emerging display technologies such as electronic paper and OLED (Organic Light-Emitting Diode) screens will be delivered on flexible substrates. This will enable bendable/ rollable displays that can be made larger than the dimension of the mobile device they are used with. E-paper could also enable inexpensive, very large digital displays to be incorporated into walls and other surfaces more widely. Speech recognition, gesture recognition, haptics, machine vision and even brain control are all improving rapidly to support more natural interactions with these new display technologies. (Haller 2008, p. 91)

The affordances of "new displays and interfaces" has been picked up by Fisher and Kanomi (2007), who have explored the migration from PC to mobile devices and point out that wireless and mobile technologies provide new opportunities for creating novel socio-technical environments that are consequently empowering, but not without potential pitfalls; they focus on "moving *'computing off the desktop'* by *'going small, large, and everywhere'*"; they provide specific examples including human-centred public transportation systems, collaborative design, and information sharing with smart physical objects. Indeed, one emerging trend is the use of screens, be they small or large, is to enhance visualization and collaboration. Haller (2008) describes some of the emerging technologies that can enable visualization: they include interactive displays, next generation interfaces, new forms of interaction and collaboration, concluding that:

> Multi-touch and interactive surfaces are becoming more interesting, because they allow a natural and intuitive interaction with the computer system . . . We are just at the beginning of a new decade, where books can be displayed on e-paper devices such as the Sony Reader. On the other hand, we will still work with traditional interfaces including paper. The integration of real notes, for example, in a digital environment seems to be a very important motivation for people using these new technologies, since it combines the affordances of a traditional medium such as paper with the capabilities of digital content and displays. (Haller 2008, p. 101)

Interactive screens offer the intriguing possibility of collaborative learning, with some of these devices being able to recognise more than one person's finger presses. Figure 14.1 below shows school pupils who are trying touch sensitive

Fig. 14.1 Teacher and pupil working with SynergyNet (Source: http://tel.dur.ac.uk/galleries/sept08media/images/00442832.jpg)

interactive desk that has been developed by Durham University's technology-enhanced learning research group:

> Researchers at Durham University observed classroom interactions then worked with manufacturers to produce the necessary software and hardware. Their SynergyNet system has a teacher's console to monitor what each child or group of children is working on. The system will be tested in primary and secondary schools and in higher education over the next 4 years. (http://news.bbc.co.uk/1/hi/education/7621213.stm)

But what are that the implications of collaboratively shared screens for mobile devices?

The above question, and the issue of the trade-off between different sized screens have been explored by Liu and Kao (2007), who describe another system of shared displays. They note that the screens of handheld devices limit the promotion of interaction among groups of learners. Consequently, they propose "a design of classrooms that incorporates personal workspace and public workspace. Students use handheld devices as private workspace and work with peers on public workspace with shared displays through their handheld devices." Empirical work conducted for this shared display system

> confirmed that students with only handheld devices did not demonstrate expected participation ratios and actively interact with group members. The proposed shared display groupware promoted shared understanding of the workspace and increased awareness of partner actions. Collaboration was enhanced by creating the opportunity for students to use handheld devices to perform ideal communication patterns and avoiding ineffective communication patterns. (Liu and Kao 2007, p 285)

The above work provides a useful answer to our second question: the new ways in which meaning is created, and data stored, represented, delivered and/or accessed do indeed influence what it means to participate and collaborate in learning. Specifically, using handhelds as the focus for individual workspaces that can be linked to public collaborative workspaces enhanced shared understanding, collaboration and communication. Furthermore, mobile/cell phones are increasingly using touch screens to enhance navigation and usability. The problem with the small screens of the mobile devices is that, with all this new multimedia that network infrastructures like IP Multimedia Subsystem (IMS) will bring (see Chapter 2), screens are going to be crammed with multiple layers of images, photos, videos, etc. This has led to recent work that attempts to "free up the screen's real estate". Microsoft have produced Seadragon in an attempt to "change the way we use screens, from wall-sized displays to mobile devices, so that visual information can be smoothly browsed regardless of the amount of data involved or the bandwidth of the network" (http://livelabs.com/seadragon/). Some screen shots are shown in Fig. 14.2 below.

A related development from Microsoft is Photosynth (http://livelabs.com/photosynth/. For a demo of the visually impressive Photosynth see: http://www.ted.com/index.php/talks/blaise_aguera_y_arcas_demos_photosynth.html), which attempts to automatically reconstruct a three-dimensional space from a collection of photos of a place or an object. Photosynth is able to create hyperlinks

Fig. 14.2 Screenshots of Seadragon (See http://www.billionswithzeroknowledge.com/wp-content/uploads/2007/03/windowslivewritermicrosoftimpressesatted2007-10ca3seadragon4.png and http://download.microsoft.com/download/f/c/6/fc694cb5-10c8-4422-b960-039bc3b97997/seadragon_on10.mp4, 20 Jun 2009)

between images stored on the internet, it does that based on the content inside the images and by using meta-tag information. In the talk given by Blaise Aguera y Arcas, an architect at Microsoft Live Labs, and creator of Seadragon and also the co-creator of Photosynth (his company developed it and was taken over by Microsoft in 2007), he demonstrates how photos from Flickr, in this case on the Notre Dame Cathedral, are used to reassemble by pastiche digital version of the Cathedral that can subsequently be drilled down into. For this technology Blaise Aguera y Arcas stresses that "cross modal and cross user social experience ... [that are generated] from the collective memory".

Thus we can see that displays really are going small, large, everywhere and interactive. An important trend is the prospect of many mobile devices emitting data projections, which we see as a significant emergent technology in the context of learning. For example, Samsung now has models with a "data projector" built in, the Samsung MBP200 with pico projector is shown below (http://www.engadget.com/2009/03/12/samsungs-mbp200-pico-pj-i7410-projector-phone-get-ship-dates/) (Fig. 14.3).

It seems to us that the overarching question is how does technological progress increasingly allow us to overcome the inherent limitations of small, portable devices in relation to screen size? There are emerging new and reliable voice recognition technologies, which may help to overcome the problems inherent when inputting data. Furthermore, the notion of projecting from a mobile is being extended by work at MIT's "SixthSense" (http://www.pranavmistry.com/projects/sixthsense/

Fig. 14.3 Samsung MBP200 with in-built pico projector (Source: http://www.blogcdn.com/www.engadget.com/media/2009/03/samsung-show-demo-mwc09.jpg, 20 Jun 2009)

index.htm) project: "This is a wearable gestural interface that augments the physical world around us with digital information and lets us use natural hand gestures to interact with that information". In the SixthSense system, which is being developed by MIT Labs, a learner can project information or pictures onto any surface and manipulate it with hand gestures (http://www.ted.com/index.php/talks/pattie_maes_demos_the_sixth_sense.html). It would seem to us that emerging technologies are indeed transforming learning from a managed activity to a ubiquitous – anywhere, anytime, with anyone – one. From the learner's perspective we may summarize that the new ways in which meaning is created, data stored, represented, delivered and/or accessed do indeed have an impact on and support learning as personal experiences in virtual community driven environments.

Emerging Infrastructures and Devices: Engaging with Interdisciplinary Discourse

Currently, learners need access to fast broadband wireless if they are to take advantage of some of the more high-end affordances of mobile devices. Logistical and infrastructural issues can thus have an impact on the adoption of mobile devices for learning. Mobile Broadband, cloud computing and other innovations like IMS (IP Multimedia Subsystem) may emerge as being key enablers for mainstream teaching and learning over the next 2–3 years. Although the following discussion often describes technical capabilities, which are being developed by large corporations for e-business purposes, we will try to illustrate the affordance of what is being developed for use by teachers and learners. In this way we hope to uncover the direction that near future mobile learning will take and provide teachers and researchers with access to discourses that will affect our students' futures. Cook and Light (2006) pointed out that as networks and digital media increasingly offer the potential to develop from connecting people to connecting the things around us, new skills and sensibilities are needed to understand the world and design for it. We need to make explicit what these new abilities are and place the means for learning these skills at the heart of society. The alternative is the gradual curtailment of democratic processes: as people lose their power to contribute to debates about their future, the services they wish to use, even the systems in their homes. This is true for mobile lifelong learning environments, as it is for other arenas in which self-determination is to be encouraged. So we can also ask: what is the most effective way to teach about the potential and impact of these structures and systems? How do we avoid a new digital divide between people who have the power to manipulate their learning and those who, because they do not understand the potential of mobile lifelong learning environments, cannot? Such a discourse should enable us to position ourselves with respect to the predictions we see emanating from policy makers and the press. For example, the website "Cellphonesinlearning" (http://www.cellphonesinlearning.com/2008/09/future-of-cell-phones-in-schools.html) posted an interesting article in September 2008 on future trend called 'What else is coming for cell phones?' As well as the pico projector mentioned above, the article by Liz Kolb mentions the following, which we have reproduced in full below as it has useful implications for schools and practice (and as such addresses many of the questions we posed in the introduction).

What else is coming for cell phones?
1) By 2010 ... you will be able to hook up to your laptop or desktop computer from anywhere using your cell phone.
How this affects schools:
Students, teachers, and parents could retrieve their school files and documents anytime from anywhere! No worries if you forgot a homework paper, or forgot to hand something in, you could do this via cell phone.
2) By 2010 most cell phones will allow you to store all of your files and documents and share them (similar to a USB Flash hard drive).
How this could affect schools:
Students could share files with each other by beaming them through cell phones (similar to Palm pilots, only now with a basic cell phone). Students could also collect research and data by using their cell phone to store the papers, journal articles, and other documents that they uncover. Always having their research with them.
3) DSL/Broadband Internet connection will be available on most cell phones by 2010.
How this could affect schools:
Students who do not have Internet access at home (As of 2007; 78% of U.S. households have a computer, 75% of U.S. households have Internet, while 82% of U.S. citizens have cell phones) could easily access the web for research, course webpages, and class assignments/projects (quickly and efficiently unlike current basic cell phones, where it is still cumbersome and clunky).
4) Cell phone will become a home remote controller. For example, if you forgot to set your coffee pot to turn on or off, you can do that virtually through your cell phone!
How this could affect schools:
Teachers may be able to use this feature to live-stream to their classroom when they are sick or at a conference. They could also use the live-streaming with students who are home sick or unable to make it to the classroom (parents could even watch the lessons so they can better help their children with their class assignments). In addition, teachers could remotely

set up their classroom for the next day activities (such as setting the DVD player, or loading their PowerPoint presentation on the classroom computer).
5) Your phone number could become as important as your social security number! You will be able to use it for e-commerce and identification.
How this could affect schools:
Students could use their cell phone as their school ID. Attendance and school purchases could be taken via cell phone. Grades and project feedback could be disseminated via cell phone.
6) Solar-Powered Cell Phones
Soon you will not be confined by electricity or have to worry about charging your cell phone, solar-powered cell phones are coming soon!
How this could affect schools:
Students can truly learn anytime, anywhere, anyplace, at any pace with solar powered cell phones. We know from the Millennial's Rising and Speak Up reports that this is how Twenty first Century student's like to learn best.

Our discussion will now turn more interdisciplinary in nature as it reports innovations of a more technical nature. We argue here that teachers and researchers from all disciplines need to engage in these discourses. Decisions on what new learning landscapes will look like will be made on our behalf if we are not able to see behind and beyond the jargon and envision the pedagogical possibilities and ethical implications of the technologies and infrastructures that are available for learning.

The Horizon (2008) report predicts that mobile broadband will appear more widely over the next 2–3 years and that

> over the time frame of this adoption horizon, it is expected that mobile broadband, full featured Internet, touch-screen interfaces, remotely upgradeable software, and high-quality displays will become as common as cameras are today ... The combination of social networking and mobility lets students and colleagues collaborate from anywhere they happen to be. Add to that connectivity the multimedia capacities of phones, and the storage they offer for podcasts, videos, photos, PDF files and even documents and spreadsheets, and it is not hard to see why phones are increasingly the portable tool of choice. (2008, p. 17)

Of course the challenge is not to replicate the mobile office, but to design a mobile lifelong learning environment. Allowing unfettered access to content is not advisable, as we saw earlier in the book; e-safety is an important issue. Furthermore, school children will need safe environments so that their privacy is not threatened by unwelcome intrusions. Another innovation that could assist us in designing such a mobile lifelong learning environment is Cloud computing or the web-on-the-go; this is the moving of applications and data storage away from the desktop or laptop to remote servers managed by high-speed networks. Computing applications and users' data archives will increasingly be accessible by different devices anytime, anywhere over fast and widely available wireless and wired networks (Horrigan 2008). Indeed, Becta (2008b, p. 11) substantiate this prediction, reporting that placing resources into the "cloud" makes it possible to improve utilisation; to create temporary project test beds; to lease capacity for temporary peak loads; and to outsource the management of infrastructure and services to specialist companies. Indeed, cloud computing increases opportunities to offer "software as a service" (SaaS) and to provide other services, such as remote data storage.

Many companies are investing in the large data centres needed to support such initiatives.

Van't Hooft (2008, p. 34, quoting Thomas Vander Wal (http://personalinfocloud.com/2006/01/the_come_to_me_.html)) describes the shift from desk to cloud computing as "going from the "I go get web" (people accessing static and information in proprietary formats created by others on a desktop computer) to the "come to me web" (people creating, finding, using/re-using, sharing and storing information in open formats across multiple devices in different locations). Consequently, whereas the focus used to be on the technology, it has now shifted to the person, demoting the technology to a serving role and following the user wherever he or she goes".

Becta (2008b, p. 12) also report that in

> addition to practical problems of maintaining connectivity, migrating applications to this remote [cloud] resource and ensuring service level agreements take proper account of bandwidth demands, capacity overruns and backup, the sheer scale of the most recent data centres creates new challenges for managing hardware, data and applications.

It appears that Amazon's "Elastic Compute Cloud" (http://aws.amazon.com/ec2/) is already available as an existing, commercial virtual hosting service. However, Becta's report (2008b, p. 12) cautions that

> Managed services in education may make increased use of virtualised resources and applications; a number of browser-based management information systems and learning platforms are already employing such techniques. Improved access to the 'cloud' could make 'anywhere, any time, any device' services more accessible to staff and students. Nevertheless, the inherent risks of moving control to third parties, such as service continuity, data security, contingency planning and backup, must be considered by managers and advisers.

Some of these issues are not new for the IT industry given the trend towards outsourcing. However, when this approach is used for educational purposes, schools need to be sure they "read the small print" of service level agreements, etc. The advantages of cloud computing could be enormous, but the vision of large "farms" of servers sitting on a commercial park, generating masses of heat is a central issue in the green IT discussion and refers to the enormous energy needed to cool professional server systems.

Above we have tried to extend the Horizon analysis of what mobile devices have to offer learning by examining trends in the wireless networks and cloud computing infrastructures that these devices and learners inhabit. This seems appropriate if we are to explore the socio-cultural ecology that these developments afford. As we mentioned in Chapter 2, the CONTSENS project uses the IP Multimedia Subsystem (IMS) as its architectural framework for delivering internet protocol (IP) and multimedia to mobile users. IMS, widely available from 2009 to 2010, we see as being significant for mobile learning. At a meeting of the CONTSENS consortium in September 2008 in Bulgaria, representatives from Eriksson outlined the advantages of IMS for mobile learning, which we summarise below.

The Erickson Ireland team made an informative presentation on IMS to the CONTSENS consortium meeting, Varna, Bulgaria, in September 2008. Eriksson (2008) describe how IMS provides several services that can be leveraged in mobile learning applications and courses. These services include new ways to perform activities on mobile devices (what IMS calls a Converged User Sessions), new ways to deliver course material and monitor student participation (through IP Based Content Delivery), and new ways to help maintain the student's focus during mobile learning activities (Presence and Group Management). The specifics of IMS are described below. However, what is important to note is that traditionally on mobile networks a session consists of one mode of communication: video, voice, web browsing, etc. With IMS a single user session can consist of multiple modes of communication at once. An example of this could be that during a mobile learning session, four students and a teacher could be involved in a teleconference with a shared whiteboard. Then, as the teacher speaks, the students can collaborate on diagrams or watch the same slides that the teacher.

A Converged User Sessions (CUS) refers to a situation where one user session consists of several IMS sessions. For example, as we pointed out above, several learners can share web-browsing during a CUS voice call. The idea is that the learners can choose how to communicate during an established session, rather than having to break the current session to start a new one. To put this in concrete terms, two History students on a field trip can show a live feed of the Cistercian Chapel in Yorkshire, described in Chapter 2, to all session participants. The teacher, sat with other students back in the school in London, can superimpose the visualisation of what the Chapel had looked like before the building was in ruins. Whilst the teacher outlines a research assignment orally to the students about what they are seeing, which can also be sent by SMS to all students, the students can use the shared whiteboard to note down issues for further research.

IP (internet protocol) Based Content Delivery is a central component of IMS. As IMS is all IP-based, i.e. it is the same as internet and web-browsing, the content can be delivered from anywhere, e.g. from dedicated servers using cloud computing or the internet etc. Furthermore, in IMS it is also very easy to monitor what has been accessed by whom and to automate some aspects of this (thus enabling context-sensitive learning). Therefore, IMS is not only useful for getting the content to the students but also getting the student's feedback/progress/results back onto some sort of centralised storage. This loop of immediate formative assessment and the ability for students to act on a task is important in Laurillard's Conversational Framework and can be supported by IMS.

Learning services delivered over IMS are claimed to be device agnostic. This means a user can pull down course material onto a phone, PDA or laptop. IMS has a way of discovering the client capabilities of the end device, for instance if the device has a microphone, camera or large screen. The appropriate content can then in theory be made available to that particular device. It is still early days to test this claim for IMS; at the time of writing, content developed for one device, say a Nokia with a Symbian operating system, cannot be played on another device, e.g. a HTC device running windows mobile operating system. This is known as an interoperability issue.

The Presence and Group Management (PGM) functions can be used to set user status on a network, in much the same way MSN, GTalk or Skype do it. Unlike these instant messengers, however, PGM allows more granularity than just online/offline/busy. Firstly, with PGM users can set their preferred modes of contact, be it voice, SMS, IM or email. Then, instead of everyone just seeing the user as online or offline, groups can be defined. So, a user might set her presence as offline to everyone in her work group, but all of her social contacts would still be able to see her online.

Finally, a Mobile Positioning System (MPS) is used to determine the geographical position of a mobile/cell phone/device and delivers the position co-ordinates to the application requesting this information. MPS is the most commonly used positioning system in the world today. MPS 9.0 supports basic accuracy positioning methods that work for all legacy handsets today (i.e. phones that are built on the way earlier versions worked, e.g. on an earlier operating system). Spatial triggering, i.e. notifications that an application can automatically generate when a user meets certain spatial conditions, e.g. moving into or out of a predefined area in the mediascape case study in the Urban Planning described in Chapter 2. Thus for example, MPS can be used to find the location of family members or learning group members and view their position on a map. This is part of a zone-based notifications/alerts system that operates through e-mail, SMS and MMS (see Fig. 14.4).

Erickson have provided a facility in some of its phones, developed with Sony, for each group member to appear as a dropdown menu; this is presented with an option to request the current location. There is a positioning history feature that allows users to track family members. Zone-based notifications can be set to be sent when a specified family member either enters or leaves the selected area. The notification uses MPS Spatial Triggers. Clearly these forms of tracking and surveillance have major ethical implications; we will return to this below. However, if the goal of enabling innovative learning from context to context is to be achieved in a pedagogically rich way, then we think IMS holds great promise.

A major insight into the characteristics and affordances that mobile/cell phones will offer over the next few years can be gained by looking at Google's mobile Android phone, called the G1, which was launch in September 2008 (http://www.telegraph.co.uk/connected/main.jhtml?xml=/connected/2008/09/22/dlgoogle122.xml) followed by the G2 in 2009. The phone runs Google's Android operating system and heralds the intervention into the mobile device market of a large new digital media corporate that has dominated search engines and advertising on the internet. In terms of functionality, the G1 is capable of running Google's range of internet applications such as its email service Gmail, productivity suite Google Docs and mapping service Google Maps. This will provide a ready made market for the G1. It also features Google's new web browser called Chrome. As direct competitor to the Apple iPhone, the G1 contains a GPS chip, allowing it to double-up as a mobile sat-nav. Google will also provide additional tools for the device to help push location-specific information to the phone's owner, such

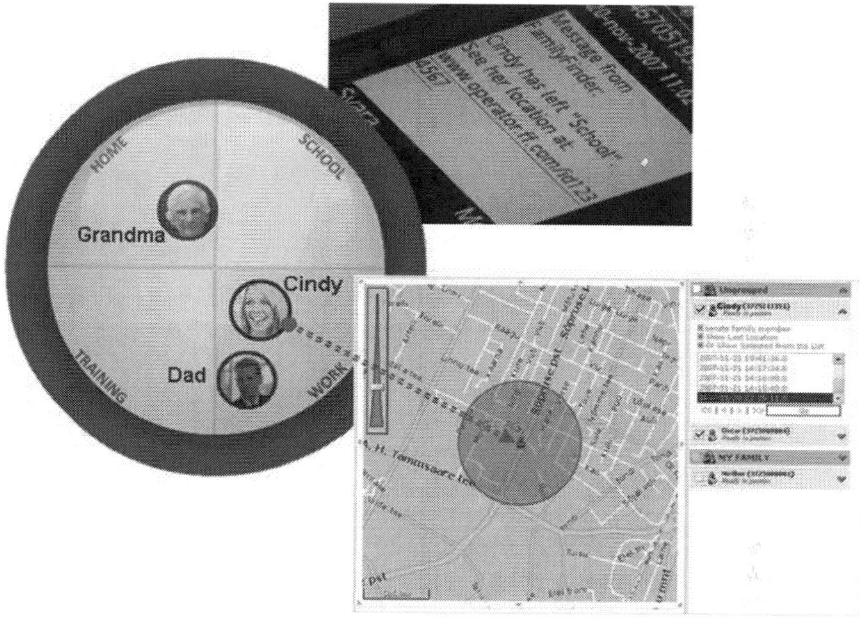

Fig. 14.4 A Mobile Positioning System exemplified (Source: http://www.ericsson.com/ericsson/corpinfo/programs/resource_documents/judy_nix_july_2008.pdf; p. 16)

as weather forecasts, travel updates and restaurant recommendations. Thus, in conjunction with IMS multimedia network or Google Wave abilities, developments like the G1 are opening wide the possibilities for mixed-reality, context, location-sensitive and ambient learning that we discussed in Chapter 2. Users of Android phones will be able to download additional software and programs for their device, in a similar way that iPhone users can add extra applications to their handset. This will enable pedagogically-orientated developments for such devices and their associated systems and networks. A problem is emerging in that the G1 operating system, Android, is in competition with Windows Mobile; the latter is used on over 90% of mobile/cell phones. This means that if learning applications are developed for one platform they may not function on another (i.e. interoperability problems may get worse). As we saw above, IMS may solve this problem. Indeed, Adobe has proposed that its new system AIR (http://www.adobe.com/products/air/) will help with the development and deployment of cross platform, rich multimedia.

The iPhone can be regarded as a major event in that, because of its easy-to-use interface, many educators can now see the possibilities of such devices for education. The Apple iPhone has proved popular, although it wasn't the first handset to use a touch screen. Taiwanese phone maker HTC beat iPhone to the market with its TouchFLO phone. Both phones make use of accelerometers, these allow the devices to react to motion and to the way they are being held. Multi-touch interfaces accept intuitive, gesture-based commands and open up possibilities for simultaneous, collaborative work. "These two innovations – accelerometer-based devices and multi-touch screens – allow users to manipulate content intuitively, using natural gestures like flicking the wrist or sweeping the fingertips over a display" (Johnson et al. 2008, p. 18). However, it is the iPhone that has won over a lot of users, as Darren Waters (Technology editor, BBC News website) put it in November 2007 (http://news.bbc.co.uk/1/hi/technology/7079098.stm):

> The greatest success of Apple's iPhone lies in the realisation that most phones you have owned previously are compromises. The iPhone is not perfect – far from it – but it genuinely re-moulds the expectations we have for mobile devices. And it provokes a reaction among gadget lovers and ordinary members of the public that no other phone can match.

The key to the innovation of the iPhone is the simple and easy-to-use touch interface that allows users to interact with the underlying operating system. Following various upgrades the functionality of the iPhone has been similar to most smartphones, and includes camera, digital radio, increased storage capacity, web browsing, bluetooth, GPS, 3G, etc; however, at the time of publication of this book it does still not support Flash. The App Store allows users to browse and download a multitude of applications of a general as well as educational nature from the iTunes Store. In early 2009 there were around 20,000 apps available to purchase and download. This number has grown significantly since to over 100,000 in late 2009 (see e.g. http://appshopper.com/ for latest figures).

> The fact that third-party applications [i.e. software or services that are developed by someone other than the mobile/cell phone producer] can be developed and deployed for our phones represents a profound shift in the way we think about mobile devices. The App Store for the Apple iPhone (http://www.apple.com/iphone/appstore/) is bursting with small applications, including software for games, productivity, education, business, health and fitness, reference, travel, and more. Other mobile platforms are emerging that will encourage similar development, such as the Android platform developed by Google and the Open Handset Alliance (http://en.wikipedia.org/wiki/Google_Android). (Horizon Report 2008, p. 25)

One controversy is that all apps that are developed have to be approved by Apple. However, we would agree with the Australasian Horizon report: the implication of these emerging devices and infrastructures for teaching and learning over the longer term are immense:

> The applications of mobile technology to teaching and learning are virtually limitless. Adoption rate and availability of bandwidth are the limiting factors. Once infrastructure is in place and students routinely carry mobile devices, they will be a natural choice for content delivery and even field work and data capture.
>
> For the newest generation of mobiles, third-party applications for language, maths, science, and elementary education are easy to find. The most obvious materials – flash cards – are already available at all levels for almost every discipline. Tools that tap into the unique capabilities of mobile devices, like the camera, the microphone, and the accelerometer are appearing by the day. Language learners can install applications on their mobiles that let them look up words and even hear the word pronounced in the language they are learning, and it is not unreasonable to project that before long, they will be able to speak

> into the phone and hear their own voice compared to a native speaker's saying the same thing.
>
> Reference materials for writing, chemistry, medicine, physics and astronomy – from dictionaries to calculators to interactive periodic tables – can be installed on mobile devices, ready for anytime, anywhere access. Pocket astronomy charts range from iAstronomica (http://artistictechworks.com/iastronomica.html), which includes planetarium-perspective illustrated star maps, to Distant Suns (http://www.distantsuns.com/index.html), a mobile version of an established desktop astronomy package. Google Earth is available for the mobile, complete with zoom and spin implemented through the touch screen. The variety and quality of content available for next-generation mobile devices is growing at a fantastic pace (Johnson et al. 2008, p. 26).

We conclude this section by observing that there is much to commend mobile devices and emerging infrastructures for learning inside and outside of school. Yet, with reference to Chapter 13, where we argued that democracy can be viewed as the possibility for equity of access to essential conceptual, cultural and social resources, it has to be re-iterated that further development of digital infrastructures is needed to guarantee access by all learner groups without excluding any one of them.

Context-Sensitive Learning

Context-sensitive and location-aware learning will be key areas for mobile learning in the future because they move beyond visual awareness related to the screen and issues surrounding how data is stored, represented and delivered. We have already looked at context-sensitive learning in Chapter 2; it refers to educational interventions being made by the mobile device or service, which are directly relevant to the educational activity that the learner engages in. Context-sensitive systems automatically log and aggregate learner usage for designing collaborative filtering systems and predictive user interfaces. Location-based learning refers to the ability to pin-point the physical location of a mobile device so that, for example, material can be offered, which are directly relevant to the location in which the users find themselves. Using established technologies such as Mobile Positioning System (MPS), GPS (Global Positioning System), RFID (Radio Frequency Identification) and QR (Quick response) Codes, content can be developed for both context-sensitive and location-based delivery. For example the CONTSENS project (http://www.ericsson.com/ericsson/corpinfo/programs/using_wireless_technologies_for_context_sensitive_education_and_training/) investigates the use of wireless technologies for context-sensitive education and training. This 2-year European Commission funded project involves a European-wide consortium headed by Ericsson Education Ireland. As described in Chapter 2, one CONTSENS partner, at the UK's London Metropolitan University, are developing a series of mobile learning applications that will make use of QR codes, location-based alerts and IMS.

Other examples of context-sensitive learning include Greenfield (2008) who describes JAPELAS, a prototype context-aware ubiquitous Japanese language instruction system developed at Tokushima University:

> One of the complications of learning to speak Japanese involves knowing which of the many levels of politeness is appropriate in a given context, and this is just what JAPELAS sets out to teach. JAPELAS determines the apposite expression for a given situation by trying to assess both the social distance between interlocutors, their respective status, and the overall context in which they're embedded. In this model of the world, context is handled straightforwardly as being a matter of where you are physically: is the setting a bar after class, a job interview, or a graduation ceremony? (Greenfield 2008, p. 7).

A more sophisticated notion of context is provided by CAGE (Context Aware Gallery Explorer), which was developed as part of the MOBIlearn project (http://www.mobilearn.org/), one aspect of this project was to enable learners context-sensitive learning in Italian art galleries.

There is some potential in the area of context- and location-aware learning for computer-adaptive assessment (CAA) or so-called "portable assessment" tools. Greenfield (2008, p. 10) notes:

> The premise of CAA is simple . . .: tests are composed dynamically, in real time, in response to the test-taker's answers to previous questions. The difficulty of successive questions can be tuned to account for patterns beyond mere correctness – for example, the time interval required to complete a given question. The arguments that are advanced for CAA include that it ostensibly increases efficiency, reduces student anxiety, and provides a more accurate picture of the test-taker's true competency than traditional methods of assessment.

Greenfield (2008, p. 9) further points out that one of "the most promising aspects of location-based learning is that it might offer new hope to those for whom learning from books or in conventional classroom settings is difficult", a group we have called "at-risk learners" in this book. "Pervasive games and simulations, in particular, appear to offer educational content in a way that is commensurate with a wider range of learning styles." Context-sensitive and location-aware learning can therefore be seen to offer great potential with respect to question two posed above, specifically with respect to new ways of meaning-making that extend beyond the classroom.

Social Operating Systems

Looking further ahead, The Horizon report (2008, p. 3) predicts the emergence of what it calls social operating systems in the longer term. There are many similarities between this concept and what we have called context sensitive systems. The report describes such systems as follows:

> The essential ingredient of next generation social networking, social operating systems, is that they will base the organization of the network around people, rather than around content. This simple conceptual shift promises profound implications for the academy, and for the ways in which we think about knowledge and learning. Social operating systems will support whole new categories of applications that weave through the implicit connections and clues we leave everywhere as we go about our lives, and use them to organize our work and our thinking around the people we know. (The Horizon Report 2008, p. 3)

Current social networking systems are unaware of the connections that users have not explicitly told them about, they do not recognise the "social graph", i.e. the network of relationships a person has: "These data and other information you use every day, analyzed with a people-centric view, can be and are being used to transparently connect the dots among files, contacts, and much more" (Horizon report 2008, p. 26). The report goes on to describe (p. 26) early applications like Xobni (www.xobni.com) and a proof-of-concept project from Yahoo known as Yahoo Life!, which – it claims – demonstrate this shift in the organisation of information. An interesting scenario is presented in the report of how a social operating system would work (admittedly for Higher Education project work but the idea is similar for schools):

> Colleagues working on the same research project share files, both by email and online using collaborative writing tools. In both cases, whenever one of them touches a document, the names and profiles of everyone else who has worked on that document are displayed in a sidebar. The application also suggests names from the scholar's network of other contacts who have not worked on the project, but whose background indicates that they might be useful contributors.

This scenario could also be described as context-aware learning. Such a conception of emerging technologies has big implications for learning.

> Placing people and relationships at the center of informational space will have a profound influence at all levels of academia. It will change the way we relate to knowledge and information; the way we do research and evaluate credibility; the way educators and students interact with each other; and the way students learn to be professionals in their chosen disciplines (p. 27).

How Ubiquitous Do You Want It?

The recent Ofcom (2008a) report does not cover education directly, in fact it covers healthcare and transport; however, the statistics presented for UK are interesting. For example, the report notes that "Wireless communications are so integral to our lives that today there are more mobile subscriptions [i.e. subscribing to a mobile/cell phone service], at 70 million, than the 60 million UK population." Indeed, the world of mobile internet devices is set to explode in the next 4 years says chip maker Intel (http://news.bbc.co.uk/1/hi/technology/7522305.stm). Furthermore, sales of smartphones are expected to overtake those of laptops in the next 12–18 months, i.e. by the end of 2009, as the mobile/cell phone completes its transition from voice communications device to multimedia computer (http://news.bbc.co.uk/1/hi/technology/7250465.stm). However, a key issue here for bridging learning in formal and informal contexts will be the ability to move seamlessly between wireless networks, like wifi and cell networks like 3G and 4G. Indeed, the position globally has seen a massive uptake of mobile devices:

> Now the mobile/cell phone is on course to replace the PC as the primary device for getting online. According to the International Telecommunication Union, 3.3 billion people, more than half the world's population, now subscribe to a mobile/cell-phone service ... so the internet at last looks set to change the whole world. (The Economist 2008, p.3)

Ethical Considerations and Suspicions

Ethics are being considered here as part of regulatory frameworks etc. In Chapter 1 we noted that appropriation within structures provides a level of reflexivity and as such ethical issues are further seen as being integral to our conception of appropriation. That said, the systems discussed above offer the promise of a flexible, distributed, context sensitive learning support environment in which we can move computing off the desktop by going small, large, and everywhere. However, there are some ethical considerations and suspicions which will need to be debated. For example, consider this application proposed in the Ofcom report (2008a):

> *In-body networks*: a "body area network" could be implanted inside a patient's body to enable doctors to monitor their recovery remotely. The in-body network sensors monitor how a patient moves or picks up vital health signs, such as blood sugar levels, and sends this information wirelessly to make an alert via a home hub or portable monitor. A number of UK universities, including Imperial College, are carrying out research in this area. These networks could use existing spectrum specifically allocated for use by sensor networks. (website (http://www.ofcom.org.uk/media/news/2008/05/nr_20080507))

Our technology is already wearable (http://www.thinkgeek.com/index.shtml) and buildings may in future start to talk to us as conversational agents are embedded in their design. Ethical questions here include: what price would we be paying for the benefits of such invasive embedding of technology? What risk is associated with the surveillance that it enables? The same could be said of context-sensitive mobile learning, which is not mentioned in the Ofcom (2008a) report. Should we be monitoring a learner's activity and location on such a fine-grained level of detail? There seem to be parallels here with Google maps, which at a fine-grained level can identify real people or their homes. Informed consent and easy opt-in opt-out would seem to apply here; but is this too simplistic and will we be given a choice? Shops can already track customers via mobile/cell phone (http:// www.timesonline.co.uk/tol/news/tech_and_web/article3945496.ece). Is the surveillance society that CCT is already promoting just a foretaste of things to come?

Bridging the Digital Divide at the Policy Level

The "infrastructure" issues mentioned above are important with respect to the widespread availability of mobile broadband and related "cloud" infrastructures; this can be equated to the provision of clean water to the home and school, they are essential and equality of access and need consideration from policy level down to the local schools. The primacy of aspects of this need appears to have been taken up by the UK Government, who take the view that a "computer with internet access is now as essential as a pen and paper in modern learning" and who announce in September 2008 (http://www.dcsf.gov.uk/pns/DisplayPN.cgi?pn_id=2008_0208) that "Children from jobless and low income families will receive a free computer and free broadband access under major plans to close the digital divide amongst young people." Becta have played a key role researching for and advising on the project and will be instrumental in implementing the initiative Becta report (http://www.becta.org.uk/homeaccesstaskforcepapera) that

> This initiative is intended to bridge the digital divide where currently more than one million children still do not have a computer at home and 35% of families have no access to the internet. This should create a level playing field for learners where every child has equal access to the internet at home to assist with their learning.
>
> Initially the programme will be piloted in two local authority areas in early 2009. This will allow time to trial the purchasing logistics and eligibility criteria, after which the wider roll-out of the programme is planned for autumn 2009 with the aim to have universal home access by 2011.

Immediate response to this UK Government initiative on the BBC news forum "Have your Say" (http://newsforums.bbc.co.uk/nol/thread.jspa?sortBy=1&forumID=5381&edition=1&ttl=20080924103820&#paginator) revealed interesting attitudes to this announcement; comments include:

"Stop spending my hard earned money on no-hopers."

"£700 for computers! Nurseries, that are run as businesses! Children need to learn to read & write...not be given a tool to be able to play games and chat to their friends."

"I don't like the computers for poor kids idea.""First, alot of those little darlings will be playing traunt [sic] so don't deserve them."

"Those that go to school have access to them there and will know enough to get them jobs with computers."

"Thirdly, people may have forgotton [sic] this, but libraries have computers for all, and for free. Kids can [and do – I've seen them many times] go after school, on saturdays and during holidays."

"Put a million poorer families online with computers and internet so we can track what they read, where they surf and what they learn."

"£300m on laptops which will go straight on ebay isn't a solution."

No claim is made about the representativeness of these quotes of the population at large. Given that a major theme of this book is to discuss how learners who are at a distance to school and even society can be encouraged to engage with school-based learning, these comments underline the potential difficulties around initiatives that they to bridge the digital divide and provide access to any where, any time, any device learning.

Conclusions

In Chapter 13 we drew on salutary work by Cuban to ask the question: has the experience of students in a typical class changed in any significant way due to the introduction of mobile devices? Well, the answer is not straightforward. Innovation is unfolding at an unprecedented pace in the area of digital devices and infrastructure and there is growing ubiquity of this technology as appropriated in the life-worlds of school children. This is leading to ubiquitous – anywhere, anytime, with anyone learning. But this is happening predominantly outside formal educational settings. Throughout this book we have provided examples of teachers as innovators, introducing into the school community policies that can engender adoption of mobile devices for pedagogical purpose. However, schools are keen to retain control. Consequently, we believe that the question posed in Chapter 13 is highly relevant: "Formal and informal learning inside and outside schools – is it still helpful to think in this way?" Assuming a future in which formal education provision by schools and other organisations remains a cornerstone of socialisation, by looking at the life-worlds of school children outside schools educators are able to more readily take into account the prerequisites of their learners. Yet, clearly, the boundaries between what is inside and what outside continue to blur further.

The co-construction of learning between teachers and students is a powerful vehicle for innovation. As Shuler (2009, p. 5) points out, not all children are alike and instruction should be adaptable to individual and diverse learners. Yet, groups of children from the same socio-cultural milieu do share characteristics, for example around risk taking. By the same token, children from different milieus differ. Shuler, in the "Pockets of Potential" report, expands on the notion of personalised learning:

> As Kurt Squire [an expert interviewed for the study] told us, "Mobile devices enable kids to develop passions and interests via their own personalized, media-enhanced environments that can transport them to different times and places." Not all children are alike; in an ideal world, instruction should vary and be adapted in relation to individual and diverse learners. Differentiated instruction is a process to approach teaching and learning that recognizes learners' varying background knowledge, readiness, language, preferences, and interests, and reacts responsively. The intent of differentiating instruction is to maximize each student's growth and individual success by meeting them where they are and assisting in the learning process... There are significant opportunities for genuinely supporting differentiated, autonomous, and individualized learning through mobile devices. (Shuler 2009, pp. 21–22)

In this chapter we saw that computing is moving off the desktop: going small, large, everywhere and getting interactive. Infrastructures such as mobile broadband, social operating systems, cloud computing and IMS are developing at a pace. We considered context-sensitive and location-aware learning as offering great potential with respect to new ways of meaning-making that extend beyond the classroom. Ethical questions have been raised throughout our discussions, and they include: what risk is associated with the surveillance that mobile technology enables? Should we be monitoring a learner's activity and location on such a fine-grained level of detail? As a consequence to these trends and ethical concerns our goal here has been to uncover the direction that near-future mobile learning might take and provide teachers and researchers with access to discourses that will affect our students' futures. However, the implications of what we have discussed go wider to the policy level and have implications for society and the world at large. In the end, it is down to the pedagogical ingenuity of educators to harness the potential of mobile devices in formal contexts for learning that clearly exists.

Chapter 15
Visions and Suspicions

Introduction

Larry Cuban (2001) cautions about technology being 'oversold and underused'; and, broadly, we agree. So here, in this concluding chapter, we recapitulate some of the issues, which we have discussed and allow ourselves the luxury of some 'visions'. Here and there too we indicate suspicions around problems, pitfalls and wrong directions in speculating about the future of mobile devices and technologies and 'mobile learning'. It is not our intention to offer solutions or clear directions; it is too early to set out clear routes to possible futures. In any case, our intention has been, and is, to stimulate a debate – as informed as it is possible to be at this time – about the potentials of mobile devices in relation to a society's educational needs, purposes and desires.

Getting Beyond 'Being Critical'

In line with the socio-cultural ecological approach taken in the book, we argue for the importance of reflexivity. Subjecting 'taken for granted', 'everyday' social practices and forms to critique, is a sine-qua-non of academic and intellectual work; it is normal, essential, inevitable. The practice of critique, the stance of 'being critical' is embedded in all aspects of such work. In that context, the use of the adjective 'critical' becomes not much more than a redundant flourish. At the same time, its use harks back to strong concerns in the 1970s, when 'critique' had a political edge. 'Critique', then, as the means of 'putting things into crisis', offered the possibility of effecting changes, away from skewed distributions of power and its effects.

The present seems neither the time to 'put things into crisis' – patently they are – nor a time when socially progressive projects can easily be articulated, advocated and hope to gain wide consent. Yet we concur with the many who insist that there is no question that 'things could be better'. We want to play our part in that, by shaping tools for *purposeful agency* in the *design*, *production* and *dissemination* of social and pedagogic conceptions founded on the interests of social actors. These could be articulated as *texts* or as *practices* and *dispositions* for actors in the 'mobile complex' that we have sketched in this book. Mobile devices enter into the picture

N. Pachler et al., *Mobile Learning*, DOI 10.1007/978-1-4419-0585-7_15,

because in their affordances, their potentials, they can be seen as 'tracking' broad social developments in relation to power, agency, diversity, provisionality. In that, they offer potentials for (selectively) amplifying or modifying these social developments; maybe at times in their use they suggest a path, and seem to lead – by virtue of their affordances – where social understandings and practices might follow. Text-messaging may be one such case in point; though we have indicated others throughout the book. We are clear, however, that in or by themselves the technologies and devices we have discussed are not, and do not offer the panacea to the solution of educational problems.

The devices and their affordances are now a part of the everyday life of very many people in the media-dominated fabric of our society – though there remain significant variation in ownership and use in terms of age, region, gender, wealth. Yet their near ubiquity, especially among the young, makes it imperative for educational systems, institutions and educators to take them seriously as an integral part of the communicational and, therefore, of the 'learning landscape'. There is a need for schools and other institutions to become clear whether or not, or how, to utilise the affordances and potentials of these devices – alongside many other technologies, new and old – to enhance possibilities for learning, for learning experiences and to attempt to understand their place – actually now and into the near future – as instruments in learning and their place in environments of learning. That much is clear; and it is more than urgent.

The devices are taken into most personal and social spaces, contexts and situations as a matter of course, so that these spaces are now connected with, have access to, and interact with the convergent media landscape, which increasingly dominates social life. The German term 'Handy' for the mobile/cell phone – meaning either 'in the hand' or, as a loanword, meaning 'practical'/'versatile' – is revealing in that respect; these devices are useful tools for the integration of divergent cultural practices across social milieus and national and geographical boundaries, due to their potential for fostering communication of all kinds. That includes the school.

One of the inherent challenges posed for their (potential) integration into institutional educational practices arises precisely from this transgression of boundaries. The school has been, and still is, an institutional site, which insists on maintaining forms, frames and boundaries: of knowledge, of authority, of site/space/location, of time, of identities. The features and affordances of the devices all go in the direction of unmaking these *social* – rather than technical – framings and boundaries. The introduction of the device thus poses the problem, first and foremost, of dealing with these social (and ideological/epistemological) issues. In that respect, the devices and their affordances are less a threat within a paradigm of *critique*, where what is at stake is access to alternative articulations of a given curricular issue with the intention of subjecting that to critique, than in a paradigm of 'new production', of *design*, arising out of the interests of students, the issue is their claim to agency in relation to the making of texts and knowledge.

The Issue of 'Recognition': The Education System and Prevailing Social/Cultural Transformations

If mobile technologies have become 'normalized', they can no longer be ignored by the education system: banning them is not a (sensible) option. The question is how to harness their affordances. That goes to the issue of 'recognition', in a number of distinct yet related dimensions: *recognition* of the potentials of the devices; *recognition* of the potential uses of their affordances for the purposes of the school; and a *recognition* above all, of the agency of students who use the devices and integrate their affordances into their everyday life-worlds. Such *recognition* would offer a start to solving one major challenge in relation to school-based education: how to gain the support of parents, of politicians, of those in authority; getting parents and others to view learning with mobile devices as absolutely serious, not as a facile pandering to orientations to entertainment, not an expression of a narrowing conceptualisation of learning.

Interestingly, this raises yet again, with new seriousness, the issue – both old and ever new – about technologies and social practices: should mobile devices be viewed as a new technology with which to do old things in new ways or whether the time has come to do the new things afforded by the technology (see e.g. Noss and Pachler 1999).

Schools, teachers and students face the deep effects of the transition from the authority of the state to the power of the market, from a particular work ethic, sense of duty and obligation to the seductive promises by the market of gratification through consumption. In that context, schools and other education institutions are facing a crisis of legitimacy. When knowledge is ubiquitously available at any time in any place, when the canonicity of knowledge is no longer guaranteed by official authority, then school can no longer function as the gatekeepers for 'knowledge' as such: their legitimacy is challenged at many points, which manifests itself in forms of refusal and avoidance of school(ing); and the use by students of alternative routes to information and knowledge.

There is another and significant problem of *recognition* from two further perspectives: an older generation does not have the *conceptual* (and *affective*) *means* to recognize what the young are *actually* doing; the younger generation in its turn has neither the experience nor the conceptual means to question the conditions of their own present – which the old see as 'fragmentation' and which the young know as 'what is'. This leads to a hugely problematic 'generational divide', in that the adult population went to school before any or some of the real impact of digital and mobile technologies had begun to be felt and consequently has no 'inwardness' with it. Yet it is these adults who are today's policy-makers and teachers, who determine curricula, while those who are the most affected in their educational experience have no real say in the formulation of those curricula.

The educational impact of the transition of authority and a shift from stability to instability is significant: 'reproduction', whether of society and its culture(s) – producing the young in the image of that society, with its knowledges and values – is no longer possible. Different curricular, conceptual, social and ethical resources are required: distinct, and apt for the social world of today and tomorrow. The effects of social fragmentation, of fast-moving cultural forms and media practices, including the effects of the technologies we have been discussing, mean that there are no longer any stable 'givens' to which curricula might be anchored, with some certainty that they would fit the society of tomorrow.

In the context of the changes to social structures and cultural practices which we have outlined, schools and other educational institutions are finding it increasingly difficult to gain their communities' assent to, or their students' engagement with *curricula of content*. In the face of this the school will have to move to curricula based on the recognition of those factors, which make for fragmentation and contestation: shifts in power, still increasing diversity, including increasingly marked *generational* divisions. The school will, as well, need to strive to give recognition to the principles and practices, and the values of their students in a world of instability and provisionality. The curricula could then provide the tools, which enable reflection, production with full awareness of the potentials of the resources used in the communicational environments – shaped by power of different kinds – for which materials would now be designed and destined.

Students are finding it increasingly difficult to engage with the characteristics of the environments of learning proposed and enacted still, by schools as agents of state power or groups of parents – whether in terms of the imagined social relations projected into forms of pedagogies enacted in classrooms, which, in terms of social relations, remain lodged in a conception of a state and its relation to (prospective) citizens no longer recognizable to the young whose subjectivities and identities are shaped by the market as consumers. This disjunction emerges in all aspects of curriculum, of pedagogy and of agency assigned, assumed and of agency denied. It emerges in the role of power in relation to knowledge; in the value given to correctness (a social issue, linked to convention) as against accuracy (an ethical issue, linked to truth); in the choice of modes for representation, which are admitted and permitted and which are marginalized or banished; of what media of dissemination are imagined and whose power is validated in them – the contrast illustrated perhaps by school-authorized materials as against the principles of Web 2.0 production by students.

The state still expects schools to fulfil this role and these functions, though now without the support of the social structures and forms which gave their strong if implicit framing, nor of the power of a state which provided legitimacy, even if through coercion.

Learning and Life-Worlds: Environments of Learning

These fundamental changes in the environments in which educational institutions operate, brought about by a large variety of factors and often accelerated by technological innovations, of which mobile technologies and devices are one part, raise fundamental questions about the constitution and focus of formal learning environments. We are not arguing that schools abandon a clear and strong sense of the significance of much of the knowledge and values traditionally conveyed by the school. What we are arguing is that the significance of that knowledge cannot be 'pressed' on students through power of various kinds – in places like the UK in forms of coercion ranging from the exclusion of children from school to the imprisonment of parents on the grounds of their children's truancy. Rather, the school's task is to propose what the communities, which it serves, continue to regard as the significant *and* essential achievements in understandings and knowledge of their cultures, based, often, on centuries of work of social agents in their production of cultural resources of all kinds.

In proposing such curricula the school will need to be aware of the principles on which learning proceeds: not on the basis of power pressing on the young – learning seen as acquisition or adaption, or accumulation – but learning seen as transformative engagement with the *curricular ground* provided by the school, in the light of the learners' interests. Framed in the light of an understanding of the principles, the interests and the assumed agency of the young, the teachers' task is to guide learners to an understanding *achieved* by them in the light of their interests and principles. In that, the school's task remains central: to act as the agent of the community, society, state in proposing the *ground* for the learners' engagement; and elucidate the issues of significance for the lives of learners in the light of the learners' interests and principles.

One such way would be for schools to *recognize* and to acknowledge the learning that takes place in many other sites, constituted around different principles of authority, power and values, as well as strategies for encouraging learning using notions of pleasure rather than necessarily only of work. There is a well-recognized danger in bringing students' everyday life into schools – taking from them their life-world and its interests and turning it into the curricular stuff of school-authority, fed back to those who initially shaped and owned it in the frames of a now extraneous authority. This links to the definition of learning we proposed in Chapter 1 of this book and it might allow schools to harness the learning that takes place in everyday life, as the result of the ceaseless, constant engagement with the world. The key notion here is that of the active, transformative engagement of young people with the world on the basis of principles, which they bring to that engagement, captured by us in the notion of 'agency' in our model of a socio-cultural ecology.

To repeat: our argument is not at all one of schools becoming superfluous or marginal – quite the opposite: we see them as continuing to have a central *social* role, albeit one that is different to what it has traditionally been: a role along the lines of the social changes that have marked the last four or five decades. Educational institutions and their professionals remain agents of culture and society; their task has become that of *proposing* 'what is to be learnt'. That implies a significant change in power relations and pedagogical practices. We see the role of schools and teachers as facilitating engagement in the materials presented by the school shaped for students in terms of their interests and principles, including 'navigational aids' for students to take further on the basis of their interests. In this way both schools' expertise and students' interest, i.e. their agency in their life-worlds, would be affirmed. In this we see the role of mobile devices as enabling both educators and learners to set up, and to integrate new environments for learning – using the facilities provided by media convergence. Mobile devices can then become an important interface with the media-rich world of young people.

We use the term 'school' as a compacted, short-hand term for a whole set of institutional factors: of those who are contemporaneously regarded as 'stake-holders', different in different contexts, with differing powers. So when we speak of a certain inability, if not reluctance, of 'schools' to change, to engage proactively with the fundamental features and factors inherent in the 'mobile complex', we do not wish to lay 'blame' at the door of schools or their staff; rather, we wish to point to a complex in which the school is the most visible entity, and the one encountered by students and parents. The 'holy grail' of education, namely '"a resurgence of thirst" for learning' (Borgman et al. 2008, p. 12) or a clear means for reconnecting the young with the school, or of integrating technologies meaningfully with the interests and purposes of schools and students, all that remains elusive and to be played for.

Participation, Social Divides and Cultural Resources

Our approach via a socio-cultural ecology is particularly timely given the (still) increasing ubiquity of mobile devices; there is a real prospect of 'everyone' owning a multifunctional mobile computing device in the near future. The cost of a 'learning-technology' thus becomes individualised, reducing the burden on the state to provide (part of) a technological infrastructure to support formal education. If, as a society, we are able to provide low cost technological tools for everyone, then democratisation in the form of access as well as contribution to cultural production through mobile devices by everyone can be part of the vision. If we are unable to do so, there is the clear likelihood of the 'digital divide' opening further. Potentially, individualisation dramatically transforms the technological infrastructure, which is available to learners. With the convergence of affordances onto a single mobile device, private, informal and formal spaces, situations and contexts become intermingled. Learning, working, entertainment, community and social communications, commerce, shopping and other activities become intertwined. But what does the prospect of such a convergent, technology-rich and – compared to prior arrangements – entirely differently framed world mean for the future of learning?

One of our main lines of arguments in the book has been and is: mobile devices are, and have to be understood as, part of a convergent media landscape. They are tools for accessing data and networks. Even if mobile devices include features such as GPRS, their connectivity, convergence options, interoperability and handling are inextricably linked with web-based technologies.

But to repeat: what will be the impact on learning, whether in institutional sites or in general?

'Situated Learning' and New Practices of Learning

Chan (2007) has recently noted that in institutionally fostered mobile learning we should aspire to context-aware, authentic, and situated learning. We agree; though just before leaving it there, it might be useful to unpack – even if belatedly – some terms. For instance: 'what is inauthentic learning?' 'what or when is learning *not* situated?' Is not the problem that students are only too aware of these things? And of course, the more important question: 'when is there not learning?'

Let us attempt careful phrasing of our concerns. For instance, a concern 'that schools or other institutions should strive to produce situation in which "what is to be learned" corresponds to core features of the environment in which the learning is to be done'; or: that schools produce environments for/of learning in which there is a congruence between the environment and that which is to be learned. Or maybe strive much more in the era of the dominance of the market to find means to link what is to be learned to concerns and interests shared by learners – rather than relying, as before, on power and sanctions to 'motivate' learners. Chan points to a key problem, namely the need for the restructuring of the school: its curricula, pedgagogies, didactics, timetables, in which the school is being transformed to respond to the ubiquity of multifunctional computing devices. He presents an intriguing map of the future that captures the relationship between the physical word (Natural Platform) and the digital world (Cyber Platform); it indicates that mobile devices will increasingly be embedded in the smart 'ubiquitous environments' that we have shown in Chapter 13, in the example of Seadragon and Photosynth.

In a more cautionary vein, Bruce (2008, p. 583) provides a useful perspective by noting that 'Education would certainly be easier to promote if we could simply identify some new technologies that would make ubiquitous learning occur. But the new technologies are neither necessary nor sufficient for this to happen'. Bruce argues that it is the vision for ubiquitous learning that matters most, not simply the technical affordances: 'We need to define ubiquitous learning in an historically legitimate way, one which recognizes the possibilities afforded by the new technologies without reducing the argument to a technocentric position.' Bruce goes beyond the concerns of Cuban by stressing that learning extends far beyond the confines of the classroom. Bruce stresses that as new technologies and media penetrate nearly every aspect of daily life, so does learning – though our qualification would be, as just stated, that there has always been and always will be learning in all aspects of daily life; the difference being the erasure now of a boundary between learning in and about everyday life and learning in institutional sites of learning.

Context Awareness

Haythornthwaite (2008) picks up on the work of Bruce by looking at the changing relationships in who learns from whom. When we learn, she suggests, we are increasingly dependent on online sources and the hidden work of retrieval algorithms; she argues that this increases the work of the learner, and raises the need for what she calls *critical media literacy,* as well as *critical retrieval* and *retrieval technology literacy*. As before, we might want to ask what learning is meant? And what actually are the real differences in kinds of learning and in what has been and is being learned. The present is also marked by massive loss of learning: of things, practices, means of relating with, and to others all of which were commonplace. And just what work does the adjective 'critical' do in these terms, not to mention the noun 'literacy' – rather than capacities, skills (of information retrieval), or competences.

What position or perspective does Haythornthwaite adopt when she suggests that 'criticality is often not a primary concern when users share personal data'? Is it conceivable that the users' criteria for evaluation are different ones, not recognized from the perspective of a different generation, or the elevation of the academics view? What do generationally different users of social networking sites such as MySpace and YouTube know about the criteria of evaluation brought by those from a younger generation?

There are questions here for those who do research as much as for those who are researched. Any move towards context-aware services and social operating systems could further intensify the situation. We propose that there is an absolute requirement for a curriculum of 'navigational aids' in relation to text-making, reading, discernment and discrimination, both for the researched and the researchers. The latter have the difficulty of labouring with inappropriate antiquated theoretical tools; while the former face the problem of practicing as they go along, without maybe some of the tools for reflection that could be provided to them by an older generation – newly informed. That is, both groups stand in need of a curriculum founded on principles of judgement and evaluation in ethical and aesthetic issues as an essential response to market principles of 'choice'.

There is a debate to be had and work to be done on both 'sides' of this divide: how best to sensitise young people to the opportunities and challenges, the pitfalls and potentials, in navigating what are seen by an older generation as increasingly fragmented and segmented media – quite decisively not experienced as such by the set of younger, contemporary users; and how best to give the older generation the means for recognition of the principles inhering in the practices employed by the younger.

Key Readings

Part I: Big Picture and Examples

Chapter 1. Charting the Conceptual Space

Beyond Current Horizons Challenge Papers (2008): http://www.beyondcurrenthorizons.org.uk/findings/research-challenges/longlist-challenge-papers/

The project, which aims to ensure that the UK education system has identified and prepared for a wide range of potential social, technological and cultural futures, commissioned a set of so-called challenge papers to identify emerging trends in society, technology and education.

Chapter 2. Mobile Learning: A Topography

Arnedillo-Sánchez, I., Sharples, M. and Vavoula, G. (eds.) (2007) *Beyond mobile learning workshop. The CSCL Alpine Rendez-Vous*. Trinity College Dublin Press. Available at: http://www.ell.aau.dk/fileadmin/user_upload/documents/research/kaleidoscope/Alpine_rendez_vous/CSCLAlpineRDV2007Report.pdf

This is a report from the 2007 Alpine Rendezvous workshop of the Kaleidoscope Mobile Learning SIG. The workshop explored new opportunities for mobile, contextual and ambient learning. The report contains the abstracts of presentations for the workshop and offers insights into the state of the art in mobile learning anno 2007 and pointers for future work.

Dourish, P. (2004) 'What we talk about when we talk about context.' In *Personal and Ubiquitous Computing 8(1)*, pp. 19–30. Also available at: http://www.ics.uci.edu/~jpd/publications/2004/PUC2004-context.pdf

This paper discussed the notion of 'context' against the background of ubiquitous and context-aware computing. It argues that the representational stance implied in traditional interpretations of the term is unhelpful in view of emerging everyday life practices around computing and suggests an alternative model with a view to providing new directions for design.

N. Pachler et al., *Mobile Learning*, DOI 10.1007/978-1-4419-0585-7,

Kukulska-Hulme, A., Sharples, M., Milrad, M., Arnwdillo-Sanchez, I. and Vavoula, G. (2009) 'Innovation in mobile learning: A European perspective.' In *Journal of Mobile and Blended Learning 1(1)*, pp. 13–35. Also available at: http://oro.open.ac.uk/12711/1/IJMBL_pre-print_19_Dec_2008.pdf

This paper offers a typology of the use of mobile technologies in European mobile learning projects. Starting with a short overview over the history of mobilelearning research, the authors describe the shift from technology-centred research to a situative, communicative, participatory and generative understanding of mobilelearning focussing on context-generation, social practices and the learner. The categories underlying the 'typology of use' are location-based, i.e. in which institutional contexts mobile learning (research) is implemented.

Sharples, M. (ed) (2007) *Big issues in mobile learning. Report of a workshop by the Kaleidoscope Network of Excellence in Mobile Learning Initiative.* Learning Sciences Research Institute, University of Nottingham. Available at: http://www.lsri.nottingham.ac.uk/Publications_PDFs/BIG_ISSUES_ REPORT_PUBLISHED.pdf

This report offers a summary of the deliberations on mobile learning of a group of researchers at a two-day workshop in Nottingham in 2006. The contributions summarise the outcomes of thematic group discussions. The report charts the rapid changes in the mobile learning landscape, in particular the growing use of mobile devices for personal and informal learning.

Sharples M., Milrad M., Arnedillo-Sánchez I., Vavoula G. (2008) 'Mobile Learning: Small devices, Big Issues'. In Balacheff, N., Ludvigsen, S., de Jong, T., Lazonder, A., Barnes, S. and Montandon, L. (eds.) *Technology enhanced learning: Principles and products*. Kaleidoscope Legacy Book. Berlin, Springer. Available at: http://www.lsri.nottingham.ac.uk/msh/Papers/KAL_Legacy_Mobile_Learning_SUBMITTED.pdf

This chapter addresses definitional questions around mobile learning and how it can be designed and evaluated. The authors offer a first outline of a theory of mobile learning.

van't Hooft, M. and Vahey, P. (eds.) *Educational technology XLVII(3). Special issue: Highly mobile computing*. Available at: http://asianvu.com/bookstoread/etp/Educational_Technology_May_June_2007.pdf

A collection of papers from the US and the UK intended to provide an introduction to mobile devices.

Chapter 3. Mobile Devices as Resources for Learning: Characteristics, Functions and Constraints

The Horizon Project, http://horizon.nmc.org/wiki/Main_Page.

This space is a place for the members of the Horizon Project Advisory Board to manage the process of selecting the topics for their Horizon Reports, which are co-published by the New Media Consortium (NMC) and the EDUCAUSE Learning Initiative (ELI). We recommend the following three reports from this workspace:

- The Horizon Report (2008). New Media Consortium and EDUCAUSE.
- The Horizon Report (2009). New Media Consortium and EDUCAUSE.
- The Horizon Report (2009). K-12 Edition. New Media Consortium and EDUCAUSE.

The reports introduce six emerging technologies or practices that are likely to enter mainstream use in learning-focused organizations within three adoption horizons over the next one to five years.

Ofcom, *or Office of Communication, is the independent regulator and competition authority for the UK communications industries. Ofcom's statutory duties, as set down in the Communications Act 2003, are: "3(1) It shall be the principal duty of Ofcom, in carrying out their functions; (a) to further the interests of citizens in relation to communications matters; and (b) to further the interests of consumers in relevant markets, where appropriate by promoting competition". Ofcom has responsibilities across television, radio, telecommunications and wireless communications services.* http://www.ofcom.org.uk/. *We recommend in particular the following five Ofcom reports:*

- Ofcom (2008a) Media literacy audit – Report on UK children's media literacy.
- Ofcom (2008b) Mobile citizens, mobile consumers.
- Ofcom (2008c) Media literacy audit: Media literacy of UK adults from ethnic minority groups.
- Ofcom (2008d) Annex 3: Media literacy audit. Report on UK adults by platform.
- Ofcom (2008e) Social networking: A quantitative and qualitative research report into attitudes, behaviours and use.

Patten, B., Sánchez, I.-A. and Tangney, B. (2006) 'Designing collaborative, constructionist and contextual applications for handheld devices.' In *Computers & Education 46*, pp. 294–308

This paper examines applications for handheld devices and their use of the attributes of handheld devices in order to facilitate learning on the basis of a functional framework, which makes reference to pedagogical underpinnings.

Price, S. (2007) 'Ubiquitous computing: Digital augmentation and learning.' In: Pachler, N. (ed) *Mobile learning: Towards a research agenda.* WLE Centre, Institute of Education, London, pp. 33–54. Available at: http://www.wlecentre.ac.uk/cms/files/occasionalpapers/mobilelearning_pachler_2007.pdf

This chapter presents an overview of digital augmentation; it illustrates the use of augmentation for learning by offering examples from research and makes some recommendations for future research.

Shuler, C. (2009) *Pockets of potential: Using mobile technologies to promote children's learning,* New York: The Joan Ganz Cooney Center at Sesame Workshop. Available: http://www.joanganzcooneycenter.org/pdf/pockets_of_potential.pdf,

This study argues that just as Sesame Street transformed television into a revolutionary learning tool for preschoolers, mobile learning technology may represent the next frontier. The report includes an inventory of over 25 examples of mobile learning.

Chapter 4. Cases of Mobile Learning

Faux, F.; McFarlane, A.; Roche, N.; Facer, K. (2006) *Handhelds: Learning with handheld technologies: Futurelab handbook.* Bristol: Futurelab. Available at: http://www.futurelab.org.uk/resources/documents/handbooks/handhelds_handbook.pdf

This report provides a comprehensive overview of mobile learning projects and describes aims, settings and activities. The underlying theories concentrate on self-responsible and collaborative learning, as well as an approach that focuses on technologies and content distribution.

Hartnell-Young, E. and Heym, N. (2008) *How mobile/cell phones help learning in secondary schools. A report to Becta.* Available at: http://schools.becta.org.uk/upload-dir/downloads/page_documents/research/ lsri_report.pdf

This project report to BECTA focuses on three different settings of mobile learning in schools: (a) use of own mobile/cell phones (24/7), (b) use of own sim cards in unlocked mobile/cell phones (24/7) and (c) unlocked smart phones with sim cards used for less than one day. A central result is that mobile/cell phones were used for specific tasks and in specific situations if it was considered by teachers and pupils to be appropriate and pragmatic only.

Jacucci, G., Oulasvirta, A. and Salovaara, A. (2007) 'Active construction of experience through mobile media: A field study with implications for recording and sharing.' In *Personal and Ubiquitous Computing 11(4)*, pp. 215–234. Also available at: http://www.cs.helsinki.fi/u/oulasvir/scipubs/jacucci-etal_revised_print.pdf

This paper reports an ethnographic study on spectators using mobile/cell phones to record and share experiences at a FIA World Rally Championship in Finland. The analysis focuses on the role of technology-mediated memories in the construction of experiences.

Naismith, L.; Lonsdale, P.; Vavoula, G.; Sharples, M. (2004) *Literature Review in Mobile Technologies and Learning: Report 11*. Bristol: Futurelab. Available at: http://www.futurelab.org.uk/resources/documents/lit_reviews/Mobile_Review.pdf

This literature review provides an overview of different learning theories with relevance for mobile learning, with focus on behaviourist, constructivist, situated, collaborative, informal and lifelong learning theories, and considering context, mobility, learning over time, informality and ownership.

Roschelle, J. and Pea, R. (2002) 'A walk on the WILD side: How wireless handhelds may change computer-supported collaborative learning.' In *International Journal of Cognition and Technology 1(1)*, pp. 145–168. Also available at: http://ctl.sri.com/publications/downloads/WalkWildSide.pdf

Drawing upon research across a range of handheld projects, the authors suggest application-level affordances of wireless internet learning devices, namely (a) augmenting physical space, (b) leveraging topological space, (c) aggregating coherently across all students, (d) conducting the class, and (e) act becomes artefact.

Stald, G. (2008) 'Mobile identity: Youth, identity, and mobile communication media'. In Buckingham, D. (ed) (2008) *Youth, identity, and digital media*. Cambridge, MA MIT Press, pp. 143–164. Available at: http://www.mitpressjournals.org/doi/pdf/10.1162/dmal.9780262524834.143

Based on research with 15–24 year-old Danes, this chapter discussed the meaning of the mobile/cell phone in young people's lives, specifically in relation to questions of identity.

Uden, L. (2007) 'Activity theory for designing mobile learning'. In: *International Journal for Mobile Learning and Organisation 1(1)*, pp. 81–102.

In order to analyse relationships, which are constructed during learning processes with mobile devices, the author proposes to use Activity Theory as describing and analytical tool.

Chapter 5. Towards a Cultural Ecology

Kress, G. and Pachler, N. (2007) 'Thinking about the 'm' in m-learning.' In: Pachler, N. (ed) *Mobile learning: Towards a research agenda*. WLE Centre, Institute of Education, London, pp. 7–32. Available at: http://www.wlecentre.ac.uk/cms/files/occasionalpapers/mobilelearning_pachler_2007.pdf

This chapter discusses the centrality and nature of learning in relation to contemporary socio-cultural and neo-liberal political trends, such as individualised risk and the commodification of education, with particular reference to mobile devices. Characteristics and potential of digital technologies are also discussed.

Laurillard, D. (2007) 'Pedagogical forms of mobile learning: Framing research questions.' In: Pachler, N. (ed) *Mobile learning: Towards a research agenda.* WLE Centre, Institute of Education, London, pp. 153–176. Available at: http://www.wlecentre.ac.uk/cms/files/occasionalpapers/mobilelearning_pachler_2007.pdf

This chapter discussed the Conversational Framework in relation to learning with mobile technologies and in informal contexts.

Sharples, M., Taylor, J. and Vavoula, G. (2007) 'A theory of learning for the mobile age.' In. Andrews, R. and Haythornthwaite, C. (eds.) *The SAGE Handbook of e-learning research.* London: Sage, pp. 221–24. Also available at: http://www.lsri.nottingham.ac.uk/msh/Papers/Theory%20of%20Mobile%20Learning.pdf

This chapter sets out a theory of mobile learning based on Activity Theory and the Conversational Framework.

Wali, E., Winters, N. and Oliver, M. (2008) 'Maintaining, changing and crossing contexts: An activity theoretic reinterpretation of mobile learning.' In *ALT-J 16(1)*, pp. 41–57

This paper critically discusses Sharples et al's 2007 theory of learning in a mobile age with particular reference to Activity Theory.

Zhao, Y. and Frank, K. (2003) 'Factors affecting technology uses in schools: An ecological perspective.' In *American Educational Research Journal 40(4)*, pp. 807–840. Also available at: http://www.msu.edu/~kenfrank/papers/Factors%20affecting%20technology%20uses%20in%20schools.pdf

This paper uses the ecological metaphor with reference to the introduction of the zebra mussel into the Great Lakes to analyse technology use in schools and to identify factors affecting it.

Part II: Mobile Devices as Resources for Learning: A Socio-Cultural Ecological Analysis of the Mobile Complex

Ball, S. (2003) 'The Risks of Social Reproduction: The middle class and education markets.' In: *London Review of Education 1(3)*, pp. 163–175.

Stephen Ball is one of the few scholars in the UK who draw on the approach of 'risk' that was introduced by the German sociologist Ulrich Beck and combines that with the concept of social distinction and habitus by Pierre Bourdieu. By explaining education as a market, Ball refers to the notion of lifestyle and consumption that is usually underlying studies on social segmentation.

Bereiter, C. and Scardamelia, M. (1993) *Surpassing ourselves. An Inquiry into the nature and implications of expertise.* Open Court: Chicaco and La Salle, Illinois

"Surpassing ourselves" explores the function of knowledge in a society characterised by individualised life worlds. Within the context of life-world segmentation, the development of knowledge is no longer determined by the standardised school curriculum but the individual competence of experts within their restricted life-worlds. To find and recognise "the hidden knowledge of experts" (p. 46ff.) is an important task of integrating informal learning into curricularized school learning.

Conway, S. (1997) 'The reproduction of exclusion and disadvantage: Symbolic violence and social class inequalities in 'Parental Choice' of Secondary Education.' In: *Sociological Research Online 2(4).* Available at: http://www.socresonline.org.uk/socresonline/2/4/4.html

The paper argues that entrance to education, paths and decisions within education and school achievement is related to social class and cultural capital, thus reproduces social inequalities. It concludes that middle class in Britain struggles to maintain social positions but people also have the resources to climb upwards in society, other than working class that seems very hesitant, traditional, without the necessary resources for social mobility.

Giddens, A. (1984) *The constitution of society: Outline of the theory of structuration.* University of California Press

The first chapter of the sociology of the constitution of a society offers a model for the interrelationship of social structures and the agency of the people, who act on different levels of consciousness within structures and for transforming structures. The "stratification model of the action ... involves treating the reflexive monitoring, rationalization and motivation of action as embedded sets of processes" (p. 3). Broadly speaking, agency is the reflexive monitoring capacity in the continuous process of action (p. 9), which takes place within structures ("rules and resources", p. 25) within a system ("reproduced relations between actors or collectives, organized as regular social practices", p 25) and its "conditions governing the continuity or transmutation of structures" (p 25). The "conditions governing the continuity or transmutation of structures, and therefore the reproduction of the social systems", is covered by the term 'structuration'.

Hall, S. (1980) 'Encoding/Decoding'. In: Hall, S. et al. (eds.): *Culture, media, language*. London: Hutchinson: pp. 128–139.

Hall, S. (ed.) (1997) *Representation. Cultural representations and signifying practices*. London: Sage

Stuart Hall, the key protagonist in the field of Cultural Studies, integrated the notion of "cultural practices" as constitutive for meaning into media studies, firstly by opening in the 1980 the transport model of media to "signifying practices". The production of media as well as their usage depends on encoding and decoding activities within or by cultural practices (1980, p. 130; 1997, p. 36). Within cultural practices he described "modes of reading" or positions of reading, which are the "dominant-hegemonic position", "negotiated position" and "oppositional position" (1980, p. 136). In the tradition of Cultural Studies the interrelationship of (a) social structures, (b) the "conditions governing the continuity or transmutation of structures", structuration, and (c) the reflexive capacity of the media user were considered by means of Giddens' stucturation model, to which Hall contributed the operazionalization of signifying practices (e.g. modes of reading) and cultural practices of media use.

Kress, G. (2008) 'New literacies, new democracies'. A challenge paper. Available online at: http://www.beyondcurrenthorizons.org.uk/wp-content/uploads/bch_challenge_paper_democracies_gunther_kress.pdf *Retrieved 26 March 2009.*

This paper discusses the contemporary changes in representation and communication as part of broader social, economic and political transformations, and relates them to education.

Kress, G. and van Leeuwen, T. (1996, 2006) *Reading images. The grammar of visual design*. Routledge, London

This book introduces the multimodal analysis framework to visual representations from a social semiotic perspective, including the notion of affordances as conceived in social semiotics.

Lave, J. and Wenger, E. (1991) *Situated learning: Legitimate peripheral participation*. Cambridge (Cambridge University Press)

A central idea of "situated learning" comes from the semiotic emphasis that meaning results not only from the interrelation of signs and the user of signs but it depends constitutively on situations. A second leading idea is that learning is a form of meaning-making. The standardised situation of instruction in schools veils the situatedness of learning as meaning-making. The constitutive dependence of learning as meaning-making to situations determines the educational and curricular options for integrating media and use-generated contexts into a curriculum.

Luckin, R., Clark, W., Garnett, F., Whitworth, A., Akass, J., Cook, J., Day, P., Ecclesfield, N., Hamilton, T. and Robertson, J. (2009) *Learner generated contexts: a framework tosupport the effective use of technology to support learning*. In Lee, M. & McLoughlin, C. (eds.) *Web 2.0-based e-learning: applying social informatics for tertiary teaching.* Hershey, PA: IGI Global

The approach of this curricular research group is to integrate the culturally new notion of user-generated contexts in curriculum-based formal learning. The focus is on technologically enhanced contexts for learning.

Pachler, N., Cook, J. and Bachmair, B. (2010) 'Appropriation of 'mobile' cultural resources for learning.' In *Journal of Mobile and Blended Learning*

This paper discusses appropriation of mobile cultural resources, which are viewed as social, cultural and media-related practices and structures attendant to the use of mobile devices.

Scardamalia, M., Bereiter, C. (1999) 'Schools as knowledge-building organizations'. In: Keating, D. and Hertzman, C. (eds.): *Today's children, tomorrow's society: The developmental health and wealth of nations*. New York: Guilford, pp. 274–289

The focus of the model of collaborative knowledge-building is on changing teacher-driven instruction to cooperative forms of project work with learning as a development of knowledge. Knowledge is not focussed on the hic et nunc, but is to be integrated into the real world. The basic idea of collaboration is informed by the model of co-operative work of an academic scientific community.

Vygotsky, L. (1978/1930) *Mind in society. The development of higher psychological processes.* Edited by M. Cole et al., Cambridge, MA. Harvard University Press

Vygotsky, L. (1986/ 1934) *Thought and language.* Edited by A. Kozulin, Cambridge, MA. MIT Press

Vygotsky worked on a model to relate the development of children and young people to curricular learning in school. Vygotsky saw children developing on the basis of the assimilation of the concepts of adults, that means the assimilation of the outside world (1986/1934, p. 154f.). But he criticised intensively the dominance of the learning object for school learning. Vygotsky proposed "that an essential feature of learning is that it creates the zone of proximal development; that is, learning awakens a variety of internal developmental processes that are able to operate only when the child is interaction with people in his environment and in cooperation with his peers. Once these processes are internalized, they become part of the child's independent developmental achievement." "Zone" can be seen in the traditional categories of child development as developmental phase or in situational categories as a specific context. The central task of a teacher is to understand "how external knowledge" are "internalized" and assimilated by the children with their "abilities" (1978/1930, p. 91). This internalization will be successful if a teacher offers the external knowledge within "zone of proximal development" (1978/1930, pp. 84ff.) of children or young people. This conceptual approach bringing together child development and curricular learning by a context, the zone of proximal development, offers scope for the theoretical integration of teaching, learning, and development with the culturally new user-generated and mediated contexts.

Part III: Perspectives for Mobile Learning: Infrastructures, Emerging Technologies and Application in Practice

Chapter 14. Emerging Technologies and Attendant Practices

Bryant, L. (2007) 'Emerging trends in social software for education.' In Becta *Emerging technologies for learning 2*, pp. 9–27. Available at: http://partners.becta.org.uk/page_documents/research/emerging_technologies07_chapter1.pdf

This discussion of social software tools is interesting inter alia for its reference to Jyri Engeström's notion of 'object-based sociality', i.e. social networking and discussion centred around shared objects (photos, videos, music, etc.) rather than just being 'about' people.

Fisher, G. and Konomi, S. (2007) 'Innovative socio-technical environments in support of distributed intelligence and lifelong learning. In *Journal of Computer Assisted Learning 23*, pp. 338–350

This paper discusses how wireless and mobile technologies can change conceptual frameworks such as the relationship between planning and situated action, context awareness, human attention, distances in collaborative design activities, and the trade-off between tools for living and tools for learning. The paper also offers examples from mobile technologies-related research projects, which focus on moving 'computing off the desktop' by 'going small, large, and everywhere'.

Greenfield, A. (2008) 'Location-based and context-aware education: Prospects and perils.' In Becta *Emerging technologies for learning 3*, pp. 47–57. Available at: http://partners.becta.org.uk/upload-dir/downloads/page_documents/research/emerging_technologies08_chapter3.pdf

This paper discusses some of the potential issues and pitfalls around implementation and reliance on location- and context-aware systems and their application in education.

Haller, M. (2008) 'Interactive displays and next-generation interfaces.' In Becta *Emerging technologies for learning 3*, pp. 91–101. Available at: http://partners.becta.org.uk/upload-dir/downloads/page_documents/research/emerging_technologies08_chapter6.pdf

This paper explores the potential of some emerging display and interface technologies to improve interaction with computers and facilitate collaborative activities in more natural and intuitive ways

Chapter 15. Visions and Suspicions

Bruce, B. (2008) 'Ubiquitous learning, ubiquitous computing, and lived experience.' Paper presented at Symposium 'Making the Transition to Ubiquitous Learning'. *Networked learning conference,* May, Greece. Available at: http://www.networkedlearningconference.org.uk/abstracts/PDFs/Bruce_583-590.pdf

Bruce notes that "education would certainly be easier to promote if we could simply identify some new technologies that would make ubiquitous learning occur. But the new technologies are neither necessary nor sufficient for this to happen". He argues that it is our vision for ubiquitous learning that matters most, not simply the technical affordances: "We need to define ubiquitous learning in an historically legitimate way, one which recognizes the possibilities afforded by the new technologies without reducing the argument to a technocentric position."

Cuban, L. (2001) Oversold and underused. Harvard University Press. Available at: https://www.hull.ac.uk/php/edskas/Cuban%20article%20-%20oversold.pdf

Cuban argues that computers can be useful when teachers sufficiently understand the technology themselves, believe it will enhance learning, and have the power to shape their own curricula. He posits that these conditions can't be met without a broader and deeper commitment to public education and needs to be paid to the civic and social goals of schooling.

Kress, G. (2005) 'Gains and losses: New forms of texts, knowledge, and learning.' In *Computers and Composition 22*, pp. 5–22

This paper looks at what might be gained and what might be lost as we move from representation primarily through writing to representation primarily though image. In so doing, the paper also considers issues related to learning, knowledge, and human agenc

References

Adami, E. (2009) 'Do YouTube? When Communication Turns into Video Enteraction.' In Toretta, D. (ed.) *Forms of migration – migrations of forms*. Atti del XXIII. Convegno Nazonale A/A. Progedit: Bari.

Albrechtslund, A. (2008) 'Online social networking as participatory surveillance.' In *First Monday 13*(3). Available at: http://www.uic.edu/htbin/cgiwrap/bin/ojs/index.php/fm/article/view/2142/1949

Alfred-Teves-Schule (2008) 'Schulwebseiten der Grund- und Hauptschule Alfred-Teves-Schule, Gifhorn.' Gewaltprävention - Die Medien AG der Alfred-Teves-Schule.' Available at: http://www.alfred-teves-schule.de/schulwebseiten/de/Medien-AG/index.php

Ally, M. (ed.) (2009) *Mobile learning. Transforming the delivery of education and training*. Edmonton, AB: AU Press, Athabasca University. Also available at: http://www.aupress.ca/books/120155/ebook/99Z_Mohamed_Ally_2009-MobileLearning.pdf.

Appadurai, A. (1996) *Modernity at large: Cultural dimensions of globalisation*. Minneapolis: University of Minnesota Press.

Arnedillo-Sánchez, I., Sharples, M. and Vavoula, G. (eds.) (2007) *Beyond mobile learning workshop. The CSCL Alpine Rendez-Vous*. Switzerland: Trinity College Dublin Press, pp. 43–53. Available at: http://www.ell.aau.dk/fileadmin/user_upload/documents/research/kaleidoscope/Alpine_rendez_vous/CSCLAlpineRDV2007Report.pdf

Arnseth, H. C. (2008) 'Activity theory and situated learning theory: Contrasting views of educational practice.' In *Pedagogy, Culture & Society 16*(*3*), pp. 289–302.

Ashley (2007) 'sony dcr-hc23 Laufwerksgeräusche, Normal???' Available at: http://www.slashcam.de/info/sony-dcr-hc23-Laufwerksgeraeusche—Normal—194459.html

Attewell, J. (2005) *Mobile technologies and learning A technology update and m-learning project summary*. LSDA. Available from: http://www.m-learning.org/docs/The%20m-learning%20project%20-%20technology%20update%20and%20project%20summary.pdf

Augsburger Allgemeine Zeitung (2007) 'Handy-Videos: Jugendliche stellen Augsburger Obdachlose im Internet bloß.' Available at: http://www.augsburger-allgemeine.de/Home/Lokales/Region/Artikel,-Jugendliche-stellen-Augsburger-Obdachlose-im-Internet-bloss-_arid,1028623_regid,2_puid,2_pageid,4634.html

Avis, J. (2009) 'Transformation of transformism: Engeström's version of activity theory?' In *Educational Review 61*(*2*), pp. 151–165.

Bachmair, B. (1986) 'Auto und Fernsehen - Objekte der Begierde. Kulturhistorische Gedanken zur Technologisierung von Mobilität und Kommunikation.' In *Pädagogik heute* (*7–8*), pp. 4–11. Available at: https://kobra.bibliothek.uni-kassel.de/bitstream/urn:nbn:de:hebis:34-2009010725597/1/BachmairAutoUndFernsehen.pdf.

Bachmair, B. (1991) 'From the motor car to the television. Cultural-historical arguments on the meaning of mobility for communication.' In *Media, Culture & Society 13*(*521–533*). doi: 10.1177/016344391013004006.

Bachmair, B. (1997) 'Ein Kinderzimmer als Text.' In *Medien Impulse* (2), pp. 59–62. Available at: https://kobra.bibliothek.uni-kassel.de/bitstream/urn:nbn:de:hebis:34-2009061028177/1/BachmairKinderzimmerAlsText.pdf.

Bachmair, B. (1999) 'Ein Kinderzimmer als Text. Bedeutungskonstitution als kulturelle Aktivität der Rezipienten.' In Neuß, N. (ed.), *Ästhetik der Kinder. Interdisziplinäre Beiträge zur ästhetischen Erfahrung von Kindern, Beiträge zur Medienpädagogik. Vol. 5.* Frankfurt: Gemeinschaftswerk der evangelischen Publizistik, pp. 189–203. Available at: https://kobra.bibliothek.uni-kassel.de/bitstream/urn:nbn:de:hebis:34-2009060328068/1/BachmairKinderzimmer.pdf.

Bachmair, B. (2006) 'Communicative modes after the coherent media – orientation within a semiotic space.' In *MedienPädagogik*. Available at: http://www.medienpaed.com/06-1/ bachmair1.pdf.

Bakardjieva, M. (2005) *Internet society.' The internet in everyday life*. London: SAGE Publications.

Bakhurst, D. (2009) 'Reflections on activity theory.' In *Educational Review 61*(2), pp. 197–210.

Barab, S. (2002) 'Human-field interaction as mediated by mobile computers.' In Koschmann, T., Hall, R. And Miyake, N. (eds.) *CSCL2. Carrying forward the conversation*. Mahwah, NJ: Erlbaum, pp. 533–537.

Barab, S., Cherkes-Julkowski, M., Swenson, R., Garrett, S., Shaw, R. and Youg, M. (1999) 'Principles of self-organization: Learning as participation in autocatakinetic systems.' In *The Journal of the Learning Sciences 8(3&4)*, pp. 349–390. Also available at: http://inkido.indiana.edu/research/onlinemanu/papers/selforg.pdf.

Barz, H. (2000) Weiterbildung und soziale Milieus. Ziel

Barz, H. and Tippelt, R. (2004) *Weiterbildung und soziale Milieus in Deutschland. Praxishandbuch Milieumarketing*. Bielefeld: Bertelsmann (DIE spezial, 1).

Bateson, G. (1972) *Steps to an ecology of mind*. Chicago: University of Chicago Press.

Bauer Media, K. G. (ed.) (2004) 'BRAVO Faktor Jugend 7: Marken und Trends.' Available at: http://www.bauermedia.com/fileadmin/user_upload/pdf/studien/zielgruppe/jugend/jugend7.pdf

Bauer Media, K. G. (ed.) (2007) 'BRAVO.de Trend-Barometer Gaming.' Available at: http://www.bauermedia.com/fileadmin/user_upload/pdf/studien/zielgruppe/jugend/Trendbarometer_Gaming_10.09.07.pdf

Baumann, Z. (2000) *Liquid modernity*. Cambridge: Blackwell.

Baur, N. and Lamnek, S. (2005) 'Einzelfallanalyse.' In Mikos, L., Wegener, C. (eds.) *Qualitative Medienforschung. Ein Handbuch*. Konstanz: UVK Verlagsgesellschaft (UTB Medien- und Kommunikationswissenschaft, Pädagogik, Psychologie, Soziologie), pp. 241–252.

Beale, R. (2007a) 'How to enhance the experience without interfering with it?' In Sharples, M. (ed.) *Big issues in mobile learning. Report of a workshop by the Kaleidoscope Network of Excellence in Mobile Learning Initiative*. Nottingham: Learning Sciences Research Institute, University of Nottingham, pp. 12–16. Available at: http://www.lsri.nottingham.ac.uk/Publications_PDFs/BIG_ISSUES_REPORT_PUBLISHED.pdf.

Beale, R. (2007b) 'Ubiquitous learning or learn how to learn and you'll never have to learn anything again?' In Arnedillo-Sánchez, I., Sharples, M., and Vavoula, G. (eds.) *Beyond mobile learning: Workshop: The CSCL Alpine Rendez-Vous*, pp. 64–65. Available at: http://mlearning.noe-kaleidoscope.org/repository/Beyond%20Mobile%20Learning%20Book%20Proceedings%2011.1.07.pdf.

Beck, U. (1986) *Risikogesellschaft. Auf dem Weg in eine andere Moderne*. Frankfurt a. M.: Suhrkamp. (1992): *Risk society: towards a new modernity*. Translated by Mark Ritter. London: Sage

Becta (2007) *Harnessing Technology Review 2007: Progress and impact of technology in education*. Coventry. Available at: http://partners.becta.org.uk/upload-dir/downloads/page_documents/ research/harnessing_technology_review07.pdf

Becta (2008a) KS3 and KS4 learners' use of Web 2.0 technologies in and out of school – Summary. Available at: http://partners.becta.org.uk/upload-dir/downloads/page_documents/research/web2_technologies_ks3_4_summary.doc

Becta (2008b). TechNews. September, Coventy. http://partners.becta.org.uk/upload-dir/downloads/page_documents/research/technews/sep08.pdf

Becta (2008c). KS3 and KS4 learners' use of Web 2.0 technologies in and out of school – Summary. http://partners.becta.org.uk/upload-dir/downloads/page_documents/research/web2_technologies_ks3_4_summary.doc

Bereiter, C. and Scardamalia, M. (1996) 'Rethinking learning.' In Olson, D. and Torrance, N. (eds.) *The handbook of education and human development: New models of learning, teaching and schooling*. Cambridge, MA: Basil Blackwell, pp. 485–513.

Bereiter, C. and Scardamelia, M. (1993) *Surpassing ourselves. An inquiry into the nature and implications of expertise*. Open Court, Chicaco and La Salle, Illinois, US

Berger, P. and Luckmann, T. (1966) *The social construction of reality. A treatise in the sociology of knowledge*. Harmondsworth, Baltimore: Penguin Books.

Bernstein, B. (1996/2000) *Pedagogy, symbolic control and identity. Theory, research, critique*. Lanham, MD: Rowman Littlefield Publisher. First edition 1996 by Taylor & Francis.

Bernstein, B. and Henderson, D. (1973) 'Social class differences in the relevance of language to socialization.' In Bernstein, B. (ed.) *Class, codes and control. Volume 2. Applied studies towards a sociology of languages*. London and Boston: Routledge & Kegan Paul, pp. 24–47.

Berson, I. and Berson, M. (2007) 'Ubiquitous mobile/cell phone technology and youth: Cross-national findings.' In van't Hooft, M. and Swan, K. (eds.) *Ubiquitous computing in education. Invisible technology, visible impact*.Mahwah, NJ: Lawrence Erlbaum, pp. 287–301.

Bezemer, J. and Kress, G. (2008). 'Writing in multimodal texts: A social semiotic account of designs for learning.' In *Written Communication 25*, pp. 166–95.

bimbofighter (2006) 'Szenenwechsel.' Available at: http://www.psd-tutorials.de/modules/Forum/68_flash-allgemein/15782-szenenwechsel.html

bimbofighter (2007a) 'After Effects Fuß finden.' Available at: http://www.slashcam.de/info/After-Effects-Fuss-finden-194772.html

bimbofighter (2007b) 'Mein Video.' Available at: http://www.pcwelt.de/forum/1272119-post1.html

bimbofighter (2008) 'Profile.' Available at: http://www.timeshot.de/profile.php?mode=viewprofile&u=6499

Biocca, F., Harms, C. and Burgoon, J. (2003) 'Towards a more robust theory and measure of social presence: Review and suggested criteria.' In *Presence 12(5)*, pp. 456–480.

Blumler, J. and Katz, E. (1974) *The uses of mass communication. Current perspectives on gratifications research*. Beverly Hills, CA: Sage.

Borgman, C., Abelson, H., Dirks, L., Johnson, R., Koedinger, K., Linn, M., Lynch, C., Oblinger, D., Pea, R., Salen, K., Smith, M. and Szalay, A. (2008) 'Fostering learning in the networked world: The cyberlearning opportunity and challenge. A 21st century agenda for the National Science Foundation.' Report of the NSF Task Force on Cyberlearning. Available at: http://www.nsf.gov/pubs/2008/nsf08204/nsf08204.pdf

Bourdieu, P. (1979) *La distinction. Critique social du jugement. Paris: Les éditions de minuit (1984) Distinction: A social critique of the judgement of taste*. London: Routledge.

Bovill, M. and Livingstone, S. (2001) 'Bedroom culture and the privatization of media use.' In Livingstone, S. and Bovill, M. (eds) *Children and their changing media environment. A European comparative study*. London: Lawrence Erlbaum, pp. 179–200.

Bradley, C., Haynes, R., Cook, J., Boyle, T. and Smith, C. (2009) 'Design and development of multimedia learning objects for mobile/cell phones.' In Mohamed, A. (ed.) *Mobile learning in education and training*. Athabasca: Athabasca University Press, pp. 157–82. Available at: http://www.aupress.ca/books/120155/ebook/99Z_Mohamed_Ally_2009-MobileLearning.pdf.

Bradley, C., Haynes, R., Smith, C., Cook, J. and Boyle, T. (2007) *Multimedia learning objects for mobiles*. Paper presented at 'Mobile Learning', 5–7 July 2007. Lisbon, Portugal.

Breck, J. (2007) 'Education's interwingled future.' In van't Hooft, M. and Vahey, P. (eds) *Educational technology XLVII(3). Special issue: Highly mobile computing*, pp. 50–54. Available at: http://asianvu.com/bookstoread/etp/Educational_Technology_May_June_2007.pdf.

Brown, J. and Adler, R. (2008) 'Minds on fire: Open education, the long tail and learning 2.0.' In *EDUCAUSE Review*, January/ February 2008, pp. 18–32. Available at: http://www.educause.edu/EDUCAUSE+Review/EDUCAUSEReviewMagazineVolume43/MindsonFireOpenEducationtheLon/162420

Brown, A. and Dowling, P. (1998) *Doing research/reading research.' A mode of interrogation for education*. London: RoutledgeFalmer.

Bruce, B. (2008) 'Ubiquitous learning, ubiquitous computing, and lived experience.' Paper presented at Symposium 'Making the Transition to Ubiquitous Learning'. Networked learning conference, May 2008, Greece. Available at: http://www.networkedlearningconference.org.uk/abstracts/PDFs/Bruce_583-590.pdf

Bruce, B. C. and Hogan, M. P. (1998) 'The Disappearance of Technology: Toward an Ecological Model of Literacy.' In Reinking, D., McKenna, M. C., Labbo,L. D., and Kieffer, R. D. (eds.) *Handbook of literacy and technology: Transformations in a post-typographic world*. London: Lawrence Erlbaum Associates, pp. 269–281. Available at: http://www.isrl.uiuc.edu/chip/pubs/disappearance.shtml.

Bruns, A. (2007) 'Beyond difference: Reconfiguring education for the user-led age.' Paper given at the *ICE3 conference*: *Digital difference*, Loch Lomond, March 23. Available at: http://produsage.org/files/Beyond%20Difference%20(ICE%203%202007).pdf

Buckingham, D. (2000) *After the death of childhood: Growing up in the age of electronic media*. New York: John Wiley.

Buckingham, D. (2006). Defining Digital Literacy: What young people need to know about digital media. Keynote presentation at Becta annual Research conference. Slides with voice over available at: http://events.becta.org.uk/display.cfm?cfid=1476190&cftoken=29154&resID=31991&page=1793&catID=1617and text from talk: http://about.becta.org.uk/content_files/corporate/resources/events/2006/november/david_buckingham.doc

Buckingham, D. and Scanlon, M. (2003) *Education, entertainment and learning in the home*. Buckingham: Open University Press.

Buckingham, D. and Willett, R. (eds.) (2006) *Digital generation. Children, young people and new media*. London: Erlbaum.

Bull, M. (2005) 'No dead air! The iPod and the culture of mobile listening.' In *Leisure Studies 24(4)*, pp. 343–355.

Bullying Online (2008) 'Bullying UK - Help us to support the UK's children.' Available at: http://bullying.co.uk/

cYRiLLPictures (2008) 'Profil - T-Shirts bedrucken und gestalten : Spreadshirt.' Available at: http://www.spreadshirt.net/de/DE/Community/Profil-2752/User/Profile/show/id/1194379

Castells, M. (2004) *The network society. A cross-cultural perspective*. Cheltenham: Elgar.

Center for Knowledge Societies (CKS) (2005a) 'Learning Lab: Inclusive Education using Mobile Devices. Paper presented on the International conference on inclusive design Royal College of Art, London, UK, 5–8 April 2005.' London.' Available at: http://www.hhc.rca.ac.uk/archive/hhrc/programmes/include/2005/proceedings/pdf/soodadityadev.pdf

Center for Knowledge Societies (CKS) (2005b) 'Learning Lab Initiative. Project report.' Available at: http://www.cks.in/html/cks_pdfs/learninglab_ppt.pdf

Center for Knowledge Societies (CKS) (2006) 'Ecology Building.' Learning Lab.' Available at: http://www.cks.in/html/ecology_htmls/cks_ecology_building01.html#section11

Chan, T.-W. (2007). AIED 2007 – Keynote. The Four Problems of Technology Enhanced Learning. Available at: http://www.g1on1.org/AIED2007updated%2011-30.ppt

channel unit – digitale Mediengesellschaft mbH (ed.) (2009) 'slashCAM Magazin.' Available at: http://www.slashcam.de

Charlton, M. and Bachmair, B. (1990) *Media communication in everyday life – interpretative studies on children's and young people's media actions*. München, New York: Saur Verlag. Available at: https://kobra.bibliothek.uni-kassel.de/bitstream/urn:nbn:de:hebis:34-2007112219705/1/BachmairMediaCommunication.pdf.

Cole, M. (1996) *Cultural psychology: A once and future discipline*. Cambridge, MA: Harvard University Press.

Cook, J., Bradley, C., Lance, J., Smith, C. and Haynes, R. (2007) 'Generating learning contexts with mobile devices.' In Pachler, N. (ed.) *Mobile learning. Towards a research agenda*. London: WLE Centre, pp. 55–74.Available at: http://www.wlecentre.ac.uk/cms/files/occasionalpapers/mobilelearning_pachler_2007.pdf. Occasional Papers in Work-based Learning, Volume 1.

Cook, J. and Light, A. (2006). New Patterns of Power and Participation? Designing ICT for Informal and Community Learning. *E-Learning*. Special Issue of ICE2 Symposium, 3(1), 51–61. Available: http://www.wwwords.co.uk/elea/content/pdfs/3/issue3_1.asp or final draft: http://homepages.north.londonmet.ac.uk/~cookj/top_files/e-learning_JC_AL_final_draft.doc

Cook, J. and Pachler, N. (2010). 'Appropriation of mobile/cell phones in and across formal and informal learning.' In Land, R. and Bayne, S. (eds.) *Digital difference*. Rotterdam: Sense Publishers.

Cook, J., Pachler, N. and Bradley, C. (2008a) 'Bridging the gap? Mobile/cell phones at the interface between informal and formal learning.' In *Journal of the Research Centre for Educational Technology. Special Issue on Learning While Mobile*. Spring. Available at: http://www.rcetj.org/?type=art&id=87827&.

Cook, J., Pachler, N. and Bradley, C. (2008b) 'Towards m-maturity: The nature and role of appropriation in mobile learning.' Paper at *mLearn 2008*. Ironbridge Gorge World Heritage Site, Shropshire, UK

Cook, J. and Smith, M. (2004). 'Beyond formal learning: Informal community eLearning.' In *Computer Education 43*, pp. 35–47.

Cook, J. and Smith, C. (2007) *Building Learning for the Future: Any Time, Anyplace*. Invited talk, Google, Belgrave House, 76 Buckingham Palace Road, London, 27 November

Cooper, G. (2002) 'The mutable world: Social theory in the wireless world.' In Brown, B., Green, N. and Harper, R. (eds.) *Wireless world: Social and interactional aspects of the mobile world*. New York: Springer, pp. 19–31.

Crook, C. and Harrison, C. (2008) Web 2.0 technologies for learning at Key Stages 3 and 4: A summary report. Coventry: Becta. Available at: http://schools.becta.org.uk/upload-dir/downloads/page_documents/research/web2_ks34_summary.pdf

Crystal, D. (2008) *Txtng: The gr8db8*. Capital Books

Cuban, L. (2001) *Oversold and underused. Computers in the classroom*. Cambridge, MA: Harvard University Press.

Dale, E. (1969) *Audiovisual methods in teaching*. 3rd edition. New York: Dryden Press.

Dannhardt, K. and Nowak, D. (2007). *Sinus-Milieus. Lebensstil, Fernsehnutzung und Umgang mit neuer Kommunikationstechnologie*. (SevenOne Media GmbH & Sinus Sociovision GmbH, Eds.). Unterföhring: SevenOne Media. Available at: http://appz. sevenonemedia.de/download/publikationen/Sinus_2007.pdf

Davies, G. (1997) 'Lessons from the past, lessons for the future: 20 years of CALL.' In Korsvold, A.-K. and Rüschoff, B. (eds.) *New technologies in language learning and teaching*. Strasbourg: Council of Europe. Available at: http://www.camsoftpartners.co.uk/coegdd1.htm.

Davies, C. (2008) 'Views of young people.' In Theorising the benefits of new technology for youth: Controversies of learning and development. The educational and social impact of new technologies on young people in Britain. Report of the seminar held on Wednesday 12 March, Department of Education, University of Oxford. ESRC. Available at: http://www.education.ox.ac.uk/esrcseries/uploaded/08_0314%20ESRC%20report_final_HR.pdf

Dehm, U. and Storll, D. (2003) 'TV-Erlebnisfaktoren. Ein ganzheitlicher Forschungsansatz zur Rezeption unterhaltender und informierender Fernsehangebote' In *Media Perspektiven 9*, pp. 425–433.

Dehm, U., Storll, D. and Beeske, S. (2004). 'TV-Erlebnistypen und ihre Charakteristika. Das heterogene Fernsehpublikum und seine Erlebnisweisen.' In *Media Perspektiven 5*, pp. 217–225.

Dehm, U., Storll, D. and Beeske, S. (2006). 'Das Internet: Erlebnisweisen und Erlebnistypen.' In *Media Perspektiven 2*, pp 91–101.

Deubelbeiss, R. (2007a) 'Das Handy an der NET. Verbote, Gebote, Lifestyle, Jugendkultur, Lernhilfe...? Begleitbrief an Eltern. Nationale Elitesportschule Thurgau.' Available at: http://metaportfolio-phsg.kaywa.ch/files/Das%20Handy%20an%20der%20NET%20Begleitbrief.pdf

Deubelbeiss, R. (2007b) 'Rahmenbedingungen Projekt "Handy".' Available at: http://metaportfolio-phsg.kaywa.ch/

Deubelbeiss, R. (ed.) (2007c) 'Beispiel-Sammlung - Weg-Zeit-Diagramm (Fabian, 3. Sek.).' Available at: http://metaportfolio-phsg.kaywa.ch/mathematik/weg-zeit-diagramm-fabian-3-sek.html

Deubelbeiss, R. (ed.) (2007d) 'Beispiel-Sammlung - Elfchen (Thamara, 1. Sek.).' Available at: http://metaportfolio-phsg.kaywa.ch/deutsch/elfchen-thamara-1-sek.html

Deubelbeiss, R. (ed.) (2007e) 'Beispiel-Sammlung - Satzglieder (Marco, 3. Sek.).' Available at: http://metaportfolio-phsg.kaywa.ch/deutsch/satzglieder-marco-3-sek.html

Deubelbeiss, R. (ed.) (2007f) 'Beispiel-Sammlung - Handy-Video zu Passé composé (Yannick, 2. Real und Marco, 2. Sek).' Available at: http://metaportfolio-phsg.kaywa.ch/franzoesisch/passe-compose-yannick-2-real.html

Deubelbeiss, R. (ed.) (2007g) 'Beispiel-Sammlung - M. est plus grand que... (Adi, 2. Sek.).' Available at: http://metaportfolio-phsg.kaywa.ch/franzoesisch/m-est-plus-grand-que-adi-2-sek.html

Deubelbeiss, R. (ed.) (2007h) 'Beispiel-Sammlung - Französisch: Objet (in)direct (von Ff, Praktikantin).' Available at: http://metaportfolio-phsg.kaywa.ch/franzoesisch/franzoesisch-objet-indirect-von-ff.html

Deubelbeiss, R. (ed.) (2007i) 'Beispiel-Sammlung - le comparatif (S2).' Available at: http://metaportfolio-phsg.kaywa.ch/franzoesisch/le-comparatif-s2.html

Dillenbourg, P. (2008) 'Integrating technologies into educational ecosystems.' In *Distance Education 29(2)*, pp. 127–140

direktindiefresse (2008a) 'Der Arbeitslosen-Channel.' YouTube - Kanal von direktindiefresse.' Available at: http://de.youtube.com/direktindiefresse

direktindiefresse (2008b) 'So ist das halt.' Available at: http://de.youtube.com/watch?v=9U4QRzJdRRk

direktindiefresse (2008c) 'Was ist 3 + 3 x 3 ?????' Available at: http://de.youtube.com/watch?v=YrzckZQ9hn4

Divitini, M. and Morken, E. (2007) 'Collaborative community-oriented mobile learning: A position statement.' In Arnedillo-Sánchez, I., Sharples, M. and Vavoula, G. (eds.) *Beyond mobile learning workshop. The CSCL Alpine Rendez-Vous*. Switzerland: Trinity College Dublin Press, pp. 12–15. Available at: http://www.ell.aau.dk/fileadmin/user_upload/documents/research/kaleidoscope/Alpine_rendez_vous/CSCLAlpineRDV2007Report.pdf.

Dourish, P. (2004) 'What we talk about when we talk about context.' In *Personal and Ubiquitous Computing 8(1)*, pp. 19–30. Also available at: http://www.ics.uci.edu/~jpd/publications/2004/PUC2004-context.pdf.

Du Gay, P. (ed.) (1997) *Production of culture/cultures of production*. London: Open University.

Dunning, J. (ed.) (2000) *Regions, globalization, and the knowledge-based economy*. Oxford: Oxford University Press.

Eckert, R., Vogelgesang, W., Wetzstein, T. and Winter, R. (1991) *Grauen und Lust – die Inszenierung der Affekte. Eine Studie zum abweichenden Videokonsum*. Pfaffenweiler: Centaurus-Verlagsgesellschaft.

Elias, N. (1979) Über den Prozess der Zivilisation. Soziogenetische und psychogenetische Untersuchungen. Bd. 1: Wandlungen des Verhaltens in den weltlichen Oberschichten des Abendlandes. Bd. 2: Wandlungen der Gesellschaft. Entwurf einer Theorie der Zivilisation. Frankfurt a. M. (Suhrkamp) 1979, 6th edition, 1st edition 1937

Endzeit (2008) 'MySpace.com - Endzeit - 18 - Männlich - Augsburg, DE - www.myspace.com/cypictures.'; Available at: http://www.myspace.com/cypictures

Engeström, Y. (1987) *Learning by expanding an activity -theoretic approach to developmental research*. Helsinki: Orienta-Konsultit Oy.

Engeström, Y. (1993) 'Developmental studies on work as a test bench of ATs.' In Chaiklin, S. and Lave, J. (eds.) *Understanding practice: Perspectives on activity and context*. Cambridge: CUP, pp. 64–103.

Engeström, Y. (2001) 'Expansive learning at work: Toward an activity theoretical reconceptualisation.' In *Journal of Education and Work 14(1)*, pp. 133–56.

Engeström, Y. (2008) *From teams to knots: Activity-theoretic studies of collaboration and learning at work.* (*Learning in doing: Social, cognitive and computational perspectives*). New York: Cambridge University Press.

Engeström, Y., Engeström, R. and Vähäaho, T. (1999) 'When the center does not hold: The importance of knotworking.' In Chaiklin, S., Hedegaard, M. and Jensen, U. (eds.) *Activity theory and social practice: Cultural-historical approaches*. Aarhus: Aarhus University Press, pp. 345–374.

Ericsson. (2008) *What is IMS? Presentation by Ericsson Ireland team to the CONTSENS consortium meeting*. Varna, Bulgaria, September.

Faux, F., McFarlane, A., Roche, N. and Facer, K. (2006) *Handhelds: Learning with handheld technologies: Futurelab Handbook.* Bristol: Futurelab.

Featherstone, M. (2006) 'Archive.' In *Theory Culture and Society 23*(2), pp. 591–597.

Fensel, D. (2004) *Ontologies: A silver bullet for knowledge management and electronic commerce*. 2nd, revised and extended edition with a Foreword by Michael L. Brodie. Berlin: Springer.

Finck, N. (2001) 'Mathematik-8: Projekt "Handy".' Lernsituation / Projekt "Gebühren und Tarife".' Available at: http://members.aol.com/nfinckx/m8handy/m8handy.htm

Fisch, S. (2004) *Children's learning from educational television: Sesame street and beyond*. Mahwah, NJ: Lawrence Erlbaum Associates.

Fischer, G. and Konomi, S. (2007). 'Innovative socio-technical environments in support of distributed intelligence and lifelong learning.' In *Journal of Computer Assisted Learning 23*, pp. 338–50.

Fisher, T., Higgins, C. and Loveless, A. (2006) *Teachers learning with digital technologies: A review of research and projects*. Bristol. Available at: http://www.futurelab.org.uk/resources/documents/lit_reviews/Teachers_Review.pdf

Fisher, G. and Kanomi, S. (2007) 'Innovative socio-technical environments in support of distributed intelligence and lifelong learning.' *Journal of Computer Assisted Learning 23*, pp. 338–350.

Foucault, M. (1972) *The archeology of knowledge*. New York: Pantheon.

Freire, P. (2000) *Pedagogy of the oppressed*. New York: Continuum, Portuguese original 1970.

Friesen, N. (2006) 'Microlearning and (Micro)Didaktik.' In Hug, T., Lindner, M., and Bruck, P. (eds.) *Micromedia & e-learning 2.0: Gaining the big picture*. Proceedings of Microlearning Conference 2006. Innsbruck: Innsbruck University Press, pp. 41–61.

GQ.com (2008a) 'Visitenkarte - bimbofighter - Gentlemen's Club - Die GQ.community.' Available at: http://www.gq-magazin.de/profil/bimbofighter/62752

GQ.com (2008b) 'Bilder - bimbofighter - Gentlemen's Club - Die GQ.community.' Available at: http://www.gq-magazin.de/profil_image/bimbofighter/62752/0/0/0/

GQ.com (2008c) 'Stylefight - bimbofighter - Gentlemen's Club - Die GQ.community.' Available at: http://www.gq-magazin.de/profil_image_fight/bimbofighter/62752/0/0/0/

GQ.com (2008d) 'GQ.com Stilblog: Das Zeug zum Gentleman - Style Diary - Mode-Blog - Street Style » Blog Archiv » Style Diary: Cyrill alias "bimbofighter".' Available at: http://community.gq-magazin.de/blog/2008/03/13/cyrill-alias-bimbofighter/

GQ.com (2008e) 'Pimp your Style - Street Style, Modetrends 2008, Berlin, München, Sartorialist - GQ.com.' Available at: http://www.gq-magazin.de/articles/stil/modetrend/street-style/2008/03/13/07684/

Gay, G., Rieger, R. and Bennington, T. (2002) 'Using mobile computing to enhance field study.' In Koschmann, T., Hall, R., and Miyake, N., (eds.) *CSCL 2: Carrying forward the conversation.* Mahwah, N.J., Lawrence Erlbaum Associates Inc.

Gergen, K. (2002) 'The challenge of the absent presence.' In Katz, J. and Aakhus, M. (eds.) *Perpetual contact: Mobile communication, private talk, public performance.* Cambridge: CUP, pp. 227–241.

Giddens, A. (1982) 'Reason without revolution? Habermas' Theorie des Kommunikativen Handelns.' In PRAXIS International 3, pp. 318–338

Giddens, A. (1984) *The constitution of society: Outline of the theory of structuration.* Cambridge: Polity Press.

Giddens, A. (1990) *The consequences of modernity.* Stanford, CA: Stanford University Press.

Giddens, A. (1991) *Modernity and self-identity. Self and society in the late modern age.* Cambridge: Polity Press, Blackwell Publishers.

Giddens, A. (1999) 'Risk and responsibility.' In *Modern Law Review 62*(*1*), pp. 1–10.

Giddens, A. (2006) *Sociology.* 5th edition. Cambridge: Polity Press.

Greenfield, A. (2008) 'Location-based and context-aware education: Prospects and perils.' In *Becta: Emerging Technologies for Learning 3*, pp. 47–57. Available at http://partners.becta.org.uk/upload-dir/downloads/page_documents/research/emerging_technologies08_chapter3.pdf.

Guardian (2008) Gr8 db8r takes on linguistic luddites. Interview with David Crystal by John Crace, 16th September. Available at: http://www.guardian.co.uk/education/2008/sep/16/academicexperts.languages

Habermas, J. (1995) *Theorie des kommunikativen Handelns. Band 1: Handlungsrationalität und gesellschaftliche Rationalisierung. Band 2: Zur Kritik der funktionalistischen Vernunft.* 1st edition. Frankfurt: Suhrkamp Verlag, 1981.

Hall, S. (1980) 'Encodung/Decoding.' In Hall, S. et al. (eds.) *Culture, media, language.* London: Hutchinson, pp. 128–139.

Hall, S. (ed.) (1997) *Representation. Cultural representations and signifying practices.* London: Sage.

Haller, M. (2008). Interactive displays and next-generation interfaces. In Research Report: Emerging technologies for learning, Volume 3. Becta, pp. 91–101. Available at: http://publications.becta.org.uk/display.cfm?resID=35877&page=1835

Hanks, W. (1991) 'Foreword.' In Lave, J. and Wenger, E. (eds.) *Situated learning: Legitimate peripheral participation.* Cambridge: Cambridge University Press, pp. 13–24.

Hardcastle, J. (2009) 'Vygotsky's Englightenment precursors.' In *Educational Review 61*(*2*), pp. 181–195.

Hardman, J. (2007) 'Making sense of the meaning maker: Tracking the Object of activity in a computer-based mathematics lesson using activity theory.' In *International Journal of Education and Development Using Information and Communication Technology 3*(*4*), pp. 110–130.

Hartnell-Young, E. (2008) Defying a cultural taboo: Using mobile/cell phones for learning in secondary schools. Paper presented at British Educational Research Association (BERA) conference, Heriot Watt University, Edinburgh from 3–6th September.

Hartnell-Young, E. and Vetere, F. (2008) 'A means of personalising learning: incorporating old and new literacies in the curriculum with mobile/cell phones.' In *Curriculum Journal 19(4)*, pp. 283–292

Haythornthwaite, C. (2008) 'Ubiquitous Transformations.' Paper presented at Symposium 'Making the Transition to Ubiquitous Learning'. Networked learning conference, May 2008, Greece. Available at: http://www.networkedlearningconference.org.uk/abstracts/PDFs/Haythornthwaite_598-605.pdf

Haythornthwaite, C., Bruce, B. C., Clark, A., Cope, B., Duffy, D. and Kalantzis, M. (2008). Making the Transition to Ubiquitous Learning. Symposium at Networked learning conference, May 2008, Greece. Available at: http://www.networkedlearningconference.org.uk/abstracts/PDFs/HaythornthwaiteIntro_574-575.pdf

Hegel, G. W. F. (1807) *System der Wissenschaft. Erster Theil, die Phänomenologie des Geistes*. Erstausgabe. Bamberg/Würzburg: Verlag Joseph Anton Goebhardt.

Hodgkinson, T. (2008) 'With friends like these ...' In *The Guardian*, January 14. Available at: http://www.guardian.co.uk/technology/2008/jan/14/facebook/print

Hoppe, U. (2007) 'How can we integrate mobile devices with broader educational scenarios?' In Sharples, M. (ed.) *Big issues in mobile learning. Report of a workshop by the Kaleidoscope Network of Excellence in Mobile Learning Initiative*. Nottingham: Learning Sciences Research Institute, University of Nottingham, pp. 32–35. Available at: http://www.lsri.nottingham.ac.uk/Publications_PDFs/BIG_ISSUES_REPORT_PUBLISHED.pdf.

Horizon Report (2008). New Media Consortium and EDUCAUSE. http://horizon.nmc.org/wiki/Main_Page

Horrigan, J. (2008) Seeding the Cloud: What Mobile Access Means for Usage Patterns and Online Content. Pew Internet and American Life Project. Available at: http://pewinternet.org/pdfs/PIP_Mobile.Data.Access.pdf

Horton, D. and Wohl, R. (1956) 'Mass communication and para-social interaction: Observations on intimacy at a distance.' In *Psychiatry 19*(*3*), pp. 215–229.

Hug, T. (ed.). (2007) *Didactics of microlearning. concepts, discourses and examples*. Münster/New York/Berlin/München: Waxmann.

Hug, T. and Lindner, M. (eds.) (2007) *Didactics of microlearning*. Münster: Waxmann.

Hug, T., Lindner, M. and Bruck, P. (eds.) (2006) *Microlearning: Emerging concepts, practices and technologies*. Proceedings of Microlearning Learning & Working in New Media Environments. Innsbruck: Innsbruck University Press.

Humboldt, W. von. (2002a) 'Theorie der Bildung des Menschen. Bruchstücke.' In Flitner, A., Giel, K. (Hrsg.) *Wilhelm von Humboldt. Werke in fünf Bänden. Band I: Schriften zur Anthropologie und Geschichte*. 4th edition. Stuttgart: Wissenschaftliche Buchgesellschaft, pp 234–240.

Humboldt, W. von. (2002b, written in the 1790s) 'Theorie der Bildung des Menschen. Bruchstücke.' In Flitner, A. and Giel, K. (eds.) *Wilhelm von Humboldt. Werke in fünf Bänden. Volume I: Schriften zur Anthropologie und Geschichte.* 4th edition. Stuttgart: Wissenschaftliche Buchgesellschaft, pp. 234–240.

Humboldt, W. von. (2002c, written in the 1797) 'Plan einer vergleichenden Anthropologie.' In Flitner, A. and Giel, K. (eds.) *Wilhelm von Humboldt. Werke in fünf Bänden. Volume I: Schriften zur Anthropologie und Geschichte.* 4th edition. Stuttgart: Wissenschaftliche Buchgesellschaft, pp. 337–375.

Humboldt, W. von. (2002d, written in the 1792) 'Ideen zu einem Versuch, die Gränzen der Wirksamkeit des Staates zu bestimmen.' In Flitner, A. and Giel, K. (eds.) *Wilhelm von Humboldt. Werke in fünf Bänden. Volume I: Schriften zur Anthropologie und Geschichte.* 4th. edition. Stuttgart: Wissenschaftliche Buchgesellschaft, pp. 56–233.

Hung, D. and Chen, V. (2007) 'Context-process authenticity in learning: Implications for identity enculturation and boundary crossing.' In *Educational Technology Research Development 55*(2), pp. 147–167.

IDG Magazine Media GmbH (ed.) (2009) 'PC-WELT'. Available at: http://www.pcwelt.de

IndiaRetailBiz (2006) 'Socio Economic Classes (SEC categories) ≪ indiaretailbiz.' Available at: http://indiaretailbiz.wordpress.com/2006/10/15/socio-economic-classifications-sec-categories/

International Association for Mobile Learning (IAMLearn) (2009) 'Mobile Learning Projects.' Available at: http://mlearning.noe-kaleidoscope.org/projects/

Internet-ABC e.V. 'Internet-ABC - Startseite.' Available at: http://internet-abc.ch/kinder

Ito, M., Horst, H., Bittanti, M., boyd, d., Herr-Stephenson, B., Lange, P., Pascoe, C. and Robinson, L. (2008) 'Living and learning with New Media'. McArthur Foundation Reports on Digital Media and Learning. Chicago, IL

Jacucci, G., Oulasvirta, A. and Salovaara, A. (2007) 'Active construction of experience through mobile media: A field study with implications for recording and sharing.' In *Personal and Ubiquitous Computing 11(4)*, pp. 215–234. Also available at: http://www.cs.helsinki.fi/u/oulasvir/scipubs/jacucci-etal_revised_print.pdf.

Jarrett, K. (2008) 'Interactivity is evil! A critical investigation of Web 2.0.' In *First Monday 13(3)*. Available at: http://www.uic.edu/htbin/cgiwrap/bin/ojs/index.php/fm/article/view/2140/1947.

Jenkins, H. (2006) 'The war between effect and meaning: Rethinking the video game violence debate.' In Buckingham, D. and Willett, R. (eds.) *Digital generation. Children, young people and new media*. London: Erlbaum, pp. 19–31.

Jenkins, H., Purushotma, R., Clinton, K., Weigel, M. and Robison, A. (2006) Confronting the challenges of participatory culture: Media education for the 21st century. An occasional paper on digital learning. Chicago, Il: The MacArthur Foundation. Available at: http://digitallearning.macfound.org/atf/cf/%7B7E45C7E0-A3E0-4B89-AC9C-E807E1B0AE4E%7D/JENKINS_WHITE_PAPER.PDF

Johnson, L., Levine, A. and Smith, R. (2008) *The horizon report: 2008 Australia–New Zealand edition*. Austin, TX: The New Media Consortium.

Johnson, L., Levine, A. and Smith, R. (2009) *The 2009 horizon report*. Austin, TX: The New Media Consortium.

Jones, A., Issroff, K. and Scanlon, E. (2007) 'Affective factors in learning with mobile devices.' In Sharples, M. (ed.) *Big issues in mobile learning. Report of a workshop by the Kaleidoscope network of excellence in mobile learning initiative*. Nottingham: Learning Sciences Research Institute, University of Nottingham, pp. 17–22. Available at: http://www.lsri.nottingham.ac.uk/Publications_PDFs/BIG_ISSUES_REPORT_PUBLISHED.pdf.

Joseph Rowntree Foundation (2008) A minimum income standard for Britain, June. http://www.jrf.org.uk/bookshop/eBooks/2226-income-poverty-standards.pdf

Kanton Zürich (2004) 'Gewalt und Pornografie auf dem Handy (E-Lesson). Kantonspolizei-Sicherheitsdirektion - Internet Kanton Zürich.' Available at: http://www.kapo.zh.ch/internet/ds/kapo/de/aktuell/E_Lesson.html

Kaptelinin, V. (2005) 'The object of activity: Making sense of the sense-maker.' In *Mind, Culture and Activity 12(1)*, pp. 2–18.

Kitchen, S., Finch, S. and Sinclair, R. (2007) *Harnessing technology schools survey 2007*. Coventry: Becta. Available at: http://partners.becta.org.uk/upload-dir/downloads/page_documents/research/harnessing_technology_schools_survey07.pdf.

Kollar, I. and Fischer, F. (2008) 'Was ist eigentlich aus der neuen Lernkultur geworden? Ein Blick auf Instruktionsansätze mit Potenzial zur Veränderung kulturell geteilter Lehr- und Lernskripts.' In *Zeitschrift für Pädagogik 54(1)*, pp. 49–62.

Koper, R., Giesbers, B., Rosmalen, P., Sloep, P., Bruggen, J., Tattersall, C., Vogten, H. and Brouns, F. (2005) 'A design model for lifelong learning networks.' In *Interactive Learning Environments 13(1–2)*, pp. 71–92.

Kress, G. (2003) *Literacy in a new media age*. London: Routledge.

Kress, G. (2008) 'New Literacies, New Democracies.' A challenge paper. Available at: http://www.beyondcurrenthorizons.org.uk/wp-content/uploads/bch_challenge_paper_democracies_gunther_kress.pdf

Kress, G. (2009) 'Social, educational and semiotic change: learning in a world marked by provisionality.' In Seipold, J. (ed.) *Media Art Culture - Medienkultur mit Blick auf die documenta 12. Kassler Beiträge zur Erziehungswissenschaft* 1. Kassel university press, pp. 339–354.

Kress, G. and Pachler, N. (2007) 'Thinking about the 'm' in m-learning.' In Pachler, N. (ed.) *Mobile learning: Towards a research agenda*. London: Institute of Education, London, pp. 7–32. Available at: http://www.wlecentre.ac.uk/cms/files/occasionalpapers/mobilelearning_pachler_2007.pdf.WLE Centre Occasional Papers 1.

Kress, G. and van Leeuwen, T. (1996, 2006) *Reading images. The grammar of visual design*. London: Routledge.

Krotz, F. (2005) 'Handlungstheorien.' In Mikos, L., Wegener, C. (eds.): Qualitative Medienforschung. Ein Handbuch. Konstanz: UVK Verlagsgesellschaft (UTB Medien- und Kommunikationswissenschaft, Pädagogik, Psychologie, Soziologie), pp. 40–49

Kukulska-Hulme, A. (2005) 'Introduction.' In Kukulska-Hulme, A., Traxler, J. (eds.) *Mobile learning. A handbook for educators and trainers. New edition.* London, New York: Routledge (The Open and Flexible Learning Series), pp. 1–6.

Kukulska-Hulme, A. and Pettit, J. (2007) 'Self-service education: Smartphones as a catalyst for informal collective and individual learning.' In *mLearn Melbourne 2007: Making the connections. Conference proceedings*, pp. 114–124. Available at: http://www.mlearn2007.org/files/mLearn_2007_Conference_Proceedings.pdf

Kukulska-Hulme, A., Sharples, M., Milrad, M., Arnedillo-Sánchez, I. and Vavoula, G. (2009) ''Innovation in mobile learning: A European perspective.' In *International Journal of Mobile and Blended Learning 1(1)*, pp. 13–35.

Kukulska-Hulme, A. and Traxler, J. (eds.) (2005) *Mobile learning: A handbook for educators and trainers.* London: Routledge.

Landesanstalt für Medien Nordrhein-Westfalen (LfM); Medienpädagogischer Forschungsverbund Südwest (mpfs) 'handysektor.' Available at: http://www.handysektor.de/

Lankshear, C. and Knobel, M. (2006) *New literacies: Everyday literacies and classroom learning.* Maidenhead and New York: Peter Lang.

Lasswell, H. (1948) 'The structure and the function of communication in society.' In Bryson, L. (ed.) *The communication of ideas. A series of addresses.* New York: Institute for Religious and Social Studies (Harper), pp. 37–51

Lasswell, H., Lerner, D. and Sola Pool de, I. (1952) *The comparative study of symbols.* Stanford: Stanford University Press.

Laurillard, D. (2002) *Rethinking university teaching: A conversational framework for the effective use of learning technologies.* 2nd edition. London: Routledge.

Laurillard, D. (2007) 'Pedagogical forms of mobile learning: Framing research questions.' In Pachler, N. (ed.) *Mobile learning: Towards a research agenda.* London, WLE Centre, Institute of Education, pp. 153–176. Available at: http://www.wlecentre.ac.uk/cms/files/occasionalpapers/mobilelearning_pachler_2007.pdf.

Laurillard, D. (2008) 'Technology enhanced learning as a tool for pedagogical innovation.' In *Journal of Philosophy of Education 42(3–4)*, pp. 521–33.

Lave, J. and Wenger, E. (1991) *Situated learning: Legitimate peripheral participation.* Cambridge: Cambridge University Press.

LeJeune, P. (1975) *Le pacte autobiographique.* Paris: Seuil.

Lefebvre, H. (1972) *Das Alltagsleben in der modernen Welt.* Frankfurt/M: Suhrkamp.

Lemke, J. (1999) 'Typological and topological meaning in diagnostic discourse.' In *Discourse Processes 27*(2), pp. 173–185. Also available at: http://academic.brooklyn.cuny.edu/education/jlemke/papers/topomed.htm.

Liu, C.-C. and Kao, L.-C. (2007) 'Do handheld devices facilitate face-to-face collaboration? Handheld devices with large shared display groupware to facilitate group interactions'. *Journal of Computer Assisted Learning 23*, 285–299.

Livingstone, S. (2001) 'Children and their changing media environment.' In Livingstone, S. and Bovill, M. (eds.) *Children and their changing media environment. A European comparative study.* London, Lawrence Erlbaum, pp. 307–333.

Lonsdale, P., Baber, C. and Sharples, M. (2004) 'A context awareness architecture for facilitating mobile learning.' In Attewell, J. and Savill-Smith, C. (eds.) *Learning with mobile devices: Research and development.* London, Learning and Skills Development Agency, pp. 79–85.

Luckin, R. (2008) 'The learner centric ecology of resources: A framework for using technology to scaffold learning.' In *Computers & Education 50*(2), pp. 449–462.

Luckin, R., Clark, W., Garnet, F., Whitworth, A., Akass, J., Cook, J. et al. (2009) 'Learner generated contexts: A framework to support the effective use of technology to support learning.' In

Mark, J. and McLoughlin, L. (eds.) *Web 2.0-based e-learning: Applying social informatics for tertiary teaching*. Hershey, PA, IGI Global.

Luckin, R., du Boulay, B., Smith, H., Underwood, J., Fitzpatrick, G., Holmberg, J., Kerawalla, L., Tunley, H., Brewster, D. and Pearce, D. (2005) 'Using mobile technology to create flexible learning contexts.' In *Journal of Interactive Media in Education 22*. Available at: http://jime.open.ac.uk/2005/22/luckin-2005-22.pdf.

McFarlane, A., Rouche, N. and Triggs, P. (2007) *Mobile learning: Research findings*. Coventry. Available at: http://partners.becta.org.uk/upload-dir/downloads/page_documents/research/mobile_learning_july07.pdf

McFarlane, A., Triggs, P. and Yee, W. (2008) *Researching mobile learning - Interim report to Becta* Period: April–December. Coventry. Available at: http://partners.becta.org.uk/upload-dir/downloads/page_documents/research/mobile_learning.pdf

Mead, G. (1934) *Mind, self and society*. Chicago: University of Chicago Press.

Medienforschung Super, R. T. L. (2000) *Kinderwelten 2000*. Köln, München: RTL Disney Fernsehen GmbH & Co. KG.

Medienforschung Super, R. T. L. (2002) *Kinderwelten 2002*. Köln, München: RTL Disney Fernsehen GmbH & Co. KG.

Medienpädagogischer Forschungsverbund Südwest (mpfs) (2008) 'JIM-Studie 2008. Jugend, Information, (Multi-) Media. Basisuntersuchung zum Medienumgang 12- bis 19-Jähriger.' Available at: http://www.mpfs.de/fileadmin/JIM-pdf08/JIM-Studie_2008.pdf

Metcalf, D. (2006) *M-learning: Mobile learning and performance in the palm of your hand*. Amherst, MA: HRD Press.

Milrad, M. (2007) 'How should learning activities using mobile technologies be designed to support innovative educational practices?' In Sharples, M. (ed.) *Big issues in mobile learning. Report of a workshop by the Kaleidoscope network of excellence in mobile learning initiative*. Nottingham, Learning Sciences Research Institute, University of Nottingham, pp. 29–31. Available at: http://www.lsri.nottingham.ac.uk/Publications_PDFs/BIG_ISSUES_REPORT_PUBLISHED.pdf.

Mizuko, I., Horst, H., Bittanti, M., Boyd, D., Herr-Stephenson, B., Lange, P., Pascoe, C. and Robinson, L. (2008) *Living and learning with new media: Summary of findings from the Digital Youth Project*. Chicago, IL: The MacArthur Foundation. Available at: http://www.macfound.org/atf/cf/%7BB0386CE3-8B29-4162-8098-E466FB856794%7D/DML_ETHNOG_WHITEPAPER.PDF.

Mobile Industry Crime Action Forum (2008) 'Out of Your Hands?' Available at: http://www.outofyourhands.com/

Moore, G. (1991) *Crossing the chasm*. New York: Harper Collins.

MySpace, Inc. (ed.) (2009) 'MySpace.de.' Available at: http://www.myspace.de

Mößle, T., Rehbein, F. and Kleimann, M. (2007) *Bildschirmmedien im Alltags von Kindern und Jugendlichen. Problematische Mediennutzungsmuster und ihr Zusammenhang mit Schulleistungen und Aggressivität*. Baden-Baden: Nomos.

NFER (2008) *Teacher Voice Omnibus Survey – November 2007*. Available at: http://www.nfer.ac.uk/what-we-offer/teacher-voice/ExampleReport.pdf

Naismith, L. and Corlett, D. (2006) 'Reflections on success: A retrospective of the mLearn conference series since 2002–2005.' Paper given at *mLearn 2006: Across generations and cultures*. Banff, Alberta. Available at: http://auspace.athabascau.ca:8080/dspace/bitstream/2149/1239/1/Naismith_Corlett+mlearn06.pdf

Naismith, L., Lonsdale, P., Vavoula, G. and Sharples, M. (2004) *Literature Review in Mobile Technologies and Learning*. Futurelab Series, Report 11. Available at: http://www.futurelab.org.uk/resources/documents/lit_reviews/Mobile_Review.pdf

Nardi, B. (1996) 'Concepts of cognition and consciousness: Four voices.' In *Australian Journal of Information Systems 4(1)*, pp. 64–79. Available at: http://dl.acs.org.au/index.php/ajis/article/view/377/343.

Nardi, B. (2002) 'Activity Theory and design.' In Koschmann, T., Hall, R. And Miyake, N. (eds.) *CSCL2. Carrying forward the conversation*. Mahwah, N.J, Erlbaum, pp. 529–32.

Nationale Elitesportschule Thurgau (2007) 'NET - Nationale Elitesportschule Thurgau. SBW Neue Medien AG.' Available at: http://www.sportschuletg.ch/index.php

New Media Consortium (2005). *A Global Imperative – the report of the 21st century literacy summit*. Available at http://www.adobe.com/education/pdf/globalimperative.pdf

Norris, C., Shin, N. and Soloway, E. (2007) 'Educational technology for the mainstream: A call for designing for simplicity and reliability.' In van't Hooft, M. and Vahey, P. (eds.) *Educational Technology XLVII (3). Special Issue: Highly mobile computing*, pp. 6–9. Available at: http://asianvu.com/bookstoread/etp/Educational_Technology_May_June_2007.pdf

Noss, R. and Pachler, N. (1999) 'The challenge of new technologies: Doing old things in a new way, or doing new things?'. In Mortimore, P. (ed.) *Understanding pedagogy and its impact on learning*. London, Sage, pp. 195–211.

Nuspliger, K. und Diel, E. (eds.) (1989) *Spielgaben für begabte Spieler, die Tradition Fröbels im Kindergarten der deutschen Schweiz*. 2nd edition. Zürich: Schweizerischer Kindergärtnerinnen-Verein.

Nyiri, K. (2002) 'Towards a philosophy of m-learning.' Presented at the IEEE International Workshop on Wireless and Mobile Technologies in Education (WMTE 2002). August 29–30, 2002

Nyíri, K. (ed) (2009) Mobile communication and the ethics of social networking. Vienna: Passagen Verlag

O'Connell, M. and Smith, J. (2007) *A guide to working with m-learning standards. A manual for teachers, trainers and developers*. Australian Flexible Learning Framework. Available standards: http://e-standards.flexiblelearning.net.au/docs/m-standards-guide-v1-0.pdf

OECD (2004) *Messages from PISA 2000*. Available at: http://www.oecd.org/dataoecd/31/19/34107978.pdf

OECD (2007) *Executive Summary PISA 2006: Science Competencies for Tomorrow's World*. Available at: http://www.oecd.org/dataoecd/15/13/39725224.pdf

Ofcom (2008a). Tomorrow's Wireless World: Ofcom's Technology Research Programme 2007/08. Available at: http://www.ofcom.org.uk/media/news/2008/05/nr_20080507

Ofcom (2008b) Media Literacy Audit - Report on UK children's media literacy. http://www.ofcom.org.uk/advice/media_literacy/medlitpub/medlitpubrss/ml_childrens08/

Ofcom (2008c) Mobile citizens, mobile consumers. http://www.ofcom.org.uk/consult/condocs/msa08

Ofcom (2008d) Media Literacy Audit: Media literacy of UK adults from ethnic minority groups. http://www.ofcom.org.uk/advice/media_literacy/medlitpub/medlitpubrss/ml_emg08/

Ofcom (2008e) Annex 3: Media Literacy Audit. Report on UK adults by platform. http://www.ofcom.org.uk/advice/media_literacy/medlitpub/medlitpubrss/ml_adult08/aannex.pdf

Ofcom (2008f) Social Networking: A quantitative and qualitative research report into attitudes, behaviours and use. http://www.ofcom.org.uk/advice/media_literacy/medlitpub/medlitpubrss/socialnetworking/

Oliver, M. (2005) 'The problem with affordance.' In *E-learning 2(4)*, pp. 402–413.

Österreichisches Institut für angewandte Telekommunikation (ÖIAT) 'Handywissen.at.' Das Handy sicher und kostengünstig nutzen.' Available at: http://www.handywissen.at/

Pachler, N., Cook, J. and Bachmair, B. (2010) 'Appropriation of mobile cultural resources for learning.' In *Journal of Mobile and Blended Learning*.

Pachler, N. (ed) *Mobile learning: Towards a research agenda*. WLE Centre, Institute of Education, London, pp. 7–32. Available at: http://www.wlecentre.ac.uk/cms/files/ occasional-papers/mobilelearning_pachler_2007.pdf

Pask, G. (1976) 'Conversational techniques in the study and practice of education.' In *British Journal of Educational Psychology 46*, pp. 12–25.

Passey, D. (2008) 'The Role of Mobile Technologies in Moving 'Digital Natives' to 'Learning Natives'. In Traxler, J., Riordan, B., and Dennett, C. (eds.) *Proceedings of the mLearn2008 Conference 'The Bridge From Text To Context'*. Wolverhampton, University of

Wolverhampton School of Computing and Information Technology, pp. 224–231. Available at: http://www.scit.wlv.ac.uk/brendan/mLearn2008.pdf.

Patten, B., Arnedillo-Sánchez, I. and Tangney, B. (2006) 'Designing collaborative, constructionist and contextual applications for handheld devices'. In *Computers & Education 46(3)*, 294–308.

Peim, M. (2009) 'Activity theory and ontology.' In *Educational Review 61(2)*, pp. 167–180.

Perry, D. (2003) *Handheld computers (PDAs) in schools*. Becta: Coventry. Available at: http://partners.becta.org.uk/index.php?section=rh&rid=13623

Peters, K. (2007) 'm-learning: Positioning educators for a mobile, connected future.' In *International Review of Research in Open and Distance Learning* 8(2). Available at: http://www.irrodl.org/index.php/irrodl/article/view/350/914.

Petersen, S. M. (2008) 'Loser generated content: From participation to exploitation.' In *First Monday 13(3)*. Available at: http://www.uic.edu/htbin/cgiwrap/bin/ojs/index.php/fm/article/view/2141/1948.

PhonepayPlus (2008) 'PHONEbrain.' Available at: http://www.phonebrain.org.uk/

Piaget, J. (1947/2001) *The psychology of intelligence*. London, New York: Routledge Classics 2001. Fist publication: *La Psychologie de l'intelligence*. Paris: Armand Colin 1947.

Piaget, J. (1955) *The construction of reality in the child*. London: Routledge and Kegan Paul.

Pickering, A. (1995) *The mangle of practice*. Chicago: University of Chicago Press.

Pietrass, M., Schmidt, B. and Tippelt, R. (2005) 'Informelles Lernen und Medienbildung.' In *Zeitschrift für Erziehungswissenschaft 8*(3), pp. 412–426.

Popper, K. (1978) *Three Worlds*. The Tanner Lecture on Human Values. Delivered at The UNiversity of Michigan. April, 7. Available at http://www.tannerlectures.utah.edu/lectures/documents/popper80.pdf

Press Trust of India (PTI) (2007) 'Karnataka bans mobile/cell phone use by school children - AOL India News.' Available at: http://www.aol.in/news/story/2007091112439022000015/index.html

Price, S. (2007) 'Ubiquitous computing: Digital augmentation and learning.' In Pachler, N. (ed.) *Mobile learning: Towards a research agenda*. London, WLE Centre, Institute of Education, pp. 33–54. Available at: http://www.wlecentre.ac.uk/cms/files/occasionalpapers/mobilelearning_pachler_2007.pdf.

Rieber, L. (1996) 'Seriously considering play: Designing interactive learning environments based on the blending of microworlds, simulations, and games.' In *Educational Technology Research and Development 44*(2), pp. 43–58.

Ritzer, G. (1993) *The McDonaldization of society*. Thousand Oaks, London: Pine Forge Press.

Rogers, Y. and Price, S. (2007) 'Using ubiquitous computing to extend and enhance learning experiences.' In van't Hooft, M. and Swan, K. (eds.) *Ubiquitous computing in education. Invisible technology, visible impact*. Mahwah, NJ, Lawrence Erlbaum, pp. 329–347.

Rogers, Y., Price, S., Randell, C., Stanton Fraser, D., Weal, M. and Fitzpatrick, G. (2004) 'Ubi-learning: Intergrating indoor and outdoor learning experiences.' In *Communications of the ACM 48*(1), pp. 55–49.

Roschelle, J. (2003) 'Unlocking the learning value of wireless mobile devices.' In *Journal of Computer Assisted Learning 19*(3), pp. 260–72.

Roschelle, J. and Pea, R. (2002) 'A walk on the WILD side: How wireless handhelds may change computer-supported collaborative learning.' In *International Journal of Cognition and Technology 1(1)*, pp. 145–168. Also available at: http://ctl.sri.com/publications/downloads/WalkWildSide.pdf.

Ryu, H. and Parsons, D. (eds.) (2008) *Innovative mobile learning: Techniques and technologies*. Hershey, NY: Information Science Reference. Also available at: http://rapidshare.com/files/170054540/Innovative_Mobile_Learning.rar.

Scardamalia, M. and Bereiter, C. (1999) 'Schools as Knowledge-Building Organizations.' In Keating, D. and Hertzman, C. (eds.) *Today's children, tomorrow's society: The developmental health and wealth of nations*. New York, Guilford, pp. 274–289. Also available at: http://www.ikit.org/fulltext/1999schoolsaskb.pdf.

Schenker, J., Kratcoski, A., Lin, Y., Swan, K. and van't Hooft, M. (2007) 'Researching ubiquity: Was to capture it all.' In van't Hooft, M.and Swan, K. (eds) *Ubiquitous computing in education. Invisible technology, visible impact*. Lawrence Erlbaum, Mahwah, NJ, pp. 167–186.

Schostak, J. (2002) *Understanding, designing and conducting qualitative research in education*. Buckingham: Open University Press.

Schulze, G. (1992) *Die Erlebnisgesellschaft. Kultursoziologie der Gegenwart*. 2nd edition. Frankfurt a.M: Campus.

Schweizer Fernsehen (SF) (2003) 'Dossier Handy. SF Wissen mySchool, SF 1.' Available at: http://www.sf.tv/sf1/myschool/detailinfo.php?docid=3193

Schön, E. (1987) Der Verlust der Sinnlichkeit oder Die Verwandlung des Lesers: Mentalitätswandel um 1800. Stuttgart: Klett-Cotta

Schütz, A. (1932) *Der sinnhafte Aufbau der sozialen Welt. Eine Einleitung in die verstehende Soziologie*. Wien, Verlag Julius Springer. English translation: The phenomenology of the social world. Northwestern University Press. Evanstone 1967

Schütz, A. and Luckmann, T. (1984) 'Strukturen der Lebenswelt'. Band 2. 3. Auflage. Frankfurt a. M.: Suhrkamp

Sefton-Green, J. (2004) *Literature Review in Informal Learning with Technology Outside School*. Futurelab Series, Report 7. Available at: http://www.futurelab.org.uk/resources/documents/lit_reviews/Informal_Learning_Review.pdf

Seipold, J. (2009) 'Mo-LeaP - The mobile learning projects database.' In Pachler, N. and Seipold, J. (eds.) *Mobile learning cultures across education, work and leisure*. Book of abstracts. Proceedings of the 3rd WLE Mobile Learning Symposium, London, 27th March 2009. London, pp. 157–161. Available at: http://www.londonmobilelearning.net/symposium/downloads/3rd_wle_mlearning_symposium__book_of_abstracts_single_page_display.pdf

Seipold, J. and The London Mobile Learning Group (LMLG) (2009) 'MoLeaP – The Mobile Learning Project Database.' Available at: http://www.moleap.net

Selwyn, N. (2008) 'Developing the technological imagination: Theorising the social shaping and consequences of new technologies.' In *Theorising the benefits of new technology for youth: Controversies of learning and development. The educational and social impact of new technologies on young people in Britain*. Report of the seminar held on Wednesday 12 March. Department of Education, University of Oxford. ESRC. pp. 18–28. Available at: http://www.education.ox.ac.uk/esrcseries/uploaded/08_0314%20ESRC%20report_final_HR.pdf

Sfard, A. (1998) 'On two metaphors for learning: And the dangers of choosing just one.' In *Educational Researcher 27*(2), pp. 4–13. Also available at: http://www.jstor.org/view/0013189x/ap040264/04a00020/0.

Shao, Y., Crook, C. and Kolevas, B. (2007) 'Designing a Mobile Group Blog to Support Cultural Learning.' In mLearn melbourne 2007. making the connections. Conference Proceedings mLearn melbourne 2007, pp. 211–215

Sharples, M. (2000) 'The design of personal mobile technologies for lifelong learning.' In *Computers and Education 34*, pp. 177–193.

Sharples, M. (2005) 'Learning as conversation: Transforming education in the Mobile Age.' Centre for Educational Technology and Distance Learning. University of Birmingham. Available at: http://www.eee.bham.ac.uk/sharplem/Papers/Theory%20of%20learning%20Budapest.pdf

Sharples, M. (2006) Becta seminar 'Future Gazing for Policy Makers', 28 March, held at the BT Government Innovation Centre, London, UK

Sharples, M. (2007a) 'Theory Of Learning For The Mobile Age. Presentation in Leicester April 2007.' Available at: http://www.slideshare.net/sharplem/theory-of-learning-for-the-mobile-age-leicester-april-2007/

Sharples, M. (ed) (2007b) *Big issues in mobile learning. Report of a workshop by the Kaleidoscope network of excellence in mobile learning initiative*. Nottingham: Learning Sciences Research Institute, University of Nottingham, pp. 5–6. Available at: http://www.lsri.nottingham.ac.uk/Publications_PDFs/BIG_ISSUES_REPORT_PUBLISHED.pdf.

Sharples, M., Corlett, D. and Westmancott, O. (2001) 'A systems architecture for handheld learning resources.' Paper presented at *CAL 2001*. Available: http://www.lsri.nottingham.ac.uk/msh/Papers/handler%20cal2001.pdf

Sharples, M., Corlett, D. and Westmancott, O. (2002) 'The design and implementation of a mobile learning resource.' In *Personal and Ubiquitous Computing 6*, pp. 220–234. Also available at: http://www.eee.bham.ac.uk/sharplem/Papers/mobile%20learning%20puc.pdf

Sharples, M., Lonsdale, P., Meek, J., Rudman, P. and Vavoula, G. (2007) 'An evaluation of MyArtSpace: A mobile learning service for school museum trips.' Paper at *mLearn 2007*. Melbourne. Preprint available from http://www.lsri.nottingham.ac.uk/msh/write.htm

Sharples, M., Milrad, M., Arnedillo-Sánchez, I. and Vavoula, G. (2008) 'Mobile Learning: Small devices, Big Issues.' In Balacheff, N., Ludvigsen, S., de Jong, T., Lazonder, A., Barnes, S. and Montandon, L. (eds.) *Technology enhanced learning: Principles and products. Kaleidoscope Legacy Book*. Berlin, Springer. Available at: http://www.lsri.nottingham.ac.uk/msh/Papers/KAL_Legacy_Mobile_Learning.pdf.

Sharples, M., Taylor, J. and Vavoula, G. (2007) 'A theory of learning for the mobile age.' In Andrews, R. and Haythornthwaite, C. (eds.) *The sage handbook of E-learning research*. London, SAGE, pp. 221–247. Available at: http://hal.archives-ouvertes.fr/docs/00/19/02/76/PDF/Sharples_et_al_Theory_of_Mobile_Learning_preprint.pdf.

Sheller, M. and Urry, J. (eds.) (2006) *Mobile technologies of the city*. London: Routledge.

Shin, N., Norris, C. and Soloway, E. (2007) 'Findings from early research on one-to-one handheld use in K-12 education.' In van't Hooft, M. and Swan, K. (eds.) *Ubiquitous computing in education. Invisible technology, visible impact*. Mahwah, NJ, Lawrence Erlbaum, pp. 19–39.

Shore, R. (2008) The Power of Pow! Wham!: Children, Digital Media and Our Nation's Future. Three Challenges for the Coming Decade. Available at: http://www. joanganzcooneycenter.org/pdf/Cooney_Challenge_advance.pdf

Shuler, C. (2009) *Pockets of potential. Using mobile technologies to promote children's learning*. New York: The Joan Ganz Cooney Centre at Sesame Workshop. Available at: http://www.joanganzcooneycenter.org/pdf/pockets_of_potential.pdf.

Silverstone, R. (1994) *Television and everyday life*. London: Routledge.

Sinus Sociovision (2007) ‚Die Milieus der Menschen mit Migrationshintergrund in Deutschland. Eine qualitative Untersuchung von Sinus Sociovision. Auszug aus dem Forschungsbericht.' Heidelberg, 16. Oktober

Sinus Sociovision (2009) *Informationen zu den Sinus-Milieus® 2009*. Heidelberg. Available at: http://www.sociovision.de/uploads/tx_mpdownloadcenter/informationen_2009.pdf

Smith, C., Cook, J. and Bradley, C. (2008) 'Engineering suitable content for context sensitive education and vocational training (CONTSENS).' Paper at *Handheld Learning* 2008, October 13–15th, London

Smith, C., Cook, J., Bradley, C., Gossett, R. and Haynes, R. (2007) 'Motivating learners: Mobile learning objects and reusable learning objects for the X-box generation.' Paper presented at *ALT-C 2007*, 14th International Conference of the Association for Learning Technology, University of Nottingham, September 2007

Spikol, D. (2008) *Exploring novel learning practices through co-designing mobile games co-design*. Paper presented at: Digital Content Creation: Creativity, Competence, Critique. The second international DREAM conference 18–20 September, University of Southern Denmark, Odense, Denmark. Available at: http://www.dreamconference.dk/nyheder/Spikol,%20David.pdf

Sprake, J. (2007) 'Sensing anomalies: An exploration of disorganisation and disturbance as productive elements in learning through location.' In Arnedillo-Sánchez, I., Sharples, M. and Vavoula, G. (eds.) *Beyond mobile learning workshop. The CSCL Alpine Rendez-Vous*. Switzerland, Trinity College Dublin Press, pp. 30–42. Available at: http://www.ell.aau.dk/fileadmin/user_upload/documents/research/kaleidoscope/Alpine_rendez_vous/CSCLAlpineRDV2007 Report.pdf.

sprd.net AG (Ed.) (2009) 'Spreadshirt.' Available at: http://www.spreadshirt.net

Stald, G. (2008) 'Mobile identity: Youth, identity, and mobile communication media.' In Buckingham, D. (ed.) *Youth, identity, and digital media*. Cambridge, MA, MIT Press, pp. 143–164. Available at: http://www.mitpressjournals.org/doi/pdf/10.1162/dmal.9780262524834.143.

Stone, C. (2008) 'The role of football in everyday life.' In *Soccer & Society 8(2/3)*, pp. 169–184.

Strauss, A. and Corbin, J. (1990) *Basics of qualitative research: Grounded theory.' Procedures and techniques*. London: SAGE Publications.

Taylor, J. (2007) 'Evaluating mobile learning. What are appropriate methods for evaluating learning in mobile environments?' In Sharples, M. (ed.) *Big issues in mobile learning. Report of a workshop by the Kaleidoscope network of excellence in mobile learning initiative*. Nottingham, Learning Sciences Research Institute, University of Nottingham, pp. 26–28. Available at: http://www.lsri.nottingham.ac.uk/Publications_PDFs/BIG_ISSUES_REPORT_PUBLISHED.pdf.

Taylor, J., Sharples, M., O'Malley, C., Vavoula, G. and Waycott, J. (2006) 'Towards a task model for mobile learning: A dialectical approach.' In *International Journal of Learning Technology 2(2–3)*, pp. 138–158. Also available at: http://kn.open.ac.uk/public/getfile.cfm?documentfileid=7175.

Thackara, J. (2005) *In the bubble: Designing in a complex world*. Cambridge, MA: The MIT Press.

The Horizon Report (2008). New Media Consortium and EDUCAUSE. Available at: http://horizon.nmc.org/wiki/Main_Page

The Horizon Report (2009). K-12 Edition. New Media Consortium and EDUCAUSE. Available at: http://horizon.nmc.org/wiki/Main_Page

The Horizon Report (2009). New Media Consortium and EDUCAUSE. Available at: http://horizon.nmc.org/wiki/Main_Page

The World Bank (2002) 'India Karnataka: Secondary Education and The New Agenda for Economic Growth. Report No. 24208-IN.' Available at: http://www-wds.worldbank.org/external/default/WDSContentServer/WDSP/IB/2002/07/27/000094946_02070204224050/Rendered/PDF/multi0page.pdf

The World Bank (2008a) 'EdStats.' Education Statistics Version 5.3. World Bank's Education Group of the Human Development Network (HDNED) and the Development Economics Data Group (DECDG) in collaboration with the UNESCO Institute for Statistics (UIS), OECD and other agencies.' Available at: http://www.worldbank.org/education/edstats/

The World Bank (2008b) 'ICT at a Glance: India.' Available at: http://devdata.worldbank.org/ict/ind_ict.pdf

The Economist (2008). Nomads at last. A special report on mobility. April 12th. Availabale at: http://www.economist.com/surveys/downloadSurveyPDF.cfm?id=10950383&surveycode=UK&submit=View+PDF or http://www.economist.com/specialreports/displayStory.cfm?STORY_ID=10950394

Thorne, S. (2003) 'Artifacts and cultures-of-use in intercultural communication.' In *Language Learning & Technology 7(2)*, pp. 38–67. Available at: http://llt.msu.edu/vol7num2/thorne/.

Thorpe, G. (2006) 'Multilevel analysis of PISA 2000. 'Reading results for the United Kingdom using pupil scale variables.' In *School Effectiveness and School Improvement 16(1)*, pp. 33–62.

Timeshot Medien GmbH & Co. KG (ed.) (2005) 'Forum: Schönstes Mädchen aus Augsburg.' Available at: http://www.timeshot.de/viewtopic.php?p=104367&sid=8f48fe3a67c26e8177c60921119b03d

Timeshot Medien GmbH & Co. KG (ed.) (2006) 'Forum: Schönstes Mädchen aus Augsburg.' Available at: http://www.timeshot.de/viewtopic.php?p=592849&sid=3038537f62eee24bd13592228c4052a0

Timeshot Medien GmbH & Co. KG (ed.) (2007) 'Forum: Lernen?!?!' Available at: http://www.timeshot.de/viewtopic.php?t=7959&sid=289e5e3cf0ce7bad45044ed1427aca9b

Timeshot Medien GmbH & Co. KG (ed.) (2009) 'Timeshot.' Available at: http://www.timeshot.de

Tippelt, R., Weiland, M., Panyr, S. and Barz, H. (2003) *Weiterbildung, Lebensstil und soziale Lage in einer Metropole*. Bielefeld: Bertelsmann (Theorie und Praxis der Weiterbildung).

Traxler, J. (2007a) 'Defining, discussing, and evaluating mobile learning: The moving finger writes and having writ. . .'. In *International Review of Research in Open and Distance Learning* 8(2). Available at: http://www.irrodl.org/index.php/irrodl/article/view/346/882.

Traxler, J. (2007b) 'Flux within change.' In mLearn Melbourne 2007: Making the connections. Conference proceedings, pp. 256–264. Available at: http://www.mlearn2007.org/files/mLearn_2007_Conference_Proceedings.pdf

Traxler, J. (2008) 'Learners: Should we leave them to their own devices?' In *Emerging Technologies*. Coventry, Becta. Available at: http://emergingtechnologies.becta.org.uk/index.php?section=etr&rid=14148

Traxler, J. and Dearden, P. (2005) *The potential for using SMS to support learning and organisation in Sub-Saharan Africa.* Available at: http://www.wlv.ac.uk/PDF/cidt-article20.pdf

Traxler, J. and Dearden, P. (2005) 'The potential for using SMS to support learning and organisation in Sub-Saharan Africa.' Development Studies Association *Connecting and promoting the development research community. Annual Conference*. Milton Keynes, 7–9th September 2005. Powerpoint Slides: http://www.devstud.org.uk/Conference05/abstracts/ITD.htm

Treumann, K. P. (2005) 'Triangulation.' In Mikos, L, Wegener, C. (eds.): *Qualitative Medienforschung*. Ein Handbuch. Konstanz: UVK Verlagsgesellschaft (UTB Medien- und Kommunikationswissenschaft, Pädagogik, Psychologie, Soziologie), pp. 209–221

Tsai, C.-C. (2004) 'Beyond cognitive and metacognitive tools: The use of the Internet as an 'epistemological' tool for instruction.' In *British Journal of Educational Technology 35*(5), pp. 525–536.

PSD-Tutorials.de (Ed.) (2009) 'PSD-Tutorials.de.' Available at: http://www.psd-tutorials.de

Urry, J. (2007) *Mobilities*. Chichester: Wiley.

Vadas, N., Ellenberger, J. and Hollenstein, S. (2007) 'Dossier Handy.' Webquest zum Film "Dossier Handy".' Available at: http://edavs.educanet2.ch/handy/.ws_gen/

Vahey, P., Roschelle, J. and Tatar, D. (2007) 'Using handhelds to link private cognition and public interaction.' In In van't Hooft, M. and Vahey, P. (eds) *Educational Technology XLVII*(3). *Special issue: Highly mobile computing*, pp. 13–16.

Vahey, P., Tatar, D. and Roschelle, J. (2007) 'Using handheld technology to move between private and public interactions in the classroom.' In van 't Hooft, M. and Swan, K. (eds.) *Ubiquitous computing in education: Invisible technology, visible impact*. Mahway, NJ, Lawrence Erlbaum Associates, pp. 187–210.

van Merriënboer, J., Clark, R. and de Croock, M. (2002) 'Blueprints for complex learning: The 4C/ID-model.' In *Educational Technology, Research and Development 50*(2), pp. 39–64.

van't Hooft, M. (2008) 'Mobile, wireless, connected Information clouds and learning.' In Becta Research Report, Volume 3: *Emerging technologies for learning*. pp. 2–18. Coventry: Becta. Available at: http://partners.becta.org.uk/upload-dir/downloads/page_ documents/research/emerging_technologies08_chapter2.pdf

van't Hooft, M. and Swan, K. (2007) 'Epilogue.' In van't Hooft, M. and Swan, K. (eds.) *Ubiquitous computing in education. Invisible technology, visible impact*. Mahwah, NJ, Lawrence Erlbaum, pp. 349–51.

Vavoula, G., Pachler, N. and Kukulska-Hulme, A. (eds) (2009) *Researching mobile learning: Frameworks, methods and research design*. Oxford: Peter Lang.

Verdejo, F., Celorrio, C., Lorenzo, E., Ruiz, A. and Sastre, T. (2007) 'Sustaining learning activity flow in a framework for ubiquitous learning.' In Arnedillo-Sánchez, I., Sharples, M. and Vavoula, G. (eds.) *Beyond mobile learning workshop. The CSCL Alpine Rendez-Vous*. Switzerland, Trinity College Dublin Press, pp. 43–53. Available at: http://www.ell.aau.dk/fileadmin/user_upload/documents/research/kaleidoscope/Alpine_rendez_vous/CSCLAlpineRDV2007Report.pdf.

Vester, M. (2006) 'Die ständische Kanalisierung der Bildungschancen: Bildung und soziale Ungleichheit zwischen Boudon und Bourdieu.' In Georg, W. (ed.) *Soziale Ungleichheit im Bildungssystem: Eine empirisch-theoretische Bestandsaufnahme*. Konstanz, UVK-Verl.-Ges. (Theorie und Methode Sozialwissenschaften), pp. 13–54.

Virilio, P. (1990) *L'intertie polaire*. Paris: Christian Bourgois Editeur.

Visions (2007) Teacher innovation: A look at the possibilities for innovation within the current education framework 4. Futurelab. Available at: http://www.futurelab.org.uk/resources/documents/vision/VISION_04.pdf

Vogelgesang, W. (1991) Jugendliche Video-Cliquen. Action- und Horrorvideos als Kristallisationspunkte einer neuen Fankultur. Opladen: Westdeutscher Verlag

Vygotsky, L. (1978/1930) *Mind in society. The development of higher psychological processes*. In Cole, M. et al. (eds.). Cambridge, MA: Harvard University Press.

Vygotsky, L. (1986/1934) *Thought and language*. In Kozulin, A. (ed.). Cambridge, MA: MIT Press.

Wagner, U., Gebel, C. and Eggert, S. (2006) ‚Muster konvergenzbezogener Medienaneignung.' In U. Wagner and H. Theunert (eds) *Neue Wege durch die konvergente Medienwelt*. Studie im Auftrag der Bayerischen Landesanstalt für neue Medien (BLM). BLM-Schriftenreihe Volume 85. München: Verlag Reinhard Fischer, pp 83–124

Wali, E., Winters, N. and Oliver, M. (2008) 'Maintaining, changing and crossing contexts: An activity theoretic reinterpretation of mobile learning.' In *ALT-J 16(1)*, pp. 41–57.

Walker, K. (2007) 'Introduction: Mapping the landscape of mobile learning.' In Sharples, M. (ed.) *Big issues in mobile learning. Report of a workshop by the Kaleidoscope Network of Excellence in Mobile Learning Initiative*. Nottingham, Learning Sciences Research Institute, University of Nottingham, pp. 5–6. Available at: http://www.lsri.nottingham.ac.uk/Publications_PDFs/BIG_ISSUES_REPORT_PUBLISHED.pdf.

Waycott, J. (2004) *The appropriation of PDAs as learning and workplace tools: An activity theory perspective*. Unpublished PhD. The Open University. Available at: http://kn.open.ac.uk/public/getfile.cfm?documentfileid=9608

Weilenmann, A. (2003) *Doing mobility*. Gothenburg: Gothenburg Studies in Informatics.

Wenger, E. (1998) *Communities of practice. Learning, meaning, and identity*. Cambridge: Cambridge University Press.

White, N. (2006) Blogs and community – launching a new paradigm for online community? *The Knowledge Tree. An e-Journal of Learning Innovation. Going Communal. 11*. Available at http://kt.flexiblelearning.net.au/tkt2006/edition-11-editorial/blogs-and-community-%E2%80%93-launching-a-new-paradigm-for-online-community/

Wikipedia (2008) 'Kannada language.' Available at: http://en.wikipedia.org/wiki/Kannada_language

Williams, R. (1974) *Television: Technology and Cultural Form*. 1st edition. London: Routledge. 1990, Schocken Books, 2nd edition.

Winter, R. (2005) 'Interpretative Ethnographie.'. In Mikos, L., Wegener, C. (eds.) *Qualitative Medienforschung. Ein Handbuch*. Konstanz: UVK Verlagsgesellschaft (UTB Medien- und Kommunikationswissenschaft, Pädagogik, Psychologie, Soziologie), pp. 553–560.

Winters, N. (2007) 'What is mobile learning?' In Sharples, M. (ed.) *Big issues in mobile learning. Report of a workshop by the Kaleidoscope network of excellence in mobile learning initiative*. Nottingham: Learning Sciences Research Institute, University of Nottingham, pp. 7–11. Available at: http://www.lsri.nottingham.ac.uk/Publications_PDFs/BIG_ISSUES_REPORT_PUBLISHED.pdf.

Wood, D., Bruner, J. and Ross, G. (1976) 'The role of tutoring in problem solving.' In *Journal of Child Psychology and Psychiatry 17*(2), pp. 89–100.

Young, M. (2006) 'Curriculum studies and the problem of knowledge; updating the Enlightenment?' In Lauder, H., Brown, P., Dillabough, J.-A., and Halsey, A. (eds.) *Education, globalization, and social change*. Oxford: Oxford University Press, pp. 734–741.

Zhao, Y. and Frank, K. (2003) 'Factors affecting technology uses in schools: An ecological perspective.' In *American Educational Research Journal 40(4)*, pp. 807–840. Available at: http://www.msu.edu/~kenfrank/papers/Factors%20affecting%20technology%20uses%20in%20schools.pdf.

Zimmer, M. (2008) 'The externalities of Search 2.0: The emerging privacy threats when the drive for the perfect search engine meets Web 2.0.' In *First Monday 13*(3). Available at: http://www.uic.edu/htbin/cgiwrap/bin/ojs/index.php/fm/article/view/2136.

Index

9572915R0

Made in the USA
Lexington, KY
15 May 2011